Alain Auguste Victor Fivas

New Grammar of French Grammars

Comprising the Substance of all the Most Approved French Grammars Extant...

Alain Auguste Victor Fivas

New Grammar of French Grammars
Comprising the Substance of all the Most Approved French Grammars Extant...

ISBN/EAN: 9783337157562

Printed in Europe, USA, Canada, Australia, Japan

Cover: Foto ©Paul-Georg Meister /pixelio.de

More available books at **www.hansebooks.com**

𝔉or tṭe 𝔘se of 𝔆olleges, 𝔖cṭools, and 𝔓ribate 𝔖tudents.

NEW GRAMMAR OF FRENCH GRAMMARS:

COMPRISING THE SUBSTANCE OF

ALL THE MOST APPROVED FRENCH GRAMMARS EXTANT,

BUT MORE ESPECIALLY OF THE STANDARD WORK,

"GRAMMAIRE DES GRAMMAIRES,"

SANCTIONED BY THE FRENCH ACADEMY AND THE UNIVERSITY OF PARIS.

WITH NUMEROUS EXERCISES AND EXAMPLES
ILLUSTRATIVE OF EVERY RULE.

BY DR. V. DE FIVAS, M.A., F.E.I.S.,
MEMBER OF THE GRAMMATICAL SOCIETY OF PARIS, ETC.

LONDON:
LOCKWOOD & CO., 7 STATIONERS' HALL COURT.
EDINBURGH: OLIVER & BOYD; JOHN MENZIES.
DUBLIN: M'GLASHAN & GILL.

THIRTY-SECOND EDITION.—1869.

PREFACE.

> "*Grammar*, as the master-key of the human mind, is the first object in the cultivation of the understanding."—
> (*The Linguist.*)
>
> "Presque partout, deux hommes d'esprit, de nation diverse, qui se rencontrent, s'accordent à parler français."—
> (*Préf. du Dict. de l'Acad. franç.*)

WE read, in a recent London publication, that there are about one hundred French Grammars for the use of English students. But, *How many of these exhibit the orthography and rules of the language as they are fixed at the present day !* It is the impossibility of satisfactorily answering this question, that first suggested to me the idea of producing a work which, without being a mere compilation, should embody the substance of the latest decisions of the French Academy, with the most lucid and concise rules of the best modern French Grammarians. The single fact of the French Academy having lately published a new edition of their Dictionary, entirely revised and greatly enlarged, shows in an obvious point of view the call that is made for a new and improved French Grammar.

My plan, in this publication, has been to give everything useful, and nothing superfluous.* I have studied to make the

---

* Some Grammarians devote fifty pages to the declensions of nouns and pronouns, while the French language has no declension.† Many encroach on the province of the Teacher, and encumber their pages by giving a repetition of all the conjugations interrogatively and negatively, when one, as a model, is quite sufficient. Others, give elaborate treatises on pronunciation, which can never be properly learned from books, and are quite unnecessary, since a good French Teacher can now be found in every town and village of the United Kingdom, from whom more knowledge of pronunciation will be obtained in one lesson than in one year from all the books ever published on this subject.

† La Langue française n'a point, et ne peut avoir, de déclinaisons; on doit purger nos Grammaires de tout ce fatras, de toutes ces superfluités qui sont plus propres à nuire qu'à servir à l'intelligence de la Langue.
　　　　　　　　　　　　DEMANDRE, *Dict. de l'Élocution française.*

definitions at once clear and precise, that they may be readily understood and easily retained. When I judged it necessary, I have also presented the rules in a new light, in order to adapt them to the capacity of youthful students. I have further endeavoured to arrange and distribute the matter, so as to embrace, within a narrow compass, much more information than is usually found in grammatical class-books. Indeed, there is not a useful Rule or Observation in the largest grammar in print that is not to be found in this.

The *Exercises* illustrate everything that can be reduced to rules in the French language. This branch of the work has, for several years, engaged my special attention. The phraseology is all founded on the highest French classical authorities; and it has been my study throughout to introduce a moral precept, an historical or a geographical fact, or a conversational phrase; and thus to impart useful information along with grammatical rules.

The present Edition of this Grammar has been carefully revised, and a considerable number of words and remarks introduced that are not to be found in any other Grammar. I have also had the advantage of being able to avail myself of the criticisms that the learned Authors of the "*Grammaire Nationale*" have made on the "*Grammaire des Grammaires*," and of the answers to those criticisms by M. Lemaire, Professor of Rhetoric at the College Louis-le-Grand, in Paris. "Tout homme qui veut bien écrire," says VOLTAIRE, "doit corriger ses ouvrages toute sa vie."

LONDON, *July* 1860.

The following are a few of the numerous Literary Notices of this Work:—

"At once the simplest and most complete Grammar of the French Language To the Pupil, the effect is almost as if he looked into a map, so well-defined is the course of study as explained by M. de Fivas."—*(Literary Gazette.)*

"This Grammar is the most systematic and distinct that we have seen:—the work is simple in its arrangement; clear and precise in its definitions; and the Exercises under each head, most appropriate and useful."—*(Chronicle.)*

"Its precision and conciseness are admirable. We cordially recommend it to Teachers and Students. Its excellence cannot fail to secure it an established reputation."—*(Standard.)*

"This Grammar is the cheapest, most concise, philosophical, and satisfactory which has come under our notice."—*(Edinburgh Journal.)*

"The distinguishing features of this work are, its embodiment of the latest changes and modifications of the French Language. In the writing and arrangement of the work, M. de Fivas has displayed great skill."—*(Scotsman.)*

"This is an excellent book—lucid and comprehensive. It contains the latest improvements made by the French Academicians."—*(Gateshead Observer.)*

"In this work everything is plain and clear to the most obtuse understanding; the Exercises are excellent, being individually easily understood, and consecutively so arranged as to carry the pupil step by step to a thorough acquaintance with the language.—One of the best recommendations of this well-written Grammar is, that it is framed on the orthography and practice of the language at the present day, which we do not believe to be the case with 5 out of the 100 at present in use."—*(Tyne Mercury.)*

"This is, beyond comparison, the best French Grammar we have ever met with. It contains everything necessary to a thorough knowledge of the language."—*(Dublin Monitor.)*

From Professor MARCEL.—" J'ai parcouru votre dernier ouvrage 'Grammaire des Grammaires,' et, frappé de sa clarté et de sa concision, je lui ai reconnu sous ce rapport une grande supériorité sur les autres grammaires, aussi me suis-je empressé de la recommander à tous ceux qui désirent se pénétrer des vrais principes de notre langue."

From Professor VOGUE.—" J'ai lu avec un vif intérêt votre Grammaire française. Je me suis convaincu de son mérite et de son utilité. Je ne manquerai pas de la recommander comme claire, exacte, et complète."

From Professor DUMAS.—" Votre ouvrage bien que peu volumineux est clair et complet. Je ne recommanderai certainement jamais d'autre grammaire."

From Professor DUVAL.—" J'approuve beaucoup votre ouvrage et je me propose d'en faire usage: il est déjà entre les mains de plusieurs de mes élèves."

From Professor MESSIEUX.—" Je me décide à donner la préférence à votre grammaire, ayant le mérite d'être mieux arrangée, plus claire, et plus correcte que celle dont je me sers."

From Professor DE CANDOLE.—" J'ai cherché du mal dans votre ouvrage, mais je n'en ai pas trouvé; je me suis fait critique, j'y ai perdu ma peine, car tout était juste, vrai. Vous avez retranché bien des inutilités dans le commencement, et dans la syntaxe que j'ai parcourue avec soin vous avez franchement abordé les difficultés et fait admirablement sentir les délicatesses de notre langue."

EXPLANATION OF THE ABBREVIATIONS AND MARKS

USED IN THE EXERCISES.

m. *stands for*	masculine.	
f. . . .	feminine.	
sing. *or* s. .	singular.	
pl. . . .	plural.	
h m. . .	*h* mute.	
h asp. . .	*h* aspirate.	
art. . . .	article.	
pr. *or* prep.	preposition.	
pron. . .	pronoun.	
inf-1. . .	present of the infinitive.	
inf-2. . .	infinitive past.	
inf-3. . .	participle present.	
inf-4. . .	participle past.	
ind-1 . .	present of the indicative.	
ind-2 *stands for*	imperfect.	
ind-3 . . .	preterite definite.	
ind-4 . . .	preterite indefinite.	
ind-5 . . .	preterite anterior.	
ind-6 . . .	pluperfect.	
ind-7 . . .	future absolute.	
ind-8 . . .	future anterior.	
cond-1 . .	conditional present.	
cond-2 . .	conditional past.	
imp. . . .	imperative.	
subj-1. . .	present of the subjunctive.	
subj-2. . .	imperfect.	
subj-3. . .	preterite.	
subj-4. . .	pluperfect.	

ACAD. for *Académie française* (French Academy), a learned Society, a literary Parliament, the highest authority on the French language.

The small figures 1, 2, 3, point out the order of the French construction when it differs from the English.—The larger figures 32, 47, etc. refer to the rule with that number, and which the student will do well to consult in cases of doubt.

* The asterisk, or little star, denotes that the English word under which it is placed, is to be omitted in French.

—— The line placed under an English word indicates that it is the same in French.

( ) When several English words are included within a parenthesis, they must be translated by the French word or words placed under them.

The English words printed in *italics*, are those to which the rules prefixed must be applied.

The substantives are generally given in the singular, the adjectives in the masculine singular, and the verbs in the present of the infinitive the student being expected to put them in their proper gender, number tense, and person.

N.B.—The student should make himself well acquainted with the use of the *Apostrophe*, page 9—with the *Contraction* of the article, p. 14—and, with the *General rule* for the place of personal pronouns, p. 237. The knowledge of these points will greatly facilitate his studies.

GRAMMAR

OF

FRENCH GRAMMARS.

Bien parler annonce la bonne éducation;
Bien écrire annonce de l'esprit.

INTRODUCTION.

1. GRAMMAR is the art which teaches to speak and write a language correctly.

To speak and to write, we make use of *words*.

Words are composed of one or more *syllables;* and syllables are composed of one or more *letters*.

2. The French Alphabet contains 25 letters, viz.:

    A B C D E F G H I J K L M
Names:—ah bay say day a eff *jay ash e *jee kah ell emm

    N O P Q R S T U V X Y Z.
enn o pay ku† err ess tay u† vay ecks eegree zaid.

[*Appellation usuelle:*— A B C D E F G H I J K L M
a bé cé dé é effe gé ache i ji ka elle emme

    N O P Q R S T U V X Y Z.
enne o pé ku erre esse té u vé ikse igrec zède.]
—*Académie française.*

3. Letters are divided into *vowels* and *consonants*. The vowels are A, E, I, O, U, and Y, which sometimes has the sound of one *i*, and sometimes of two. All the other letters are consonants.

The French make use of the W only in words borrowed from other languages; as, *Washington, whist.*

---

* *j* has here the sound of *s* in *pleasure*.

† The sound of *u* must be learned from the Teacher; unless you know how to pronounce *u* in the Scotch words *gude* (good), or *schule* (school).

OF ACCENTS AND OTHER MARKS.

4. The orthographical signs used in the French language are,—the *accents,* the *apostrophe,* the *hyphen,* the *diæresis,* the *cedilla,* the *parenthesis,* and the different marks of *punctuation.*

OF THE ACCENTS.

5. *Accents* are small marks placed upon vowels, either to point out their true pronunciation, or to distinguish the meaning of one word from that of another which is spelt alike, but has a different meaning.—Ex. *pêche,* peach; *péché,* sin; *pêcher,* to fish; *pécher,* to sin.

6. There are three accents in French,—the *acute,* the *grave,* and the *circumflex.*

7. The *acute* accent (´) is never used but over the vowel *e,* as in *vérité,* truth; *été,* summer; *café,* coffee.

8. The *grave* accent (`) is used over the vowels *a, e, u,* as in *voilà,* there is; *père,* father; *règle,* rule; *où,* where. It is placed—

Over the preposition *à,* to, in order to distinguish it from the third person singular of the verb *avoir, il a,* he has;

Over the adverb *là,* there, to distinguish it from the article *la,* the, or the pronoun *la,* her, it;

Over the adverb or pronoun *où,* (where, in which, to which), to distinguish it from the conjunction *ou,* or;

Over the preposition *dès,* from, since, to distinguish it from the compound article *des,* of the, some.

9. The *circumflex* accent (ˆ) is used with any of the vowels, the sound of which it always lengthens; as in *âge,* age; *tête,* head; *épître,* epistle; *dôme,* cupola; *flûte,* flute; *apôtre,* apostle. It is placed—

Over the adjective *sûr,* sure, to distinguish it from the preposition *sur,* upon;

Over the adjective *mûr,* ripe, to distinguish it from the substantive *mur,* wall;

Over *dû*, participle past of *devoir*, to owe, to distinguish it from the compound article *du*, of the, some; but the accent is only used in the singular masculine of the participle, as there can be no mistake in the feminine singular, nor in the plural of either gender;

Over *tû*, participle past of *taire*, to be silent, to distinguish it from the pronoun *tu*, thou;

Over *crû*, past participle of *croître*, to grow, to distinguish it from *cru*, past participle of *croire*, to believe.

OF THE APOSTROPHE.

10. The *Apostrophe* is a small mark in the form of a comma ('), which is placed over the line between two letters, to point out the elision or suppression of a vowel at the end of a word before another word beginning with a vowel, or *h* mute, as in *l'âme*, the soul; *l'homme*, the man; *s'il*, if he; instead of *la âme, le homme, si il*.

A, E, I, are the only vowels liable to be thus cut off.

11. The A is suppressed only in *la*, article or pronoun.

12. The elision of the E occurs, not only in the masculine article and pronoun *le*, but also in the monosyllables *je, me, te, se, ce, de, ne, que;* and, moreover—

(1.) In *jusque*, before *à, au, aux, ici;* as, *jusqu'à Rome*.

(2.) In *lorsque, puisque,* and *quoique,* before *il, ils, elle, elles, on, un, une,* or a word with which these conjunctions are immediately connected; as—*Lorsqu'ils viendront.—Puisqu'ainsi est.—Puisqu'il le veut.—Quoiqu'elle soit*.

(3.) In *quelque*, before *un, une;* as, *quelqu'un, quelqu'une;* and also in *quel qu'il soit, quelle qu'elle soit*. But we write *quelque autre; quelque historien*.

(4.) In *presque*, in the compound word *presqu'île*, peninsula; and likewise in *grande*, in the words *grand'mère* and *grand'tante*.

We also say and write:—*La grand'messe.—Avoir grand'faim.—Faire grand'chère.—C'est grand'pitié.—Il eut grand'peur.—Ce n'est pas grand'chose*.

13. The I is cut off only in the conjunction *si* (if) before the pronoun *il* and its plural *ils*, but never before *elle* or *elles*, nor any other word whatever.

14. But no elision of the *a* or *e* takes place in *le, la, de, ce, que,* before *oui, huit, huitaine, huitième, onze,* and *onzième;* neither in the pronouns *le* or *la,* after a verb in the imperative mood, nor in the adverb *là:* so we say, *le oui et le non; le huit ou le onze du mois; menez-le à Paris; ira-t-il là avec vous?*

15. The final *e* of the preposition *entre* is retained before the pronouns *eux, elles,* and before *autres;* and is only retrenched when *entre* forms a compound word with another word beginning with a vowel; as—*entr'acte, entr'ouvrir, s'entr'accuser, s'entr'aider.*

OF THE HYPHEN.

16. The *Hyphen* (in French, *tiret* or *trait d'union*) is a short horizontal line, thus -, which is used principally in connecting compound words, and between a verb and a pronoun, when a question is asked, as in *arc-en-ciel,* rainbow; *chef-d'œuvre,* master-piece; *parlez-vous?* do you speak? *avez-vous?* have you?

OF THE DIÆRESIS.

17. The *Diaresis* (in French, *tréma* or *diérèse*) is a mark of two points, thus ¨, put over the vowels *e, i, u,* to intimate that they form a distinct syllable from the vowels that precede them, as in the words *ciguë,* hemlock; *Moïse,* Moses; *Saül,* Saul; which are pronounced *Ci-gu-e, Mo-ise, Sa-ul.*

OF THE CEDILLA.

18. The *Cedilla* is a small mark placed under the letter *C,* to indicate that it is to be pronounced like *S,* before the vowels A, O, U, as in *Français,* French; *garçon,* boy; *maçon,* mason; *reçu,* received.

The signs of punctuation, and all other marks and characters, are the same in French as in English.

OF NUMBER.

19. There are two numbers in French; the *singular* and the *plural*. The singular denotes one person or thing; the plural denotes more than one.

OF CASES.

20. The French language has no *Cases*, properly so called, and consequently no declensions. The French express by prepositions, and especially by *de* (of or from), and *à* (to or at), the relations which the Greeks and the Romans indicated by the change of the different terminations of their nouns.

OF GENDER.

21. The French language has only two genders, the *masculine* and the *feminine*. The gender of *animate* or *living* beings presents no difficulty, as all males are *masculine*, and all females are *feminine ;* but it is only by practice that one can learn the gender of *inanimate* objects, and of animals whose names are the same for the male and female, such as *éléphant,* elephant; *buffle,* buffalo ; *cygne,* swan ; *perdrix,* partridge ; *baleine,* whale ; *truite,* trout; *saumon,* salmon.

It is not possible to give general and precise rules by means of which one may, on every occasion, distinguish the gender of a noun from its mere aspect. Several Grammarians, however, have given treatises on the genders; but those treatises are extremely incomplete; some of their rules are vague, and above all liable to numberless exceptions. The truth is, the perfect knowledge of the gender of substantives can only be the work of time. It is by reading with attention, and by having recourse, in cases of doubt, to a dictionary, that one will insensibly acquire a complete knowledge of the genders. Nevertheless in cases of doubt, and in the absence of a dictionary, it may be of some practical utility to know that about nine tenths of the nouns ending in *e* not accented are feminine; the final *e* mute being, in French, the distinctive mark of the feminine gender.

The French call the termination in *e* mute, a feminine termination; any other is called masculine. This distinction arises probably from the circumstance that most nouns of the feminine gender end with an *e* mute; thus, *la table, la rue, la plante, la tête, la fenêtre, la chambre, la plume, l'encre.*

22. Names of *states, empires, kingdoms,* and *provinces* are of the gender which their terminations indicate; thus: *Danemarck, Piémont, Tyrol, Portugal,* etc., are masculine; but: *Angleterre, Irlande, Ecosse, France, Espagne, Italie, Suisse, Belgique, Hollande, Allemagne, Prusse,* etc. which end in *e* mute, are feminine. *Le Hanovre, le Bengale, le Mexique,* and perhaps a few more, are exceptions.

23. The preceding rule is applicable to towns; every name of a town ending with an *e* mute is generally feminine, any other termination is masculine; thus: *Rome, Mantoue, Toulouse, Marseille,* are feminine; but: *Paris, Lyon, Rouen, Toulon, Amsterdam,* are masculine. *Jérusalem* is feminine; *Londres* is masculine. So we say, *Londres est florissant; Marseille est florissante.*

But, when one is uncertain of the gender of a town, the best way to get out of the difficulty is to put the word *ville* before the name of the town, and say: *la ville de Bruxelles, la ville de Lisbonne,* etc.

24. To the student who understands Latin, it may not be unimportant to know, that of nouns derived from that language, those from feminine nouns are mostly feminine, and those from masculine or neuter nouns, masculine; as *foi* from fides, *loi* from lex, *fourmi* from formica, *génie* from genius, *collége* from collegium, *poëme* from poëma, *incendie* from incendium, *fleuve* from fluvius, &c.

The gender of Nouns has been generally marked, in the Exercises throughout this work, in order to facilitate the acquirement of this part of French Grammar.

PART I.

25. There are, in French, as in English, nine sorts of words, usually called PARTS OF SPEECH; namely,

1. ARTICLE.
2. SUBSTANTIVE or NOUN.
3. ADJECTIVE.
4. PRONOUN.
5. VERB.
6. ADVERB.
7. PREPOSITION.
8. CONJUNCTION.
9. INTERJECTION.

CHAPTER I.

OF THE ARTICLE.

26. The *Article* is a word placed before a noun, to point it out, and to show the extent of its meaning.

The French article is *le, la, les,* the.

As the French language has borrowed much from the Latin, there is every reason to think that we have formed our *le* and our *la* from the pronoun *ille, illa, illud.* From the last syllable of the masculine word *ille*, we have made *le;* and from the last syllable of the feminine *illa*, we have made *la;* it is thus also that from the first syllable of that word, we have made our pronoun *il* (he), which we use with verbs, as likewise from the feminine *illa* we have made *elle* (she).

We use *le* before substantives masculine in the singular; *la* before substantives feminine, also in the singular; and, as the letter *s,* in the French language, is the sign of the plural when it is added to the singular, we have formed *les* from the singular *le.* *Les* serves equally for both genders.

When *le* or *la* comes before a noun beginning with a vowel or *h* mute, the *e* or *a* is cut off, and an apostrophe is put instead of the letter omitted. (See page 9.)

27. From the foregoing remarks it follows that the learner is to translate the English article

The, by
{
le before a noun masculine singular.
la before a noun feminine singular.
l' before a noun, either masculine or feminine singular, beginning with a vowel or *h* mute.
les before any noun in the plural.
}

A or *an* is translated by:
{
un before a noun masculine.
une before a noun feminine.
}

28. The English prepositions *to* and *at* are generally rendered in French by *à*; and *of* and *from* by *de*, or *d'* if the word begins with a vowel or an *h* mute.

EXERCISE I.

The father. — *The* mother. — *The* children. — *The* brother.—
    père m.   *mère* f.   *enfants* pl.   *frère* m.

The sister. — *The* uncle.— *The* aunt.— *The* relations.— *A* son.—
   sœur f.   *oncle* m.   *tante* f.   *parents* pl. *fils* m.

A daughter. — *The* man. —   *The* women. — *A* boy.—
  fille f.   *homme* h.m.   *femmes* pl.   *garçon* m

The day. — *The* night. — *The* sun.   — *The* moon. — *The*
  jour m.   *nuit* f.   *soleil* m.   *lune* f

stars. — *A* history. — *The* school. — *A* book. — *The* page.
étoiles pl. *histoire* f.   *école* f.   *livre* m.   *page* f.

29. CONTRACTION OF THE ARTICLE.

Whenever the prepositions *à* (*to* or *at*) or *de* (*of* or *from*) precede the article *le* before a noun masculine singular, beginning with a consonant or *h* aspirate, *à le* is contracted into *au*, and *de le* into *du*; and before plural nouns of either gender, *à les* is changed into *aux*, and *de les* into *des*.

A and *de* are not contracted with *le* before nouns which begin with a vowel or *h* mute, but then the article suffers elision.

Nor are *à* and *de* ever contracted with *la*.

The learner will therefore translate

To the, or at the, by
{
au { before a noun masculine singular, beginning with a consonant, or *h* aspirate.
à la { before a noun feminine singular, beginning with a consonant, or *h* aspirate.
à l' { before a noun masculine or feminine, in the singular, beginning with a vowel, or *h* mute.
aux before any noun in the plural.
}

OF THE ARTICLE.

Of the, or from the, by
- **du** before a noun masculine singular, beginning with a consonant, or *h* aspirate.
- **de la** before a noun feminine singular, beginning with a consonant, or *h* aspirate.
- **de l'** before a noun masculine or feminine, in the singular, beginning with a vowel, or *h* mute.
- **des** before any noun in the plural.

To a, to an, at a, at an, are translated by
- **à un** before a noun masculine.
- **à une** before a noun feminine.

Of or from a or an, by
- **d' un** before a noun masculine.
- **d' une** before a noun feminine.

EXERCISE II.

To the king.—To the queen.—To the hero.—To the scholars.—
   roi m.   *reine* f.   *héros* h asp.   *écoliers* pl.
Of the master.—Of the house.—Of the church.—Of the coat.—
   maître m.   *maison* f.   *église* f.   *habit* h m.
Of the curtains.—To a dictionary.—Of a grammar.—To a pen.—
   rideaux pl. *dictionnaire* m. *grammaire* f. *plume* f.
Of a penknife.—At the hotel.—From the garden.—To the
   canif m.   *hôtel* h m.   *jardin* m.
town.—Of the harp.—To a watch.—From a clock.—
ville f.   *harpe* f. h asp. *montre* f.   *horloge* f.
Of the ladies.—At an inn.—From a village to a town.
   dames pl. *auberge* f.   ——m.

GENERAL RULES ON THE ARTICLE.

30.—I. The article must always agree in gender and number with its noun.

31.—II. The article and the prepositions *à* and *de*, whether contracted or not, are generally repeated in French before every noun, although often omitted in English.

EXAMPLE.

| Le lis est le symbole de la candeur, de l'innocence, et de la pureté. | The *lily is* the *emblem* of *candour, innocence, and purity* |

EXERCISE III.

The lion is the king of animals.—The fox is the
   —m. *est* *roi* m. art. *animaux* pl. *renard* m.
emblem of cunning.—The rose is the queen of flowers.—
emblème m art. *ruse* f.   —f.   *reine* f. art. *fleurs* pl.

Idleness is the mother of all vices.— The love of
art. *paresse* f.   *mère* f. *de tous* art. — pl.   *amour* m.

life is natural to man. — She (is learning)
art. *vie* f.   *naturel* art. *homme* h m.   *Elle apprend*

drawing, music, and dancing.—I write to the
art. *dessin* m. art. *musique* f.   *et* art. *danse* f. *J'écris*

nephew and the niece.—The Creator of heaven and
neveu m.   pr.   *nièce* f.   *Créateur* m. art. *ciel* m.

earth.—The vigour of mind and body.
pr. art. *terre* f.   *vigueur* f.   art. *esprit* m.   pr. art. *corps* m.

32.—III. OF THE ARTICLE *du, de la, de l', des*, USED IN A
PARTITIVE SENSE, *i. e.* implying a part, not the whole.

Du for the masculine, *de la* for the feminine, *de l'* before a vowel or *h* mute, *des* for the plural, answering to the English words SOME or ANY, expressed or *understood*, must be repeated before every noun in French.

EXAMPLES.

Envoyez-nous *du* pain, *de la* viande, | Send us some bread, meat, and
et *des* pommes de terre. | potatoes.
Avez-vous *de la* monnaie? | Have you got any change?

EXERCISE IV.

Give me *some* paper, . ink, and pens.— Take
Donnez-moi *papier* m. *encre* f. *et plumes* pl. *Prenez*

some tea or coffee. — Put in *some* sugar and cream.—
thé m. *ou café* m. *Mettez-y* *sucre* m. *crême* f.

Offer him *some* cheese, eggs, butter, and milk.—
Offrez-lui *fromage* m. *œufs* pl. *beurre* m. *lait* m.

Drink *some* wine, *some* beer, or *some* water. — Eat
Buvez *vin* m. *bière* f. *eau* f. *Mangez*

some hash. — Bring me *some* oil, mustard,
hachis m. h asp. *Apportez-moi* *huile* h m. *moutarde* f.

pepper, and salt. — Have you got *any* money? — Has she *any*
poivre m. *sel* m. *Avez-vous* *argent* m. *A-t-elle*

wool or thread?—Is there *any* ripe fruit in the garden?
laine f. *fil* m. *Y a-t-il* *mûr* [1]—m. *dans* *jardin* m.

Yes; there are apricots, peaches, pears, and apples.
il y a *abricots, pêches, poires, pommes.*

CHAPTER II.
OF THE SUBSTANTIVE OR NOUN.

33. A *Substantive* or *Noun* is the name of any person or thing that exists, or of which we have any notion; as, *Alexandre*, Alexander; *Londres*, London; *homme*, man; *maison*, house; *vertu*, virtue.

Substantives are either *proper* or *common*.

The substantive *proper*, or *proper name*, is the name appropriated to one person, or one thing only; as, *Calvin, Milton, France, Paris, Dublin*.

The *common* noun is that which belongs to persons, or things of the same kind; as, *homme*, man; *arbre*, tree; which appellation equally suits all men, all trees.

Among common nouns, we must distinguish the *collective nouns;* so called, because, although used in the singular number, they present to the mind the idea of several persons or things.

Collective nouns are divided into *general* and *partitive*. The former express a whole body; as, *armée*, army; *forêt*, forest. The latter express only a partial number; as, *multitude*, multitude; *quantité*, quantity.

OF THE FORMATION OF THE PLURAL OF FRENCH SUBSTANTIVES.

GENERAL RULE.

34. The plural of Substantives, either masculine or feminine, is formed by adding an *s* to the singular; as,

le père,	*the father.*	les pères,	*the fathers.*
la mère,	*the mother.*	les mères,	*the mothers.*
l'enfant,	*the child.*	les enfants,*	*the children.*
le moment,	*the moment.*	les moments,*	*the moments.*

---

* It was formerly a general practice, and it is still retained by some, to leave out the *t* in the plural of nouns and adjectives ending in *ant* and *ent*, but at the present day the adjective *tout* (all) is the only word in which the French Academy drops the *t* in the plural masculine; as,

Tous les parents.	*All the relations.*
Tous les habitants.—*(Académie.)*	*All the inhabitants.*

To *tout* might be added *gent*, plural *gens;* but *gent* singular is only used in familiar poetry; as, *la gent marécageuse*, the marshy tribe.

OF THE SUBSTANTIVE.

EXCEPTIONS TO THE GENERAL RULE.

35. Exception I.—Nouns ending in *s*, *x*, or *z*, in the singular, remain the same in the plural; as,

le lis,	the lily.	les lis,	the lilies.
la voix,	the voice.	les voix,	the voices.
le nez,	the nose.	les nez,	the noses.

EXERCISE V.

The *trees* of their *orchards*.—The *flowers* of our *gardens*.—
    arbre leurs verger   fleur nos jardin
The *palaces* of the *kings*.—Buy me four *pounds* of *walnuts*.
    palais   roi Achetez-moi quatre livre   noix
—The *fashions* of the *French*.—The *crosses* of the *knights*.—
    mode   Français   croix   chevalier
The *laws* of those *countries*.—The *movements* of the *armies*.—
    loi   ces   pays   mouvement   armée
The *spoons* and *forks* are on the table.— He has
    cuiller et art. fourchette sont sur ——f. Il a
three *sons* and two *daughters*.—The *lilies* of the *fields*.
trois fils deux fille   champ

36. Exception II.—Nouns ending in *au*, *eu*, *œu*, or *ou*, take an *x* instead of an *s* in the plural; as,

chapeau,	hat.	chapeaux,	hats.
jeu,	game.	jeux,	games.
vœu,	vow.	vœux,	vows.
bijou,	jewel.	bijoux,	jewels.
hibou,	owl.	hiboux,	owls.

37. The following nouns in *ou*, conform to the general rule, taking an *s* in the plural:

clou,	nail.	licou,	halter.
coucou,	cuckoo.	sou,	penny.
filou,	pickpocket.	trou,	hole.
fou,	fool.	verrou,	bolt.

EXERCISE VI.

A *fleet* of twenty *ships*.— The *boats* of the *sailors*.—
  flotte f. vingt vaisseau   bateau   matelot
He (found himself) between two *fires*.— *Owls* are
Il se trouva   entre deux feu art. sont des
nocturnal birds.—The *knives* are on the *sideboard*.—
²nocturnes ¹oiseau   couteau   sur   buffet m.
(There are) many *pickpockets* in London and Paris.—
Il y a beaucoup de filou à Londres et à ——

Fill up those *holes*. — Give him six *pence*. — Our doors
Remplissez ces   *Donnez-lui* — *sou*   *Nos porte*
have   *bolts*.—He has sold the *pictures* and the *jewels*.
ont 32 *verrou*   *vendu*   *tableau*

38. EXCEPTION III.—Most nouns ending in *al* or *ail* in the singular, form their plural by changing the final *al* or *ail* into *aux*; as,

canal,	canal.	canaux,	canals.
hôpital,	hospital.	hôpitaux,	hospitals.
travail,	work.	travaux,	works.

39. The following nouns in *al* and *ail* take an *s* in the plural:

attirail,	apparatus,	imple-	éventail,	fan.	
bal,	ball.	[ments.	gouvernail,	helm, rudder.	
carnaval,	carnival.		portail,	portal.	
détail,	detail, particulars.		régal,	treat.	

40. AÏEUL, CIEL, ŒIL, have two plurals.

Singular.	Meaning.		Plural.
aïeul	{ grandfather, - - - - -		aïeuls.
	ancestor, forefather, - - - - -		aïeux.
ciel	{ sky, heaven, - - - - -		cieux.
	sky in a picture; or, tester of a bed,	-	ciels
œil	eye, - - - - - - - -		yeux.

(*œil-de-bœuf*, bull's-eye, (architectural term), makes in the plural, *œils-de-bœuf*.)

Bétail, subst. masc. sing., and *Bestiaux*, subst. masc. pl., are synonymous, both meaning *cattle*.

EXERCISE VII.

The *horses* of the *generals*. — The *marshals* of France. —
      cheval   *général*   *maréchal* ———
The English *admirals*.—These *corals* are beautiful.—The *balls*
   ²*anglais* ¹*amiral*   *Ces corail sont superbes*.   *bal*
of the nobility. — He sells   *fans*. — Our   Saviour
     noblesse f.   *Il vend* 32 *éventail Notre Sauveur*
ascended into *heaven* in presence of his disciples.—Open
monta   *à* art. *ciel* pl. *en présence de ses* ——— *Ouvrez*
your   *eyes*.—She has the portraits of her two *grandfathers*.
   * art. *œil*   *Elle a*   ——— *ses deux*
— His *forefathers* have filled   high   stations.
         ont rempli de grandes charges.

CHAPTER III.

OF THE ADJECTIVE.

41. An *Adjective* is a word which expresses some quality or distinction ascribed to a substantive.

Adjective, from the Latin *adjectus*, signifies *added to*.

A word is known to be an adjective, when it can be properly joined with the word *personne*, person; or *chose*, thing. Thus, *fidèle*, faithful, and *agréable*, agreeable, are adjectives, because we can say, *une personne fidèle*, a faithful person; *une chose agréable*, an agreeable thing.

In English, the adjectives never vary on account of gender and number, but in French they change their termination, in order to agree, in gender and number, with the nouns or pronouns to which they relate.

OF THE FORMATION OF THE FEMININE OF ADJECTIVES.

GENERAL RULE.

42. The feminine of adjectives is formed by adding an *e* mute to the masculine singular; as,

Masc.	Fem.		Masc.	Fem.	
prudent,	prudente,	*prudent.*	joli,	jolie,	*pretty.*
grand,	grande,	*great.*	âgé,	âgée,	*old, aged.*
court,	courte,	*short.*	petit,	petite,	*little, small.*

EXCEPTIONS.

43. EXCEPTION I.—Adjectives ending in *e* mute (that is, *e* not accented), remain the same in the feminine; as,

un jeune garçon, *a young boy.* | une jeune fille, *a young girl.*

EXERCISE VIII.

Their house   is *small,* but it   is   very *pretty.*—
Leur maison f. est   mais elle est très

That street is *narrow* and *dark.*—The meat is *cold;* the
Cette rue f.   étroit   et obscur   viande f. froid

water is *hot.*— This   pear   (is not)   *ripe.*— Avoid
eau f. chaud Cette poire f. n'est pas   mûr   Évitez

OF THE ADJECTIVE.

bad company.—That girl is very cunning.—She
art mauvais compagnie f. fille f. rusé Elle
has a black gown and a red scarf.—The eldest sister
a ²noir ¹robe f. ²rouge ¹écharpe f. ²aîné ¹sœur
is a model of filial piety.—(She is) a clever woman.
modèle m. ² ¹piété f. C'est habile femme.

44. Exception II.—Adjectives ending in *f* change
that letter into *ve* for the feminine; as,

Masc.	Fem.		Masc.	Fem.	
actif,	active,	active.	neuf,	neuve,	new.
bref,	brève,	brief, short.	vif,	vive,	lively.

45. Exception III.—Adjectives ending in *x* change
the *x* into *se*; as,

Masc.	Fem.		Masc.	Fem.	
heureux,	heureuse,	happy.	paresseux,	paresseuse,	idle.
jaloux,	jalouse,	jealous.	vertueux,	vertueuse,	virtuous.

46. The following in *x* form their feminine thus:

Masc.	Fem.		Masc.	Fem.	
doux,	douce,	sweet, mild.	roux,	rousse,	red.
faux,	fausse,	false.	vieux,	vieille,	old.

EXERCISE IX.

Is she attentive?—Catherine de Médicis was ambitious,
Est-elle attentif — — — était ambitieux
imperious, and superstitious; she was a native of Florence.—
impérieux et superstitieux * natif de —
Joshua (brought down) the walls of the proud Jericho.—
Josué fit tomber mur orgueilleux Jéricho f.
The Italian language is sweet and harmonious.—That
²italienne ¹langue f. doux harmonieux Cette
news is false.—The new tower is in the old town.
nouvelle f. faux ²neuf ¹tour f. dans vieux ville f.

47. Exception IV.—Adjectives ending in *el*, *eil*, *ien*,
on, and *et*, form their feminine by doubling the last consonant, and adding an *e* mute after it; as,

Masc.	Fem.		Masc.	Fem.	
cruel,	cruelle,	cruel.	chrétien,	chrétienne,	Christian.
pareil,	pareille,	similar.	bon,	bonne,	good.
ancien,	ancienne,	ancient.	net,	nette,	clean.

☞ Prêt, ready, makes prête in the feminine.

OF THE ADJECTIVE.

48. The following adjectives in *et* and *er* follow the *general rule*, but take a grave accent over the *e* before the final *t* or *r* in the feminine:

Masc.	*Fem.*	
complet,	complète,	*complete.*
incomplet,	incomplète,	*incomplete.*
discret,	discrète,	*discreet.*
indiscret,	indiscrète,	*indiscreet.*
inquiet,	inquiète,	*uneasy.*
secret,	secrète,	*secret.*
cher,	chère,	*dear.*
fier,	fière,	*proud.*
premier,	première,	*first.*
dernier,	dernière,	*last.*

EXERCISE X.

The soul is *immortal.*—I (am reading) ancient history.—
âme f. est immortel   Je   lis   art.²ancien ¹histoire f. h m.
We are in the nineteenth century of the Christian
Nous sommes dans dix-neuvième siècle m.   ²chrétien
era.— She (is not) pretty, but she is good.— That poor
¹ère f. Elle n'est pas joli mais est   Cette pauvre
woman is *dumb.* — Are you *ready,* my *dear* sister?—Your
femme muet   Etes-vous   ma   sœur ? Votre
mother is very *uneasy.*—That person is extremely *indiscreet.*
mère très   personne f. extrêmement

49. EXCEPTION V.—Adjectives ending in *eur*, formed from a participle present by the change of *ant* into *eur*, make *euse* in the feminine; as,

Participle.	*Masc.*	*Fem.*	
connaiss*ant*,	connaisseur,	connaisseuse,	*knowing, a judge.*
flatt*ant*,	flatteur,	flatteuse,	*flattering, a flatterer.*
ment*ant*,	menteur,	menteuse,	*lying, a liar.*
tromp*ant*,	trompeur,	trompeuse,	*deceiving, deceitful.*

OBSERVATION.—Words of this sort are real adjectives, though for the most part used as substantives. About a hundred of them follow this rule.

50. The following must be excepted, as they form their feminine by changing *eur* into *eresse:*

Masc.	*Fem.*	
demandeur,	demanderesse,	*a plaintiff.*
défendeur,	défenderesse,	*a defendant.*
enchanteur,	enchanteresse,	*enchanting.*
pécheur,	pécheresse,	*a sinner.*
vengeur,	vengeresse,	*avenging, an avenger.*

51. *Inventeur,* inventor; *inspecteur,* inspector; *persécuteur,* persecutor, make, in the feminine, *inventrice, inspectrice,* and *persécutrice.*

52. As to the adjectives, or rather nouns used adjectively, ending in *teur,* which, though derived from verbs, are not formed from a participle present, by the change of *ant* into *eur,* they change *teur* into *trice* for the feminine; as,

Masc.	*Fem.*	
accusateur,	accusa*trice,*	*an accuser.*
bienfaiteur,	bienfai*trice,*	*a benefactor, a benefactress.*
conducteur,	conduc*trice,*	*a conductor, a conductress.*
instituteur,	institu*trice,*	*a schoolmaster, a governess.*

Upwards of fifty nouns follow this rule.

Those who know Latin will see that most nouns ending in *teur* and *trice* are derived from the Latin words in *tor* and *trix;* as, *accusator, accusatrix,* etc.

53. Adjectives ending in *eur,* not derived from verbs, and conveying an idea of *opposition* or *comparison,* follow the general rule of taking an *e* mute in the feminine; as,

Masc.	*Fem.*		*Masc.*	*Fem.*	
antérieur,	antérieure,	*anterior.*	majeur,	majeure,	*major.*
citérieur,	citérieure,	*citerior.*	mineur,	mineure,	*minor.*
extérieur,	extérieure,	*exterior.*	postérieur,	postérieure,	*posterior.*
intérieur,	intérieure,	*interior.*	supérieur,	supérieure,	*superior.*
inférieur,	inférieure,	*inferior.*	ultérieur,	ultérieure,	*ulterior.*
meilleur,	meilleure,	*better.*			

54. *Empereur,* emperor; *ambassadeur,* ambassador; *gouverneur,* governor; *serviteur,* servant, make in the feminine *impératrice, ambassadrice, gouvernante, servante.*

Chasseur, hunter, has two feminines—*chasseuse* in prose, and *chasseresse* in poetry.

Chanteur, singer, has also two feminines—*chanteuse* and *cantatrice.* The latter is used in speaking of an eminent professional female vocalist.

55. Words expressing *professions, trades,* &c., usually followed by men, have no feminine, even when exercised by women; as,

graveur,	*an engraver.*	imprimeur,	*a printer.*
sculpteur,	*a sculptor.*	docteur,	*a doctor.*

24   OF THE ADJECTIVE.

professeur,   *a professor.* | traducteur,   *a translator.*
auteur,   *an author.* | &c.   &c.

EXAMPLES.

Mademoiselle de Schurman, née à Cologne en 1606, était *peintre, graveur, sculpteur, géomètre.*—(DICT. DE BIOGRAPHIE.)	*Mademoiselle de Schurman, born at Cologne in 1606, was a painter, an engraver, a sculptor, and a geometrician.*
Madame de Staël est un de nos plus grands *écrivains.*—(BOISTE.)	*Madame de Staël is one of our greatest writers.*
Une femme *auteur.*—(ACAD.)	*A female author.*
Madame Deshoulières était un *poète* aimable.—(ACAD.)	*Madame Deshoulières was an amiable poetess.*

☞ *Poétesse*, s. f. (a female poet) is a word seldom used.—(ACAD.)

EXERCISE XI.

She is   a great   *talker*   and a great   *laugher.* — Is she
C'est   *grand parleur*   *rieur*   *Est-elle*

quarrelsome ? — Joan of Arc was the *avenger* of France.—
querelleur   Jeanne d'Arc fut   *vengeur*   art. ——f.

She is the *benefactress* of the poor. — She is a good *actress*,
C'est   *bienfaiteur*   pauvre pl.   *bon acteur*

and a celebrated *singer.*—Minerva was the *protectress* of the
                 célèbre   Minerve était   *protecteur*

fine arts. —The city of Troy was in   Asia *Minor.*—
beaux-arts.   ville f. Troie dans art. *Asie* f. *Mineur*

(There is) a *superior*   power.— That is a *flattering* promise.
Il y a   ²*supérieur* ¹*puissance* f. *C'*   ²   ¹*promesse* f.

56. There are seven adjectives ending in *c* which form their feminine thus:

Masc.	*Fem.*		*Masc.*	*Fem.*	
blanc,	blanche,	*white.*	public,	publique,	*public.*
caduc,	caduque,	*infirm.*	sec,	sèche,	*dry.*
franc,	franche,	*frank, open.*	turc,	turque,	*Turkish.*
grec,	grecque,	*Greek, Grecian.*			

57. The six following terminations in *s* take *se* in the feminine:

Masc.	*Fem.*		*Masc.*	*Fem.*	
bas,	basse,	*low.*	gras,	grasse,	*fat.*
épais,	épaisse,	*thick.*	gros,	grosse,	*big.*
exprès,	expresse,	*express.*	las,	lasse,	*tired.*

OF THE ADJECTIVE.

58. The following adjectives form their feminine irregularly:

Masc.	Fem.		Masc.	Fem.	
beau,	belle,*	*fine.*	long,	longue,	*long.*
bénin,	bénigne,	*benign.*	malin,	maligne,	*malignant*
favori,	favorite,	*favourite.*	mou,	molle,*	*soft.*
fou,	folle,*	*foolish.*	nouveau,	nouvelle,*	*new.*
frais,	fraiche,	*fresh.*	nul,	nulle,	*null.*
gentil,	gentille,	*genteel.*	sot,	sotte,	*silly.*
jumeau,	jumelle,	*twin.*	traître,	traîtresse,	*treacherous*

* REMARK.—The feminines, *belle, folle, molle, nouvelle,* are formed from the masculines, *bel, fol, mol, nouvel,* which are used before a vowel, or *h* mute.

EXERCISE XII.

(Here is) a handsome white gown.—His public life is
Voici beau ²blanc ¹robe f. Sa ²public ¹vie f. est

irreproachable. — This table is too low. — This board is
irréprochable. Cette —f. trop bas planche f.

too long and too thick. — This soup is too fat. — It is
long épais soupe f. gras C'est

a new discovery. — Have you seen my favourite flower.
nouveau découverte f. Avez-vous vu ma ²favori ¹fleur f.

the rose, so fresh and so sweet? — That is a fine tree.
— f. si frais doux Voilà arbre m.

PLURAL OF FRENCH ADJECTIVES.

GENERAL RULE.

59. Adjectives form their plural, like substantives, by the simple addition of an *s* to the singular; as,

Singular.	Plural.	
grand, *masc.*	grands,	} *great.*
grande, *fem.*	grandes,	
savant, *masc.*	savants,	} *learned.*
savante, *fem.*	savantes,	

This rule is without any exceptions for the feminine, but the masculine has the three following:

60.—EXCEPTION I. Adjectives ending in *s* or *x* do not change their termination in the plural masculine; as, *gras,* fat; *gros,* big; *heureux,* happy.

61.—EXCEPTION II. Adjectives ending in *au* take *x* in the plural masculine; as, *beau*, handsome; *nouveau*, new; plural, *beaux, nouveaux.*

62.—EXCEPTION III. Adjectives ending in *al* change this termination into *aux* for the plural masculine; as, *égal*, equal; *moral*, moral; plural, *égaux, moraux.*

_{A few adjectives ending in *al* follow the general rule, and take *s* in the plural, and others have no plural masculine; but these are adjectives seldom used.}

63. *Tout*, all, is the only adjective that changes *t* into *s* for the plur. masc., but it makes *toutes* in the plur. fem.

EXERCISE XIII.

Give some *entertaining* books to those *pretty little* girls.
Donnez   ²*amusant* ¹*livre* m.   *ces*   *joli*   *petit*   *fille*

—He has *powerful* enemies, but their efforts (will be)
Il a de puissant ennemi m. *mais leurs* —— m. *seront*

vain and *useless*.—These chickens are *big* and *fat*, but those
vain et inutile   *Ces poulet* m. *sont gros* *gras*

partridges are very *lean*. — *All* the *general* officers were
perdrix f.   *très maigre* *Tout* ²*général* ¹*officier étaient*

present. — The *old* and the *new* soldiers did won-
présent   *vieux*   *soldat firent* 32 mer-

ders.— I agree to *all* those conditions, they are reasonable.
veille Je consens   *ces* —— f. *elles raisonnable*

OF THE DEGREES OF COMPARISON.

64. There are three degrees of comparison; the *Positive*, the *Comparative*, and the *Superlative*.

The *Positive* is the adjective itself, merely expressing the quality of an object, without any comparison; as,

_{Un enfant *sage* et *studieux*. | A well-behaved *and* studious *child.*}

EXERCISE XIV.

She is *satisfied* with her lot. — Merit is *modest.* —
Elle est content de son sort. art. *mérite* m. *modeste.*

Socrates and Plato were two great philosophers.—
Socrate   *Platon étaient deux grand philosophe*

Virgil had a *fine* and *delicate* taste.—The style of
Virgile avait ²*fin* ³*et* ⁴*délicat* ¹*goût* m.   — m.

Fénélon is *harmonious*.—The Alps   are *high* and *steep*.—
——— *est harmonieux.*   *Alpes* f. pl. *sont haut*   *escarpés*
The city of Rome is *full* of *ancient* and *modern* monuments.
ville f. ——— *rempli* ²*ancien* ³*et* ⁴*moderne* ¹———— m.

65. The *Comparative Degree* expresses a comparison between two or more objects. There are three sorts of comparatives, viz. of *superiority*, *inferiority*, and *equality*.

The comparative of *superiority* is formed by putting the adverb *plus*, more, before the adjective, and the conjunction *que*, than, after it; as,

Athènes a été *plus* illustre *que* Lacédémone. | *Athens was* more *illustrious* than *Lacedæmon.*

N.B.—The comparative degree is often formed in English by adding *r* or *er* to the positive; as, *wise*, *wiser; great, greater;* and as these letters stand for the adverb *more*, they must be rendered in French by its corresponding adverb *plus ;* thus, *wiser*, plus sage; *greater*, plus grand.

Plus must be repeated before every adjective.

EXERCISE XV.

Virtue   is *more* precious *than*   riches. — He is
art. *vertu* f. est   *précieux*   art. *richesses* pl.   *Il*
happier than a king.—He is *more* fortunate *than* wise. — It is
content   roi.   *heureux*   *sage*. *Il*
more   noble to forgive *than* to (avenge one's self). —
         ——— *de pardonner*   *de*   *se venger.*
The simplicity of   nature is *more* pleasing *than* all the
 simplicité f. art. ——— f.   *agréable*   *tout*
embellishments of   art. — London   is *more* populous
 ornement m.   art. — *Londres* m.   *peuplé*
than Paris, but   France is *larger* and *more* populous *than*
     ——— *mais* art. ——— f. *grand et*
     England. — The Thames is *deeper than* the Seine.
art. *Angleterre.*   *Tamise* f. *profond*   ——— f.

66. The comparative of *inferiority* is formed by placing the adverb *moins*, less, before the adjective, and *que*, than, after it; as,

L'Afrique est *moins* peuplée *que* l'Europe. | *Africa is less populous than Europe.*

Moins is to be repeated before every adjective.

The comparative of *inferiority* may also be formed by putting the verb in the negative, with *si*, so, before the adjective, and *que*, as, after it; as,

L'Afrique n'est pas *si* peuplée *que* l'Europe. | *Africa is not so populous as Europe.*

EXERCISE XVI.

Death is *less* fatal *than* the pleasures which attack
art. *mort* f. est   *funeste*   *plaisir   qui attaquent*
virtue.—He is *less* polite and obliging *than* his brother.—
art. *vertu* f. Il   *poli   obligeant   son frère.*
She is *less* amiable *than* her sister.—Cæsar (was not) *less* brave
Elle   aimable   sa sœur.   César n'était pas
than Alexander.—They are *less* happy *than* you think.—He
Alexandre.   Ils   heureux   vous ne pensez.
(is not) *so* rich *as* his brother-in-law.—His family is much
n'est pas   riche   beau-frère.   Sa famille f. bien
less numerous *than* ours.—He is *less* rich *than* you.
nombreux   la nôtre.

67. The comparative of *equality* is formed by placing the adverb *aussi*, as, before the adjective, and *que*, as, after it; as,

Aristide était *aussi* vaillant *que* juste. | *Aristides was as valiant as just.*

Aussi must be repeated before every adjective.

EXERCISE XVII.

Is he *as* clever, and *as* docile *as* his cousin?—He is *as*
Est-il   habile   son ――― m. Il est
tall *as* you.—Your niece is *as* pretty *as* that girl.—She is
grand   vous. Votre nièce   joli   cette fille.
as good *as* beautiful.—Socrates was *as* valiant *as* wise.
          beau   Socrate était   vaillant   sage.
— Cicero was *as* pious *as* eloquent.—It is *as* easy to do
Cicéron   pieux   éloquent.   Il   aisé de faire
good *as* to do evil. History is *as* useful *as*
art. *bien* m.   art. *mal* m. art. *histoire* h m.   *utile*
agreeable. — This house is *as* large *as* yours.
agréable.   Cette   maison f.   *grand   la vôtre.*

68. The *Superlative Degree* expresses the quality in the highest or lowest degree. There are two sorts of superlatives, the *relative* and the *absolute*.

The superlative *relative* expresses a relation or comparison with another object; it is formed by putting the article *le, la, les*, before the comparative.

EXAMPLES.

Le chien est l'animal *le plus* fidèle.	The dog is the most *faithful animal.*
Ce sont les hommes *les plus* sages de l'assemblée.—(ACAD.)	They are the wisest *men in the assembly.*

The superlative *relative* may also be formed by placing before the comparative one of the possessive adjectives, *mon, ma, mes,* my; *ton, ta, tes,* thy; *son, sa, ses,* his or her; *notre, nos,* our; *votre, vos,* your; *leur, leurs,* their.

EXAMPLES.

Mon plus puissant protecteur.	My most *powerful protector.*
Votre plus grand ennemi.	Your greatest *enemy.*

EXERCISE XVIII.

Gold   is *the* purest, *the most* precious, *the most* ductile,
art. *or* m. *est*   pur,   précieux,   ———
and, after   platina, *the heaviest* of   all   metals.—
      après art. *platine* m.   pesant   tout art. *métal* m.
The *least* excusable of all   errors   is   that which is
      ———   art. *erreur* f.   *celle qui*
wilful.— The elephant   is *the strongest* of all   animals.—
volontaire.   *éléphant* m.   *fort*   art. *animal* m.
I prefer my house to *the finest* palace. — Our greatest
Je préfère ma maison   *beau palais* m.   *Nos grand*
interests. — *Your most* cruel enemies. — My *prettiest* rings.
intérêt m. *Vos*   *cruel ennemi* m. *Mes*   *bague* f.

69. The superlative *absolute* does not imply any relation to another object, but merely expresses the quality in the highest or lowest degree; it is formed by putting before the adjective one of these words, *très,** *fort,*† *bien,* very; *extrêmement,* extremely; *infiniment,* infinitely; *excessivement,* excessively; or any other adverb expressing a very high degree.

EXERCISE XIX.

Mr and Mrs Fox are *very* happy. They are both *very*
                    heureux.   *tous deux*
capricious.—Dublin is a *very* large and *very* fine city.—That
capricieux. —— *est*   *grand*   *beau ville* f. *Cette*
lady is *very* charitable.—He is a *very* unfortunate man.—He
dame   ——   *C'est* " *¹malheureux* ²*homme Il.*

---

* *Très,* from the Greek τρις, thrice; *très-heureux,* thrice happy.

† *Fort,* abbreviation of *fortement* strongly.

OF THE ADJECTIVE.

(is not) *very* clever. — This soup is *very* hot. — The
n'est pas   *habile.*   *Cette soupe* f.   *chaud*
tea and the sugar are *very* bad. — That work
thé m.   *sucre* m.   *mauvais.*   *Cet ouvrage* m.
is *very* much esteemed by the learned. — Madame Dacier
    *   *estimé de*   *savant* m. pl.
was *extremely* learned. — God is *infinitely* just.
était   *savant*   *Dieu*   *juste.*

70. The adjectives, *bon, mauvais,* and *petit,* and the adverbs, *bien, mal,* and *peu,* form their degrees in the following manner:

	Positive.		Comparative.		Superlative.	
Adjectives.	bon,	good.	meilleur,	better.	le meilleur,	the best.
	mauvais,	bad.	pire,	worse.	le pire,	the worst.
	petit,	little.	moindre,	less.	le moindre,	the least.
Adverbs.	bien,	well.	mieux,	better.	le mieux,	the best.
	mal,	badly.	pis,	worse.	le pis,	the worst.
	peu,	little.	moins,	less.	le moins,	the least.

Plus mauvais, plus petit, plus mal, are also used, but never *plus bon, plus bien, plus peu.*

EXERCISE XX.

That wine is *good,* but this is *better.* — Lend me
   Ce vin m. *est*   *mais celui-ci*   *Prêtez-moi*
the best book in your library. — He writes *well,* but his
       livre m. *de votre bibliothèque. Il écrit*   *sa*
sister writes still *better.* — The life of a slave is *worse*
sœur   *encore*   *vie* f. *esclave* m.
than death itself. — He was a *little better,* but he is
que art. *mort* f. *même. se portait*   *mais est*
now *worse* than ever. — She speaks *little.* — Speak *less.*—
maintenant que jamais.   *parle*   *Parlez*
(It is) his *least* misfortune. — The remedy is *worse* than
C'est son   *malheur* m.   *remède* m. *est*
the disease. — Temperance is *the best* doctor.
   mal m. art. *tempérance* f.   *médecin* m.

There are some adjectives which have neither comparatives nor superlatives, because the qualities which they express are in themselves the highest degree of perfection, worth, etc.; such are *éternel, immortel, suprême,* etc.

OF NUMERAL ADJECTIVES.

71. The Adjectives of Number are divided into *Cardinal* and *Ordinal*.

The *Cardinal* numbers are used to count and express the quantity or number of persons or things.

The *Ordinal* numbers mark the order or rank which persons or things hold with regard to one another.

All numeral adjectives are of both genders, with the exception of *un*, *premier*, and *second*, which take an *e* in the feminine.

Cardinal Numbers.	Ordinal Numbers.
1 Un.	1st Premier.
2 Deux.	2d Second, *or* Deuxième.
3 Trois.	3d Troisième.
4 Quatre.	4th Quatrième.
5 Cinq.	5th Cinquième.
6 Six.	6th Sixième.
7 Sept.	7th Septième.
8 Huit.	8th Huitième.
9 Neuf.	9th Neuvième.
10 Dix.	10th Dixième.
11 Onze.	11th Onzième.
12 Douze.	12th Douzième.
13 Treize.	13th Treizième.
14 Quatorze.	14th Quatorzième.
15 Quinze.	15th Quinzième.
16 Seize.	16th Seizième.
17 Dix-sept.	17th Dix-septième.
18 Dix-huit.	18th Dix-huitième.
19 Dix-neuf.	19th Dix-neuvième.
20 Vingt.	20th Vingtième.
21 Vingt et un.	21st Vingt et unième.
22 Vingt-deux.	22d Vingt-deuxième.
23 Vingt-trois.	23d Vingt-troisième.
24 Vingt-quatre.	24th Vingt-quatrième.
25 Vingt-cinq.	25th Vingt-cinquième.
26 Vingt-six.	26th Vingt-sixième.
27 Vingt-sept.	27th Vingt-septième.
28 Vingt-huit.	28th Vingt-huitième.
29 Vingt-neuf.	29th Vingt-neuvième.
30 Trente.	30th Trentième.

OF THE ADJECTIVE.

CARDINAL NUMBERS.	ORDINAL NUMBERS.
31 Trente et un.	31st Trente et unième.
32 Trente-deux.	32d Trente-deuxième.
33 Trente-trois.	33d Trente-troisième.
34 Trente-quatre.	34th Trente-quatrième.
35 Trente-cinq.	35th Trente-cinquième.
36 Trente-six.	36th Trente-sixième.
37 Trente-sept.	37th Trente-septième.
38 Trente-huit.	38th Trente-huitième.
39 Trente-neuf.	39th Trente-neuvième.
40 Quarante.	40th Quarantième.
41 Quarante et un.	41st Quarante et unième.
42 Quarante-deux.	42d Quarante-deuxième.
43 Quarante-trois.	43d Quarante-troisième.
44 Quarante-quatre.	44th Quarante-quatrième.
45 Quarante-cinq.	45th Quarante-cinquième
46 Quarante-six.	46th Quarante-sixième.
47 Quarante-sept.	47th Quarante-septième.
48 Quarante-huit.	48th Quarante-huitième.
49 Quarante-neuf.	49th Quarante-neuvième.
50 Cinquante.	50th Cinquantième.
51 Cinquante et un.	51st Cinquante et unième.
52 Cinquante-deux.	52d Cinquante-deuxième.
53 Cinquante-trois.	53d Cinquante-troisième.
54 Cinquante-quatre.	54th Cinquante-quatrième.
55 Cinquante-cinq.	55th Cinquante-cinquième.
56 Cinquante-six.	56th Cinquante-sixième.
57 Cinquante-sept.	57th Cinquante-septième.
58 Cinquante-huit.	58th Cinquante-huitième.
59 Cinquante-neuf.	59th Cinquante-neuvième.
60 Soixante.	60th Soixantième.
61 Soixante et un.*	61st Soixante et unième.
62 Soixante-deux.	62d Soixante-deuxième.
63 Soixante-trois.	63d Soixante-troisième.
64 Soixante-quatre.	64th Soixante-quatrième.
65 Soixante-cinq.	65th Soixante-cinquième.
66 Soixante-six.	66th Soixante-sixième.
67 Soixante-sept.	67th Soixante-septième.
68 Soixante-huit.	68th Soixante-huitième.
69 Soixante-neuf.	69th Soixante-neuvième.
70 Soixante et dix.*	70th Soixante et dixième.
71 Soixante et onze.	71st Soixante et onzième.
72 Soixante-douze.	72d Soixante-douzième.

* We say also, but less frequently, and not so well for euphony *soixante-un, soixante-dix.*—(FRENCH ACADEMY.)

OF THE ADJECTIVE.

CARDINAL NUMBERS.	ORDINAL NUMBERS.
73 Soixante-treize.	73[d] Soixante-treizième.
74 Soixante-quatorze.	74th Soixante-quatorzième.
75 Soixante-quinze.	75th Soixante-quinzième.
76 Soixante-seize.	76th Soixante-seizième.
77 Soixante-dix-sept.	77th Soixante-dix-septième.
78 Soixante-dix-huit.	78th Soixante-dix-huitième.
79 Soixante-dix-neuf.	79th Soixante-dix-neuvième.
80 Quatre-vingts.	80th Quatre-vingtième.
81 Quatre-vingt-un.	81st Quatre-vingt-unième.
82 Quatre-vingt-deux.	82[d] Quatre-vingt-deuxième.
83 Quatre-vingt-trois.	83[d] Quatre-vingt-troisième.
84 Quatre-vingt-quatre.	84th Quatre-vingt-quatrième.
85 Quatre-vingt-cinq.	85th Quatre-vingt-cinquième.
86 Quatre-vingt-six.	86th Quatre-vingt-sixième.
87 Quatre-vingt-sept.	87th Quatre-vingt-septième.
88 Quatre-vingt-huit.	88th Quatre-vingt-huitième.
89 Quatre-vingt-neuf.	89th Quatre-vingt-neuvième.
90 Quatre-vingt-dix.	90th Quatre-vingt-dixième.
91 Quatre-vingt-onze.	91st Quatre-vingt-onzième.
92 Quatre-vingt-douze.	92[d] Quatre-vingt-douzième.
93 Quatre-vingt-treize.	93[d] Quatre-vingt-treizième.
94 Quatre-vingt-quatorze.	94th Quatre-vingt-quatorzième.
95 Quatre-vingt-quinze.	95th Quatre-vingt-quinzième.
96 Quatre-vingt-seize.	96th Quatre-vingt-seizième.
97 Quatre-vingt-dix-sept.	97th Quatre-vingt-dix-septième.
98 Quatre-vingt-dix-huit.	98th Quatre-vingt-dix-huitième.
99 Quatre-vingt-dix-neuf.	99th Quatre-vingt-dix-neuvième.
100 Cent.	100th Centième.
101 Cent un.	101st Cent-unième.
102 Cent deux.	102[d] Cent-deuxième.
200 Deux cents.	200th Deux centième.
1000 Mille.	1000th Millième.
10,000 Dix mille.	10,000[th] Dix millième.
1,000,000 Million.	1,000,000[th] Millionième.

Among the words which express number, there are some which are real *substantives;* these are divided into three sorts, called *collective, distributive,* and *proportional.*

The *collective* denotes a certain quantity or collection of things; as, *une douzaine,* a dozen; *une vingtaine,* a score; *un million,* a million.

The *distributive* expresses a part of a whole; as, *la moitié,* the half; *le quart,* the quarter.

The *proportional* denotes the progressive increase of things; as, *le double*, the double; *le triple*, the triple; *le centuple*, a hundred-fold.

72. REMARKS.—I. The *ordinal* numbers, the *collective* and *distributive* nouns take an *s* in the plural; as,

Les premières douzaines.	The first dozens.
Les sept huitièmes.	The seven eighths.

73. II. *Vingt* and *cent* are the only *cardinal* numbers which take an *s* in the plural, that is, when preceded by another number which multiplies them; as,

Quatre-*vingts* chevaux.	Eighty horses.
Cinq *cents* soldats.	Five hundred soldiers.

The preceding remark holds good when the noun is understood; as,

Nous étions deux *cents*.	We were two hundred (persons.)

74. III. But, when *vingt* and *cent* are followed by another number, or used for the date of the year, they do not take an *s*; as,

Quatre-*vingt*-dix chevaux.	Ninety horses.
Cinq *cent* vingt soldats.	Five hundred and twenty soldiers.
L'an mil sept *cent* quatre-vingt.	In the year one thousand seven hundred and eighty.

75. IV. *Mille*, a thousand, never takes an *s* in the plural; but, *mille*, a mile, takes one: thus, *dix mille* is ten thousand, and *dix milles* means ten miles. In mentioning the Christian era, *mille* is abridged into *mil*; as,

Napoléon mourut en MIL huit cent vingt et un.	Napoleon died in one THOUSAND eight hundred and twenty-one.

76. V. The French make use of the *cardinal* numbers,—1st, In mentioning all the days of the month, except the *first*: thus we say, *le deux mars*, the second of March; *le quatre mai*, the fourth of May; and, *le premier mai*, the first of May; *le premier juin*, the first of June.

Note.—Voltaire used to say, *le deux de mars, le quatre de mai*; and Racine *le deux mars, le quatre mai*. With regard to grammatical correctness, the first construction is certainly preferable; but if we follow usage, which, as to language, is the rule of opinion, we must say *le deux mars, le quatre mai*. It is thus that our good authors almost always express themselves, as well as those persons who pique themselves on speaking purely, and who avoid every kind of affectation.

OF THE ADJECTIVE. 35

2d, In speaking of sovereigns; as, *Guillaume quatre*, William the fourth. The *first* of the series is excepted, for we say *Jacques premier, Henri premier*, and not *Jacques un, Henri un*; but we say indifferently, *deux* or *second*.

Henri *deux*, roi de France.	*Henry* the second, *king of France*.
Catherine *deux*, Impératrice de Russie.—(ACAD.)	*Catharine* the second, *empress of Russia*.
François *second* succéda à Henri *second*.—(GIRARD.)	*Francis* the second *succeeded Henry* the second.

In speaking of the Emperor Charles V, and of Pope Sixtus V, we say *Charles-Quint, Sixte-Quint*.

EXERCISE XXI.

America was discovered by Christopher Columbus, in
art. *Amérique* f. *fut découverte par Christophe Colomb* *
the year *one thousand four hundred and ninety-two*.—We have
an m.* * Nous avons
eighty (men of war) ready to sail, we (shall soon have)
vaisseaux de guerre prêts faire voile en aurons bientôt
two hundred.— Our troops took *five thousand* prisoners. —
Nos troupes firent prisonnier
(It is) *four miles* from this.— Send me the *first* *two dozens*.
Il y a mille m. ici. Envoyez-moi
— Your letter of the *fifteenth* of January (reached me) on
Votre lettre f. * janvier m'est parvenue *
the *first* of February. — I arrived on the *second*.
* février. suis arrivé *

EXERCISE XXII.

Louis *the sixteenth*, Louis *the eighteenth*, and Charles *the tenth*,
———— ———— ————
were brothers.— Francis *the first*, king of France, and
étaient frère François ————
Frederick *the second*, king of Prussia, were great warriors.
Frédéric Prusse, étaient de grand guerrier
—Louis *the thirteenth* was the founder of the French Academy.
est fondateur ² ¹*Académie* f.
—Charles *the fifth*, king of France, was surnamed the wise.—
fut surnommé sage.

Pope Sixtus *the fifth* was contemporary to Philip *the second*,
art. pape était contemporain de Philippe
son of the emperor Charles *the fifth*.—James I, and Henry IV

OF THE ADJECTIVE.

Observations on Words which are alike in French and English.

77. There are many nouns and adjectives which are alike in both languages, with the exception of the difference in pronunciation, and that some require accents in French; and there are others which differ merely in their termination.

Most words are alike in both languages, when ending in—

ace, ice,	as,	place, préface, race, trace, face, grimace, avarice, justice, injustice, service, vice, etc.
ade, ude,	„	arcade, brigade, cavalcade, sérénade, fortitude, multitude, prélude, prude, etc.
ance, ence,	„	distance, ignorance, tempérance, éloquence, évidence, patience, silence, etc.
ant, ent,	„	constant, élégant, éléphant, instant, absent, accident, compliment, excellent, etc.
ile, ule,	„	docile, ductile, reptile, versatile, globule, bile, mule, ridicule, etc.
acle,	„	miracle, obstacle, oracle, réceptacle, spectacle, tabernacle, etc.
al,	„	cardinal, fatal, local, moral, principal, général, naval, royal, libéral, radical, etc.
ble,	„	câble, charitable, fable, table, probable, Bible, éligible, visible, noble, double, etc.
ge,	„	âge, cage, charge, image, page, rage, collége, déluge, refuge, forge, orange, siége, etc.
ine,	„	- doctrine, famine, héroïne, machine, etc.
ion,	„	action, éducation, instruction, légion, nation, opinion, passion, question, etc.

78. Most English words ending in *ary, ory, our, or, ous, cy, ty,* and *y,* become French by changing these terminations in the following manner:—

ary	-		into *aire,*	as	military,	*militaire.*
ory	-	-	„ *oire,*	„	victory,	*victoire.*
our	-		„ *eur,*	„	favour,	*faveur.*
or	-	-	„ *eur,*	„	doctor,	*docteur.*
ous	-		„ *eux,*	„	famous,	*fameux.*
cy	-	-	„ *ce,*	„	constancy,	*constance.*

OF THE ADJECTIVE. 37

ty (after a vowel) into *té*, as beauty, *beauté*.

y { (other than the preceding) } „ *ie*, „ fury, *furie*; modesty, *modestie*.

79. Most proper names of women and goddesses ending in *a*, become French by changing that *a* into *e* mute; as,

| Julia, | Julie. | Minerva, | Minerve. |
| Sophia, | Sophie. | Diana, | Diane. |

EXERCISE XXIII.

The sagacity of that animal is admirable. — That
      f.   cet   m.   est
instrument is very harmonious. — The history of the Royal
m.   très   h mu.
Society.—The rector of an academy.—He has the approbation
[1] f.   f.   a   f.
of the nation.—His memory is extraordinary.—The valour of
     f.   Sa   f.   f.
that general is regulated by   prudence. — His courage is
ce   réglée par art.   f.   Son m.
invincible. — The number of   stars is incalculable. —
                nombre m.   art. étoile
Give this nosegay to Maria or Louisa.—Flora was the
Donnez ce bouquet m. à   ou à   était
goddess of   flowers, and Pomona, the goddess of fruits.
déesse   art. fleur   art. ——

EXERCISE XXIV.

The weathercock is the symbol of   inconstancy.—The
    girouette f.   symbole m.   art.
prosperity of the wicked   is not durable. — An ambitious
f.   méchants pl.   [2]
soul is seldom capable of moderation. — It is sometimes
[1] âme f.   rarement   quelquefois
difficult to distinguish the copy from the original.—The sublimity
difficile de distinguer   f.   m.   f.
of his sentiments is still superior to the energy of his
ses   m.   encore   f.   ses
expressions.—Magistrates and physicians formerly rode
     f.   art. magistrat   art. médecin [2]autrefois [1]allaient
on   mules.—Thalia is the muse of comedy, Urania that
sur d s   ——f. art. f.   celle
of   astronomy. — The unicorn is a fabulous animal.
art.   f   licorne f.   [2]   [1]

CHAPTER IV.

OF PRONOUNS.

80. The word *Pronoun* is formed of the word *noun*, and of the Latin preposition *pro*, which means *for* or *instead of*.

In the French language, there are five kinds of Pronouns, viz. the *Personal*, the *Possessive*, the *Demonstrative*, the *Relative*, and the *Indefinite*.

81. § I. OF PERSONAL PRONOUNS.

Personal pronouns are used instead of the names of persons or things, to avoid the repetition of the nouns which they represent.

There are *three persons:* the first is, the person speaking; the second, the person spoken to; the third, the person or thing spoken of.

82. PRONOUNS OF THE FIRST PERSON.

	Singular.		Examples.	
Subject,	Je,	*I.*	Je donne,	I *give.*
Object,	{ moi,	{ me.	suivez-*moi*,	*follow* me.
		{ to me.	écoutez-*moi*,	*listen to* me.
	{ me,	{ me.	Il *me* flatte,	he *flatters* me.
		{ to me.	Il *me* parle,	he *speaks* to me.
	Plural.			
Subject,	nous,	*we.*	nous donnons,	we *give.*
Object,	nous,	{ us.	Il *nous* voit,	he *sees* us.
		{ to us.	Il *nous* parle,	he *speaks* to us.

The pronouns of the *first* and *second* persons are both masculine and feminine, that is, of the same gender as the person or persons they represent.

83. PARTICULAR OBSERVATIONS.—The Personal Pronouns are generally placed before the verb, *except*—

(1.) When the pronouns take a preposition before them in French; as, *il parle de* nous, he speaks of us.

(2.) In interrogative sentences; as, *parlez*-vous? do you speak?

(3.) When the verb is in the first person plural, or

in either of the second persons of the Imperative, without a negative; as, *parlez*-moi, speak to me. But if the Imperative is used with a negative, the personal pronouns are placed before the verb; as, *ne* me *parlez pas*, do not speak to me.

EXERCISE XXV.

I speak French.—*I* have said that.—Lend *me* your pencil.—
    parle français.   ai dit cela.   Prêtez   votre crayon m.
Help *me*. — Believe *me*.—Write *to me*.—Do not write *to me*.
Aidez   Croyez   Écrivez
—He hurts *me*. — He sees *me*. — This picture   pleases *me*
    Il blesse   voit   Ce tableau m. plaît
more than the other. — *We* praise God. — He knows *us*.—
plus que   autre.   louons Dieu.   connaît
We tell   him the truth,   but he (will not) believe *us*.—
    ²disons ¹lui   vérité f. mais   ne veut pas croire
He related *to us* the history   of his misfortunes.
    a raconté   histoire h m.   ses malheur

84. PRONOUNS OF THE SECOND PERSON.

	Singular.		Examples.	
Subject,	tu,	thou.	tu es heureux,	thou *art happy*.
Object,	toi,	thee.	je parle pour toi,	*I speak for* thee.
	te,	thee.	Dieu te voit,	*God sees* thee.
		to thee.	je te parle,	*I speak* to thee.
	Plural.			
Subject,	vous,	you.	vous chantez,	*you sing*.
Object,	vous,	you.	il vous connaît,	*he knows* you.
		to you.	je vous parle,	*I speak* to you.

85. REMARK.—When from politeness we use *vous* (you), instead of the singular *tu* (thou), the verb is put in the plural, but the adjective or participle following remains in the singular, and takes the feminine termination if we speak to a female; as,

Monsieur, vous êtes bien *bon*. | *Sir, you are very good.*
Madame, vous êtes bien *bonne*. | *Madam, you are very good.*

EXERCISE XXVI.

Thou fearest God.—He (will do) it for *thee*.—He praises
        crains Dieu.   Il ²fera ¹le pour   loue
thee. — He will speak *to thee*.—*You* have spoiled this book.—
            parlera   avez gâté   ce livre m.

How troublesome *you* are!—How good *you* are!—Ladies,
Que ³*importun* ¹m. ²*êtes* ³*bon* ¹f. ² *Mesdames*,
how amiable *you* are!—I bring *you* the newspaper.— You
³*aimable* ¹ ² *apporte* *journal* m.
(are fond of) flowers; if *you* like, I will give *you* this
aimez art. *fleur* *si* *voulez* *donnerai* *ce*
fine nosegay.— Are *you* pleased, my dear little friend?
beau bouquet m. *Êtes* *content* *ma* 48 *amie* f.

86.   PRONOUNS OF THE THIRD PERSON.

Singular. *Examples.*

Subject,	{ il, *m.*	he, it.	il donne,	he *gives.*
	elle, *f.*	she, it.	elle donne,	she *gives.*
Object,	{ lui, *m.*	{ him. to him.	Il parle de *lui*,	he speaks *of* him.
	lui, *f.*	to her.	Il *lui* parle,	he speaks to him.
	elle, *f.*	her.	Je *lui* parlerai,	I *will speak* to her.
			Il parle d'*elle*,	he speaks *of* her.

Plural.

Subject,	{ ils, *m.*	they.	*ils* mangent,	they *eat.*
	elles, *f.*	they.	*elles* chantent,	they *sing.*
Object,	{ eux, *m.*	them.	venez avec *eux*,	come *with* them.
	elles, *f.*	them.	c'est pour *elles*,	it is *for* them.
	leur, *m. & f.*	to them.	Je *leur* parlerai,	I *will speak* to them.

87.   OF THE PRONOUNS *le, la, les.*

These pronouns always accompany a *verb*, and are thus easily distinguished from the articles *le, la, les,* (see p. 14), which constantly accompany a *noun.*

EXAMPLES.

le, *masc.*	{ him, it,	je *le* connais,	*I know* him.
		{ voilà un bon livre, lisez-*le*,	{ *there is a good book, read* it.
la, *fem.*	{ her, it,	je *la* vois,	*I see* her.
		{ vous avez la clef, donnez-*la* moi,	{ *you have the key, give it* me.
les, *for both gend.*	} them,	{ vous *les* trouverez dans mon tiroir,	{ *you will find* them *in my drawer.*
		il *les* connaît,	*he knows* them.

In this phrase, *Je connais* les *princes et* les *princesses, je* les *vois souvent,* (I know the princes and the princesses, I see them often), the first two *les* are articles, the third is a pronoun.

☞ These three personal pronouns, *le, la, les,* are called "Relative" by some Grammarians.

OF PERSONAL PRONOUNS.

EXERCISE XXVII.

He has done his duty. — She sings well. — I (am writing)
   a   fait son devoir.   chante bien.   écris
to him. — What (shall I say) to her? — They speak to them.
           Que   dirai-je   m. parlent
— They will return with them. — (Do not come) without them.
   f. reviendront   m.   Ne venez pas sans   f.
— They prefer the country to the town. — Prosperity
  m. préfèrent   campagne f.   ville f. art. prospérité f.
gets us friends and   adversity tries them.
fait   32 ami   art.   éprouve

88. OF THE PERSONAL PRONOUNS, *SE, SOI*.

Se, soi, Pronouns of the third person are used both for persons and things. *Se* is placed before a verb, and *soi* generally after a preposition.

EXAMPLES.

SE,
- *himself*, il se loue, — *he praises* himself.
- *herself*, elle se flatte, — *she flatters* herself.
- *itself*, il se détruit, — *it destroys* itself.
- *oneself*, se louer, — *to praise* oneself.
- *themselves*, ils or elles se flattent, — *they flatter* themselves.
- *to himself*, il s'attribue, — *he attributes* to himself.
- *to herself*, elle s'attribue, — *she attributes* to herself.
- *to oneself*, se prescrire, — *to prescribe* to oneself.
- *to themselves*, ils or elles se prescrivent, — *they prescribe* to themselves.

SOI,
- *himself*, chacun pour soi, — *every one for* himself.
- *itself*, cela est bon en soi, — *that is good in* itself.
- *oneself*, il faut songer à soi, — *one must think of* oneself.
- *themselves*, on doit parler rarement de soi, — *people should seldom speak of* themselves.

EXERCISE XXVIII.

He submits himself to your orders. — That lady praises
    soumet   vos ordre   Cette dame loue
herself (too much.) — She gives herself (a great deal) of
       trop.   donne   beaucoup
trouble. — They expose themselves to   danger. — They
peine.   exposent   art. —— m.
will accustom themselves (to it.) — (Every one) works for
[3]accoutumeront   1   [2]y   Chacun travaille pour
himself. — The loadstone attracts   iron   to itself. —
                aimant m. attire   art. fer m.
  Virtue is amiable in itself. — He will soon correct himself.
art. vertu f. est aimable de   * [3]bientôt [2]corrigera [1]

89. § II. OF POSSESSIVE PRONOUNS.

The *Possessive*, as well as the *Demonstrative* Pronouns, are of a mixed nature, partaking of the properties both of pronouns and adjectives; therefore some Grammarians class them among the *adjectives*; others refuse them the name of *pronouns* or *adjectives*, and place them in the rank of *articles*. Indeed, it would be difficult to state, within a moderate compass, the various opinions of Grammarians respecting this part of speech. As for us, we shall follow here the classification adopted by the French Academy, and by the most correct modern writers, and divide the Possessive Pronouns of the old Grammarians into two classes:

    1st, *Possessive Adjectives;*
    2d, *Possessive Pronouns;*

And, from the affinity these two kinds of words have with each other, we shall place them one after the other in separate articles.

90.   OF POSSESSIVE ADJECTIVES.

The *Possessive* adjectives denote possession or property, and are called *adjectives* rather than *pronouns*, because they do not stand *for* a noun, but, on the contrary, are always joined to a noun. They are:

Singular.		*Plural.*	
Masc.	*Fem.*	For both genders.	
mon	ma	mes	*my*
ton	ta	tes	*thy*
son	sa	ses	*his, her, its*
notre	notre	nos	*our*
votre	votre	vos	*your*
leur	leur	leurs	*their*

91. Observe.—(1.) The *possessive adjectives*, as well as the preposition which may accompany them, must be repeated before every noun, and agree with it in gender and number.

OF POSSESSIVE PRONOUNS.

92. (2.) The *possessive adjectives* always agree in French with the noun following, and never with the preceding one; that is to say, they agree with the object *possessed*, and not with the *possessor*, as in English.

93. (3.) For the sake of euphony, *mon, ton, son,* are used instead of *ma, ta, sa,* before a feminine noun beginning with a vowel or *h* mute.

EXERCISE XXIX.

My father, mother, and brothers are in the country. —
    père   mère   frère   sont à   campagne f.
His uncle, aunt, and cousins are in Wales. — I
    oncle   tante   m. *sont dans le pays de Galles.*
have seen Paris, *its* theatres, and buildings. — *Our* perseverance
    ai vu   théâtre m.   édifice m.   persévérance f.
and *our* efforts. — *Your* country and *your* friends. — *Their*
          m.   pays m.   ami m.
house and *their* servants. — *Her* son is learned. — *His* sister
maison f. domestique   fils est savant.   sœur
is married. — *My* ambition, *thy* honesty,   and *his* friendship.
mariée.   f.   honnêteté f. h m.   amitié f.
— *My* brother has lost *his* pen, *his* pencil, and *his* books. —
         a perdu   plume f.   crayon m.   livre m.
My mother has sold *her* house and *her* garden.
              vendu   jardin m.

94.   OF POSSESSIVE PRONOUNS.

These pronouns always relate to some noun spoken of before, with which they agree in gender and number.

The possessive pronouns are:

Singular.		*Plural.*		
Masc.	*Fem.*	*Masc.*	*Fem.*	
le mien	la mienne	les miens	les miennes	*mine*
le tien	la tienne	les tiens	les tiennes	*thine*
le sien	la sienne	les siens	les siennes	*his, hers, its*
		Pl. for both genders.		
le nôtre	la nôtre	les nôtres		*ours*
le vôtre	la vôtre	les vôtres		*yours*
le leur	la leur	les leurs		*theirs*

EXERCISE XXX.

(Here is) your   hat,   (don't take) mine. — His
 Voici   chapeau m. ne prenez pas

house   and *mine* have been burnt, but *theirs* (has not)
maison f. et   ont   été brûlées mais   n'a point
suffered.—Your books   are better bound than *mine.* — My
souffert.   *livre* m.   sont   reliés   que
watch   (does not go) so well as *hers.*—Your garden   is
montre f. ne va pas si   que   *jardin* m. est
 larger   than *ours,* but our orchard   is larger than *yours.*—
plus grand   *verger* m.
You have taken my gloves,   and   (I have) taken *yours.*—
       avez pris   *gant* m.   moi j'ai
I know your relations,   but I (don't know) *theirs.*
  connais   *parent* m. pl.   *ne connais pas*

95. § III. OF DEMONSTRATIVE PRONOUNS.

We shall divide the Demonstrative pronouns, as we have done the Possessive, into two classes:

      1st, *Demonstrative Adjectives;*
      2d, *Demonstrative Pronouns.*

96. OF DEMONSTRATIVE ADJECTIVES.

The *Demonstrative* adjectives always precede a substantive, which they designate and point out. They are:

This, or *that,*
{ CE, before a noun masculine singular, beginning with a consonant, or *h* aspirate.
CET, before a noun masculine singular, beginning with a vowel, or *h* mute.
CETTE, before any feminine noun. }

These, or *those,* { CES, before any noun in the plural, whether masculine or feminine.

97. RULE.—The Demonstrative adjectives must be repeated in French before every noun, though in English *this, that, these, those,* are frequently used before the first noun only, and understood before the others; as,

  Ces hommes, *ces* femmes, et *ces* | These men, women, and children
  enfants jouent. | are playing.

EXERCISE XXXI.

This picture,   *that* bird,   *this* doll,   *these* flowers, and
  tableau m.   *oiseau* m.   *poupée* f.   *fleur*   et
those shells   are (my sister's).— Taste *this* wine. — Take
  coquillage sont à ma sœur.   Goûtez   vin m. Prenez
one of *these* biscuits. — *Those* boys and girls (are going) to
       —— m.   garçon   fille   vont

school. — Give him *this* book and *that* slate. — *These*
art. *école   Donnez-lui   livre* m.   *ardoise* f.

cups and saucers (are not) clean.—*This* cake is for you.
tasse   soucoupe ne sont pas propre   gâteau m. *pour*

98. OF DEMONSTRATIVE PRONOUNS.

These pronouns serve to point out the persons or things which they represent. They are:

Singular.			Plural.		
Masc.	*Fem.*		*Masc.*	*Fem.*	
ce	- -	*this, that, it.*	No plural.		
celui	celle	*that.*	ceux	celles	*those.*
celui-ci	celle-ci	*this.*	ceux-ci	celles-ci	*these.*
celui-là	celle-là	*that.*	ceux-là	celles-là	*those.*
ceci	- -	*this.*	} No plural.		
cela	- -	*that.*			

CE, demonstrative *pronoun*, differs from *ce*, demonstrative *adjective*, in this, that the former is always joined to the verb *être*, to be, or followed by *qui*, or *que;* whereas the latter is always followed by a substantive. Thus, in this phrase: CE *qui me plaît,* C'EST *sa modestie*, what (*that which*) pleases me is his modesty, CE is a demonstrative *pronoun;* and it is a demonstrative *adjective* in the following: CE *juge est incorruptible,* that judge is incorruptible.

When *ce* does not come immediately before a substantive, it answers for both numbers and genders; as,

De toutes les vertus celle qui se fait le | *Of all the virtues, that which makes itself*
plus chérir, c'est l'humanité. | *most beloved is humanity.*
Ce furent les Phéniciens qui inven- | *It was the Phœnicians who invented*
tèrent l'écriture.—(BOSSUET.) | *writing.*

The French Academy remark that *ce* joined to the verb *être* generally forms a gallicism.

99. The Pronouns *celui, celle, ceux, celles,* always relate to a noun expressed before; as,

Voici votre livre, où est *celui* de votre | *Here is your book, where is that of your*
frère? | *brother?*
J'admire les traductions de Pope et | *I admire the translations of Pope and*
celles de Delille. | *those of Delille.*

OF DEMONSTRATIVE PRONOUNS.

100. When two or more objects have been spoken of, *celui-ci, celle-ci, ceux-ci, celles-ci* are used with reference to the nearest, and *celui-là, celle-là, ceux-là, celles-là* refer to the most distant, or first-mentioned object; as,

Voici deux pistolets, lequel choisissez-vous, *celui-ci* ou *celui-là ?*	*Here are two pistols, which do you choose,* this *or* that?
Le corps périt, l'âme est immortelle; cependant nous négligeons *celle-ci*, et nous sacrifions tout pour *celui-là.*	*The body perishes, the soul is immortal; yet we neglect* the latter, *and sacrifice everything for* the former.

This last example shows also that the English words, *the former*, are likewise expressed by *celui-là, celle-là, ceux-là, celles-là*, and *the latter* by *celui-ci, celle-ci, ceux-ci, celles-ci*, according to the gender and number of the substantive to which they relate.

REMARK. — LÀ means *there*, and CI is an abbreviation of ICI, *here;* so that CELUI-CI is equivalent to *this here*, and CELUI-LÀ, to *that there*.

101. *Ceci*, this, and *cela*, that, are never followed by a noun, nor used with reference to a noun mentioned before; they stand for something pointed at, but not named; they have no plural, and are both masculine.

Ceci est bon, mais *cela* est mauvais.	*This* is good, *but that* is bad.
Donnez-moi *ceci*, et gardez *cela*.	*Give me* this, *and keep* that.

EXERCISE XXXII.

It is a misfortune. — (Here is) your umbrella, and *that* of
  est   malheur m.   Voici   parapluie m.
your cousin. — Bring my scissors, and *those* of my
  —— m. *Apportez* ciseaux m. pl.
sister. — Which of these watches (will you have), *this* or
sœur. *Laquelle*   montre f. voulez-vous   ou
that? — (Here are) fine pictures, buy *these* or *those*.—
      Voici de beau tableau m. *achetez*

Give *this* to (the lady) and *that* to (the gentleman). — An
Donnez   madame   monsieur.
upright magistrate and a brave officer are equally
[1]*intègre* [1]*magistrat* m.   —— officier m. sont également
estimable; *the former* makes war against domestic
——   fait art. guerre f. à art.[2]*domestique*
enemies, *the latter* protects us against foreign enemies
[1]*ennemi* m. pl.   *protége* contre art.[2]*extérieur* [1]

102. § IV. OF RELATIVE PRONOUNS.

Relative Pronouns are those which relate to a noun or pronoun, or phrase going before, which is thence called the *antecedent*.

The relative pronouns are: *qui, que, quoi, lequel, dont, où, en, y.*

OF *qui, que, quoi, lequel, dont.*

103. QUI, QUE, QUOI, are of both genders and numbers.

EXAMPLES.

qui,	{ *who,* *which,*	Dieu *qui* est juste, la dame *qui* parle, les oiseaux *qui* chantent,	God who *is just.* the lady who *is speaking.* the birds which *are singing.*
à *qui,* said of persons only,	} *to whom,*	{ le garçon à *qui* j'écris,	} the boy to whom *I am writing.*
que,	{ *whom, which,*	l'homme *que* vous voyez, les livres *que* vous lisez,	the man whom *you see.* the books which *you read.*
quoi,	*what,*	{ voilà de *quoi* je voulais vous parler,	} that is what *I wished to speak to you about.*

REMARK.—*Que* loses the *e* before a vowel; *qui* never changes.

104. LEQUEL is a compound of *quel*, and of the article *le*, with which it incorporates in the following manner:

Singular.   *Plural.*

lequel	laquelle	lesquels	lesquelles	*which.*
duquel	de laquelle	desquels	desquelles	*of which.*
auquel	à laquelle	auxquels	auxquelles	*to which.*

This pronoun is used with reference to persons and things, with which it always agrees in gender and number.

EXAMPLES of *lequel.*

lequel, *m. which,*	{ le fauteuil sur *lequel* je suis assis,	{ the arm-chair on which *I am sitting.*
laquelle, *f. which,*	{ c'est une raison à *laquelle* il n'y a point de réplique,	{ it is a reason to which there can be no reply.
laquelle, *f. which,*	{ c'est une de ses sœurs, mais je ne sais *laquelle,*	{ it is one of his sisters, but I do not know which

105. DONT is of both genders and numbers, and is used when speaking of persons or things: it supplies the place of *duquel, de laquelle, desquels, desquelles, de quoi*, but is never used in asking a question.

Note.—Dont is never used in asking a question, that is—you never begin a question with *dont*; but, in the body of an interrogative phrase, the word is perfectly correct; as, *Où est la femme* DONT *vous parlez?* Where is the woman *of whom* you speak?

EXAMPLES of *dont*.

dont,	*of which,*	c'est une maladie *dont* on ne connaît pas la cause,	*it is an illness, the cause of which is unknown.*
	of whom,	l'homme *dont* vous parlez,	*the man of whom you speak.*
	whose,	la nature *dont* nous ignorons les secrets,	*nature, whose secrets are unknown to us.*

106. *Qui, que, quoi, lequel,* are called relative pronouns *absolute,* when they have no antecedent, and only present to the mind a vague and indeterminate idea.

In this case *qui* is employed only in speaking of persons, *que* and *quoi* in speaking of things.

Lequel marks a distinction, and is used in interrogative sentences, when asking which person or thing among several.

EXAMPLES.

qui,	*who,*	*qui (quelle personne)* est là?	*who is there?*
		je ne sais *qui* est arrivé,	*I don't know who has arrived.*
	whom,	*qui* appelez-vous?	*whom do you call?*
		consultez *qui* vous voudrez,	*consult whom you please.*
que,	*what,*	*que (quelle chose)* cherchez-vous?	*what are you seeking?*
		je ne sais *que* faire,	*I don't know what to do.*
quoi,	*what,*	à *quoi (à quelle chose)* pensez-vous?	*what are you thinking of?*
		quoi de plus aimable que la vertu?	*what more amiable than virtue?*
lequel, *m. which,*		*lequel* préférez-vous?	*which do you prefer?*
		choisissez *lequel* vous voudrez,	*choose which you please.*
laquelle, *f. which,*		*laquelle* de ses sœurs est mariée?	*which of his sisters is married?*

107. Of the Relative Pronoun *où*.

Où is a relative pronoun when used instead of *lequel, laquelle, lesquels, lesquelles*, preceded by a preposition. This pronoun is employed only in speaking of things, and is of both genders and numbers.

EXAMPLES.

L'instant où nous naissons est un pas vers la mort.—(VOLTAIRE.)	The instant in which *we are born is a step towards death.*
La maison où je demeure. (ACAD.)	The house in which *I live.*
Les pays par où j'ai passé.	The countries through which *I have passed.*

EXERCISE XXXIII.

The man *who* reasons. — The lady *whom* I see. — The
       raisonne.   dame   vois.
sciences   *to which* he applies. — Here is the gentleman
—— f. pl.   s'applique.   Voici   monsieur
of whom you speak. — With *whom* do you live ? — What
     parlez.   Avec   demeurez-vous?
(shall we do)   to-day? — *Which* (do you like) best of those
ferons-nous aujourd'hui?   aimez-vous
three pictures? — The child *to whom* everything yields
  tableau m.   enfant m.   tout   cède
is the most unhappy. — The state *in which* I find myself.
   malheureux.   état m.   me trouve.

108. Of the Relative Pronoun *en*.

EN, a pronoun of both genders and numbers, is sometimes used in speaking of persons, although it is chiefly said of things, and places: its principal function is to avoid the repetition of a word or phrase already expressed. It signifies *of him, of her, of it, from it, of them, some of it, some of them, any,* &c.

EXAMPLES.

Il aime les auteurs français, il EN parle souvent.	*He likes French authors, he often speaks* of them.
Cette maladie est dangereuse, il pourrait EN mourir.	*That illness is dangerous, he might die* of it.
A-t-il des protecteurs? oui, il EN a de très-puissants.	*Has he any protectors? yes, he has some very powerful* ones.
Vous parlez d'argent, EN avez-vous? oui, j' EN ai.	*You talk of money, have you* any? *yes, I have* some.

109. OF THE RELATIVE PRONOUN *y*.

Y, a pronoun of both genders and numbers, is sometimes employed with reference to persons, but its use is almost strictly confined to things: it corresponds to the English *to him, to her, to it, to them, in it, in them, therein,* &c.

EXAMPLES.

Je connais cet homme, je ne m'y fie pas.	*I know that man, I do not trust to him.*
Il aime l'étude et s'y livre entièrement.	*He loves study, and devotes himself entirely to it.*
J'ai reçu sa lettre, j'y répondrai.	*I have received his letter, I shall answer* (to) *it.*
Vos raisons sont bonnes, je m'y rends.	*Your reasons are good, I yield to them.*
J'y ai remarqué quelques fautes.	*I observed some faults in it, or in them.*

☞ Some Grammarians class *en* and *y* among the personal pronouns.

N. B.—The pronouns *en* and *y* are always placed before the verb, except with an Imperative affirmative.

[See, in the Chapter on the Adverb, what is said upon y, adverb.]

EXERCISE XXXIV.

Read his letter, and tell me what you think *of it.* —
Lisez   lettre f.   dites-moi ce que   pensez

Give me that, I (am in want) *of it.* — Are you going to
Donnez-moi   ai besoin   Allez-vous

Edinburgh? I come *from it.*—(Here are) strawberries, will
Édimbourg   viens   Voici 32 fraise   voulez

you have any? — I will give you *some.* — Take *some*
    *   donnerai   Prenez

more. — I consent *to it.* — Put your signature *to it.*—
davantage.   consens   Mettez   ———

Those arguments are conclusive; I see no reply
——— m. sont concluant   n' vois point de réplique

to them. — The undertaking is difficult, but you
    entreprise f.   difficile mais

(will succeed) *in it.* — They will gain nothing (*by it*).
réussirez   n' gagneront rien   y

110. § V. OF INDEFINITE PRONOUNS.

Some pronouns are called *Indefinite*, because they denote persons or things in an indefinite or general manner.

They are the following: *on, quiconque, quelqu'un, chacun, autrui, personne, l'un l'autre, l'un et l'autre.*

111. ON, *one, they, we, people, it*, &c. *On* is a contraction of the Latin word *homo*, man. This pronoun is of very extensive use in the French language; it is employed when speaking in general terms, without designating any particular person: it has commonly a plural meaning, but always requires the verb to be in the third person singular.

EXAMPLES.

On ne peut lire Télémaque sans devenir meilleur.	One *cannot read Telemachus without becoming better.*
On dit que nous aurons bientôt la paix.	They, *or people, say we shall soon have peace.*
On pense que la nouvelle est vraie.	It *is thought that the news is true.*
On apprend mieux ce que l'on comprend, que ce que l'on ne comprend pas.	We *learn better what we understand, than what we do not.*

REMARK.—For the sake of euphony, the pronoun *on* takes an *l*, with an apostrophe (l'), after the words *et, si, où, que, qui,* and *quoi;* as,

Et *l'*on dit,
Si *l'*on savait,
Où *l'*on veut,
Ce que *l'*on comprend,
Ceux à qui *l'*on doit,

instead of

et on dit.
si on savait.
où on veut.
ce qu'on comprend.
ceux à qui on doit.

However, *on* remains the same when the word following it is *le, la,* or *les;* we say: *et on le dit, si on le savait,* and not *et l'on le dit, si l'on le savait.*

L'on for *on* should never begin a sentence, although some authors have not always observed this rule.

112. QUICONQUE, *whoever, whosoever, any person whatever.* This pronoun has no plural, and is used only with reference to persons; as,

Quiconque a dit cela n'a pas dit la vérité.	Whoever *said so, has not spoken the truth.* [*punished.*
Quiconque me trompera sera puni.	Whoever *deceives me shall be*

Quiconque is generally masculine; however, when it evidently relates to a female, the adjective is put in the feminine; as,

Mesdames, *quiconque* de vous sera assez *hardie* pour médire de moi, je l'en ferai repentir.—(ACAD.)	Ladies, *whoever of you shall be bold enough to speak ill of me, I will make her repent it.*

113. QUELQU'UN, *somebody, some one.*

EXAMPLES.

J'attends *quelqu'un*.	*I wait for* somebody.
Quelqu'un me l'a dit.	Somebody *told me so.*

This pronoun takes gender and number; thus:—

Quelqu'un, *m.* }
Quelqu'une, *f.* } some one, somebody.

Quelques-uns, *m. pl.* }
Quelques-unes, *f. pl.* } some, several, out of a greater number.

Quelqu'un de ces messieurs.	Some one *of these gentlemen.*
Quelqu'une de ces dames.	Some one *of these ladies.*
Quelqu'un m'a dit.	Somebody *told me.*
J'ai lu *quelques-uns* de ces livres.	*I have read* some *of those books.*
Connaissez-vous *quelques-unes* de ces dames?	*Do you know* any *of those ladies?*
Oui, j'en connais *quelques-unes*.	*Yes, I know* some *of them.*

114. CHACUN, *m.*, CHACUNE, *f.*, *every one, each;* without plural.

Chacun vit à sa manière.	Every one *lives after his own way.*
Chacune de ces demoiselles.	Each *of these young ladies.*

Un chacun, much used by old writers, is now obsolete.

[See page 55, what is said on *chaque*, every, each.]

115. AUTRUI, *others, other people.* (From the Latin *alterius*, gen. of *alter*, other.) This pronoun is masculine, and has no plural; it is generally preceded by a preposition, and is used in speaking of persons only.

La charité se réjouit du bonheur d'*autrui*.	*Charity rejoices in the happiness of* others.
Ne faites pas à *autrui* ce que vous ne voudriez pas qu'on vous fît.	*Do not to* others, *what you would not wish others to do to you.*

116. PERSONNE. This pronoun is always masculine and singular. When it means *no person, nobody, no one,* it requires the negative *ne* before the verb.

EXAMPLES.

Personne ne sera assez hardi.	Nobody *will be bold enough.*
Je n'ai vu *personne.*	*I have seen* nobody.

When *personne* is used without a negative in interrogative sentences, and those expressing doubt and uncertainty, it means *any person, any body, any one.*

EXAMPLES.

Y a-t-il *personne* d'assez hardi ?	*Is there* any body *bold enough ?*
Je doute que *personne* y réussisse.—(ACAD.)	*I doubt whether* any one *will succeed in it.*

PERSONNE, as a noun, is always feminine, and is used both in the singular and plural; it means *a person, a man* or *woman, people.*

EXAMPLES.

C'est une *personne* de mérite.	*He is a* man *of merit.*
C'est une *personne* très-instruite.	*She is a very well-informed* person.
Des *personnes* bien intentionnées.	*Well-intentioned* people.

117. L'UN L'AUTRE, *m.*, L'UNE L'AUTRE, *f.*; LES UNS LES AUTRES, *m. pl.*, LES UNES LES AUTRES, *f. pl.*; *one another, each other.*

This pronoun is employed in speaking of persons and things. *L'un l'autre* is used with reference to two, and *les uns les autres* with reference to more than two.

If there be any preposition, it must be placed between *l'un l'autre*, and not before, as is the case in English before *one another* or *each other.*

EXAMPLES.

Ils se louent *l'un l'autre.*	*They praise* one another.
Les soldats s'excitaient *les uns les autres.*	*The soldiers excited* one another.
Ils parlent mal *l'un DE l'autre.*	*They speak ill OF each other.*

118. L'UN ET L'AUTRE, *m.*, L'UNE ET L'AUTRE, *f.*; LES UNS ET LES AUTRES, *m. pl.*, LES UNES ET LES AUTRES, *f. pl.*; *the one and the other, both.*

EXAMPLES.

L'un et l'autre sont bons.	Both *are good.*
L'une et l'autre rapportent le même fait.	Both *relate the same circumstance.*
Ils se réunissaient *les uns et les autres* contre l'ennemi.	*They all united against the enemy.*

When *l'un et l'autre* is followed by a noun, it is no longer an indefinite pronoun, but an adjective; as, *l'un et l'autre* CHEVAL, both horses; *l'une et l'autre* SAISON, both seasons; *l'une et l'autre* DEMANDE, both requests.

☞ Many Grammarians class TEL among the *Indefinite pronouns;* but it is a real adjective, and agrees in gender and number with a noun either expressed or understood; as, *une telle action,* such an action; *de tels animaux,* such animals; *tel* (*homme* understood) *rit aujourd'hui,* such as laughs to-day; *telle* (*femme* understood) *se croit belle,* such a one thinks herself beautiful.

[For any further explanation respecting the Pronouns, see the Syntax.]

EXERCISE XXXV.

One has often need of a (person inferior) to oneself.—
a   souvent besoin   plus petit m. que soi.

They say he is learned — God (will punish) *whosoever*
dit qu' est Dieu punira

transgresses his laws. — Somebody has taken my umbrella. —
transgresse loi a pris parapluie m

Every one (will read) in his turn. —We (must not) covet
lira à tour m. Il ne faut pas désirer

the property of *other people*. — Pride becomes *nobody*.
bien m. art. orgueil m. convient à

EXERCISE XXXVI.

Fire and water destroy *each other.* — I have
art. *feu* m. art. *eau* f. *se détruisent* ai

read the Iliad and the Eneid, *both* have delighted me.—
lu Iliade f. Énéide f. ont enchanté

People who have (little to do) are very great talkers;
art. *gens* m. peu d'affaires de parleur

the less *one* thinks, the more *one* speaks.—*Each* of them resolved
moins pense plus parle. résolut

to live as a gentleman. —He who chooses badly for himself,
de vivre en * gentilhomme. * choisit soi

chooses badly for *others.*—*Some* assert the contrary.
assurent contraire m.

119. OF INDEFINITE PRONOMINAL ADJECTIVES.

We shall treat here of the *indefinite pronominal adjectives*, on account of their affinity with the indefinite pronouns; these adjectives are: *chaque, nul, aucun, pas un, même, plusieurs, tout, quelconque, quel, quelque.*

120. CHAQUE, *every, each*, is of both genders, and without plural. This word must not be confounded with *chacun*; *chaque* is always followed by a noun; *chacun*, on the contrary, is never joined to a noun (see page 52).

EXAMPLES.

Chaque âge a ses plaisirs.	Every *age has its pleasures*.
Chaque science a ses principes.	Every *science has its principles*.

121. NUL, *m.*, NULLE, *f.*; AUCUN, *m.*, AUCUNE, *f.*; PAS UN, *m.*, PAS UNE, *f.*; *none, no, no one, not one, not any.*

These expressions have nearly the same meaning when accompanied by the negative *ne* placed before the verb.

EXAMPLES.

Nul homme n'est parfait.	No *man is perfect*.
Vous n'avez *aucune* preuve; non, pas une.	You *have* no *proof;* no, not one.

N.B.—*No*, in answer to a question, is translated by *non*.

122. MÊME, *same, self, like, alike;* plural, MÊMES; of both genders.

EXAMPLES.

C'est le *même* homme, la *même* personne.	It *is the* same *man, the* same *person.*
Les cendres du berger et du roi sont les *mêmes*.	*The ashes of the shepherd and the king are* alike.

Même is often placed after a substantive or a pronoun, to give more energy to the expression.

EXAMPLES.

C'est la bonté *même*.	She *is kindness* itself.
Le roi lui-*même* s'y opposa.	*The king* himself *opposed it.*
Nous le ferons nous-*mêmes*.	*We will do it* ourselves.

Même is also an adverb; then it is invariable, and means *even, also*. This is the *etiam* of the Latin.

EXAMPLE.

Les femmes et *même* les enfants furent tués.	*Women* and even *children* were killed.

123. PLUSIEURS, *several, many.* It is of both genders and has no singular.

EXAMPLES.

Plusieurs historiens ont raconté.	Several *historians have related.*
En *plusieurs* occasions.	*On* several *occasions.*
Plusieurs de vos amis.	Many *of your friends.*

124. TOUT. There are various kinds of this word.

(1.) *Tout,* indefinite pronominal adjective, meaning *every, each, any, any one;* the *quisque* of the Latin. In this sense, *tout* never takes an article nor a pronoun, and is always singular. — EXAMPLES:

Tout citoyen doit servir son pays.	Every *citizen ought to serve his country.*
Toute peine mérite salaire.—(Ac.)	Every *labour deserves a reward.*

(2.) *Tout,* adjective, *all, whole;* in Latin, *totus, omnis:*

Tout le monde; *toute* la terre; *tous* les hommes.	All *the world;* all *the earth;* all *men.*
Tout l'homme ne meurt pas.	*The* whole *man does not die.*

(3.) *Tout,* adverb, *quite, entirely, however;* in Latin, *omninò, planè:*

Elle fut *tout* étonnée.	*She was* quite *astonished.*
Nos vaisseaux sont *tout* prêts.	*Our vessels are* quite *ready.*

☞ *Tout,* adverb, becomes adjective, or at least agrees like one, in gender and number, when immediately followed by an adjective or participle feminine, beginning with a consonant, or *h* aspirate; as,

Elle était *toute* changée.	*She was* quite *altered.*
Elle en est *toute* honteuse.	*She is* quite *ashamed of it.*
Toutes spirituelles qu'elles sont.	*Witty as they are.*

(4.) *Tout,* substantive masculine, *the whole;* the *totum* of the Latin:

Ne prenez pas le *tout.*	*Do not take the* whole.

125. QUELCONQUE, *whatever, whatsoever.* When used with a negative, it is nearly synonymous with *nul, aucun;* it is invariable, and is always placed after a noun; as,

Il n'y a homme *quelconque.*	*There is no man* whatever.
Il n'y a raison *quelconque.*	*There is no reason* whatsoever.

When used without a negative, it admits of a plural; as,

Deux points *quelconques.*–(ACAD.)	*Two points* whatsoever.

OF INDEFINITE PRONOMINAL ADJECTIVES.

126. QUEL, *m.*, QUELLE, *f.*; QUELS, *m. pl.*, QUELLES, *f. pl.*, *what*. This pronominal adjective is used principally in interrogations and exclamations, or to express uncertainty and doubt. It is always followed by a noun expressed or understood, with which it agrees in gender and number.

EXAMPLES.

Quel maître?—Quelle dame?	What *master?*—What *lady?*
Quels livres, quelles brochures lisez-vous?	What *books*, what *pamphlets* do *you read?*
Quel bonheur!	What *happiness!*
Quel homme vous êtes!	What *a man you are!*
Il ne sait quel parti prendre.	*He knows not* what *course to take.*
J'ai des nouvelles à vous apprendre.—Quelles (nouvelles) sont-elles?	*I have news to tell you.*—What *is it?*

127. QUELQUE, *s.*, QUELQUES, *pl.*, *some*, is of both genders, and is always joined to a noun.

EXAMPLES.

Quelque auteur en a parlé.	Some *author has mentioned it.*
Il y a quelques difficultés.	*There are some difficulties.*

Quelque, in this sense, corresponds to the *aliquis* of the Latin.—(*Acad.*, and the modern Grammarians.)

Quelque, with *que* before the succeeding verb, means *whatever*. This is the *quantuscunque, quantacunque* of the Latin.

EXAMPLES.

Quelque soin qu'on prenne.	Whatever *care one may take.*
Quelque raison qu'il ait.	Whatever *reason he may have.*
Quelques efforts que vous fassiez.	Whatever *efforts you may make.*

But should *quelque* be followed by the verb *être*, to be, it is written in two words *(quel que)*; in this case, *quel* must agree in gender and number with the subject of the verb. This expression answers to the *qualiscunque* of the Latin.

EXAMPLES.

Quelle que soit votre intention.	Whatever *your intention may be.*
Quels que soient vos desseins.	Whatever *your designs may be.*
Quelles que soient vos vues. (ACAD.)	Whatever *your views may be.*

Quelque, followed by an adverb or an adjective without a noun, is considered as an adverb, and is invariable; it corresponds to the English *however, howsoever*, and to the Latin adverb *quantumvis;* as,

Quelque bien écrits que soient ces ouvrages, ils ont peu de succès.	However well *written these works may be, they have little success.*
Quelque puissants qu'ils soient, je ne les crains point.—(ACAD.)	However powerful *they may be, I do not fear them.*

Quelque, when immediately followed by a cardinal number, is also considered as an adverb; then, it means *about, nearly, some*, and answers to the *circiter* of the Latin. In this sense, *quelque* is of the familiar style; as,

Alexandre perdit *quelque* trois cents hommes, lorsqu'il défit Porus.	Alexander lost some *three hundred men, when he defeated Porus.*

EXERCISE XXXVII.

Every country has its customs.—*No one* is dissatisfied with
   pays m. *a* coutume   n'est mécontent de
his own understanding.—*No* reason can justify a
•   jugement m.   raison f. ne peut justifier le
falsehood. — It is the *same* sun that (gives light to) *all*
mensonge m. C'est   soleil m. qui   éclaire
the nations of the earth. — It is virtue *itself.*—Divide the
——— f. pl. terre f.   art. vertu f.   Divisez
whole into *several* parts.—The *whole* fleet is at sea.—*Every*
en   partie ² ¹ flotte f. est en mer.
truth (is not) proper (to be told).—Any pretext *whatever.*
vérité f. n'est pas bon à dire. Un prétexte m.

EXERCISE XXXVIII.

No one is satisfied with his fortune, nor dissatisfied with his
 n' content de   ——— f. ni
own wit. — *No* road of flowers conducts to glory.—
* esprit m. chemin m.   ne conduit art. 78
What lesson have you learnt?—(There are) *some* defects in
 leçon f. avez- apprise? Il y a   défaut dans
that picture. — *Whatever* your talents (may be), you
 tableau m.   ——— m. pl. soient
(will not succeed) without application.—She is *quite* wet. —
ne réussirez pas sans ———   mouillée.
These ladies were *quite* surprised to see him.
   furent   surprises de ²voir ¹

CHAPTER V.
OF THE VERB.

128. FRENCH VERBS are divided into five kinds: *Active, Passive, Neuter, Pronominal,* and *Impersonal,* or rather *Unipersonal,* besides the two Auxiliary Verbs, *avoir,* to have, and *être,* to be.

There are FOUR CONJUGATIONS in French, which are distinguished by the termination of the Present of the Infinitive.

 The first   ends in ER, as, *parler,* to speak.
 ... second   ... IR, ... *finir,* to finish.
 ... third   ... OIR, ... *recevoir,* to receive.
 ... fourth   ... RE, ... *vendre,* to sell.

In each of these Conjugations, there are *regular, irregular,* and *defective* verbs.

A verb is called *regular,* when all its tenses take exactly the terminations of one of the four model conjugations, which are inserted hereafter in their proper places. A verb is called *irregular,* when, in some of its tenses, it takes terminations different from those of the conjugation to which it belongs; and it is termed *defective,* when it is not used in some tenses or persons.

As the compound tenses of all verbs are formed by the help of *avoir,* to have, and *être,* to be, for which reason these two are called *auxiliary* verbs, they take precedence of the four principal Conjugations, instead of being classed among the irregular verbs to which they belong.

"It may not," says Lindley Murray, "be generally proper for young persons beginning the study of grammar, to commit to memory all the tenses of the verbs. If the *simple* tenses be committed to memory, and the rest carefully perused, the business will not be tedious to the scholars, and their progress will be rendered more obvious and pleasing."

Without wishing to dictate any particular method of tuition, we think the preceding remark of the celebrated English Grammarian peculiarly applicable to the learning of French verbs. Let the scholar be first made familiar with the *simple* tenses, and he will find the rest an extremely easy task.

The most part of Anglo-French Grammarians mix the simple and compound tenses; in this Grammar they are kept separate, but presented at one view, side by side; so that while the student is learning a *simple* tense, he also forms an acquaintance with its *compound.*

129. CONJUGATION OF THE AUXILIARY VERB
AVOIR, TO HAVE.

INFINITIVE.

PRESENT.		PAST.	
Avoir,	to have.	Avoir eu,	to have had.
PARTICIPLE PRESENT.		**COMPOUND OF PARTICIPLE PRESENT.**	
Ayant,	having.	Ayant eu,	having had.

PARTICIPLE PAST.—Eu, *m.*, eue, *f.*, had.

INDICATIVE.

Simple Tenses.   *Compound Tenses.*

PRESENT.		PRETERITE INDEFINITE.	
J'ai,*	I have.	J'ai eu,	I have had.
tu as,	thou hast.	tu as eu,	thou hast had.
il, *or* elle a,	he, *or* she has.	il a eu,	he has had.
nous avons,	we have.	nous avons eu,	we have had.
vous avez,†	you have.	vous avez eu,	you have had.
ils, *or* elles ont,	they have.	ils ont eu,	they have had.

IMPERFECT.		PLUPERFECT.	
J'avais,	I had.	J'avais eu,	I had had.
tu avais,	thou hadst.	tu avais eu,	thou hadst had.
il avait,	he had.	il avait eu,	he had had.
nous avions,	we had.	nous avions eu,	we had had.
vous aviez,	you had.	vous aviez eu,	you had had.
ils avaient,	they had.	ils avaient eu,	they had had.

PRETERITE DEFINITE.		PRETERITE ANTERIOR.	
J'eus,‡	I had.	J'eus eu,	I had had.
tu eus,	thou hadst.	tu eus eu,	thou hadst had.
il eut,	he had.	il eut eu,	he had had.
nous eûmes,§	we had.	nous eûmes eu,	we had had.
vous eûtes,§	you had.	vous eûtes eu,	you had had.
ils eurent,	they had.	ils eurent eu,	they had had.

---

* We write *j'ai*, and pronounce *jè*.

† All the second persons plural of the *simple tenses* end with z or s—with z, when the preceding e is pronounced with the sound of a in the English alphabet; as, *vous avez, vous parliez*—and with s, when the same e is not pronounced at all; as, *vous êtes, vous faites*, &c.

‡ *J'eus* is pronounced *j'u*.

§ The first and second person plural of the *Preterite Definite* of all verbs take a circumflex accent over the vowel that terminates the last syllable but one

AUXILIARY VERB *AVOIR.*

Simple Tenses.   *Compound Tenses.*

FUTURE ABSOLUTE.

J'aurai,	*I shall have.*		
tu auras,	*thou shalt have.*		
il aura,	*he shall have.*		
nous aurons,	*we shall have.*		
vous aurez,	*you shall have.*		
ils auront,	*they shall have.*		

FUTURE ANTERIOR.

J'aurai eu,	*I shall* ⎫
tu auras eu,	*thou shalt* ⎪
il aura eu,	*he shall* ⎬ *have had.*
nous aurons eu,	*we shall* ⎪
vous aurez eu,	*you shall* ⎪
ils auront eu,	*they shall* ⎭

CONDITIONAL.

PRESENT.

J'aurais,	*I should have.*
tu aurais,	*thou shouldst have.*
il aurait,	*he should have.*
nous aurions,	*we should have.*
vous auriez,	*you should have.*
ils auraient,	*they should have.*

PAST.

J'aurais eu,	*I should* ⎫
tu aurais eu,	*thou shouldst* ⎪
il aurait eu,	*he should* ⎬ *have had.*
nous aurions eu,	*we should* ⎪
vous auriez eu,	*you should* ⎪
ils auraient eu,	*they should* ⎭

IMPERATIVE.

Aie,	*Have (thou).*
qu'il ait,	*let him have.*
ayons,	*let us have.*
ayez,	*have (ye).*
qu'ils aient,	*let them have.*

SUBJUNCTIVE.

PRESENT.

Que j'aie,	*That I may*
que tu aies,	*that thou mayst*
qu'il ait,	*that he may*
que nous ayons,	*that we may*
que vous ayez,	*that you may*
qu'ils aient,	*that they may*

⎬ *have.*

PRETERITE.

Que j'aie eu,	*That I may* ⎫
que tu aies eu,	*that thou mayst* ⎪
qu'il ait eu,	*that he may* ⎬ *have had.*
que nous ayons eu,	*that we may* ⎪
que vous ayez eu,	*that you may* ⎪
qu'ils aient eu,	*that they may* ⎭

IMPERFECT.

Que j'eusse,	*That I might*
que tu eusses,	*that thou mightst*
qu'il eût,*	*that he might*
que nous eussions,	*that we might*
que vous eussiez,	*that you might*
qu'ils eussent,	*that they might*

⎬ *have.*

PLUPERFECT.

Que j'eusse eu,	*That I might* ⎫
que tu eusses eu,	*that thou mightst* ⎪
qu'il eût eu,	*that he might* ⎬ *have had.*
que nous eussions eu,	*that we might* ⎪
que vous eussiez eu,	*that you might* ⎪
qu'ils eussent eu,†	*that they might* ⎭

---

* The third person singular of the Imperfect of the Subjunctive of all verbs takes a circumflex accent over the vowel that precedes the final *t*; as, *qu'il eût, qu'il chantât, qu'il finît, qu'il récût,* &c.

† By omitting *que,* this tense is also used for the Conditional past.

EXERCISES ON *AVOIR*.

130. REMARK I. In the following Exercises, the noun being used in a partitive sense, it will be necessary to place before the noun either *du, de la, de l'*, or *des*, according to the directions given, Rule III., page 16.

EXERCISE XXXIX.

INDICATIVE. PRES.—I have money.—He has wealth.—
       argent m.   *bien* m.
She has patience and sweetness.—We have relations and
    —— f. *douceur* f.   *parent*
friends.—You have gold and silver. — They have ambition
ami   or m. *argent* m. m.   —— f.
and perseverance.—They have pomegranates and pineapples.
persévérance f. f.   *grenade* f. *ananas* m.

IMPERF.—We had umbrellas and cloaks. — You had
    parapluie m. *manteau* m.
muskets, rifles, pistols, and artillery. — They had
fusil m. *carabine* f. *pistolet* m. *artillerie* f.
swords, lances, pikes, pitchforks, bows, and arrows.
épée f. —— f. *pique* f. *fourche* f. *arc* m. *flèche* f.

PRETERITE DEFIN.—I had strawberries.—She had raspberries.
    fraise f.   *framboise* f.
We had gooseberries.—You had cherries.—They had grapes.
 groseille f.   *cerise* f. f. *raisin* m.

EXERCISE XL.

Peter has talent and experience. — You have courage and
Pierre —— m. *expérience* f.   —— m.
firmness.—John and James have walnuts and filberts. — Jane
fermeté f. *Jean* *Jacques* *noix* f. *aveline* f. *Jeanne*
had prudence and riches. — He has had good luck. — We
ind-2 —— f. *richesse* pl.   *bonheur* m.
shall have soup or fish. — Andrew shall have oranges and
 soupe f. *poisson* m. *André*   —— f.
lemons. — Louisa and Martha shall have figs and plums.—
citron m. 79   79   *figue* f. *prune* f.
That we may have had snow, rain, and wind. — Having
    neige f. *pluie* f. *vent* m.
eyes, see ye not? Having ears, hear ye not?
40 *ne voyez- point?* *oreille* f. *n'entendez-*

EXERCISES ON *AVOIR*. 63

131. REMARK II.—The addition of an adjective, *after* the noun, makes no difference as to the use of *du, de la, de l', des*. But, the adjective must agree with the noun, in gender and number.—See Rules, p. 20 and 25.

EXERCISE XLI.

INDIC. PRES.—I have red ink. —She has clear and
   ²*rouge* ¹*encre* f. ²*clair*

just ideas.—We have ripe pears.—You have sincere friends.
²*juste* ¹*idée* f. ²*mûr* ¹*poire* f. ²*sincère* ¹

—Margaret and Sophia have green parasols and purple shawls.
Marguerite Sophie ²*vert* ¹——m. ²*violet* ¹*châle* m.

FUT. ABS.—We shall have white curtains. —You will have
   ²*blanc* ¹*rideau* m.

true and real pleasures. — They will have new houses.
²*vrai* ³*réel* ¹*plaisir* m. ²*neuf* ¹*maison* f.

SUBJ. PRES.—In order that I may have ready money.—
   Afin ²*comptant* ¹

That you may have enlightened judges and faithful servants.
   ²*éclairé* ¹*juge* m. ²*fidèle* ¹*domestique*

132. REMARK III.—But, if the adjective comes *before* the noun, then, only *de*, or *d'*, is to be used before the adjective, instead of *du, de la, de l', des*, without any regard to the gender or number of the noun.

I have some good snuff. —He has good brandy, and ex-
   47 *tabac* m. *eau-de-vie* f.

cellent wine. — We have beautiful walks in our town.—
77 *vin* m. *beau promenade* f. *dans*

She had great qualities.—We shall have had long sufferings.—
   ind-2 *grand qualité* f. 58 *souffrance* f.

I should have fine pictures and pretty engravings.—You would
   58 *tableau* m. *joli gravure* f.

have great advantages. —That you may have good reasons to
   avantage m. *raison* f.

give him.— Have you not better pens to lend me?—
donner lui N' *pas* 70 *plume* f. *à prêter*

I have very good pens, but bad ink, and bad paper.
   très *mais mauvais* *papier* m.

Recapitulatory EXERCISE *upon the three foregoing Remarks.*

He has credit, power, authority, and riches. — We
crédit m. *puissance* f. *autorité* f. *richesse* f. pl.
shall have wine, beer, and cider.—Let us have politeness.—
bière f. *cidre* m. *politesse* f.
We have white bread, delicate meat, and delicious wines.—
²*blanc* ¹*pain* m. ²*délicat* ¹*viande* f. ²*délicieux* ¹
That they may have prepossessing manners.—She has excellent
²*prévenant* ¹*manière* f.
qualities.—They have small apricots, but large peaches.
petit abricot m. *gros pêche* f.

---

133. CONJUGATION OF THE AUXILIARY VERB

ÊTRE, TO BE.

INFINITIVE.

PRESENT.		PAST.	
Être,	to be.	Avoir été,	to have been.
PARTICIPLE PRESENT.		COMPOUND OF PARTICIPLE PRESENT.	
Étant,	being.	Ayant été,	having been.

PARTICIPLE PAST.—Été,* been.

INDICATIVE.

Simple Tenses.		*Compound Tenses.*	
PRESENT.		**PRETERITE INDEFINITE.**	
Je suis,	I am.	J'ai été,	I have been.
tu es,	thou art.	tu as été,	thou hast been.
il, or elle est,	he, or she is.	il a été,	he has been.
nous sommes,	we are.	nous avons été,	we have been.
vous êtes,	you are.	vous avez été,	you have been.
ils, or elles sont,	they are.	ils ont été,	they have been.
IMPERFECT.		**PLUPERFECT.**	
J'étais,	I was.	J'avais été,	I had been.
tu étais,	thou wast.	tu avais été,	thou hadst been.
il était,	he was.	il avait été,	he had been.
nous étions,	we were.	nous avions été,	we had been.
vous étiez,	you were.	vous aviez été,	you had been.
ils étaient,	they were.	ils avaient été,	they had been.

---

* *Été* never changes its termination.

AUXILIARY VERB *ÊTRE*.

Simple Tenses.
PRETERITE DEFINITE.

Je fus,	I was.
tu fus,	thou wast.
il fut,	he was.
nous fûmes,	we were.
vous fûtes,	you were.
ils furent,	they were.

FUTURE ABSOLUTE.

Je serai,	I shall be.
tu seras,	thou shalt be.
il sera,	he shall be.
nous serons,	we shall be.
vous serez,	you shall be.
ils seront,	they shall be.

Compound Tenses.
PRETERITE ANTERIOR.

J'eus été,	I had been.
tu eus été,	thou hadst been.
il eut été,	he had been.
nous eûmes été,	we had been.
vous eûtes été,	you had been.
ils eurent été,	they had been.

FUTURE ANTERIOR.

J'aurai été,	I shall have ⎫
tu auras été,	thou shalt have ⎪
il aura été,	he shall have ⎬ been.
nous aurons été,	we shall have ⎪
vous aurez été,	you shall have ⎪
ils auront été,	they shall have ⎭

CONDITIONAL
PRESENT.

Je serais,	I should be.
tu serais,	thou shouldst be.
il serait,	he should be.
nous serions,	we should be.
vous seriez,	you should be.
ils seraient,	they should be.

PAST.

J'aurais été,	I should have ⎫
tu aurais été,	thou shouldst have ⎪
il aurait été,	he should have ⎬ been.
nous aurions été,	we should have ⎪
vous auriez été,	you should have ⎪
ils auraient été,	they should have ⎭

IMPERATIVE.

Sois,	Be (thou).
qu'il soit,	let him be.
soyons,	let us be.
soyez,	be (you).
qu'ils soient,	let them be.

SUBJUNCTIVE.
PRESENT.

Que je sois,	That I may be.
que tu sois,	that thou mayst be.
qu'il soit,	that he may be.
que nous soyons,	that we may be.
que vous soyez,	that you may be.
qu'ils soient,	that they may be.

PRETERITE.

Que j'aie été,	That I may ⎫
que tu aies été,	that thou mayst ⎪
qu'il ait été,	that he may ⎬ have been.
que nous ayons été,	that we may ⎪
que vous ayez été,	that you may ⎪
qu'ils aient été,	that they may ⎭

IMPERFECT.

Que je fusse,	That I might be.
que tu fusses,	that thou mightst be.
qu'il fût,	that he might be.
que nous fussions,	that we might be.
que vous fussiez,	that you might be.
qu'ils fussent,	that they might be.

PLUPERFECT.

Que j'eusse été,	That I might ⎫
que tu eusses été,	that thou mightst ⎪
qu'il eût été,	that he might ⎬ have been.
que nous eussions été,	that we might ⎪
que vous eussiez été,	that you might ⎪
qu'ils eussent été,	that they might ⎭

E

134. General Rule.—The adjective must be of the same gender and number as the noun or pronoun which is the subject of the verb *être*.— See Rules, p. 20 and 25.

EXERCISE XLII.

INDIC. Pres.—I am ready.—She is inquisitive.—We are
            f.   47   *curieux*

busy. —Your sisters are careful. — Men are mortal.
occupé   *soigneux*   art.   *mortel*

Imperf.—I was uneasy.—Mary was tall.—She was prudent
         f.   48   *Marie*   *grand*   ——

and discreet.—Her manners were full of dignity.—We were
  48   *manière* f.   *plein*   78   f.

all present when the thing happened.—They were absent.
tout   *lorsque*   *chose* f.   *arriva.*   m.

Pret. Def.—The country was not ungrateful to him.
           patrie f. *ne*   *point*   *ingrat envers*

—The ides of March were fatal to Julius Cæsar.
   —f.   *mars*   ——   *Jules César.*

Pret. Indef. — Your aunts have always been good and
                           toujours

charitable.— Ladies, you have not been disinterested enough.
     ——   *Mesdames,*   n'   *pas*   ²*désintéressé* ¹*assez*

EXERCISE XLIII.

Pluperf.—She had been too hasty. —We had been idle
               prompt   *paresseux*

and prodigal. —They had been economical and temperate.
  prodigue   *économe*   *sobre*

Fut. Abs.—His memory will be immortal.—We shall be
         mémoire f.   *immortel*   f.

attentive and more diligent.—They will be very glad to see you.
    ——   *plus*   ——   *bien aise de voir*

Fut. Ant.— She will have been proud, whimsical, and jealous.
                      48   *fantasque*   *jaloux*

—They will have been very much pleased and very grateful.
  f.   *très*   *   *satisfait*   *reconnaissant*⸮

Impera.—Let us be poor in gold, and rich in virtues.
            pauvre en   *riche*

— Rich people, be humane, kindhearted, and generous.
  m. pl.   *   *humain*   *tendre*   *généreux*

OF REGULAR VERBS.

PRELIMINARY OBSERVATIONS.

135. (1.) There are, in French, as we have already said (No. 128), but four conjugations, because all verbs terminate in the Present of the Infinitive, in one of four different manners: in *er*, *ir*, *oir*, or *re*.

136. (2.) To conjugate, with greater facility, one verb by another, it is necessary to observe, that in all verbs there are *radical* and *final* letters. The first are like the root of the verb, and contain its meaning: these never change throughout all the different tenses and persons. The *final* letters constitute the termination of the verb, and vary according to tenses and persons. Thus, in *parler*, to speak, the termination common to all verbs of the first conjugation being *er*, the radical letters are *parl*.

137. (3.) Among the simple tenses of a verb, there are five which serve to form all the others, and on that account are called *primitive:* these are, the *Present of the Infinitive*, the *Participle present*, the *Participle past*, the *Present of the Indicative*, and the *Preterite definite*.

138. From the *Present of the Infinitive* are formed:—

1st, The *Future absolute*, by changing *r*, *oir*, or *re*, into *rai*; as, Parler, je parlerai; Finir, je finirai; Recevoir, je recevrai; Vendre, je vendrai.

2d, The *Conditional present*, by changing *r*, *oir*, or *re*, into *rais*; as, Parler, je parlerais; Finir, je finirais; Recevoir, je recevrais; Vendre, je vendrais.

<small>Some Grammarians form the Conditional present, by adding an *s* to the Future, which is the simplest way, when the Future is known.</small>

139. From the *Participle present* are formed:—

1st, The *three persons plural of the Present of the Indicative*, by changing *ant* into *ons, ez, ent*; as, Parlant, nous parlons, vous parlez, ils parlent; Finissant, nous finissons, vous finissez, ils finissent, &c.

<small>EXCEPTION.—Verbs of the Third Conjugation form the third person plural of the Present of the Indicative, from the first person singular of the same tense, by changing *s* into *vent*; as, Je reçois, ils reçoivent.</small>

2d, The *Imperfect of the Indicative*, by changing *ant* into *ais;* as, *Parlant, je parlais; Finissant, je finissais; Recevant, je recevais; Vendant, je vendais.*

3d, The *Present of the Subjunctive*, by changing *ant* into *e;* as, *Parlant, que je parle; Finissant, que je finisse; Vendant, que je vende.*

EXCEPTION.—Verbs of the Third Conjugation form only the first and second persons plural from the Participle present, as, *Recevant, que nous recevions, que vous receviez.* The others are formed from the first person singular of the Present of the Indicative, by changing *s* into *ve;* as, *Je reçois, que je reçoive, que tu reçoives, qu'il reçoive, qu'ils reçoivent.*

140. From the *Participle past* are formed all the compound tenses, by means of the auxiliary verbs *avoir* and *être;* as, *avoir parlé, j'ai fini, j'avais reçu, j'aurai vendu.*

141. From the *Present of the Indicative* is formed the Imperative, by omitting the pronouns; as, *je parle, parle; nous finissons, finissons; vous recevez, recevez.*

142. From the *Preterite definite* is formed the Imperfect of the Subjunctive, by changing *ai* into *asse* for the first conjugation; as, *je parlai, que je parlasse;* and, by adding *se* for the three others; as, *je finis, que je finisse; je reçus, que je reçusse; je vendis, que je vendisse.*

143.   TABLE

OF THE PRIMITIVE TENSES OF REGULAR VERBS.

INFINITIVE Present.	PARTICIPLE Present.	PARTICIPLE Past.	INDICATIVE Present.	PRETERITE Definite.
FIRST CONJUGATION.				
Parl-*er*.	Parl-*ant*.	Parl-*é*.	Je parl-*e*.	Je parl-*ai*.
SECOND CONJUGATION.				
Fin-*ir*.	Fin-*issant*.	Fin-*i*.	Je fin-*is*.	Je fin-*is*.
THIRD CONJUGATION.				
Rec-*evoir*.	Rec-*evant*.	Reç-*u*.	Je reç-*ois*.	Je reç-*us*.
FOURTH CONJUGATION.				
Ven-*dre*.	Ven-*dant*.	Ven-*du*.	Je ven-*ds*.	Je ven-*dis*.

144. § I. CONJUGATION OF ACTIVE VERBS.

An *Active* verb expresses an action done by the subject, and has an object, either expressed or understood. In this phrase: *Jean aime Dieu*, John loves God, *Jean* is the subject, *aime* the verb active, and *Dieu* the object.

MODEL OF THE FIRST CONJUGATION IN *ER*.
145. *PARLER*, TO SPEAK.

INFINITIVE.

PRESENT.		PAST.	
Parler,	*to speak.*	Avoir parlé,	*to have spoken*

PARTICIPLE PRESENT.		COMPOUND OF PART. PRESENT.	
Parlant,	*speaking.*	Ayant parlé,	*having spoken.*

PARTICIPLE PAST.—Parlé, *spoken.*

INDICATIVE.

Simple Tenses.   *Compound Tenses.*

PRESENT.		PRETERITE INDEFINITE.	
Je parle,	*I speak.**	J'ai parlé,	*I have* ⎫
tu parles,	*thou speakest.*	tu as parlé,	*thou hast*
il parle,	*he speaks.*	il a parlé,	*he has*
nous parlons,	*we speak.*	nous avons parlé,	*we have* ⎬ *spoken.*
vous parlez,	*you speak.*	vous avez parlé,	*you have*
ils parlent,	*they speak.*	ils ont parlé,	*they have* ⎭

IMPERFECT.		PLUPERFECT.	
Je parlais,	*I was* ⎫	J'avais parlé,	*I had* ⎫
tu parlais,	*thou wast*	tu avais parlé,	*thou hadst*
il parlait,	*he was* ⎬ *speaking.*	il avait parlé,	*he had* ⎬ *spoken.*
nous parlions,	*we were*	nous avions parlé,	*we had*
vous parliez,	*you were*	vous aviez parlé,	*you had*
ils parlaient,	*they were* ⎭	ils avaient parlé,	*they had* ⎭

PRETERITE DEFINITE.		PRETERITE ANTERIOR.	
Je parlai,	*I spoke.*	J'eus parlé,	*I had* ⎫
tu parlas,	*thou spokest.*	tu eus parlé,	*thou hadst*
il parla,	*he spoke.*	il eut parlé,	*he had* ⎬ *spoken.*
nous parlâmes,	*we spoke.*	nous eûmes parlé,	*we had*
vous parlâtes,	*you spoke.*	vous eûtes parlé,	*you had*
ils parlèrent,	*they spoke.*	ils eurent parlé,	*they had* ⎭

* I speak, I do speak, *or*, I am speaking. See N. B. p. 279.

FIRST CONJUGATION IN ER

Simple Tenses.   *Compound Tenses.*

FUTURE ABSOLUTE.

Je parlerai,	*I shall*	⎫
tu parleras,	*thou shalt*	⎪
il parlera,	*he shall*	⎬ *speak.*
nous parlerons,	*we shall*	⎪
vous parlerez,	*you shall*	⎪
ils parleront,	*they shall*	⎭

FUTURE ANTERIOR.

J'aurai parlé,
tu auras parlé,
il aura parlé,
nous aurons parlé,
vous aurez parlé,
ils auront parlé,
   —*I shall have spoken.*

CONDITIONAL.

PRESENT.

Je parlerais, *I should*
tu parlerais, *thou shouldst*
il parlerait, *he should*   *speak.*
nous parlerions, *we should*
vous parleriez, *you should*
ils parleraient, *they should*

PAST.

J'aurais parlé,
tu aurais parlé,
il aurait parlé,
nous aurions parlé,
vous auriez parlé,
ils auraient parlé,
   —*I should have spoken.*

IMPERATIVE

Parle,   *Speak (thou).*
qu'il parle,   *let him speak.*
parlons,   *let us speak.*
parlez,   *speak (you).*
qu'ils parlent,   *let them speak.*

SUBJUNCTIVE.

PRESENT.

Que je parle,
que tu parles,
qu'il parle,
que nous parlions,
que vous parliez,
qu'ils parlent,
   —*That I may speak.*

PRETERITE.

Que j'aie parlé,
que tu aies parlé,
qu'il ait parlé,
que nous ayons parlé,
que vous ayez parlé,
qu'ils aient parlé,
   —*That I may have spoken.*

IMPERFECT.

Que je parlasse,
que tu parlasses,
qu'il parlât,
que nous parlassions,
que vous parlassiez,
qu'ils parlassent,
   —*That I might speak.*

PLUPERFECT.

Que j'eusse parlé,
que tu eusses parlé,
qu'il eût parlé,
que nous eussions parlé,
que vous eussiez parlé,
qu'ils eussent parlé,
   That I might have spoken.

146. Conjugate in the same manner all the regular Verbs terminating in *er;* as,

Accepter,	*to accept.*	fermer,	*to shut.*
chanter,	*to sing.*	flatter,	*to flatter.*
chercher,	*to seek.*	garder,	*to keep.*
danser,	*to dance.*	louer,	*to praise.*
demander,	*to ask.*	montrer,	*to show.*
donner,	*to give.*	porter,	*to carry.*
éviter,	*to avoid.*	raconter,	*to relate.*

EXERCISE XLIV.

INDICATIVE. PRESENT.—I study   geography and
                    étudier art. *géographie* f.
history. — He dines at five o'clock.—We admire the
art. *histoire* f. *h* m.   *dîner*   *heure*   *admirer*
beauty of that landscape. — You forgive your enemies.—
beauté f.   *paysage* m.   *pardonner à*   *ennemi*
Your brothers and   sisters sing and dance very well.
               91

IMPERF. — I was accusing my friend. — He was listening
           accuser   *ami*   *écouter*
attentively. — We were blaming our neighbours. — You were
attentivement.   *blâmer*   *voisin*
proposing a salutary advice.—They were praising your prudence
proposer   ²   ¹*avis* m.   —f.
—The ancient Peruvians worshipped the sun.
    ancien Péruvien   *adorer*   *soleil* m.

EXERCISE XLV.

PRET. DEF.—I approved his action.—She sung two or three
        approuver 93   — f.
songs. — He borrowed money.—We declined his offer.—
chanson   *emprunter* 32 *argent* m.   *refuser* 93 *offre* f.
You rewarded the servant. — They declared war.
   récompenser domestique m.   *déclarer* art. *guerre* f.
PRET. INDEF.—I have surmounted all the difficulties. — He
              surmonter tout *difficulté* f.
has offended his Majesty. —We have bought an estate. —They
 offenser *Majesté* f.   *acheter* . *terre* f.
have considered the justice of his demand. — At all times,
   considérer   —f.   *demande* f. *Dans* art.
  gold has been looked upon as the most precious metal.
art.   *regarder comme*   *des* pl.

EXERCISE XLVI.

PLUPERF.—I had asked his consent. — The queen had
demander   consentement m.
manifested her   displeasure. — We had consulted   men
montrer   mécontentement m.   *consulter* 32
of honour. — You had emptied the bottle. — They
honneur h m.   *vider   bouteille* f.
had repaired the house. — He had tuned my piano.
réparer   maison f.   *accorder   —* m.

FUT. ABSOL.—I shall cross the river. — She will travel
traverser   rivière f.   *voyager*
with us.—We will breakfast with you.—You will shut the
avec   déjeuner   fermer
shutters. — They will bring letters and newspapers.
volet m.   *apporter* 32 *lettre* f.   32 *journal* m.

CONDIT. PRESENT.—I would explain the rule.—He would
expliquer   règle f.
avoid his company. — She would prepare the ball dresses.—
compagnie f.   *préparer   habit de bal.*
We would walk faster. — They would gain the victory.
marcher plus vite.   remporter   victoire f.

EXERCISE XLVII.

IMPERATIVE.— Give me his address and yours.—Let us
Donner   adresse f.
frequent   good company.—James, carry this letter to the
fréquenter art.   *porter   lettre* f.
post-office.—Ask, and it shall be given you; seek, and you
poste f.   on   ind-7
shall find; knock, and it shall be opened unto you.
trouver frapper   on   *ouvrira*

SUBJ. PRESENT.—That I may re-enforce my party. — That
renforcer   parti m.
he may appease his anger. — That you may find friends.
apaiser   colère f.   *des*

IMPERF.—That I might prove the truth. — That she might
prouver   vérité f.
remain in town. — That they might take advantage of the
rester en ville.   profiter
circumstances. — That you might imitate his conduct.
circonstance f.   *imiter   conduite* f.

MODEL OF THE SECOND CONJUGATION IN *IR*.
147.   *FINIR,** TO FINISH.

INFINITIVE.

PRESENT.		PAST.	
Finir,	to finish.	Avoir fini,	to have finished.

PARTICIPLE PRESENT.		COMPOUND OF PART. PRESENT.	
Finissant,	finishing.	Ayant fini,	having finished.

PARTICIPLE PAST.—Fini, *finished.*

Simple Tenses.   *Compound Tenses.*

INDICATIVE.

PRESENT.		PRETERITE INDEFINITE.	
Je finis,	*I finish.*	J'ai fini,	*I have finished.*
tu finis,	*thou finishest.*	tu as fini,	*thou hast finished.*
il finit,	*he finishes.*	il a fini,	*he has finished.*
nous finissons,	*we finish.*	nous avons fini,	*we have finished.*
vous finissez,	*you finish.*	vous avez fini,	*you have finished.*
ils finissent,	*they finish.*	ils ont fini,	*they have finished.*

IMPERFECT.		PLUPERFECT.	
Je finissais,	*I was* ⎫	J'avais fini,	*I had* ⎫
tu finissais,	*thou wast*	tu avais fini,	*thou hadst*
il finissait,	*he was* ⎬ *finishing.*	il avait fini,	*he had* ⎬ *finished.*
nous finissions,	*we were*	nous avions fini,	*we had*
vous finissiez,	*you were*	vous aviez fini,	*you had*
ils finissaient,	*they were* ⎭	ils avaient fini,	*they had* ⎭

PRETERITE DEFINITE.		PRETERITE ANTERIOR.	
Je finis,	*I finished.*	J'eus fini,	*I had* ⎫
tu finis,	*thou finishedst.*	tu eus fini,	*thou hadst*
il finit,	*he finished.*	il eut fini,	*he had* ⎬ *finished.*
nous finîmes,	*we finished.*	nous eûmes fini,	*we had*
vous finîtes,	*you finished.*	vous eûtes fini,	*you had*
ils finirent,	*they finished.*	ils eurent fini,	*they had* ⎭

FUTURE ABSOLUTE.		FUTURE ANTERIOR.	
Je finirai,	*I shall finish.*	J'aurai fini,	*I shall have* ⎫
tu finiras,	*thou shalt finish.*	tu auras fini,	*thou shalt have*
il finira,	*he shall finish.*	il aura fini,	*he shall have* ⎬ *finished.*
nous finirons,	*we shall finish.*	nous aurons fini,	*we shall have*
vous finirez,	*you shall finish.*	vous aurez fini,	*you shall have*
ils finiront,	*they shall finish.*	ils auront fini,	*they shall have* ⎭

* The final R of the Infinitive of the 2d Conjugation is always sounded.

SECOND CONJUGATION IN *IR*.

Simple Tenses.   *Compound Tenses.*

CONDITIONAL.

PRESENT.   PAST.

Je finirais,	I should	J'aurais fini,	I should
tu finirais,	thou shouldst	tu aurais fini,	thou shouldst
il finirait,	he should	il aurait fini,	he should
nous finirions,	we should	nous aurions fini,	we should
vous finiriez,	you should	vous auriez fini,	you should
ils finiraient,	they should	ils auraient fini,	they should

(finish.)   (have finished.)

IMPERATIVE.

Finis,	Finish (thou).
qu'il finisse,	let him finish.
finissons,	let us finish.
finissez,	finish (you).
qu'ils finissent,	let them finish.

SUBJUNCTIVE.

PRESENT.   PRETERITE.

Que je finisse,	That I may	Que j'aie fini,	
que tu finisses,	that thou mayst	que tu aies fini,	
qu'il finisse,	that he may	qu'il ait fini,	
que nous finissions,	that we may	que nous ayons fini,	
que vous finissiez,	that you may	que vous ayez fini,	
qu'ils finissent,	that they may	qu'ils aient fini,	

(finish.)   (That I may have finished.)

IMPERFECT.   PLUPERFECT.

Que je finisse,		Que j'eusse fini,
que tu finisses,		que tu eusses fini,
qu'il finît,		qu'il eût fini,
que nous finissions,		que nous eussions fini,
que vous finissiez,		que vous eussiez fini,
qu'ils finissent,		qu'ils eussent fini,

(That I might finish.)   (That I might have finished.)

148. Conjugate in the same manner:—

Abolir,	to abolish.	enrichir,	to enrich.
adoucir,	to soften.	établir,	to establish.
affermir,	to strengthen.	fléchir,	to soften.
agir,	to act.	fournir,	to furnish.
applaudir,	to applaud.	franchir,	to leap over.
avertir,	to warn.	frémir,	to shudder.
bâtir,	to build.	garantir,	to warrant.
choisir,	to choose.	guérir,	to cure.
démolir,	to demolish.	nourrir,	to nourish, to feed
divertir,	to divert.	obéir,	to obey.
embellir,	to embellish.	punir,	to punish.
emplir,	to fill.	réussir, &c.	to succeed, &c.

EXERCISE XLVIII.

INDICAT. PRES.—I shudder when I think (of it).—He
         quand ²*penser* ¹*y*
fulfils his promise. — Your sister enjoys good
remplir *promesse* f.   *jouir d'une*
health. — You act as a master.—They punish the idlers.
santé f.   *en * maître.*   *paresseux*
 IMPERF.—I was varnishing a picture. — He was climbing
      vernir *tableau* m.   *gravir*
the hill. — They were building a bridge and fortifications.
colline f.   *bâtir* *pont* m. 32 ——f.
 PRET. DEF.—I warned my sister of her danger. — You
     avertir   —— m.
chose a pretty colour.—They succeeded in their undertaking.—
 joli couleur f.   *réussir*   *entreprise* f.
That victory strengthened him on his throne.
          trône m.

EXERCISE XLIX.

PRET. INDEF.—I have chosen it (out of) a thousand. —
           *entre **
He has enriched science with new discoveries.—You
  enrichir art. ——f. *de nouveau découverte* f.
have grown tall. — The greatest empires have perished.
 grandir   —— m.   *périr*
 PRET. ANT.—I had done before him. — When he had
     finir avant lui. Quand
filled his pockets with pears and apples, he went away.
remplir *poche de poire* *de pomme* *s'en alla.*
 PLUPERF. — That merchant had supplied this house
      marchand m. *fournir*   *maison* f.
with wine.—The king had ennobled him.—They had disobeyed
de   *anoblir*   *désobéir*
my orders. — He had warranted my watch for six months.
à *ordre* m.   *montre* f.   *mois.*

EXERCISE L.

FUT. ABSOL.—I will search into that affair. — That will
     approfondir *affaire* f.
cure him.—We will rebuild our country-house. — I hope
guérir 87   *rebâtir* *maison de campagne. espérer*
 you will succeed.—They will obey the laws of the country.
que *réussir*   *obéir à* *loi* f.   *pays* m.

Fut. Ant.—I shall have finished my exercise before dinner.—
thème m. avant dîner.
That bad news will have cooled his ardour.
nouvelle f. refroidir 93 ardeur f.
CONDIT. Pres.—I would mitigate the punishment.—
adoucir punition f.
If he (were to do) that good action, everybody would
faisait ——f. tout le monde
²applaud ¹him.—He would stun the neighbourhood.
applaudir lui étourdir voisinage m.

EXERCISE LI.

IMPERATIVE.—Let us banish vice and cherish
bannir art. —m. chérir
virtue.—Act as a man of honour.—Choose of the
art. vertu f. en * honneur h m.
two.—Reflect for a moment.—Blush with shame.
Réfléchir * —— m. rougir de honte h asp.
SUBJ. Pres.—That I may accomplish my design.—That
accomplir dessein m.
you may establish communications between these two towns.
établir 32 —— entre
Imperf.—That she might match the colours.—That you
assortir couleur f.
might enjoy your glory.—That they might soften his heart.
jouir de gloire. attendrir cœur m.

EXERCISE LII.

That we might have fathomed that mystery.—That they
approfondir mystère m.
might have fed the poor, and cured the sick.—All
pauvre pl. malade pl. Tout
that we build is of short duration.—Let him bless
ce que court durée f. bénir art.
Providence.—God will punish the ungrateful.—I shall finish
—— f. Dieu ingrat m. pl.
my translation this evening.—I have converted him.—That
traduction f. soir m. convertir
town was swallowed up by an earthquake.—The
engloutir un tremblement de terre.
torpedo benumbs the hand of him who touches it.
torpille f. engourdir celui toucher

MODEL OF THE THIRD CONJUGATION IN *OIR*.
149.   *RECEVOIR*, TO RECEIVE.

INFINITIVE.

PRESENT.		PAST.	
Recevoir,	to receive.	Avoir reçu,	to have received

PARTICIPLE PRESENT.		COMPOUND OF PART. PRESENT.	
Recevant,	receiving.	Ayant reçu,	having received.

PARTICIPLE PAST.—Reçu, *received.*

Simple Tenses.   *Compound Tenses.*

INDICATIVE.

PRESENT.		PRETERITE INDEFINITE.	
Je reçois,	I receive.	J'ai reçu,	I have ⎫
tu reçois,	thou receivest.	tu as reçu,	thou hast ⎪
il reçoit,	he receives.	il a reçu,	he has ⎬ received.
nous recevons,	we receive.	nous avons reçu,	we have ⎪
vous recevez,	you receive.	vous avez reçu,	you have ⎪
ils reçoivent,	they receive.	ils ont reçu,	they have ⎭

IMPERFECT.		PLUPERFECT.	
Je recevais,	I was ⎫	J'avais reçu,	I had ⎫
tu recevais,	thou wast ⎪	tu avais reçu,	thou hadst ⎪
il recevait,	he was ⎬ receiving.	il avait reçu,	he had ⎬ received.
nous recevions,	we were ⎪	nous avions reçu,	we had ⎪
vous receviez,	you were ⎪	vous aviez reçu,	you had ⎪
ils recevaient,	they were ⎭	ils avaient reçu,	they had ⎭

PRETERITE DEFINITE.		PRETERITE ANTERIOR.	
Je reçus,	I received.	J'eus reçu,	I had ⎫
tu reçus,	thou receivedst.	tu eus reçu,	thou hadst ⎪
il reçut,	he received.	il eut reçu,	he had ⎬ received.
nous reçûmes,	we received.	nous eûmes reçu,	we had ⎪
vous reçûtes,	you received.	vous eûtes reçu,	you had ⎪
ils reçurent,	they received.	ils eurent reçu,	they had ⎭

FUTURE ABSOLUTE.		FUTURE ANTERIOR.	
Je recevrai,	I shall ⎫	J'aurai reçu,	I shall ⎫
tu recevras,	thou shalt ⎪	tu auras reçu,	thou shalt ⎪
il recevra,	he shall ⎬ receive.	il aura reçu,	he shall ⎬ have received.
nous recevrons,	we shall ⎪	nous aurons reçu,	we shall ⎪
vous recevrez,	you shall ⎪	vous aurez reçu,	you shall ⎪
ils recevront,	they shall ⎭	ils auront reçu,	they shall ⎭

THIRD CONJUGATION IN OIR.

Simple Tenses.   *Compound Tenses.*

CONDITIONAL.

PRESENT.		PAST.	
Je recevrais,	*I should* ⎫	J'aurais reçu,	*I should* ⎫
tu recevrais,	*thou shouldst* ⎪	tu aurais reçu,	*thou shouldst* ⎪
il recevrait,	*he should* ⎬ *receive.*	il aurait reçu,	*he should* ⎬ *have received.*
nous recevrions,	*we should* ⎪	nous aurions reçu,	*we should* ⎪
vous recevriez,	*you should* ⎪	vous auriez reçu,	*you should* ⎪
ils recevraient,	*they should* ⎭	ils auraient reçu,	*they should* ⎭

IMPERATIVE.

Reçois,	*Receive (thou).*
qu'il reçoive,	*let him receive.*
recevons,	*let us receive.*
recevez,	*receive (you).*
qu'ils reçoivent,	*let them receive.*

SUBJUNCTIVE.

PRESENT.		PRETERITE.	
Que je reçoive,	⎫	Que j'aie reçu,	⎫
que tu reçoives,	⎪	que tu aies reçu,	⎪
qu'il reçoive,	⎬ *That I may receive.*	qu'il ait reçu,	⎬ *That I may have received.*
que nous recevions,	⎪	que nous ayons reçu,	⎪
que vous receviez,	⎪	que vous ayez reçu,	⎪
qu'ils reçoivent,	⎭	qu'ils aient reçu,	⎭

IMPERFECT.		PLUPERFECT.	
Que je reçusse,	⎫	Que j'eusse reçu,	⎫
que tu reçusses,	⎪	que tu eusses reçu,	⎪
qu'il reçût,	⎬ *That I might receive.*	qu'il eût reçu,	⎬ *That I might have received.*
que nous reçussions,	⎪	que nous eussions reçu,	⎪
que vous reçussiez,	⎪	que vous eussiez reçu,	⎪
qu'ils reçussent,	⎭	qu'ils eussent reçu,	⎭

This Conjugation has only seven verbs, which are:—

Recevoir, *to receive,* which is given as a model; and,

Apercevoir,	*to perceive.*	redevoir,	*to remain in debt; to owe still.*
concevoir,	*to conceive.*		
décevoir,	*to deceive.*	percevoir,	*to collect* (rents, income, taxes.)
devoir,	*to owe.*		

☞ In all tenses in which c comes before o or u, it takes a cedilla, in order that it may retain the soft sound of s which it has in the Infinitive Present.

EXERCISE LIII.

INDICAT. PRES.—I perceive the steeple of the village.—
  apercevoir clocher m.   —— m.

From his window, he perceives the top   of a mountain.
        fenêtre f.   sommet m. montagne f.

IMPERF.—He owed a large sum to his partner.—You
     devoir grand somme f.   associé m.

were collecting the taxes.—They owed a thousand pounds.
  percevoir   impôt m.   livres sterling.

PRET. DEF.—We perceived several men coming towards
                 123   qui venaient à

us.—The besieged   received succour.
       assiégé m. pl.   32 secours pl.

PRET. INDEF.—I received a letter this morning.—That
              lettre f.   matin m.

regiment has received recruits.—We have perceived
régiment m.   32 recrue f.

you from afar.—The soldiers have received provisions for
  loin.   soldat   32   vivre m.

three days.—My sister has received your parcel.
                                paquet m.

EXERCISE LIV.

FUTURE ABSOL.—I shall receive your letter on the fifteenth.
                                      76

She will receive some visits.—He will still owe thirteen
          visite   redevoir

guineas.—They will owe their misfortunes to their faults.
guinée f.   devoir   malheur m.   faute f.

COND. PRES.—I would conceive the greatest hopes.—You
           concevoir   espérance f.

ought to behave differently.—He would receive a blow.
devoir vous conduire autrement.   coup m.

IMPERATIVE.—Receive this as a mark of my
             101 comme marque f. 92

confidence and   esteem.—Let us receive his apology.—
confiance f. de mon estime f.   93 excuse f.

Conceive the horror of his situation.—Receive him
Concevoir horreur h m. 92 —— f.

kindly.—Receive everybody with civility.
avec bonté.   tout le monde   honnêteté.

MODEL OF THE FOURTH CONJUGATION IN *RE*.
150. *VENDRE*, TO SELL.

INFINITIVE.

PRESENT.		PAST.	
Vendre,	*to sell.*	Avoir vendu,	*to have sold.*

PARTICIPLE PRESENT.		COMPOUND OF PART. PRESENT.	
Vendant,	*selling.*	Ayant vendu,	*having sold.*

PARTICIPLE PAST.—Vendu, *sold.*

Simple Tenses.   *Compound Tenses.*

INDICATIVE.

PRESENT.

Je vends,	*I sell.*
tu vends,	*thou sellest.*
il vend,	*he sells.*
nous vendons,	*we sell.*
vous vendez,	*you sell.*
ils vendent,	*they sell.*

PRETERITE INDEFINITE.

J'ai vendu,	*I have* ⎫
tu as vendu,	*thou hast*
il a vendu,	*he has*
nous avons vendu,	*we have* —sold.
vous avez vendu,	*you have*
ils ont vendu,	*they have* ⎭

IMPERFECT.

Je vendais,	*I was selling.*
tu vendais,	*thou wast selling.*
il vendait,	*he was selling.*
nous vendions,	*we were selling.*
vous vendiez,	*you were selling.*
ils vendaient,	*they were selling.*

PLUPERFECT.

J'avais vendu,	*I had* ⎫
tu avais vendu,	*thou hadst*
il avait vendu,	*he had*
nous avions vendu,	*we had* —sold.
vous aviez vendu,	*you had*
ils avaient vendu,	*they had* ⎭

PRETERITE DEFINITE.

Je vendis,	*I sold.*
tu vendis,	*thou soldest.*
il vendit,	*he sold.*
nous vendîmes,	*we sold.*
vous vendîtes,	*you sold.*
ils vendirent,	*they sold.*

PRETERITE ANTERIOR.

J'eus vendu,	*I had* ⎫
tu eus vendu,	*thou hadst*
il eut vendu,	*he had*
nous cûmes vendu,	*we had* —sold.
vous eûtes vendu,	*you had*
ils eurent vendu,	*they had* ⎭

FUTURE ABSOLUTE.

Je vendrai,	*I shall sell.*
tu vendras,	*thou shalt sell.*
il vendra,	*he shall sell.*
nous vendrons,	*we shall sell.*
vous vendrez,	*you shall sell.*
ils vendront,	*they shall sell.*

FUTURE ANTERIOR.

J'aurai vendu,	*I shall* ⎫
tu auras vendu,	*thou shalt*
il aura vendu,	*he shall*
nous aurons vendu,	*we shall* —have sold.
vous aurez vendu,	*you shall*
ils auront vendu,	*they shall* ⎭

FOURTH CONJUGATION IN *RE*.

Simple Tenses.   *Compound Tenses.*

CONDITIONAL.

PRESENT.		PAST.	
Je vendrais,	*I should*	J'aurais vendu,	*I should*
tu vendrais,	*thou shouldst*	tu aurais vendu,	*thou shouldst*
il vendrait,	*he should*	il aurait vendu,	*he should*
nous vendrions,	*we should*	nous aurions vendu,	*we should*
vous vendriez,	*you should*	vous auriez vendu,	*you should*
ils vendraient,	*they should*	ils auraient vendu,	*they should*

(*sell.* / *have sold.*)

IMPERATIVE.

Vends,	*Sell (thou).*
qu'il vende,	*let him sell.*
vendons,	*let us sell.*
vendez,	*sell (you).*
qu'ils vendent,	*let them sell.*

SUBJUNCTIVE.

PRESENT.		PRETERITE.	
Que je vende,		Que j'aie vendu,	
que tu vendes,		que tu aies vendu,	
qu'il vende,	*That I may sell.*	qu'il ait vendu,	*That I may have sold.*
que nous vendions,		que nous ayons vendu,	
que vous vendiez,		que vous ayez vendu,	
qu'ils vendent,		qu'ils aient vendu,	

IMPERFECT.		PLUPERFECT.	
Que je vendisse,		Que j'eusse vendu,	
que tu vendisses,		que tu eusses vendu,	
qu'il vendît,	*That I might sell.*	qu'il eût vendu,	*That I might have sold.*
que nous vendissions,		que nous eussions vendu,	
que vous vendissiez,		que vous eussiez vendu,	
qu'ils vendissent,		qu'ils eussent vendu,	

151. Conjugate in the same manner:—

Attendre,	*to wait for.*	pendre,	*to hang.*
correspondre,	*to correspond.*	perdre,	*to lose.*
défendre,	*to defend.*	prétendre,	*to pretend.*
dépendre,	*to depend.*	rendre,	*to render.*
descendre,	*to descend.*	répandre,	*to spread.*
entendre,	*to hear.*	répondre,	*to answer.*
fendre,	*to split.*	suspendre,	*to suspend.*
fondre,	*to melt.*	tordre,	*to twist.*
mordre,	*to bite.*	&c.	&c.

F

EXERCISE LV.

INDICAT. PRESENT.—I hear the children.—That depends
                                enfant
on circumstances.—He understands English (a little.)—That
des circonstance f.   *entendre* ²*l'anglais* ⋅ ¹
dog bites. — He defends his sister. — We expect several
chien m.   *attendre*
friends to dinner.— You claim a half. — They confound
          à dîner.   *prétendre moitié* f.   *confondre*
the arts with the sciences.—He is splitting some wood.
 — m.   —— f.   *bois* m.

IMPERF.—I was waiting for the steam-boat. — He was
           attendre *   *bateau à vapeur* m.
coming down with David.—They were wasting their time.
  descendre   *perdre*   *temps* m.

EXERCISE LVI.

PRET. DEF.—I alighted at the hôtel de France — He
           descendre   *h* m.
answered in a few words.—We aimed at an honest end.—
      en peu de mots.   *tendre*   ²*honnête* ¹*but* m.
They lost their lawsuit. — The storm burst upon the town.
       procès m.   *orage* m. *fondre*

PRET. INDEF. — I have heard that musician. — He has
                          entendre   *musicien* m
restored the money. — The sun has melted the snow. — The
rendre   *fondre*   *neige* f.
thermometer has fallen four degrees since yesterday.
thermomètre m. *descendre de*   *degré* m. *depuis*   *hier.*
—You have defended him with much talent. — Ladies,
       défendre   *beaucoup de* —— *Mesdames*
have you heard the music of the new opera?
                musique f.   *nouvel opéra* m.

EXERCISE LVII.

FUTURE. — Make haste, I will wait for you. — It is a
         Dépêchez-vous   *attendre* *   C'
thing to which he will never condescend. — You will
chose f.   *ne* ²*jamais* ¹*condescendre*
wait a long time. — They will shear their sheep.
attendre * *longtemps.*   *tondre*   *brebis* pl

COND. PRES.—I would correspond regularly with
      correspondre régulièrement
my friends. — Your hens would lay eggs every day.
     poule f. *pondre tous les jours.*
 IMPERATIVE.—Let us answer their letter. — Wait
      répondre à   *Attendre*
till to-morrow. — Hang up your hat and your
jusqu'à demain. *Pendre* * *chapeau* m.
cloak. — Render unto Cæsar (the things which are Cæsar's.)
manteau m. *à César ce qui appartient à César.*

---

152. CONJUGATION

OF A VERB WITH A NEGATIVE.

PRELIMINARY REMARKS.

153. The English negatives *no* and *not* are rendered in French by *ne*, which is placed immediately after the subject or nominative, whether it be a noun or pronoun, and *pas* or *point* after the verb in simple tenses, and between the auxiliary and the participle in compound tenses.

"When the verb is in the Present of the Infinitive, it is optional to place *pas* and *point* before or after the verb. *Pour ne* POINT *souffrir.—Pour ne souffrir* POINT. The first manner of speaking, however, is more used."—
       (FR. ACAD. "Dict. crit. de *Féraud,*" &c.)

The same rules are applicable to other negatives, such as, *ne jamais,* never; *ne rien,* nothing; *ne plus,* no more, not any more, no longer.

154. When the negative is followed by a noun, *de* is used instead of the definite article; as, *Je n'ai pas* DE *livres,* I have no books; *elle n'a point* DE *place,* she has no room.

155. The words *do* or *did,* which precede an English verb in some tenses, are not expressed in French.

156. MODEL

FOR THE CONJUGATION OF A VERB USED NEGATIVELY.

INFINITIVE.

Simple Tenses.   *Compound Tenses.*

PRESENT.   PAST.

Ne pas parler, *not to speak.* | N'avoir pas parlé, *not to have spoken.*

PARTICIPLE PRESENT.   COMPOUND OF PART. PRESENT.

Ne parlant pas, *not speaking.* | N'ayant pas parlé, *not having spoken.*

INDICATIVE

PRESENT.		PRETERITE INDEFINITE	
Je ne parle pas,		Je n'ai pas parlé,	
tu ne parles pas,		tu n'as pas parlé,	
il ne parle pas,	*I do not speak.*	il n'a pas parlé,	*I have not spoken.*
nous ne parlons pas,		nous n'avons pas parlé,	
vous ne parlez pas,		vous n'avez pas parlé,	
ils ne parlent pas,		ils n'ont pas parlé,	

IMPERFECT.		PLUPERFECT.	
Je ne parlais pas,		Je n'avais pas parlé,	
tu ne parlais pas,		tu n'avais pas parlé,	
il ne parlait pas,	*I was not speaking.*	il n'avait pas parlé,	*I had not spoken.*
nous ne parlions pas,		nous n'avions pas parlé,	
vous ne parliez pas,		vous n'aviez pas parlé,	
ils ne parlaient pas,		ils n'avaient pas parlé,	

PRETERITE DEFINITE.		PRETERITE ANTERIOR.	
Je ne parlai pas,		Je n'eus pas parlé,	
tu ne parlas pas,		tu n'eus pas parlé,	
il ne parla pas,	*I did not speak.*	il n'eut pas parlé,	*I had not spoken.*
nous ne parlâmes pas,		nous n'eûmes pas parlé,	
vous ne parlâtes pas,		vous n'eûtes pas parlé,	
ils ne parlèrent pas,		ils n'eurent pas parlé,	

FUTURE ABSOLUTE.		FUTURE ANTERIOR.	
Je ne parlerai pas,		Je n'aurai pas parlé,	
tu ne parleras pas,		tu n'auras pas parlé,	
il ne parlera pas,	*I shall not speak.*	il n'aura pas parlé,	*I shall not have spoken.*
nous ne parlerons pas,		nous n'aurons pas parlé,	
vous ne parlerez pas,		vous n'aurez pas parlé,	
ils ne parleront pas,		ils n'auront pas parlé,	

Simple Tenses.   *Compound Tenses.*

CONDITIONAL.

PRESENT.   **PAST.**

Je ne parlerais pas,	Je n'aurais pas parlé,
tu ne parlerais pas,	tu n'aurais pas parlé,
il ne parlerait pas,	il n'aurait pas parlé,
nous ne parlerions pas,	nous n'aurions pas parlé,
vous ne parleriez pas,	vous n'auriez pas parlé,
ils ne parleraient pas,	ils n'auraient pas parlé,

I should not speak.   *I should not have spoken.*

IMPERATIVE.

Ne parle pas,	*Do not speak.*
qu'il ne parle pas,	*let him not speak.*
ne parlons pas,	*let us not speak.*
ne parlez pas,	*do not speak.*
qu'ils ne parlent pas,	*let them not speak.*

SUBJUNCTIVE.

PRESENT.   **PRETERITE.**

Que je ne parle pas,	Que je n'aie pas parlé,
que tu ne parles pas,	que tu n'aies pas parlé,
qu'il ne parle pas,	qu'il n'ait pas parlé,
que nous ne parlions pas,	que nous n'ayons pas parlé,
que vous ne parliez pas,	que vous n'ayez pas parlé,
qu'ils ne parlent pas,	qu'ils n'aient pas parlé,

That I may not speak.   *That I may not have spoken.*

IMPERFECT.   **PLUPERFECT.**

Que je ne parlasse pas,	Que je n'eusse pas parlé,
que tu ne parlasses pas,	que tu n'eusses pas parlé,
qu'il ne parlât pas,	qu'il n'eût pas parlé, [parlé
que nous ne parlassions pas,	que nous n'eussions pas
que vous ne parlassiez pas,	que vous n'eussiez pas parlé
qu'ils ne parlassent pas,	qu'ils n'eussent pas parlé.

That I might not speak.   *That I might not have spoken.*

EXERCISE LVIII.

INDICAT. PRES.—I have *no* change.—The butcher has
                        monnaie.   boucher m.

no mutton.—My sister *does not* sing. — We *do not* speak of
   mouton.   chanter

that.—You *do not* answer   his letters.—They are not playing
                répondre à   lettre   jouer

IMPERF.—I *did not* expect that of you.—She was *not*
                          attendre
dancing.—You were *not* thinking of him.—They were *not*
 danser   penser à
happy. — The king was penniless, the queen had *no* money.
 heureux   sans le sou   argent.

EXERCISE LIX.

PRET. DEF.—I *did not* receive his note in time.—He
                                billet m. à temps.
did not forget his promise.—She *did not* hear him.
    oublier   promesse f.   entendre
PRET. INDEF.—I have *not* yet received his answer.—
                         encore   réponse f.
He has *never* spoken to his colonel.—You have *not* brought
                                                     apporter
the parcel. — Your brothers have *not* passed this way.
  paquet m.   passer par ici.
PLUPERF.—I had *not* finished my exercise when you came.
                                thème m. quand   vintes.

EXERCISE LX.

FUT.—I shall *not* speak to him *any more*.—We will *not* travel
                                                       voyager
this year. — You will *never* succeed in that undertaking.
    année f.   réussir   entreprise f.
COND. PRES. — I would owe *nothing*.—You would *not*
                          devoir
wait   long. —They would *never* pardon him.
attendre longtemps.   pardonner lui.
IMPERA.—Let us *not* imitate his conduct. — Do *not* lose
                         imiter   conduite f.   perdre
your time. — *Don't* shut the window.—*Don't* wait for me.
 temps m.   fermer   fenêtre f.   attendre
—*Never*   yield   to the violence of thy passions.—Let us
      t' abandonner   — f.   — f.
not act against him. — Receive *no more* of his letters.—Do
    agir   lui.
not spread that bad   news. —*Do not* be so idle.
     répandre   mauvais nouvelle f.   paresseux

157. CONJUGATION
OF A VERB INTERROGATIVELY.

PRELIMINARY REMARKS.

158. (1.) To conjugate a verb *interrogatively*, which can be done only in the Indicative and Conditional Moods, we place the pronoun, which serves as the subject or nominative, after the verb, connecting them by a hyphen; as, *Avez-vous?* have you? *Jouez-vous?* do you play?

159. (2.) In *compound tenses*, the pronoun is placed between the auxiliary and the participle, joined to the former by a hyphen; as, *Ai-je parlé?* have I spoken? *Ont-ils dîné?* have they dined?

160. (3.) When the third person singular of a verb ends with a vowel, for the sake of euphony, we place between the verb and the pronoun, the letter *t*, preceded and followed by a hyphen; as, *Aura-t-il?* will he have? *Danse-t-elle?* does she dance?

161. (4.) When the subject or nominative of a verb is a noun, that noun comes first, and one of the pronouns *il, elle, ils, elles*, is placed after the verb, and joined to it by a hyphen; as, *Mes frères parlent-ils?* do my brothers speak? *Votre sœur aurait-elle chanté?* would your sister have sung?

162. (5.) When the first person singular of a verb ends with an *e* mute, an *acute accent* is placed over that *e*, which is a sign to pronounce it; as, *Parlé-je?* do I speak? *Chanté-je?* do I sing?

163. (6.) Questions are often asked by *Est-ce que*, and then the subject or nominative precedes the verb; as, *Est-ce que vous lisez Horace?* do you read Horace?— This mode of interrogation is also used with verbs that have but one syllable in the first person singular of the Present of the Indicative; so instead of saying, *Vends-je? rends-je? mens-je? perds-je? fonds-je? pars-je?* and the like, we say, *Est-ce que je vends? est-ce que je rends?* &c. By employing the former mode of expression, we

sometimes could not even be understood; as, for instance, *Vends-je? rends-je? mens-je?* might be mistaken for the Imperative *venge, range, mange.* Usage, however, permits us to say, *Ai-je? suis-je? dis-je? fais-je? dois-je? vois-je? vais-je?* because there is no ambiguity nor any harshness of sound.

164. MODEL
FOR THE CONJUGATION OF A VERB USED INTERROGATIVELY.

INDICATIVE.

Simple Tenses.   *Compound Tenses.*

PRESENT.   **PRETERITE INDEFINITE.**

Donné-je?	Do I give?	Ai-je donné?	Have I
donnes-tu?	dost thou give?	as-tu donné?	hast thou
donne-t-il?	does he give?	a-t-il donné?	has he
donnons-nous?	do we give?	avons-nous donné?	have we
donnez-vous?	do you give?	avez-vous donné?	have you
donnent-ils?	do they give?	ont-ils donné?	have they

    given?

IMPERFECT.   **PLUPERFECT.**

Donnais-je?	Was I	Avais-je donné?	Had I
donnais-tu?	wast thou	avais-tu donné?	hadst thou
connait-il?	was he	avait-il donné?	had he
donnions-nous?	were we	avions-nous donné?	had we
donniez-vous?	were you	aviez-vous donné?	had you
donnaient-ils?	were they	avaient-ils donné?	had they

   giving?   *given?*

PRETERITE DEFINITE.   **PRETERITE ANTERIOR.**

Donnai-je?	Did I give?	Eus-je donné?	Had I
donnas-tu?	didst thou give?	eus-tu donné?	hadst thou
donna-t-il?	did he give?	eut-il donné?	had he
donnâmes-nous?	did we give?	eûmes-nous donné?	had we
donnâtes-vous?	did you give?	eûtes-vous donné?	had you
donnèrent-ils?	did they give?	eurent-ils donné?	had they

    given?

FUTURE ABSOLUTE.   **FUTURE ANTERIOR.**

Donnerai-je?	Shall I	Aurai-je donné?	Shall I
donneras-tu?	shalt thou	auras-tu donné?	shalt thou
donnera-t-il?	shall he	aura-t-il donné?	shall he
donnerons-nous?	shall we	aurons-nous donné?	shall we
donnerez-vous?	shall you	aurez-vous donné?	shall you
donneront-ils?	shall they	auront-ils donné?	shall they

   give?   *have given?*

EXERCISES ON VERBS WITH INTERROGATION. 89

Simple Tenses.   Compound Tenses.

CONDITIONAL.

PRESENT.   PAST.

Donnerais-je?	Should I	Aurais-je donné?	
donnerais-tu?	shouldst thou	aurais-tu donné?	—Should I
donnerait-il?	should he	aurait-il donné?	have given?
donnerions-nous?	should we	aurions-nous donné?	
donneriez-vous?	should you	auriez-vous donné?	
donneraient-ils?	should they	auraient-ils donné?	

EXERCISE LXI.

INDICATIVE. Pres.—Have I friends?—Is she pleased?
satisfait

Does he bring good news? — Does she dance well?—
apporter   nouvelle f.   *danser*

Has she a watch?—Is breakfast ready?—Do you call?
montre f.   *déjeuner* m. *prêt*   *appeler*

Imperf.—Was he waiting for your arrival?—Were you
attendre   *arrivée* f.

speaking to our captain?—Had the traveller a pistol?
capitaine   *voyageur* m. *pistolet* m.

Pret. Def.—Did he prefer your house to hers?—Did
préférer   *maison* f.

they clear up his doubts?—Was he bold enough?
éclaircir   *doute* m.   ²*hardi* ¹

EXERCISE LXII.

Pret. Indef.—Has the king rewarded his services?—
récompenser   —— m.

Has your mother received my letter?—Have your partners
associé m.

sold my goods? — Have you bought a pencil-case?
marchandise f.   *porte-crayon* m.

Pluperf.—Had she offended her mistress?—Had you
offenser   *maîtresse*

forgotten the date?—Had he lost his pocket-book?
oublier —— f.   *perdre* *portefeuille* m.

Fut.—Shall I have that pleasure?—Will Miss Isabella
plaisir m.

sing?—Shall we alight here?—When shall we dine?
chanter   *descendre*   *dîner*

165. MODEL

FOR THE CONJUGATION OF A VERB USED INTERROGATIVELY AND NEGATIVELY.

REMARK.—To add the negative form to a verb used interrogatively, *ne* is placed before the verb, and *pas* or *point* after the personal pronoun, both in the simple and compound tenses.

Simple Tenses.   *Compound Tenses.*

INDICATIVE.

PRESENT.		PRETERITE INDEFINITE.	
Est-ce que je ne perds pas? (*for* ne perds-je pas?)	*Do I not lose?*	N'ai-je pas perdu?	*Have I not lost?*
ne perds-tu pas?		n'as-tu pas perdu?	
ne perd*-il pas?		n'a-t-il pas perdu?	
ne perdons-nous pas?		n'avons-nous pas perdu?	
ne perdez-vous pas?		n'avez-vous pas perdu?	
ne perdent-ils pas?		n'ont-ils pas perdu?	

IMPERFECT.		PLUPERFECT.	
Ne perdais-je pas?	*Was I not losing?*	N'avais-je pas perdu?	*Had I not lost?*
ne perdais-tu pas?		n'avais-tu pas perdu?	
ne perdait-il pas?		n'avait-il pas perdu?	
ne perdions-nous pas?		n'avions-nous pas perdu?	
ne perdiez-vous pas?		n'aviez-vous pas perdu?	
ne perdaient-ils pas?		n'avaient-ils pas perdu?	

PRETERITE DEFINITE.		PRETERITE ANTERIOR.	
Ne perdis-je pas?	*Did I not lose?*	N'eus-je pas perdu?	*Had I not lost?*
ne perdis-tu pas?		n'eus-tu pas perdu?	
ne perdit-il pas?		n'eut-il pas perdu?	
ne perdîmes-nous pas?		n'eûmes-nous pas perdu?	
ne perdîtes-vous pas?		n'eûtes-vous pas perdu?	
ne perdirent-ils pas?		n'eurent-ils pas perdu?	

---

* D takes the sound of *t*, when at the end of a verb followed by one of the pronouns *il, elle, on*.—(*Dumarsais, Féraud, Bouillette, Demandre,* etc.)

VERB INTERROGATIVELY AND NEGATIVELY.

Simple Tenses.
FUTURE ABSOLUTE.
Ne perdrai-je pas?
ne perdras-tu pas?
ne perdra-t-il pas?
ne perdrons-nous pas?
ne perdrez-vous pas?
ne perdront-ils pas?
} —*Shall I not lose?*

Compound Tenses.
FUTURE ANTERIOR.
N'aurai-je pas perdu?
n'auras-tu pas perdu?
n'aura-t-il pas perdu?
n'aurons-nous pas perdu?
n'aurez-vous pas perdu?
n'auront-ils pas perdu?
} *Shall I not have lost?*

CONDITIONAL.

PRESENT.
Ne perdrais-je pas?
ne perdrais-tu pas?
ne perdrait-il pas?
ne perdrions-nous pas?
ne perdriez-vous pas?
ne perdraient-ils pas?
} —*Should I not lose?*

PAST.
N'aurais-je pas perdu?
n'aurais-tu pas perdu?
n'aurait-il pas perdu?
n'aurions-nous pas perdu?
n'auriez-vous pas perdu?
n'auraient-ils pas perdu?
} *Should I not have lost?*

EXERCISE LXIII.

INDICAT. PRES. — Am I not troublesome? — Is she not
importun
attentive? — Does your sister not draw? — Do we not walk
dessiner *marcher*
too fast? — Do you not hear the drum? — Do they not
trop vite? *entendre* *tambour* m.
ask (too much?) — Has he not enough money?
demander *trop?* *assez d'*

IMPERF. — Did he not deserve your esteem and mine? —
mériter *estime* f.
Had he not a short coat and a cloak above it?
²*court* ¹*habit* m. *manteau* m. *par-dessus* *

EXERCISE LXIV.

PRET. DEF. — Why did he not answer your question?
Pourquoi *répondre à* —— f.
— Did she not turn the box topsyturvy?
renverser *boîte* f. *sens dessus dessous?*

PRET. INDEF. — Has he not sold again his country-house? —
revendre *maison de campagne* f
Have you not signed the letter? — Have they not been here
signer *ici?*

Fut. Abs.—Will he not betray your confidence?—Will you
trahir *confiance* f.
not consult your lawyer?—Will she not invite your sister?
consulter *avocat ?* *inviter*

---

166. § II. CONJUGATION OF PASSIVE VERBS.

The *Passive* verb expresses an action received or suffered by its subject or nominative.

There is only one mode of conjugating passive verbs; it is by adding to the verb *être* through all its tenses, the past participle of the active verb.

167. Every past participle employed with the verb *être*, must agree in *gender* and *number* with the subject of *être*. To form the feminine, an *e* is added, and to form the plural, an *s*.

168. It has already been said (page 39), that the participle must be put in the singular, when the pronoun *vous* is used instead of *tu;* thus, we must say, in speaking to a man, *vous êtes loué;* and, in speaking to a female, *vous êtes louée*.

169. MODEL
FOR THE CONJUGATION OF A PASSIVE VERB.

INFINITIVE.

PRESENT.		PAST.	
Être loué,	*to be praised.*	Avoir été loué,	*to have been praised.*

PARTICIPLE PRESENT.		PARTICIPLE PAST.	
Étant loué,	*being praised.*	Ayant été loué,	*having been praised.*

Simple Tenses. — *Compound Tenses.*

INDICATIVE.

PRESENT.		PRETERITE INDEFINITE.	
Je suis	{ loué, *m.*	J'ai été	{ loué, *m.*
tu es		tu as été	
il *or* elle est	{ louée, *f.*	il *or* elle a été	{ louée, *f.*
nous sommes	{ loués, *m.*	nous avons été	{ loués, *m.*
vous êtes		vous avez été	
ils *or* elles sont	{ louées, *f.*	ils *or* elles ont été	{ louées, *f.*

— *I am praised.* — *I have been praised.*

CONJUGATION OF A PASSIVE VERB.

Simple Tenses.

IMPERFECT.

J'étais ⎫
tu étais ⎬ { loué, *m.*
il *or* elle était ⎬ { louée, *f.* } — *I was praised.*
nous étions ⎬ { loués, *m.*
vous étiez ⎬
ils *or* elles étaient ⎭ { louées, *f.*

PRETERITE DEFINITE.

Je fus ⎫
tu fus ⎬ { loué, *m.*
il *or* elle fut ⎬ { louée, *f.* } — *I was praised.*
nous fûmes ⎬ { loués, *m.*
vous fûtes ⎬
ils *or* elles furent ⎭ { louées, *f.*

FUTURE ABSOLUTE.

Je serai ⎫
tu seras ⎬ { loué, *m.*
il *or* elle sera ⎬ { louée, *f.* } — *I shall be praised.*
nous serons ⎬ { loués, *m.*
vous serez ⎬
ils *or* elles seront ⎭ { louées, *f.*

Compound Tenses.

PLUPERFECT.

J'avais été ⎫
tu avais été ⎬ { loué, *m.*
il *or* elle avait été ⎬ { louée, *f.* } — *I had been praised.*
nous avions été ⎬ { loués, *m.*
vous aviez été [été] ⎬
ils *or* elles avaient ⎭ { louées, *f.*

PRETERITE ANTERIOR.

J'eus été ⎫
tu eus été ⎬ { loué, *m.*
il *or* elle eut été ⎬ { louée, *f.* } — *I had been praised.*
nous eûmes été ⎬ { loués, *m.*
vous eûtes été ⎬
ils *or* elles eurent été ⎭ { louées, *f.*

FUTURE ANTERIOR.

J'aurai été ⎫
tu auras été ⎬ { loué, *m.*
il *or* elle aura été ⎬ { louée, *f.* } — *I shall have been praised.*
nous aurons été ⎬ { loués, *m.*
vous aurez été ⎬
ils *or* elles auront été ⎭ { louées, *f.*

CONDITIONAL.

PRESENT.

Je serais ⎫
tu serais ⎬ { loué, *m.*
il *or* elle serait ⎬ { louée, *f.* } — *I should be praised.*
nous serions ⎬ { loués, *m.*
vous seriez ⎬
ils *or* elles seraient ⎭ { louées, *f.*

PAST.

J'aurais été ⎫
tu aurais été ⎬ { loué, *m.*
il *or* elle aurait été ⎬ { louée, *f.* } — *I should have been praised.*
nous aurions été ⎬ { loués, *m.*
vous auriez été [été] ⎬
ils *or* elles auraient ⎭ { louées, *f.*

IMPERATIVE.

Sois ⎫ { loué, *m.*
qu'il *or* qu'elle soit ⎬ { louée, *f.* } *Be (thou) praised.*
soyons ⎬ { loués, *m.*
soyez ⎬
qu'ils *or* qu'elles soient ⎭ { louées, *f.*

SUBJUNCTIVE.

PRESENT.

Que je sois ⎫
que tu sois ⎬ { loué, *m.*
qu'il *or* qu'elle soit ⎬ { louée, *f.* } *That I may be praised.*
que nous soyons ⎬ { loués, *m.*
que vous soyez ⎬
qu'ils *or* qu'elles soient ⎭ { louées, *f.*

PRETERITE.

Que j'aie été ⎫
que tu aies été [été] ⎬ { loué, *m.*
qu'il *or* qu'elle ait ⎬ { louée, *f.* } *That I may have been praised.*
que nous ayons été ⎬ { loués, *m.*
que vous ayez été ⎬
qu'ils *or* qu'elles aient été ⎭ { louées, *f.*

Simple Tenses.

IMPERFECT.

Que je fusse	{ loué, m.	*That I might be praised.*
que tu fusses		
qu'il *or* qu'elle fût	{ louée, f.	
que nous fussions	} loués, m.	
que vous fussiez		
qu'ils *or* qu'elles fussent	{ louées, f.	

Compound Tenses.

PLUPERFECT.

Que j'eusse été	{ loué, m.	*That I might have been praised.*
que tu eusses été		
qu'il *or* qu'elle eût été	{ louée, f.	
que nous eussions été	} loués, m.	
que vous eussiez été		
qu'ils *or* qu'elles eussent été	{ louées, f.	

EXERCISE LXV.

INDICAT. PRES.— He is loved and esteemed by everybody.
     aimer estimer de tout le monde.

PRET. DEF.—The city of Rome was several times sacked.
    ville f. ——   fois f. saccagé

He was saved from a great danger by (his youngest son.)
  délivrer   ——m. par le plus jeune de ses fils.

She was accused of theft by her mistress.—The Gauls
   accuser vol m. par   Gaules f. pl.

were conquered by Cæsar.—The two generals were wounded.
 conquis par   blesser

PRET. INDEF. — Your work has been praised in a very
      ouvrage m.   d' ²fort

delicate manner by an academician.—The Jews have been
 ³ ¹manière f. par académicien Juif

punished by God.—She has not been well rewarded.
   de   récompenser

FUT. ABS.—You will be recognised.—Your conduct will
       reconnu   conduite f.

be approved by wise and enlightened people.
  de art. ² ³éclairé ¹personne f. pl.

170. § III. OF NEUTER VERBS.

The *Neuter* verb expresses merely the state of its subject; as, *J'existe*, I exist; or else an action limited to the subject which produces it; as, *Je marche*, I walk.

A *neuter* verb may be easily known by its not admitting immediately after it the words *quelqu'un*, somebody, or *quelque chose*, something. We cannot say: *Je*

CONJUGATION OF NEUTER VERBS. 95

marche quelqu'un, je languis quelque chose; marcher and *languir*, therefore, are neuter verbs.

There are, in French, nearly six hundred *neuter* verbs; about five hundred take the auxiliary *avoir* in their compound tenses.

171. The following form their compounds with *être:*—

Aller,	*to go.*	parvenir,	*to attain.*
arriver,	*to arrive.*	provenir,	*to come from.*
décéder,	*to die.*	redevenir,	*to become again.*
déchoir,	*to decay.*	rentrer,	*to come in again.*
devenir,	*to become.*	repartir,	*to set out again.*
disconvenir,	*to deny, to disown.*	rester,	*to remain, to stay.*
échoir,	*to become due.*	retomber,	*to fall again.*
éclore,	*to blow, to be hatched.*	retourner,	*to go back.*
entrer,	*to come in.*	revenir,	*to come back.*
mourir,	*to die.*	survenir,	*to happen.*
naitre,	*to be born.*	tomber,	*to fall.*
partir,	*to set out.*	venir,	*to come.*

172. The following neuter verbs take *avoir* or *être* in their compound tenses, according to the idea one wishes to express. *Avoir* is used when we consider the action, and *être* when regard is had to the result of the action.

Aborder,	*to land.*	descendre,	*to go down.*
accourir,	*to run to.*	disparaitre,	*to disappear*
accroitre,	*to increase.*	échapper,	*to escape.*
apparaitre,	*to appear.*	grandir,	*to grow.*
croitre,	*to grow.*	monter,	*to go up.*
déborder,	*to overflow.*	passer,	*to pass.*
demeurer,	*to remain.*	remonter,	*to go up again.*

173. § IV. OF PRONOMINAL VERBS.

Pronominal Verbs are those which are conjugated with two pronouns of the same person; as, *je me repens,* I repent; *il se propose,* he intends; *nous nous flattons,* we flatter ourselves.

174. Pronominal Verbs are called *reflected*, when they express an action or a state which relates only to the subject of the verb; as, *se blesser*, to hurt oneself;

se réjouir, to rejoice. They are called *reciprocal*, when they express a reciprocity of action between two or more subjects; as, *s'entr'aimer*, to love each other; *s'entr'aider*, to help one another.

175. Pronominal Verbs have no conjugation peculiar to themselves; they follow the one to which they belong, which is known by the termination of the Infinitive. In their compound tenses, they take the verb *être*, to be, contrary to the English expression, which requires *have*.

176. CONJUGATION OF A PRONOMINAL VERB.

INFINITIVE.

PRESENT.	PAST.
Se promener, *to walk, to take a walk.*	S'être promené, *or* promenée, *f.* } *to have walked.*

PARTICIPLE PRESENT.	PARTICIPLE PAST.
Se promenant, *walking.*	S'étant promené, *or* promenée, *f.* } *having walked.*

Simple Tenses.   *Compound Tenses.*

INDICATIVE.

PRESENT.		PRETERITE INDEFINITE.	
Je me promène,	*I walk.*	Je me suis promené,	⎫
tu te promènes,	*thou walkest.*	tu t'es promené,	⎬ *I have*
il se promène,	*he walks.*	il s'est promené,	⎬ *walked.*
nous nous promenons,	*we walk.*	nous nous sommes promenés,	⎬
vous vous promenez,	*you walk.*	vous vous êtes promenés,	⎬
ils se promènent,	*they walk.*	ils se sont promenés,	⎭

IMPERFECT.		PLUPERFECT.	
Je me promenais,	⎫	Je m'étais promené,	⎫
tu te promenais,	⎬	tu t'étais promené,	⎬
il se promenait,	⎬ *I was*	il s'était promené,	⎬ *I had*
nous nous promenions,	⎬ *walking.*	nous nous étions promenés,	⎬ *walked.*
vous vous promeniez,	⎬	vous vous étiez promenés,	⎬
ils se promenaient,	⎭	ils s'étaient promenés,	⎭

PRETERITE DEFINITE.		PRETERITE ANTERIOR.	
Je me promenai,	⎫	Je me fus promené,	⎫
tu te promenas,	⎬	tu te fus promené,	⎬
il se promena,	⎬ *I*	il se fut promené,	⎬ *I had*
nous nous promenâmes,	⎬ *walked.*	nous nous fûmes promenés,	⎬ *walked.*
vous vous promenâtes,	⎬	vous vous fûtes promenés,	⎬
ils se promenèrent,	⎭	ils se furent promenés,	⎭

CONJUGATION OF A PRONOMINAL VERB.

Simple Tenses.
FUTURE ABSOLUTE.
Je me promènerai,
tu te promèneras,
il se promènera,
nous nous promènerons,
vous vous promènerez,
ils se promèneront,
I shall walk.

Compound Tenses.
FUTURE ANTERIOR.
Je me serai promené,
tu te seras promené,
il se sera promené,
nous nous serons promenés,
vous vous serez promenés,
ils se seront promenés,
I shall have walked.

CONDITIONAL.

PRESENT.
Je me promènerais,
tu te promènerais,
il se promènerait,
nous nous promènerions,
vous vous promèneriez,
ils se promèneraient,
I should walk.

PAST.
Je me serais promené,
tu te serais promené,
il se serait promené,
nous nous serions promenés,
vous vous seriez promenés,
ils se seraient promenés,
I should have walked.

IMPERATIVE.

Promène-toi,   *Walk (thou).*
qu'il se promène,   *let him walk.*
promenons-nous,   *let us walk.*
promenez-vous,   *walk (you).*
qu'ils se promènent,   *let them walk.*

SUBJUNCTIVE.

PRESENT.
Que je me promène,
que tu te promènes,
qu'il se promène,
que nous nous promenions,
que vous vous promeniez,
qu'ils se promènent,
That I may walk.

PRETERITE.
Que je me sois promené,
que tu te sois promené,
qu'il se soit promené,
que nous nous soyons promenés,
que vous vous soyez promenés,
qu'ils se soient promenés,
That I may have walked.

IMPERFECT.
Que je me promenasse,
que tu te promenasses,
qu'il se promenât,
que nous nous promenassions,
que vous vous promenassiez,
qu'ils se promenassent,
That I might walk.

PLUPERFECT.
Que je me fusse promené,
que tu te fusses promené,
qu'il se fût promené, [menés,
que nous nous fussions pro-
que vous vous fussiez promenés,
qu'ils se fussent promenés,
That I might have walked.

177.   Conjugate in the same manner:—

S'accorder,   *to agree.*
s'adresser,   *to apply.*
s'avancer,   *to come or go forward.*
se baigner,   *to bathe.*
se baisser,   *to stoop.*
se dépêcher,   *to make haste.*
se déterminer, *to resolve upon.*
s'emporter,   *to fly into a passion.*
s'enrhumer,   *to catch cold.*
s'envoler,   *to fly away.*
se fâcher,   *to be angry.*
se hâter,   *to make haste.*
s'imaginer,   *to fancy.*
se lever, &c.   *to rise, &c.*

G

EXERCISE LXVI.

INDIC. PRES.—That woman nurses herself too much.—
s'écouter *trop.*
You wonder at that. — We take a walk (every day).
s'étonner de 101 *se promener tous les jours.*
IMPERF.—I was riding (on horseback). — We were
se promener à cheval.
fatiguing ourselves (to no purpose). — You were amusing
se fatiguer *inutilement.* *s'amuser*
yourself in the garden.—They quarrelled with everybody.
dans *se disputer tout le monde.*
PRET. DEF.—I presented myself to the assembly.—He
se présenter *assemblée* f.
lost himself in the crowd.—She laughed at his advice.—
se perdre *foule* f. *se moquer de* *avis* m.
We applied to the prime minister. — You perceived
s'adresser *premier ministre.* *s'apercevoir de*
the snare. — They met several times in the street.
piége m. *se rencontrer* 123 *fois* *rue* f.

EXERCISE LXVII.

PRET. INDEF.—I have exposed myself. — He has amused
s'exposer *s'amuser*
himself.—She has revenged herself.—Where did you stop?
se venger *s'arrêter*
PLUPERF.—I had fallen asleep. — They had grown rich
s'endormir *s'enrichir*
at your expense. — He had got up at four o'clock.
dépens pl. *se lever* *heures.*
FUT. ABS. — I shall bathe to-morrow. — You will
se baigner *demain.*
catch cold.—I shall warm myself.—He will grow bold.—
s'enrhumer *se chauffer* *s'enhardir*
They will defend themselves well.—They will fly away.
se défendre
IMPERA. — Let us rest under the shade of this
se reposer à *ombre* f.
tree. — Rise from there, that is not your place.
arbre m. *se lever* *là* *ce* ——f.

178. MODEL
OF A REFLECTED VERB CONJUGATED NEGATIVELY

INFINITIVE.

Simple Tenses.   *Compound Tenses.*

PRESENT.   **PAST.**

Ne pas se lever, { *not to rise, not to get up.* | Ne s'être pas levé, or levée, f. { *not to have risen.*

PARTICIPLE PRESENT.   **PARTICIPLE PAST.**

Ne se levant pas, *not rising.* | Ne s'étant pas levé, or levée, f. { *not having risen.*

INDICATIVE.

PRESENT.   **PRETERITE INDEFINITE.**

Je ne me lève pas,	Je ne me suis pas levé,
tu ne te lèves pas,	tu ne t'es pas levé,
il ne se lève pas,	il ne s'est pas levé, [levés,
nous ne nous levons pas,	nous ne nous sommes pas
vous ne vous levez pas,	vous ne vous êtes pas levés,
ils ne se lèvent pas,	ils ne se sont pas levés,

I do not rise.   *I have not risen.*

IMPERFECT.   **PLUPERFECT.**

Je ne me levais pas,	Je ne m'étais pas levé,
tu ne te levais pas,	tu ne t'étais pas levé,
il ne se levait pas,	il ne s'était pas levé, [levés,
nous ne nous levions pas,	nous ne nous étions pas
vous ne vous leviez pas,	vous ne vous étiez pas levés,
ils ne se levaient pas,	ils ne s'étaient pas levés,

I was not rising.   *I had not risen.*

PRETERITE DEFINITE.   **PRETERITE ANTERIOR.**

Je ne me levai pas,	Je ne me fus pas levé,
tu ne te levas pas,	tu ne te fus pas levé,
il ne se leva pas,	il ne se fut pas levé, [levés,
nous ne nous levâmes pas,	nous ne nous fûmes pas
vous ne vous levâtes pas,	vous ne vous fûtes pas levés,
ils ne se levèrent pas,	ils ne se furent pas levés,

I did not rise.   *I had not risen.*

FUTURE ABSOLUTE.   **FUTURE ANTERIOR.**

Je ne me lèverai pas,	Je ne me serai pas levé,
tu ne te lèveras pas,	tu ne te seras pas levé,
il ne se lèvera pas,	il ne se sera pas levé, [levés,
nous ne nous lèverons pas,	nous ne nous serons pas
vous ne vous lèverez pas,	vous ne vous serez pas levés
ils ne se lèveront pas,	ils ne se seront pas levés,

I shall not rise.   *I shall not have risen.*

CONDITIONAL.

Simple Tenses.   *Compound Tenses.*

PRESENT.   **PAST.**

Je ne me lèverais pas,   *I should not rise.*   Je ne me serais pas levé,   *I should not have risen.*
tu ne te lèverais pas,
il ne se lèverait pas,
nous ne nous lèverions pas,
vous ne vous lèveriez pas,
ils ne se lèveraient pas,

tu ne te serais pas levé,
il ne se serait pas levé, [levés
nous ne nous serions pas
vous ne vous seriez pas levés
ils ne se seraient pas levés,

IMPERATIVE.

Ne te lève pas,   *Do not rise.*
qu'il ne se lève pas,   *let him not rise.*
ne nous levons pas,   *let us not rise.*
ne vous levez pas,   *do not rise.*
qu'ils ne se lèvent pas,   *let them not rise.*

SUBJUNCTIVE.

PRESENT.   **PRETERITE.**

That I may not rise, &c.   *That I may not have risen, &c.*
Que je ne me lève pas.   Que je ne me sois pas levé.
que tu ne te lèves pas.   que tu ne te sois pas levé.
qu'il ne se lève pas.   qu'il ne se soit pas levé.
que nous ne nous levions pas.   que nous ne nous soyons pas levés.
que vous ne vous leviez pas.   que vous ne vous soyez pas levés.
qu'ils ne se lèvent pas.   qu'ils ne se soient pas levés.

IMPERFECT.   **PLUPERFECT.**

That I might not rise, &c.   *That I might not have risen, &c.*
Que je ne me levasse pas.   Que je ne me fusse pas levé.
que tu ne te levasses pas.   que tu ne te fusses pas levé.
qu'il ne se levât pas.   qu'il ne se fût pas levé.
que nous ne nous levassions pas.   que nous ne nous fussions pas levés.
que vous ne vous levassiez pas.   que vous ne vous fussiez pas levés.
qu'ils ne se levassent pas.   qu'ils ne se fussent pas levés.

179. REFLECTED VERB, INTERROGATIVELY.
INDICATIVE.

Simple Tenses.		*Compound Tenses.*	
PRESENT.		**PRETERITE INDEFINITE.**	
Me coupé-je? *or,* Est-ce que je me coupe? te coupes-tu? se coupe-t-il? nous coupons-nous? vous coupez-vous? se coupent-ils?	*Do I cut myself?*	Me suis-je coupé? t'es-tu coupé? s'est-il coupé? nous sommes-nous coupés? vous êtes-vous coupés? se sont-ils coupés?	*Have I cut myself?*
IMPERFECT.		**PLUPERFECT.**	
Me coupais-je? te coupais-tu? se coupait-il? nous coupions-nous? vous coupiez-vous? se coupaient-ils?	*Was I cutting myself?*	M'étais-je coupé? t'étais-tu coupé? s'était-il coupé? nous étions-nous coupés? vous étiez-vous coupés? s'étaient-ils coupés?	*Had I cut myself?*
PRETERITE DEFINITE.		**PRETERITE ANTERIOR.**	
Me coupai-je? te coupas-tu? se coupa-t-il? nous coupâmes-nous? vous coupâtes-vous? se coupèrent-ils?	*Did I cut myself?*	Me fus-je coupé? te fus-tu coupé? se fut-il coupé? nous fûmes-nous coupés? vous fûtes-vous coupés? se furent-ils coupés?	*Had I cut myself?*
FUTURE ABSOLUTE.		**FUTURE ANTERIOR.**	
Me couperai-je? te couperas-tu? se coupera-t-il? nous couperons-nous? vous couperez-vous? se couperont-ils?	*Shall I cut myself?*	Me serai-je coupé? te seras-tu coupé? se sera-t-il coupé? nous serons-nous coupés? vous serez-vous coupés? se seront-ils coupés?	*Shall I have cut myself?*

CONDITIONAL

PRESENT.		**PAST.**	
Me couperais-je? te couperais-tu? se couperait-il? nous couperions-nous? vous couperiez-vous? se couperaient-ils?	*Should I cut myself?*	Me serais-je coupé? te serais-tu coupé? se serait-il coupé? nous serions-nous coupés? vous seriez-vous coupés? se seraient-ils coupés?	*Should I have cut myself?*

180. REFLECTED VERB CONJUGATED INTERROGATIVELY AND NEGATIVELY.

INDICATIVE.

Simple Tenses.

PRESENT.
Ne me flatté-je pas?
Do I not flatter myself?
ne te flattes-tu pas? &c.
dost thou not flatter thyself? &c.

IMPERFECT.
Ne me flattais-je pas? &c.
Was I not flattering myself? &c.

PRETERITE DEFINITE.
Ne me flattai-je pas? &c.
Did I not flatter myself? &c.

FUTURE ABSOLUTE.
Ne me flatterai-je pas? &c.
Shall I not flatter myself? &c.

Compound Tenses.

PRETERITE INDEFINITE.
Ne me suis-je pas flatté?
Have I not flattered myself?
ne t'es-tu pas flatté? &c.
hast thou not flattered thyself? &c.

PLUPERFECT.
Ne m'étais-je pas flatté? &c.
Had I not flattered myself? &c.

PRETERITE ANTERIOR.
Ne me fus-je pas flatté? &c.
Had I not flattered myself? &c.

FUTURE ANTERIOR.
Ne me serai-je pas flatté? &c.
Shall I not have flattered myself? &c.

CONDITIONAL.

PRESENT.
Ne me flatterais-je pas? &c.
Should I not flatter myself? &c.

PAST.
Ne me serais-je pas flatté? &c.
Should I not have flattered myself? &c.

EXERCISE LXVIII.

I do not flatter myself. — She is not getting up. — We
　　se flatter　　　　　　　　　　*se lever*
do not intend to travel this year. — You do not
　se proposer de voyager　　　*année f.*
make haste. — She will not catch cold. — I would not
se dépêcher　　　　　　*s'enrhumer*
expose myself so rashly. — Is he washing himself? — Do
s'exposer si témérairement.　　　*se laver*
you hide yourself? — Are they amusing themselves? —
　　se cacher　　　　　　　　　　*s'amuser*

Was he rejoicing at his good fortune? — Do you not
  se réjouir de   —— f.
deceive yourself? — Have we not flattered ourselves without
se tromper   *sans*
foundation? — Will they not lose themselves in the wood? —
fondement   *se perdre*   *bois* m.
We never rise before seven o'clock in winter. — Is she not
     avant   *heures* *hiver.*
getting up? — Have they not risen too late this morning?
         ind-4   *tard* *matin* m

---

181. § V. OF IMPERSONAL OR UNIPERSONAL VERBS.

The Verbs to which the old Grammarians give generally the name of *impersonal,* and the modern that of *unipersonal,** are those which are used only in the third person singular of their tenses; as, *il faut,* it is necessary; *il y a,* there is, there are.

Unipersonal Verbs have their inflections according to the conjugation to which they belong; and, in their compound tenses, some take *avoir,* as, *il a plu, il a tonné;* and others take *être,* as, *il est résulté, il est arrivé;* but in either case, the past participle is invariable.

182. LIST of the Unipersonal Verbs of most general occurrence:—

Il pleut,	*it rains.*	il convient,	*it becomes.*
il neige,	*it snows.*	il faut,	*it is necessary.*
il grêle,	*it hails.*	il importe,	*it matters.*
il tonne,	*it thunders.*	il paraît,	*it appears.*
il éclaire,	*it lightens.*	il semble,	*it seems.*
il gèle,	*it freezes.*	il s'ensuit que,	*it follows that*
il dégèle,	*it thaws.*	il sied,	*it is becoming.*
il arrive,	*it happens.*	il y a,	*there is, there are*

IMPERSONAL means. *without a person;* UNIPERSONAL, *with one person.*

183. CONJUGATION OF THE UNIPERSONAL VERB
PLEUVOIR, TO RAIN.

Pres. Part.	pleuvant,	raining.	*Past Part.*	plu, rained.
Ind. Pres.	il pleut,	it rains.	*Pret. Indef.*	il a plu.
Imperf.	il pleuvait,	it was raining.	*Pluperf.*	il avait plu.
Pret. Def.	il plut,	it rained.	*Pret. Ant.*	il eut plu.
Fut. Abs.	il pleuvra,	it will rain.	*Fut. Ant.*	il aura plu.
Cond. Pres.	il pleuvrait,	it would rain.	*Past,*	il aurait plu.

(*No Imperative.*)

Subj. Pres.	qu'il pleuve,	that it may rain.	*Pret.*	qu'il ait plu.
Imperf.	qu'il plût,	that it might rain.	*Pluperf.*	qu'il eût plu.

184. CONJUGATION OF THE UNIPERSONAL VERB
NEIGER, TO SNOW.

Ind. Pres.	il neige,	it snows.	*Pret. Indef.*	il a neigé.
Imperf.	il neigeait,	it was snowing.	*Pluperf.*	il avait neigé.
Pret. Def.	il neigea,	it snowed.	*Pret. Ant.*	il eut neigé.
Fut. Abs.	il neigera,	it will snow.	*Fut. Ant.*	il aura neigé.
Cond. Pres.	il neigerait,	it would snow.	*Past,*	il aurait neigé.

(*No Imperative.*)

Subj. Pres.	qu'il neige,	that it may snow.	*Pret.*	qu'il ait neigé.
Imperf.	qu'il neigeât,	that it might snow.	*Pluperf.*	qu'il eût neigé.

185. CONJUGATION OF THE UNIPERSONAL VERB
GELER, TO FREEZE.

Ind. Pres.	il gèle,	it freezes.	*Pret. Indef.*	il a gelé.
Imperf.	il gelait,	it was freezing.	*Pluperf.*	il avait gelé.
Pret. Def.	il gela,	it froze.	*Pret. Ant.*	il eut gelé.
Fut. Abs.	il gèlera,	it will freeze.	*Fut. Ant.*	il aura gelé.
Cond. Pres.	il gèlerait,	it would freeze.	*Past,*	il aurait gelé.

(*No Imperative.*)

Subj. Pres.	qu'il gèle,	that it may freeze.	*Pret.*	qu'il ait gelé.
Imperf.	qu'il gelât,	that it might freeze.	*Pluperf.*	qu'il eût gelé.

186. Y AVOIR, THERE TO BE.

Pres. Part.	y ayant,	there being.
Past Part.	y ayant eu,	there having been.
Ind. Pres.	il y a,	there is, or there are.
Pret. Indef.	il y a eu,	there has been, or there have been.
Imperf.	il y avait,	there was, or there were.
Pluperf.	il y avait eu,	there had been.
Pret. Def.	il y eut,	there was, or there were.
Pret. Ant.	il y eut eu,	there had been.
Fut. Abs.	il y aura,	there will be.
Fut. Ant.	il y aura eu,	there will have been.
Cond. Pres.	il y aurait,	there would be.
Past,	il y aurait eu,	there would have been.

(*No Imperative.*)

Subj. Pres.	qu'il y ait,	that there may be.
Pret.	qu'il y ait eu,	that there may have been.
Imperf.	qu'il y eût,	that there might be.
Pluperf.	qu'il y eût eu,	that there might have been.

Examples of the same verb used interrogatively, negatively, &c.

Y a-t-il?	is there?
il n'y a pas,	there is not.
y avait-il?	was there, or were there?
n'y a-t-il pas eu?	has there not been?
il n'y avait pas eu,	there had not been.
y aura-t-il?	will there be?
il n'y aura pas,	there will not be.
y aura-t-il eu?	will there have been?

N.B.—This verb remains always in the singular in French, although it is used in the plural in English, when followed by a substantive plural.

187. FALLOIR, TO BE NECESSARY.

Pres. Part.	none. [it must.	Past Part.	fallu.
Ind. Pres.	il faut, *it is necessary*,	Pret. Indef.	il a fallu.
Imperf.	il fallait.	Pluperf.	il avait fallu.
Pret. Def.	il fallut.	Pret. Ant.	il eut fallu.
Fut. Abs.	il faudra.	Fut. Ant.	il aura fallu.
Cond. Pres.	il faudrait.	Past,	il aurait fallu

(*No Imperative.*)

Subj. Pres.	qu'il faille.	Pret.	qu'il ait fallu.
Imperf.	qu'il fallût.	Pluperf.	qu'il eût fallu.

188. REMARKS.—The usual construction of the verb *falloir* is to place the conjunction *que* after *il faut, il fallait*, &c. then to use the subject or nominative of the English verb *must*, as a subject to the second verb in

French, which must be put in the subjunctive; as, *Il faut que je vende ma maison,* I must sell my house. *Il faut que nous allions à la douane,* We must go to the custom-house.

Another construction is to allow the second verb to remain in the infinitive, as in English; then the personal pronoun which is the subject of the verb *must*, is to be expressed by one of the pronouns *me, te, lui, nous, vous, leur,* placed after the impersonal pronoun *il;* as, *Il me faut commencer mon ouvrage,* I must begin my work.

All expressions implying necessity, obligation, or want, may be rendered by *falloir;* as,

Il lui faut un habit.—(ACAD.)	*He wants a coat.*
Il me faut un dictionnaire.	*I want a dictionary*

EXERCISE LXIX.

N.B.—*The Tenses will now be used promiscuously.*

Does it *rain?*—*Was* it not *raining?*—I think it *thunders.*
            crois qu'

Does it not *lighten?*—Did it *freeze* last night?—
       ind-4 art. ²dernier ¹nuit f.

Does it *snow* this morning?— *There is* nothing to do.—
      matin m.   faire.

There are many people.— *There were* more than a
    beaucoup de gens.   de *

thousand persons.— *There has been* a great battle.— *There*
              bataille f.

would be no harm.— In Australia *there are* black swans.
     mal.   Australie   32 ² ¹cygne m.

EXERCISE LXX.

Children *must* obey their parents.—I *must* sell my horse.—
      obéir à   ——   cheval m.

You *must* speak to him.— How much do you *want?*— They
           Combien

must answer.— *Must* I show you my work?— It
  répondre   montrer   ouvrage m.

was necessary to consent to that bargain.— *It would be*
        * consentir   marché m.

necessary (to inquire about it.)— *I want* a French grammar.
    s'en informer   ² ¹

EXERCISE LXXI.

Go and see if *it rains.*—*It does* not *rain,* but *it will rain*
Allez * *voir*   *mais*

soon. — *It does* not *snow.*—*It will snow* to-morrow.—Do you
bientôt.   *demain.*

think *it freezes?*—*It is freezing* very hard.—I do not think so;
croyez- subj-1   *très fort.*   ²*crois* ¹*le*

it seems, on the contrary, that *it thaws.*—*It* often *hails* in this
            à   78   ²*souvent*   ¹

country. — *There arrived* some persons whom we did not
pays m.   *Il*   ind-3   *personne*   *que*

expect. — *It appears* that you (have not attended) to that
attendre ind-2   *ne vous êtes pas occupé de*

business.—*It is* not *becoming* in you to contradict your father.
affaire f.   *   *de contrarier*

—*There are* crocodiles in the Nile and in some other rivers
              32   ——   *Nil* m.   *quelques*   *fleuve*

EXERCISE LXXII.

Is there anyone here?—*There is* nobody.—*Were there* any
          quelqu'un   116

cavalry at the review?—*There would be* more happiness
cavalerie f.   *revue* f.   *plus de bonheur*

if everyone knew how to moderate his desires.— *There would*
   chacun savait * * *modérer*   *désir*

not *be* so many duels, if people were to reflect that
         tant de ——   *l'on* * * *réfléchir* ind-2

one of the first obligations of a Christian is to forgive
   f.   —— f.   *chrétien* *de pardonner* art.

injuries.—I wish *that there were* more order in his conduct.
injure   *voudrais* subj-2   *d'*   *conduite* f.

—*It is* not *necessary* to be a conjurer to guess his motives.—
              * * *sorcier pour deviner*   *motif*

Somebody asked Diogenes at what hour people should
   On   ind-2 à *Diogène*   *il falloir* ind-2

dine: If one is rich, replied he, when one likes; if one is
        l'on   *répondre*   *quand on veut*

poor, when one can.
                peut.

Before giving the conjugation of the *Irregular Verbs*, we shall give examples of several verbs, which, although regular in their conjugation, present a peculiarity in the orthography of some of their tenses.

189. § I. MODEL FOR THE CONJUGATION OF VERBS ENDING IN *GER*.

MANGER, to eat.

Part. Pres. mangeant.   *Part. Past,* mangé.

Ind. Pres.	Je mange,	tu manges,	il mange;
	nous mangeons,	vous mangez,	ils mangent.
Imp.	Je mangeais,	tu mangeais,	il mangeait;
	nous mangions,	vous mangiez,	ils mangeaient.
Pret.	Je mangeai,	tu mangeas,	il mangea;
	nous mangeâmes,	vous mangeâtes,	ils mangèrent.
Fut.	Je mangerai,	tu mangeras,	il mangera;
	nous mangerons,	vous mangerez,	ils mangeront.
Cond.	Je mangerais,	tu mangerais,	il mangerait;
	nous mangerions,	vous mangeriez,	ils mangeraient.
Imper.		mange,	qu'il mange;
	mangeons,	mangez,	qu'ils mangent.
Subj. Pres.	que je mange,	tu manges,	il mange;
	que nous mangions,	vous mangiez,	ils mangent.
Imp.	que je mangeasse,	tu mangeasses,	il mangeât;
	que nous mangeassions,	vous mangeassiez,	ils mangeassent.

190. Conjugate in the same manner :—

Abréger,	*to abridge.*	engager,	*to engage.*
arranger,	*to arrange.*	gager,	*to bet.*
bouger,	*to stir.*	juger,	*to judge.*
corriger,	*to correct.*	négliger,	*to neglect.*
déranger,	*to disorder.*	partager,	*to divide, to share.*
diriger,	*to direct.*	songer,	*to think.*
encourager,	*to encourage.*	venger,	*to revenge, &c.*

Remark. — Verbs ending in *ger*, require an *e* mute after the *g*, when that consonant is followed by the vowel *a* or *o*, in order that the *g* may preserve its soft sound; as, *mangeant, mangeons, mangeais;* but we write without *e* mute, *mangions, mangèrent,* because the *g* is not followed by the vowels *a, o*.

EXERCISE LXXIII.

The eye *judges* of colours; the ear *judges* of
    œil m.   art. *couleur* f.   *oreille* f.

sounds.—Where do you *direct* your steps?—He *disturbed*
art. *son* m.   *pas* m.   *déranger*

everybody. — The example of the general *encouraged* the
tout le monde.   *exemple* m.

army. — Have you *corrected* your exercise? — I *would wager*
armée f   *thème* m.   *gager*

a hundred francs (that it is not so.)—*Abridge* your speech. —
*   —— m. *que cela n'est pas*.   *discours* m.

Don't *stir*. — We *protect* the widow and the orphan.
               protéger   *veuve*   *orphelin*

191. § II. MODEL FOR THE CONJUGATION OF VERBS ENDING IN *ÉER*.

AGRÉER, TO ACCEPT, TO PLEASE.

Part. Pres. agréant.   *Part. Past*, agréé.

Ind. Pres.	J'agrée, nous agréons,	tu agrées, vous agréez,	il agrée; ils agréent.
Imp.	J'agréais, nous agréions,	tu agréais, vous agréiez,	il agréait; ils agréaient.
Pret.	J'agréai, nous agréâmes,	tu agréas, vous agréâtes,	il agréa; ils agréèrent.
Fut.	J'agréerai, nous agréerons,	tu agréeras, vous agréerez,	il agréera; ils agréeront.
Cond.	J'agréerais, nous agréerions,	tu agréerais, vous agréeriez,	il agréerait; ils agréeraient.
Imper.	—— agréons,	agrée, agréez,	qu'il agrée; qu'ils agréent.
Subj. Pres.	que j'agrée, que nous agréions,	tu agrées, vous agréiez,	il agrée; ils agréent.
Imp.	que j'agréasse, que nous agréassions,	tu agréasses, vous agréassiez,	il agréât; ils agréassent

192. Conjugate in the same manner:—

Créer,	to create.	suppléer,	to supply.
récréer,	to divert.	&c.	&c.

REMARK.—The Past Participle of verbs in *éer* requires an additional *e* to form the feminine. In the Future and Conditional where there are two, the poets usually suppress one.

Votre cœur d'Ardaric *agrérait*-il la flamme?—(CORNEILLE.)
Nos hôtes *agréront* les soins qui leur sont dus.—(LA FONTAINE.)

In prose, that suppression would be an error.

193. § III MODEL FOR THE CONJUGATION OF VERBS ENDING IN *CER*.

AVANCER, TO ADVANCE.

Part. Pres. avançant.   Part. Past, avancé.

IND. Pres.	J'avance,	tu avances,	il avance ;
	nous avançons,	vous avancez,	ils avancent.
Imp.	J'avançais,	tu avançais,	il avançait ;
	nous avancions,	vous avanciez,	ils avançaient.
Pret.	J'avançai,	tu avanças,	il avança ;
	nous avançâmes,	vous avançâtes,	ils avancèrent.
Fut.	J'avancerai,	tu avanceras,	il avancera ;
	nous avancerons,	vous avancerez,	ils avanceront.
COND.	J'avancerais,	tu avancerais,	il avancerait ;
	nous avancerions,	vous avanceriez,	ils avanceraient.
IMPER.		avance,	qu'il avance ;
	avançons,	avancez,	qu'ils avancent.
SUBJ. Pres.	que j'avance,	tu avances,	il avance ;
	que nous avancions,	vous avanciez,	ils avancent.
Imp.	que j'avançasse,	tu avançasses,	il avançât ;
	que nous avançassions,	vous avançassiez,	ils avançassent.

194. Conjugate in the same manner :—

Amorcer,	to bait.	énoncer,	to express, utter.
annoncer,	to announce.	percer,	to pierce.
bercer,	to rock.	pincer,	to pinch.
commencer,	to begin.	rincer,	to rinse, wash.
devancer,	to outrun.	sucer,	to suck.
enfoncer,	to sink, break open.	&c.	&c.

REMARK.—In all these verbs the *c* takes a cedilla, when followed by the vowel *a* or *o*.

The same rule applies to those verbs in which it is followed by *u*, whenever it is required to give the *c* the soft pronunciation of *s*; as, *il reçut, il a aperçu.*

EXERCISE LXXIV.

God *created* man after his own image.—God has *created*
art. à * —f.

heaveu and earth.—His proposal was *accepted.*—
art. *ciel* m. art. *proposition* f. *agréer*

I shall *make up* the rest.—He *announced* that news to all
suppléer *nouvelle* f.

his friends.—It *was beginning* to rain when we set out.—A
quand *partîmes.*

ball *pierced* his clothes. — Wash these glasses.
balle f. *habit* m. pl. *Rincer* *verre* m.

195. § IV. MODEL FOR THE CONJUGATION OF VERBS ENDING IN *UER*.

JOUER, TO PLAY.

Part. Pres. jouant.   *Part. Past,* joué.

IND. } Pres. }	Je joue, nous jouons,	tu joues, vous jouez,	il joue; ils jouent.
Imp.	Je jouais, nous jouions,	tu jouais, vous jouiez,	il jouait; ils jouaient.
Pret.	Je jouai, nous jouâmes,	tu jouas, vous jouâtes,	il joua; ils jouèrent.
Fut.	Je jouerai, nous jouerons,	tu joueras, vous jouerez,	il jouera; ils joueront.
COND.	Je jouerais, nous jouerions,	tu jouerais, vous joueriez,	il jouerait; ils joueraient.
IMPER.	jouons,	joue, jouez,	qu'il joue; qu'ils jouent.
SUBJ. } Pres. }	que je joue, que nous jouions,	tu joues, vous jouiez,	il joue; ils jouent.
Imp.	que je jouasse, que nous jouassions,	tu jouasses, vous jouassiez,	il jouât; ils jouassent.

196. Conjugate in the same manner:—

Avouer,	*to avow, confess.*	distribuer,	*to distribute.*
attribuer,	*to attribute.*	nouer,	*to tie.*
clouer,	*to nail.*	secouer,	*to shake off.*
contribuer,	*to contribute.*	tuer,	*to kill.*
dénouer,	*to untie.*	&c.	&c.

REMARK.—In verbs of the first conjugation, when the termination *er* of the infinitive is preceded by a vowel, as in *jouer, prier, avouer,* etc. the *e* of the termination may be preserved or suppressed, in poetry, in the Future and Conditional; but, if it be suppressed, a circumflex accent is placed over the vowel preceding. So poets write *je jouerai* or *je joûrai; j'avouerai* or *j'avoûrai; je prierais* or *je prîrais.*

197. § V. MODEL FOR THE CONJUGATION OF VERBS ENDING IN *ELER.*

APPELER, TO CALL.

Part. Pres. appelant. *Part. Past,* appelé.

IND. ⎱	J'appelle,	tu appelles,	il appelle ;
Pres. ⎰	nous appelons,	vous appelez,	ils appellent.
Imp.	J'appelais,	tu appelais,	il appelait ;
	nous appelions,	vous appeliez,	ils appelaient.
Pret.	J'appelai,	tu appelas,	il appela ;
	nous appelâmes,	vous appelâtes,	ils appelèrent.
Fut.	J'appellerai,	tu appelleras,	il appellera ;
	nous appellerons,	vous appellerez,	ils appelleront.
COND.	J'appellerais,	tu appellerais,	il appellerait ;
	nous appellerions,	vous appelleriez,	ils appelleraient.
IMPER.		appelle,	qu'il appelle ;
	appelons,	appelez,	qu'ils appellent.
SUBJ. ⎱ Que	j'appelle	tu appelles,	il appelle ;
Pres. ⎰	nous appelions,	vous appeliez,	ils appellent.
Imp. Que	J'appelasse,	tu appelasses,	il appelât ;
Que	nous appelassions,	vous appelassiez,	ils appelassent.

198. Conjugate in the same manner:—

Amonceler,	*to heap up.*	épeler,	*to spell.*
atteler,	*to put horses to.*	niveler,	*to level.*
chanceler,	*to totter, stagger.*	rappeler,	*to recall.*
dételer,	*to unyoke.*	renouveler, &c.	*to renew, &c.*

199. REMARKS.—As has been exemplified in *appeler*, verbs ending in *eler*, double the *l* before an *e* mute: *J'appelle, tu nivelles, il étincelle, ils renouvelleraient*, etc. ; but we write with a single *l: nous appelons, vous nivelez, ils étincelaient*, etc., because the vowel which follows the *l* is not an *e* mute.

200. *Geler*, to freeze ; *dégeler*, to thaw ; *harceler*, to harass ; *peler*, to peel, do not double the *l*, but the *e*, which precedes it, takes a grave accent: *Il gèle, il dégèlera, il harcèle, je pèle, ils pèleraient*, etc.

201. *Recéler*, to receive and conceal stolen things, to contain ; *révéler*, to reveal, &c. being terminated by *éler*, and not *eler*, never double the *l: Je recèle, tu révèles*, etc.

EXERCISE LXXV.

Do you *play* on the violin ? — The children *are playing* at
    de *violon* m.   *à*

blindman's buff. — He was *killed* by a (cannon shot). — The
colin-maillard.   *de* *coup de canon* m.

bells *call* to   church. — *Call* them (as you please.) —
cloche f. art. *église* f.   *comme il vous plaira*.

He is (near falling), he *staggers*. — We have *renewed*
  près de tomber

acquaintance. — *Spell* that word. — She *is peeling* an apple.
connaissance.   *mot* m.

202. § VI. MODEL FOR THE CONJUGATION OF VERBS ENDING IN *ETER*.

JETER, TO THROW.

Part. Pres. jetant.   *Part. Past,* jeté.

IND. *Pres.*	Je jette,	tu jettes,	il jette ;
	nous jetons,	vous jetez,	ils jettent.
Imp.	Je jetais,	tu jetais,	il jetait ;
	nous jetions,	vous jetiez,	ils jetaient.
Pret.	Je jetai,	tu jetas,	il jeta ;
	nous jetâmes,	vous jetâtes,	ils jetèrent.
Fut.	Je jetterai,	tu jetteras,	il jettera ;
	nous jetterons,	vous jetterez,	ils jetteront.

114 CONJUGATION OF VERBS ENDING IN *ETER.*

Cond,	Je jetterais,	tu jetterais,	il jetterait;
	nous jetterions,	vous jetteriez,	ils jetteraient.
Imper.		jette,	qu'il jette;
	jetons,	jetez,	qu'ils jettent.
Subj. Pres.	Que je jette,	tu jettes,	il jette;
	Que nous jetions,	vous jetiez,	ils jettent.
Imp.	Que je jetasse,	tu jetasses,	il jetât;
	Que nous jetassions,	vous jetassiez,	ils jetassent.

Conjugate in the same manner:—

Cacheter, *to seal.* | Projeter, *to project,* &c.

203. *Acheter,* to buy; *étiqueter,* to ticket, make *j'achète, j'achèterai, ils étiquètent,* &c. and not *j'achette, j'achetterai, ils étiquettent.*—(Acad.)

204. § VII. MODEL FOR THE CONJUGATION OF VERBS ENDING IN *YER.*

EMPLOYER, to employ.

Part. Pres. employant.   *Part. Past,* employé.

Ind. Pres.	J'emploie,	tu emploies,	il emploie;
	nous employons,	vous employez,	ils emploient.
Imp.	J'employais,	tu employais,	il employait;
	nous employions,	vous employiez,	ils employaient.
Pret.	J'employai,	tu employas,	il employa;
	nous employâmes,	vous employâtes,	ils employèrent.
Fut.	J'emploierai,	tu emploieras,	il emploiera;
	nous emploierons,	vous emploierez,	ils emploieront.
Cond.	J'emploierais,	tu emploierais,	il emploierait;
	nous emploierions,	vous emploieriez,	ils emploieraient
Imper.		emploie,	qu'il emploie;
	employons,	employez,	qu'ils emploient
Subj. Pres.	Que j'emploie,	tu emploies,	il emploie;
	Que nous employions,	vous employiez,	ils emploient.
Imp.	Que j'employasse,	tu employasses,	il employât;
	Que nous employassions,	vous employassiez,	ils employassent.

205. Conjugate in the same manner verbs in *yer*, and in general all those whose Present Participle ends in *yant;* as :—

Balayer,	*to sweep.*	nettoyer,	*to clean.*
effrayer,	*to frighten.*	appuyer,	*to prop; to rest upon.*
essayer,	*to try.*	essuyer,	*to wipe.*
payer,	*to pay.*	ennuyer,	*to tire.*

206. *Envoyer*, to send; and *renvoyer*, to send back, deviate from the preceding model of conjugation in the Future and Conditional, making—*J'enverrai, j'enverrais; je renverrai, je renverrais,* instead of *j'envoierai,* &c.

207. REMARK.—In the preceding verbs, the *y* is preserved in every part of the verb, except before the *mute* terminations *e, es, ent,* where it is changed into *i; Je paie,** tu nettoies, ils appuient.* Moreover, these verbs take a *y* and an *i* in the two first persons plural of the Imperfect of the Indicative and Present of the Subjunctive; that is, the *y* of the radical part (as *employ*), and the *i* of the final part *ions, iez*.

EXERCISE LXXVI.

That *throws* me into a great dilemma. — He *threw* himself
               dans   embarras m.

into the midst of the enemy. — Have you *sealed* your
à   milieu m.   ennemi m. pl.

letter?—He *is cleaning* his gun. — All that he takes, he
                    fusil m.   ce qu'   prend

    pays (ready money). — I *shall endeavour* to persuade
le   argent comptant.   essayer   de persuader

them. — He *will support* you with all his credit. — He
            appuyer   de   crédit m.

employs everybody to obtain that place.—That *tires* me
    tout le monde pour   f.

to death.—Don't *frighten* the child.—I *shall send* a man.
art. mort f.   enfant.

---

* The *French Academy* leaves the choice of writing *il paye,* or *il paie; je payerai,* or *je paierai,* or even *je pairai;* but the best modern Grammarians are agreed on the change of the *y* into *i,* and present usage is conformable to their opinion.

208. § VIII. MODEL FOR THE CONJUGATION OF VERBS ENDING IN *IER*.

PRIER, TO PRAY, TO REQUEST.

Part. Pres. priant.   *Part. Past*, prié.

Ind. Pres.	Je prie,	tu pries,	il prie;
	nous prions,	vous priez,	ils prient
Imp.	Je priais,	tu priais,	il priait;
	nous priions,	vous priiez,	ils priaient.
Pret.	Je priai,	tu prias,	il pria;
	nous priâmes,	vous priâtes,	ils prièrent.
Fut.	Je prierai,	tu prieras,	il priera;
	nous prierons,	vous prierez,	ils prieront.
Cond.	Je prierais,	tu prierais,	il prierait;
	nous prierions,	vous prieriez,	ils prieraient.
Imper.		prie,	qu'il prie;
	prions,	priez,	qu'ils prient.
Subj. Pres.	que je prie,	tu pries,	il prie;
	que nous priions,	vous priiez,	ils prient.
Imp.	que je priasse,	tu priasses,	il priât;
	que nous priassions,	vous priassiez,	ils priassent.

209. Conjugate in the same manner all verbs ending in *ier*; as,

Certifier,	*to certify.*	nier,	*to deny.*
crier,	*to cry.*	oublier,	*to forget.*
étudier,	*to study.*	plier,	*to bend.*
lier,	*to tie.*	relier,	*to bind.*
manier,	*to handle.*	remercier,	*to thank.*

REMARK.—*Prier* and all verbs whose Present Participle ends in *iant*, take *ii* in the first and the second person plural of the Imperfect of the Indicative and Present of the Subjunctive; that is, the *i* of the radical part (as *pri*), and the *i* of the termination: *Nous priions, vous priiez; que nous liions, que vous liiez.*

EXERCISE LXXVII.

I *thank* you for the honour   you do me.—He *studies*
        de   que   faites

night and day.—The plank   *was bending* under him.—
                    planche f.   sous

I *shall* never *forget* (what I owe you). — *Request* him to
                    ce que je vous dois.   de
come and (speak to me). — One (does not become) learned
       *   me parler.   On   ne devient pas
without *studying*.—In *handling* that vase, he broke it.
    sans   inf-1   ——— m.   briser ind-4

OF IRREGULAR AND DEFECTIVE VERBS.

210. However irregular a verb may be, its irregularities never occur in the compound tenses, for which reason we shall, except in a very few instances, dispense with these tenses in the various conjugations of irregular verbs.

§ I. IRREGULAR VERBS OF THE FIRST CONJUGATION.

The only irregular verbs of this conjugation are *aller*, to go; *s'en aller*, to go away; *envoyer*, to send; and *renvoyer*, to send back.

211. *ALLER*, TO GO.

Part. Pres. allant.   *Part. Past*, allé.

Ind. Pres.	Je vais, nous allons,	tu vas, vous allez,	il va; ils vont.
Imp.	J'allais, nous allions,	tu allais, vous alliez,	il allait; ils allaient.
Pret.	J'allai, nous allâmes,	tu allas, vous allâtes,	il alla; ils allèrent.
Fut.	J'irai, nous irons,	tu iras, vous irez,	il ira; ils iront.
Cond. Pres.	J'irais, nous irions,	tu irais, vous iriez,	il irait; ils iraient.
Imper.	allons,	va, allez,	qu'il aille; qu'ils aillent.
Subj. Pres.	que j'aille, que nous allions,	tu ailles, vous alliez,	il aille; ils aillent.
Imp.	que j'allasse, que nous allassions,	tu allasses, vous allassiez,	il allât; ils allassent.

212. Remarks.—*Aller* is conjugated with the auxiliary *être*, in all its compound tenses; *Je suis allé, j'étais allé,* &c.

The Imperative *va* takes an *s*, when followed by *en* or *y*; as, *vas en savoir des nouvelles; vas-y.*

We sometimes say, *je fus, j'ai été, j'avais été, j'aurais été,* instead of *j'allai, je suis allé, j'étais allé, je serais allé.* These expressions, however, have this difference, that *avoir été* implies the return, and *être allé* does not. Thus: *il a été à Rome,* means, that he went to Rome, and is returned, or that he has been in Rome, and has left it; but *il est allé à Rome* means only, that he is gone to Rome.—(ACAD.)

213. S'EN ALLER, TO GO AWAY.

INFINITIVE.

PRESENT.	PAST.
S'en aller, *to go away.*	S'en être allé, *to have gone away.*
PARTICIPLE PRESENT.	COMP. OF PARTICIPLE PRESENT.
S'en allant, *going away.*	S'en étant allé, *having gone away*

PARTICIPLE PAST.—En allé, *gone away.*

INDICATIVE.

Simple Tenses.   *Compound Tenses.*

PRESENT.		PRETERITE INDEFINITE.	
Je m'en vais,		Je m'en suis allé,	
tu t'en vas,		tu t'en es allé,	
il s'en va,	*I go, or am going away.*	il s'en est allé,	*I have gone away.*
nous nous en allons,		nous nous en sommes allés,	
vous vous en allez,		vous vous en êtes allés,	
ils s'en vont,		ils s'en sont allés,	

IMPERFECT.		PLUPERFECT.	
Je m'en allais,		Je m'en étais allé,	
tu t'en allais,		tu t'en étais allé,	
il s'en allait,	*I was going away.*	il s'en était allé,	*I had gone away.*
nous nous en allions,		nous nous en étions allés,	
vous vous en alliez,		vous vous en étiez allés,	
ils s'en allaient,		ils s'en étaient allés,	

PRETERITE DEFINITE.		PRETERITE ANTERIOR.	
Je m'en allai,		Je m'en fus allé,	
tu t'en allas,		tu t'en fus allé,	
il s'en alla,	*I went away.*	il s'en fut allé,	*I had gone away.*
nous nous en allâmes,		nous nous en fûmes allés,	
vous vous en allâtes,		vous vous en fûtes allés,	
ils s'en allèrent,		ils s'en furent allés,	

CONJUGATION OF THE VERB S'EN ALLER.

Simple Tenses. *Compound Tenses.*

FUTURE ABSOLUTE. FUTURE ANTERIOR.

Je m'en irai,		Je m'en serai allé,
tu t'en iras,		tu t'en seras allé,
il s'en ira,	*I shall go away.*	il s'en sera allé,
nous nous en irons,		nous nous en serons allés,
vous vous en irez,		vous vous en serez allés,
ils s'en iront,		ils s'en seront allés,	*I shall have gone away.*

CONDITIONAL.

PRESENT. PAST.

Je m'en irais,		Je m'en serais allé,
tu t'en irais,		tu t'en serais allé,
il s'en irait,	*I would or should go away.*	il s'en serait allé,
nous nous en irions,		nous nous en serions allés,
vous vous en iriez,		vous vous en seriez allés,
ils s'en iraient,		ils s'en seraient allés,	*I should have gone away.*

IMPERATIVE.

Affirmatively. *Negatively.*

Va-t'en,		Ne t'en va pas,
qu'il s'en aille,	*Go (thou) away.*	qu'il ne s'en aille pas,
allons-nous-en,		ne nous en allons pas,
allez-vous-en,		ne vous en allez pas,
qu'ils s'en aillent,		qu'ils ne s'en aillent pas,	*Do not go away.*

SUBJUNCTIVE.

PRESENT. PRETERITE.

Que je m'en aille,		Que je m'en sois allé,
que tu t'en ailles,		que tu t'en sois allé,
qu'il s'en aille,	*That I may go away.*	qu'il s'en soit allé,
que nous nous en allions,		que nous nous en soyons allés,
que vous vous en alliez,		que vous vous en soyez allés,
qu'ils s'en aillent,		qu'ils s'en soient	*That I may have gone away.*

IMPERFECT. PLUPERFECT.

Que je m'en allasse,		Que je m'en fusse allé,
que tu t'en allasses,		que tu t'en fusses allé,
qu'il s'en allât,	*That I might go away.*	qu'il s'en fût allé,
que nous nous en allassions,		que nous nous en fussions allés,
que vous vous en allassiez,		que vous vous en fussiez allés,
qu'ils s'en allassent,		qu'ils s'en fussent	*That I might have gone away.*

214. When *S'en aller* is used interrogatively, we say, *M'en irai-je, t'en iras-tu, s'en ira-t-il, nous en irons-nous, vous en irez-vous, s'en iront-ils?*

215. *Envoyer*, to send, and *renvoyer*, to send back, to dismiss, are regular, except in the Future and the Conditional, which, as we have already said (p. 115), make *j'enverrai, j'enverrais; je renverrai, je renverrais.*

EXERCISE LXXVIII.

I am going to pay some visits.—He goes from town to town.
   faire *visite* f.   *en*
They are going to the country. — Blue and pink go
      campagne f. art. *bleu* m. art. *rose* m.
well together.—We went by land.—She is gone to church.—
       terre.   art. *église* f.
Let us go away from here.— Why do you go away so soon?
       Pourquoi   *tôt*
—I will send my servant to the post-office.—She would
    domestique m. *poste* f.
dismiss her chambermaid.—They would send back their horses.
   femme de chambre.

216. § II. IRREGULAR AND DEFECTIVE VERBS OF THE SECOND CONJUGATION.

ABSTENIR (S'), *to abstain*, is conjugated like *Tenir*, which is exemplified farther on.

ACCOURIR, *to run to*, is conjugated like *Courir*, with this difference, that its compound tenses are sometimes formed with *avoir*, and sometimes with *être*, according as it denotes state or action. (See No. 172.)

ACCUEILLIR, *to receive;* see *Cueillir*.

217. *ACQUÉRIR*, TO ACQUIRE.

   Part. Pres. acquérant. *Part. Past*, acquis.

IND. } Pres. }	J'acquiers, nous acquérons,	tu acquiers, vous acquérez,	il acquiert; ils acquièrent.
Imp.	J'acquérais, nous acquérions,	tu acquérais, vous acquériez,	il acquérait; ils acquéraient.
Pret.	J'acquis, nous acquîmes,	tu acquis, vous acquîtes,	il acquit; ils acquirent.
Fut.	J'acquerrai, nous acquerrons,	tu acquerras, vous acquerrez,	il acquerra; ils acquerront.

Cond.	J'acquerrais,	tu acquerrais,	il acquerrait;
Pres.	nous acquerrions,	vous acquerriez,	ils acquerraient.
Imper.		acquiers,	qu'il acquière;
	acquérons,	acquérez,	qu'ils acquièrent.
Subj.	que j'acquière,	tu acquières,	il acquière;
Pres.	que nous acquérions,	vous acquériez,	ils acquièrent.
Imp.	que j'acquisse,	tu acquisses,	il acquît;
	que nous acquissions,	vous acquissiez,	ils acquissent.

218. Conjugate in the same manner:—

Conquérir, *to conquer,* { seldom used but in the infinitive, the preterite definite, the imperfect of the subjunctive, and the compound tenses.

Requérir, *to request, to require,* } chiefly used in law.

S'enquérir, *to inquire,* { seldom used but in the infinitive, and compound tenses.

Querir, to fetch, is used after the verbs *aller, venir, envoyer;* as, *allez querir,* go and fetch; *envoyez querir,* send for. It is confined to familiar conversation, and is getting obsolete. (*Querir* is better than *Quérir.*)

219. *ASSAILLIR,* TO ASSAULT.

Part. Pres. assaillant.   Part. Past, assailli.

Ind.	J'assaille,	tu assailles,	il assaille;
Pres.	nous assaillons,	vous assaillez,	ils assaillent.
Imp.	J'assaillais,	tu assaillais,	il assaillait;
	nous assaillions,	vous assailliez,	ils assaillaient.
Pret.	J'assaillis,	tu assaillis,	il assaillit;
	nous assaillîmes,	vous assaillîtes,	ils assaillirent.
Fut.	J'assaillirai,	tu assailliras,	il assaillira;
	nous assaillirons,	vous assaillirez,	ils assailliront.
Cond.	J'assaillirais,	tu assaillirais,	il assaillirait;
Pres.	nous assaillirions,	vous assailliriez,	ils assailliraient.
Imper.		assaille,	qu'il assaille;
	assaillons,	assaillez,	qu'ils assaillent.
Subj.	que j'assaille,	tu assailles,	il assaille;
Pres.	que nous assaillions,	vous assailliez,	ils assaillent.
Imp.	que j'assaillisse,	tu assaillisses,	il assaillît;
	que nous assaillissions,	vous assaillissiez,	ils assaillissent.

Conjugate in the same manner *tressaillir*, to start.

Note.—J. J. Rousseau, and other writers, have, for the sake of euphony, written in the present of the Indicative, *il tressaillit*, instead of *il tressaille*.

EXERCISE LXXIX.

He had *acquired* great influence over his contemporaries.—
     une ——f. *sur* *contemporain* m.
He *would acquire* honour and reputation.—
      32 *honneur* m. *h* m. 32 *réputation* f.
Alexander *conquered* a great part of Asia.—A *conquered*
    ind-3   *partie* f. art.   2
province. — We were *overtaken* by a furious storm. — At
¹—— f.   ind-3 *assaillir* d' *tempête* f.
every word they said to him about his son, the good
chaque qu' on *disait* * *de*
old man leaped for joy. — She *started* with fear.
vieillard tressaillir ind-2 *de joie.* ind-3 *de peur.*

220. BÉNIR, *to bless*, is conjugated like *finir* (see p. 73), and is only irregular in its past participle, which makes *bénit, bénite;* and *béni, bénie.*

Benit, bénite, is used only in speaking of things consecrated by a religious ceremony; as, *du pain bénit,* consecrated bread; *de l'eau bénite,* holy water.

221. *BOUILLIR,* TO BOIL.

Part. Pres. bouillant. *Part. Past,* bouilli.

IND. Pres.	Je bous, nous bouillons,	tu bous, vous bouillez,	il bout; ils bouillent.
Imp.	Je bouillais, nous bouillions,	tu bouillais, vous bouilliez,	il bouillait; ils bouillaient.
Pret.	Je bouillis, nous bouillîmes,	tu bouillis, vous bouillîtes,	il bouillit; ils bouillirent.
Fut.	Je bouillirai, nous bouillirons,	tu bouilliras, vous bouillirez,	il bouillira; ils bouilliront.
COND. Pres.	Je bouillirais, nous bouillirions,	tu bouillirais, vous bouilliriez,	il bouillirait; ils bouilliraient.
IMPER.	bouillons,	bous, bouillez.	qu'il bouille; qu'ils bouillent.

OF THE SECOND CONJUGATION.   123

SUBJ.   *que* je bouille,   tu bouilles,   il bouille;
Pres.   nous bouillions, vous bouilliez,   ils bouillent.
Imp.   *que* je bouillisse,   tu bouillisses,   il bouillît;
              nous bouillissions, vous bouillissiez, ils bouillissent.

This verb is seldom used in French, except in the third persons singular and plural; as, *L'eau bout*, the water boils; *ces choux ne bouillaient pas*, these cabbages did not boil. But when *to boil* has a noun or pronoun for its object, the French then make use of the different tenses of the verb *faire* before the infinitive *bouillir*; as, *Je fais bouillir, nous faisons bouillir*, &c. Therefore say, *Je fais bouillir de la viande*, I boil some meat, and not *je bous*.

Rebouillir, to boil again, is conjugated in the same manner, and follows the same rules.

Ébouillir, to boil away, is seldom used but in the Infinitive and past participle *ébouilli*, m; *ébouillie*, f.

222. *COURIR*, TO RUN.
Part. Pres. courant.   *Part. Past*, couru.

IND.   Je cours,   tu cours,   il court;
Pres. nous courons,   vous courez,   ils courent.
Imp.   Je courais,   tu courais,   il courait;
       nous courions,   vous couriez,   ils couraient.
Pret. Je courus,   tu courus,   il courut;
       nous courûmes,   vous courûtes,   ils coururent.
Fut.   Je courrai,   tu courras,   il courra;
       nous courrons,   vous courrez,   ils courront.
COND. Je courrais,   tu courrais,   il courrait;
Pres. nous courrions,   vous courriez,   ils courraient.
IMPER.   cours,   qu'il coure;
       courons,   courez,   qu'ils courent.
SUBJ. *que* je coure,   tu coures,   il coure;
Pres.   nous courions, vous couriez,   ils courent.
Imp.   *que* je courusse, tu courusses,   il courût;
              nous courussions, vous courussiez, ils courussent.

223. Conjugate in the same manner:—

Accourir,	*to run to.*	encourir,	*to incur.*
concourir,	*to concur.*	parcourir,	*to run over*
discourir,	*to discourse.*	secourir,	*to succour*

EXERCISE LXXX.

God had *blessed* the race of Abraham. — Does the water
—— f.

boil? — We *were boiling* some potatoes. — *Boil* that
              pommes de terre.

meat *again*, it is not (done enough). — You *run* faster
viande f.   *assez cuite.*   *plus vite*

than I. — *Will* men always *run* after shadows?
moi.   art.   32 *chimère* f. pl.

—Socrates passed the last day of his life in *discoursing*
    passer   *à* inf-1

on the immortality of the soul. — You *would incur* the
   immortalité

displeasure of the prince. — I have *run over* the whole town
disgrâce f.   2   1

to find him. — This sauce has ²*boiled away* ¹too much
pour trouver 87   —— f. est   f.   *trop*

COUVRIR, *to cover;* see *Ouvrir.*

224. CUEILLIR, TO GATHER.

  Part. Pres. cueillant.   *Part. Past,* cueilli.

IND. } *Pres.* }	Je cueille, nous cueillons,	tu cueilles, vous cueillez,	il cueille ; ils cueillent.
Imp.	Je cueillais, nous cueillions,	tu cueillais, vous cueilliez,	il cueillait ; ils cueillaient.
Pret.	Je cueillis, nous cueillîmes,	tu cueillis, vous cueillîtes,	il cueillit ; ils cueillirent.
Fut.	Je cueillerai, nous cueillerons,	tu cueilleras, vous cueillerez,	il cueillera ; ils cueilleront.
COND. } *Pres.* }	Je cueillerais, nous cueillerions,	tu cueillerais, vous cueilleriez,	il cueillerait ; ils cueilleraient.
IMPER.	cueillons,	cueille, cueillez,	qu'il cueille ; qu'ils cueillent.
SUBJ. } *Pres.* }	Que je cueille, Que nous cueillions,	tu cueilles, vous cueilliez,	il cueille ; ils cueillent.
Imp.	Que je cueillisse, Que nous cueillissions,	tu cueillisses, vous cueillissiez,	il cueillît ; ils cueillissent.

225. Conjugate in the same manner :—

Accueillir, *to receive, to welcome* | recueillir, *to collect.*

226. *DORMIR*, TO SLEEP.

Part. Pres. dormant.   *Part. Past*, dormi.

Ind. Pres.	Je dors,	tu dors,	il dort;
	nous dormons,	vous dormez,	ils dorment.
Imp.	Je dormais,	tu dormais,	il dormait;
	nous dormions,	vous dormiez,	ils dormaient.
Pret.	Je dormis,	tu dormis,	il dormit;
	nous dormîmes,	vous dormîtes,	ils dormirent.
Fut.	Je dormirai,	tu dormiras,	il dormira;
	nous dormirons,	vous dormirez,	ils dormiront.
Cond. Pres.	Je dormirais,	tu dormirais,	il dormirait;
	nous dormirions,	vous dormiriez,	ils dormiraient
Imper.		dors,	qu'il dorme;
	dormons,	dormez,	qu'ils dorment.
Subj. Pres.	que je dorme,	tu dormes,	il dorme;
	que nous dormions,	vous dormiez,	ils dorment.
Imp.	que je dormisse,	tu dormisses,	il dormît;
	que nous dormissions,	vous dormissiez,	ils dormissent.

227. Conjugate in the same manner:—

Endormir, *to lull asleep.*   se rendormir, *to fall asleep*
s'endormir, *to fall asleep.*   *again.*

228. FAILLIR, *to fail.* This verb is used only in the present of the Infinitive; in the Participle past *failli;* in the Preterite definite, *je faillis, tu faillis, il faillit; nous faillîmes, vous faillîtes, ils faillirent;* and in the compound tenses, *j'ai failli, j'avais failli,* &c.

Its derivative *défaillir,* to faint, to fail, is scarcely ever used but in the first and third persons plural of the present of the Indicative, *nous défaillons, ils défaillent;* in the Imperfect, *je défaillais,* &c.; in the Preterite definite, *je défaillis,* &c.; in the Preterite indefinite, *j'ai défailli,* &c.; and in the Infinitive *défaillir.*

229. FLEURIR, *to blossom,* in its *literal sense,* is regular; but used *figuratively,* signifying to be in a prosperous state, to flourish, to be in repute, it makes *florissant* in the present Participle, and *florissait, florissaient,* in the Imperfect of the Indicative.

EXERCISE LXXXI.

I *will gather* you some fine flowers. — We *shall collect* in
                            fleur f.   *dans*
       ancient history,   important   and   valuable   facts. —
art.   ²   ¹   32   ²   ³*précieux* ¹*fait* m.

The   hare   generally   *sleeps* with its   eyes open. —
     lièvre m. ²*ordinairement*   ¹   *   *   art.   *ouvert*

That song *lulls* one *asleep*. — I *fell asleep* about   three o'clock.
            *   ind-4   *vers* art.

— He (*was near*)   losing his   life. — His strength
      faillir ind-3   *inf*-1   *   art.   *force* f. pl.

fails   (every day). — Athens *flourished* under Pericles.
défaillir tous les jours.   Athènes   ind-2   *sous Périclès*.

230. *FUIR*, TO FLY, TO RUN AWAY, TO SHUN.

         Part. Pres. fuyant.   *Part. Past*, fui.

IND. Pres.	Je fuis, nous fuyons,	tu fuis, vous fuyez,	il fuit; ils fuient.
Imp.	Je fuyais, nous fuyions,	tu fuyais, vous fuyiez,	il fuyait; ils fuyaient.
Pret.	Je fuis, nous fuîmes,	tu fuis, vous fuîtes,	il fuit; ils fuirent.
Fut.	Je fuirai, nous fuirons,	tu fuiras, vous fuirez,	il fuira; ils fuiront.
COND. Pres.	Je fuirais, nous fuirions,	tu fuirais, vous fuiriez,	il fuirait; ils fuiraient.
IMPER.	fuyons,	fuis, fuyez,	qu'il fuie; qu'ils fuient.
SUBJ. Pres.	que je fuie, que nous fuyions,	tu fuies, vous fuyiez,	il fuie; ils fuient
Imp.	que je fuisse, que nous fuissions,	tu fuisses, vous fuissiez,	il fuît; ils fuissent.

231. Conjugate after the same manner, *s'enfuir*, to run away. In the Imperative we say, *enfuis-toi*, and not *enfuis-t'en*, nor *fuis-t'en*.

232. GÉSIR, *to lie, to lie down*, is obsolete. We, however, still say, *Il gît, nous gisons, vous gisez, ils gisent. Je gi-*

sais, tu gisais, il gisait; nous gisions, vous gisiez, ils gisaient. Gisant.—(ACAD.)

Ci-gît (here lies) is the usual form by which an epitaph is begun.

233. *HAÏR*, TO HATE.

Part. Pres. haïssant.   *Part. Past*, haï.

IND. } Pres. }	Je hais, nous haïssons,	tu hais, vous haïssez,	il hait; ils haïssent.
Imp.	Je haïssais, nous haïssions,	tu haïssais, vous haïssiez,	il haïssait; ils haïssaient.
Pret.	Je haïs, nous haïmes,	tu haïs, vous haïtes,	il haït; ils haïrent.
Fut.	Je haïrai, nous haïrons,	tu haïras, vous haïrez,	il haïra; ils haïront.
COND. } Pres. }	Je haïrais, nous haïrions,	tu haïrais, vous haïriez,	il haïrait; ils haïraient.
IMPER.	haïssons,	hais, haïssez,	qu'il haïsse; qu'ils haïssent.
SUBJ. } Pres. }	que je haïsse, que nous haïssions,	tu haïsses, vous haïssiez,	il haïsse; ils haïssent.
Imp.	que je haïsse, que nous haïssions,	tu haïsses, vous haïssiez,	il haït; ils haïssent.

234. REMARKS.—The *h* is aspirated in this verb, and a diæresis (¨) is placed over the *i*, throughout all the tenses, to show that it is to be pronounced separately from the preceding vowel *a*; as, *ha-i*; except, however, the three persons singular of the present of the Indicative, and the second person singular of the Imperative, which, forming only one syllable, are written without the diæresis, thus: *Je hais, tu hais, il hait; hais,* and pronounced—*Je hê, tu hê, il hê; hê.*

This verb is seldom used in the second person singular of the Imperative, the Preterite definite, or the Imperfect of the Subjunctive, and in these two last tenses, instead of making use of the circumflex accent: *nous haïmes, vous haïtes; qu'il haït*, we use the diæresis, *nous haïmes, vous haïtes; qu'il haït.*

MENTIR, *to lie, to utter falsehood*, is conjugated like *sentir.*

235. *MOURIR,* TO DIE.

Part. Pres. mourant.   *Part. Past,* mort.

IND. Pres.	Je meurs, nous mourons,	tu meurs, vous mourez,	il meurt; ils meurent.
Imp.	Je mourais, nous mourions,	tu mourais, vous mouriez,	il mourait; ils mouraient.
Pret.	Je mourus, nous mourûmes,	tu mourus, vous mourûtes,	il mourut; ils moururent.
Fut.	Je mourrai, nous mourrons,	tu mourras, vous mourrez,	il mourra; ils mourront.
COND. Pres.	Je mourrais, nous mourrions,	tu mourrais, vous mourriez,	il mourrait; ils mourraient.
IMPER.	mourons,	meurs, mourez,	qu'il meure; qu'ils meurent
SUBJ. Pres.	Que je meure, Que nous mourions,	tu meures, vous mouriez,	il meure; ils meurent.
Imp.	Que je mourusse, Que nous mourussions,	tu mourusses, vous mourussiez,	il mourût; ils mourussent.

Mourir is conjugated with the auxiliary *être* in its compound tenses.—The double *r* of the Future and Conditional must be sounded strongly.

When this verb takes the reflected form, *se mourir*, it means *to be at the point of death;* but, in this sense, it is seldom used except in the present and imperfect of the Indicative.—(ACAD.)

236. OUÏR, *to hear.* (Active and defective verb.)

Part. past, ouï. IND. *pret.* j'ouïs, tu ouïs, &c. SUBJ. *imperf.* que j'ouïsse, qu tu ouïsses, qu'il ouït, &c.

This verb is chiefly used in the *compound tenses,* which are generally followed by another verb in the infinitive; as,

Je l'ai ouï prêcher.—(ACAD.)	*I have heard him preach.*
Je l'avais ouï dire.	*I had heard it said.*

OF THE SECOND CONJUGATION.

EXERCISE LXXXII.

(Let us make haste), time *flies*.—I cannot meet him,
Hâtons-nous   art.   *ne puis rencontrer*

he *shuns* me.—I *hate* falsehood. — *Let us hate* vice. —
              art. *mensonge* m.   art. —— m.

He *died* some time after. — John Calvin, the celebrated
       127   *célèbre*

reformer, *died* at Geneva, on the 27th May 1564. — He
réformateur   *

is dying. — All the witnesses have been *heard*. — Anger
se mourir   *témoin* m.   art. *colère* f.

soon *dies* in a kind heart.—Here *lies* an honest man.
²*promptement* ¹   *bon*   *honnête*

237. *OUVRIR*, TO OPEN.

Part. Pres. ouvrant.   *Part. Past*, ouvert.

IND. Pres.	J'ouvre, nous ouvrons,	tu ouvres, vous ouvrez,	il ouvre; ils ouvrent.
Imp.	J'ouvrais, nous ouvrions,	tu ouvrais, vous ouvriez,	il ouvrait; ils ouvraient.
Pret.	J'ouvris, nous ouvrîmes,	tu ouvris, vous ouvrîtes,	il ouvrit; ils ouvrirent.
Fut.	J'ouvrirai, nous ouvrirons,	tu ouvriras, vous ouvrirez,	il ouvrira; ils ouvriront.
COND. Pres.	J'ouvrirais, nous ouvririons,	tu ouvrirais, vous ouvririez,	il ouvrirait; ils ouvriraient.
IMPER.	ouvrons,	ouvre, ouvrez,	qu'il ouvre; qu'ils ouvrent.
SUBJ. Pres.	que j'ouvre, que nous ouvrions,	tu ouvres, vous ouvriez,	il ouvre; ils ouvrent.
Imp.	que j'ouvrisse, que nous ouvrissions,	tu ouvrisses, vous ouvrissiez,	il ouvrît; ils ouvrissent.

238. Conjugate in the same manner :—

Couvrir,	*to cover.*	recouvrir,	*to cover again.*
découvrir,	*to discover, to uncover.*	rouvrir,	*to open again.*
offrir,	*to offer.*	souffrir,	*to suffer.*

239. *PARTIR*, TO SET OUT, TO GO AWAY.

Part. Pres. partant.   *Part. Past*, parti.

IND Pres	Je pars, nous partons,	tu pars, vous partez,	il part; ils partent.

I

Imp.	Je partais,	tu partais,	il partait;
	nous partions,	vous partiez,	ils partaient.
Pret.	Je partis,	tu partis,	il partit;
	nous partîmes,	vous partîtes,	ils partirent.
Fut.	Je partirai,	tu partiras,	il partira;
	nous partirons,	vous partirez,	ils partiront.
Cond.	Je partirais,	tu partirais,	il partirait;
	nous partirions,	vous partiriez,	ils partiraient.
Imper.		pars,	qu'il parte;
	partons,	partez,	qu'ils partent.
Subj.	que je parte,	tu partes,	il parte;
Pres.	que nous partions,	vous partiez,	ils partent.
Imp.	que je partisse,	tu partisses,	il partît;
	que nous partissions,	vous partissiez,	ils partissent.

240. Conjugate in the same manner, *repartir*, to go back, to set out again, to reply.

Répartir (with an accent over the *é*), to divide, to distribute, is regular, and conjugated like *finir*.

EXERCISE LXXXIII.

Open this press. — Harvey *discovered* the circulation of the
    armoire f.   ——— f.
blood. — I *offer* you my services with all my heart. — The
sang m.   ——— *de*   *cœur* m.
house has not been *covered again* since the roof
maison f.   *depuis que*   *toit* m.
was burnt down. — That effort *opened* his wound *again*.—
ind-4 *brûlé*   *   ——— m.   *plaie* f.
He *suffers* more than you think. — We *set out* to-morrow for
    plus que   *ne pensez.*   *demain*
the country. — He *will set out* in two or three days. —
campagne f.   *dans*
That coach *starts* every day at (twelve o'clock.)
  voiture f.   *tous les jours*   *midi.*

241. *SENTIR*, TO FEEL, TO SMELL.

Part. Pres. sentant.   Part. Past, senti.

Ind.	Je sens,	tu sens,	il sent:
Pres.	nous sentons,	vous sentez,	ils sentent.
Imp.	Je sentais,	tu sentais,	il sentait;
	nous sentions,	vous sentiez,	ils sentaient.

OF THE SECOND CONJUGATION.

Pret.	Je sentis,	tu sentis,	il sentit;
	nous sentîmes,	vous sentîtes,	ils sentirent.
Fut.	Je sentirai,	tu sentiras,	il sentira;
	nous sentirons,	vous sentirez,	ils sentiront.
Cond. ⎱	Je sentirais,	tu sentirais,	il sentirait;
Pres. ⎰	nous sentirions,	vous sentiriez,	ils sentiraient.
Imper.		sens,	qu'il sente;
	sentons,	sentez,	qu'ils sentent.
Subj. ⎱	que je sente,	tu sentes,	il sente;
Pres. ⎰	que nous sentions,	vous sentiez,	ils sentent.
Imp.	que je sentisse,	tu sentisses,	il sentît;
	que nous sentissions,	vous sentissiez,	ils sentissent.

242. Conjugate in the same manner:—

Consentir,	*to consent.*	ressentir,	*to resent.*
mentir,	*to lie.*	se repentir,	*to repent.*
pressentir,	*to foresee.*	&c.	&c.

243. *SERVIR*, TO SERVE, TO HELP TO.

Part. Pres. servant.   *Part. Past,* servi.

Ind. ⎱	Je sers,	tu sers,	il sert;
Pres. ⎰	nous servons,	vous servez,	ils servent.
Imp.	Je servais,	tu servais,	il servait;
	nous servions,	vous serviez,	ils servaient.
Pret.	Je servis,	tu servis,	il servit;
	nous servîmes,	vous servîtes,	ils servirent.
Fut.	Je servirai,	tu serviras,	il servira;
	nous servirons,	vous servirez,	ils serviront.
Cond. ⎱	Je servirais,	tu servirais,	il servirait;
Pres. ⎰	nous servirions,	vous serviriez,	ils serviraient.
Imper.		sers,	qu'il serve;
	servons,	servez,	qu'ils servent.
Subj. ⎱	que je serve,	tu serves,	il serve;
Pres. ⎰	que nous servions,	vous serviez,	ils servent.
Imp.	que je servisse,	tu servisses,	il servît;
	que nous servissions,	vous servissiez,	ils servissent.

244. Conjugate in the same manner, *desservir*, to clear the table.

Asservir, to enslave, to subject, is regular, and conjugated like *finir*.

EXERCISE LXXXIV.

He who *serves* well his country (has no need) of ancestors.—
    *   *n'a pas besoin*   40
You *will feel* the effects of it.—*Smell* this rose.—Shall we
                     effet m. 108   —f.
consent to that bargain?—Never (*tell a falsehood*).—I *foresaw*
                 marché m.   *mentir*
all those misfortunes.—He *repents* of his   bad   conduct.—
      malheur m.   *mauvais conduite* f
He *serves* his friends with warmth.—*Help*   the gentleman
                chaleur.   ³à * ⁴*monsieur*
to some partridge.—Shall I have the honour to *help* you *to*
 ¹   ²*perdrix* f.   *de*
a wing of a chicken?—*Clear the table.*
  aile f.   *

245. SORTIR, TO GO OUT, TO COME OUT.

Part. Pres. sortant.   *Part. Past,* sorti.

IND. Pres.	Je sors, nous sortons,	tu sors, vous sortez,	il sort; ils sortent.
Imp.	Je sortais, nous sortions,	tu sortais, vous sortiez,	il sortait; ils sortaient.
Pret.	Je sortis, nous sortimes,	tu sortis, vous sortites,	il sortit; ils sortirent.
Fut.	Je sortirai, nous sortirons,	tu sortiras, vous sortirez,	il sortira; ils sortiront.
Cond. Pres.	Je sortirais, nous sortirions,	tu sortirais, vous sortiriez,	il sortirait; ils sortiraient.
Imper.	sortons,	sors, sortez,	qu'il sorte; qu'ils sortent.
Subj. Pres.	Que je sorte, Que nous sortions,	tu sortes, vous sortiez,	il sorte; ils sortent.
Imp.	Que je sortisse, Que nous sortissions,	tu sortisses, vous sortissiez,	il sortît; ils sortissent.

246. Conjugate in the same manner, *ressortir,* to go out again.

EXERCISE LXXXV.

I *go out* every morning before breakfast. — The
  tout art. *matin* m. pl. *avant*
fox *comes out* of his hole. — We *went out* of the town
renard m.   *terrier* m.
after him. — Everybody is *gone out*.—I *shall go out* in half
après   Tout le monde
an hour. — If I were as ill as you, I *would* not *go out*.—
                    malade
Do not *go out* to-day. — He (is just) *gone out*.—He *went*
           aujourd'hui.   *vient de*   inf-1
out again immediately.—I *will* not *go out again* this evening.
sur-le-champ.   *soir* m.

247. TENIR, TO HOLD, TO KEEP.

Part. Pres. tenant.   *Part. Past*, tenu.

IND. Pres.	Je tiens, nous tenons,	tu tiens, vous tenez,	il tient; ils tiennent.
Imp.	Je tenais, nous tenions,	tu tenais, vous teniez,	il tenait; ils tenaient.
Pret.	Je tins, nous tînmes,	tu tins, vous tîntes,	il tint; ils tinrent.
Fut.	Je tiendrai, nous tiendrons,	tu tiendras, vous tiendrez,	il tiendra; ils tiendront.
COND. Pres.	Je tiendrais, nous tiendrions,	tu tiendrais, vous tiendriez,	il tiendrait; ils tiendraient.
IMPER.	tenons,	tiens, tenez,	qu'il tienne; qu'ils tiennent.
SUBJ. Pres.	que je tienne, que nous tenions,	tu tiennes, vous teniez,	il tienne; ils tiennent.
Imp.	que je tinsse, que nous tinssions,	tu tinsses, vous tinssiez,	il tînt; ils tinssent.

248. Conjugate in the same manner:—

S'abstenir, *to abstain.* | maintenir, *to maintain.*
appartenir, *to belong.* | obtenir, *to obtain.* [retain.
contenir, *to contain.* [verse. | retenir, *to get hold again; to*
entretenir, *to keep up; to con-* | soutenir, *to sustain.*

☞ Observe that in these verbs the *n* is doubled, whenever it is followed by *e* mute; but in no other case.

EXERCISE LXXXVI.

I *hold* it fast, it shall not escape from me. — Liberality
   bien   échapper *   art.
holds a medium between prodigality and avarice. —
  le milieu m. entre   art.   art. —— f.
This garden is well *kept*.—He *abstained* from drinking on
   jardin m.   boire *
that day. — These horses *belong* to our general. — England
ce jour-là.   art.
and the principality of Wales *contain* fifty-two counties. —
            principauté f.   Galles   comté m.
They *conversed* about trifles. — I shall *maintain* it
     s'   de bagatelles.
everywhere.—Do not *maintain* so absurd an opinion. — Has
  partout.   ²si ³absurde   ¹—— f.
he *obtained* permission ? — *Detain* not the wages of a
           —— f.   retenir   gages m. pl.
servant. — That column *supports* all the building.
domestique m.   colonne f. soutenir   bâtiment m.

249. *VENIR*, to come.

Part. Pres. venant.   Part. Past, venu.

Ind. Pres.	Je viens, nous venons,	tu viens, vous venez,	il vient; ils viennent.
Imp.	Je venais, nous venions,	tu venais, vous veniez,	il venait; ils venaient.
Pret.	Je vins, nous vînmes,	tu vins, vous vîntes,	il vint; ils vinrent.
Fut.	Je viendrai, nous viendrons,	tu viendras, vous viendrez,	il viendra; ils viendront.
Cond. Pres.	Je viendrais, nous viendrions,	tu viendrais, vous viendriez,	il viendrait; ils viendraient.
Imper.	venons,	viens, venez,	qu'il vienne; qu'ils viennent.
Subj. Pres.	Que je vienne, Que nous venions,	tu viennes, vous veniez,	il vienne; ils viennent.
Imp.	Que je vinsse, Que nous vinssions,	tu vinsses, vous vinssiez,	il vînt; ils vinssent.

250. *Venir* is conjugated like *tenir;* but with this

OF THE SECOND CONJUGATION.

difference, that in its compound tenses it always takes the auxiliary *être*.

251. Conjugate in the same manner:—

Convenir,	*to agree; to suit.*	prévenir,	*to anticipate; to prevent.*
devenir,	*to become.*	se ressouvenir,	*to recollect.*
disconvenir,	*to deny.* [*terfere.*	revenir,	*to come back.*
intervenir,	*to intervene; to in-*	se souvenir,	*to remember.*
parvenir,	*to attain.*	subvenir,	*to relieve.*

252. *Prévenir* and *Subvenir* are conjugated in their compound tenses with the auxiliary *avoir*. *Convenir*, when it signifies *to agree*, takes *être;* but *avoir*, when it signifies *to suit*.

253. VÊTIR, TO CLOTHE.

Part. Pres. vêtant.   *Part. Past,* vêtu.

IND. ⎱ Pres. ⎰	Je vêts, nous vêtons,	tu vêts, vous vêtez,	il vêt; ils vêtent.
Imp.	Je vêtais, nous vêtions,	tu vêtais, vous vêtiez,	il vêtait; ils vêtaient.
Pret.	Je vêtis, nous vêtîmes,	tu vêtis, vous vêtîtes,	il vêtit; ils vêtirent.
Fut.	Je vêtirai, nous vêtirons,	tu vêtiras, vous vêtirez,	il vêtira; ils vêtiront.
COND. ⎱ Pres. ⎰	Je vêtirais, nous vêtirions,	tu vêtirais, vous vêtiriez,	il vêtirait; ils vêtiraient.
IMPER.	vêtons,	vêts, vêtez,	qu'il vête; qu'ils vêtent.
SUBJ. ⎱ Pres. ⎰	que je vête, que nous vêtions,	tu vêtes, vous vêtiez,	il vête; ils vêtent.
Imp.	que je vêtisse, que nous vêtissions,	tu vêtisses, vous vêtissiez,	il vêtît; ils vêtissent.

254. *Vêtir*, in the singular of the Present of the Indicative, and in the singular of the Imperative, is seldom used. It is most frequently reflected, and then it signifies *to dress oneself*. In this sense it is conjugated in its compound tenses, like all other pronominal verbs, with the auxiliary *être: Je me* SUIS *vêtu ; nous nous* SOMMES *vêtus*.

Conjugate in the same manner:—

Dévêtir, *to divest, to strip*. | Revêtir, *to clothe, to invest*.

EXERCISE LXXXVII.

I *come* from London. — You *come* very seasonably. — He
                                                                                     fort   à propos.
came on foot. — *Come* on Saturday morning, at ten o'clock. — He
ind-4 *à pied.*   *   *heures.*
will come back before the end of this month. — We have *agreed*
                        fin f.   *mois* m.
about the conditions. — That she *might become* more prudent. —
     de   —— f.
Do you *deny* the fact? — He *will* not *interfere* with that
        de   *fait* m.   *dans*
affair. — We *shall attain* our end. — *Remember* your
affaire f.   *à*   *but* m.   *de*
promises. — They have *relieved* all his wants. — He only
promesse f. On Ill   *à*   *besoin* m.   *ne*
passed for a traveller, but lately he has *assumed* the
ind-2 *que voyageur depuis peu revêtir*
character of an envoy. — He *dressed himself* in haste.
caractère m. * *envoyé* m.   *à* art. *hâte* f. *h* a.

---

255. § III. IRREGULAR AND DEFECTIVE VERBS OF
THE THIRD CONJUGATION.

256. ASSEOIR, *to set*, is an active verb; but it is principally used as a reflected verb, and is conjugated as follows:—

S'ASSEOIR, TO SEAT ONESELF, TO SIT, TO SIT DOWN.

    Part. Pres. s'asseyant.   *Part. Past*, assis.

IND. ⎱ Je m'assieds,   tu t'assieds,   il s'assied;
Pres. ⎰ nous nous asseyons, vous vous asseyez, ils s'asseient.
  Imp. Je m'asseyais,   tu t'asseyais,   il s'asseyait;
       nous nous asseyions, vous vous asseyiez, ils s'asseyaient.
  Pret. Je m'assis,   tu t'assis,   il s'assit;
       nous nous assîmes, vous vous assîtes, ils s'assirent.
  Fut. Je m'assiérai.   tu t'assiéras,   il s'assiéra;
       nous nous assiérons, vous vous assiérez, ils s'assiéront.

OF THE THIRD CONJUGATION. 137

COND. *Pres*.

Je m'assiérais, tu t'assiérais, il s'assiérait ;
nous nous assiérions, vous vous assiériez, ils s'assiéraient.

IMPERATIVE.

                           assieds-toi,   qu'il s'asseie ;
asseyons-nous,   asseyez-vous,   qu'ils s'asseient.

SUBJ. *Pres*.

Que je m'asseie, tu t'asseies, il s'asseie ;
Que nous nous asseyions, vous vous asseyiez, ils s'asseient.

Imperfect.

Que je m'assisse, tu t'assisses, il s'assît ;
Que nous nous assissions, vous vous assissiez, ils s'assissent.

Conjugate in the same manner, *rasseoir*, to set again, to sit down again, to calm.

AVOIR, *to have*, is conjugated at length, p. 60.

257. CHOIR, *to fall*. This verb is not much used; it is sometimes employed in the Infinitive, especially in poetry, where it is a very expressive term, when well brought in.

The Past Participle, *chu, chue*, is also used, but rather in verse than in prose, and rather in the jocular and familiar than in the serious and dignified style.

DÉCHOIR, *to decay, to fall off*. Past participle, *déchu*. This verb is seldom used in any other tense.

258. ÉCHOIR, *to fall to; to expire, to be due*. Part. pres. *échéant*. Part. past, *échu, échue*. Indic. pres. *il échoit*, sometimes pronounced, and even written, *il échet*. Pret. *j'échus*. Fut. *j'écherrai*. Cond. *j'écherrais*. Imperf. Subj. *que j'échusse*.—(ACAD.)

FALLOIR, *to be necessary*, is a unipersonal verb, the conjugation of which has been given, page 105.

EXERCISE LXXXVIII.

Set the child in an arm-chair. — Why do you not *sit*
                             fauteuil m. *Pourquoi*
down? — He *sat down* under the shade of a tree. — Shall
                     à   *ombre* f.   *arbre* m.
we sit down here? — *Let us sit down*, my friends.—*Sit down*

on this form. — I (had risen)   to go out, but he made me
sur   banc m.   m'étais levé pour   ²fit   ¹
sit down again. — He is much *fallen* in the esteem of the
                          fort déchoir   estime f.
public. — This bill   of exchange *is due*   to-day.
———. m.   lettre f.   change   aujourd'hui.

259. *MOUVOIR*, to move.

Part. Pres. mouvant.   *Part. Past,* mu.

IND. Pres.	Je meus,	tu meus,	il meut;
	nous mouvons,	vous mouvez,	ils meuvent.
Imp.	Je mouvais,	tu mouvais,	il mouvait;
	nous mouvions,	vous mouviez,	ils mouvaient.
Pret.	Je mus,	tu mus,	il mut;
	nous mûmes,	vous mûtes,	ils murent.
Fut.	Je mouvrai,	tu mouvras,	il mouvra;
	nous mouvrons,	vous mouvrez,	ils mouvront.
COND. Pres.	Je mouvrais,	tu mouvrais,	il mouvrait;
	nous mouvrions,	vous mouvriez,	ils mouvraient.
IMPER.		meus,	qu'il meuve;
	·mouvons,	mouvez,	qu'ils meuvent.
SUBJ. Pres.	que je meuve,	tu meuves,	il meuve;
	que nous mouvions,	vous mouviez,	ils meuvent
Imp.	que je musse,	tu musses,	il mût;
	que nous mussions,	vous mussiez,	ils mussent.

260. Conjugate in the same manner, *émouvoir*, to stir up, to move; and *promouvoir*, to promote. This last verb is seldom used but in the Infinitive, and in the compound tenses.

PLEUVOIR, *to rain;* see page 104.

261. *POURVOIR*, to provide.

Part. Pres. pourvoyant.   *Part. Past,* pourvu.

IND. Pres.	Je pourvois,	tu pourvois,	il pourvoit;
	nous pourvoyons,	vous pourvoyez,	ils pourvoient.
Imp.	Je pourvoyais,	tu pourvoyais,	il pourvoyait;
	nous pourvoyions,	vous pourvoyiez,	ils pourvoyaient.

Pret.	Je pourvus, nous pourvûmes,	tu pourvus, vous pourvûtes,	il pourvut; ils pourvurent.
Fut.	Je pourvoirai, nous pourvoirons,	tu pourvoiras, vous pourvoirez,	il pourvoira; ils pourvoiront.
Cond. *Pres.*	Je pourvoirais, nous pourvoirions,	tu pourvoirais, vous pourvoiriez,	il pourvoirait; ils pourvoiraient.
Imper.	 pourvoyons,	pourvois, pourvoyez,	qu'il pourvoie; qu'ils pourvoient.
Subj. *Pres.*	que je pourvoie, que nous pourvoyions,	tu pourvoies, vous pourvoyiez,	il pourvoie; ils pourvoient.
Imp.	que je pourvusse, que nous pourvussions,	tu pourvusses, vous pourvussiez,	il pourvût; ils pourvussent.

262. *POUVOIR*, TO BE ABLE. (To can.—*Walker.*)

Part. Pres. pouvant.   *Part. Past*, pu.

Ind. *Pres.*	Je puis, *or* je peux, tu peux, nous pouvons,	vous pouvez,	il peut; ils peuvent.
Imp.	Je pouvais, nous pouvions,	tu pouvais, vous pouviez,	il pouvait; ils pouvaient.
Pret.	Je pus, nous pûmes,	tu pus, vous pûtes,	il put; ils purent.
Fut.	Je pourrai, nous pourrons,	tu pourras, vous pourrez,	il pourra; ils pourront.
Cond. *Pres.*	Je pourrais, nous pourrions,	tu pourrais, vous pourriez,	il pourrait; ils pourraient.
	(No Imperative.)		
Subj. *Pres.*	que je puisse, que nous puissions,	tu puisses, vous puissiez,	il puisse; ils puissent.
Imp.	que je pusse, que nous pussions,	tu pusses, vous pussiez,	il pût; ils pussent.

263. REMARKS.—In the Future and Conditional of this verb, one *r* only is pronounced, although written with two.

In the Present of the Indicative, we say *je puis* or *je peux;* however, *je puis* is much more used, and ought to be preferred, since interrogatively we always say *puis-je ?*

Quels vœux *puis-je* former?—(*La Harpe.*)
Que *puis-je* ajouter à cet éloge?—(*C. Delavigne.*)

Moreover, *je puis*, and not *je peux*, is the expression employed in the writings of the best French authors.

. . . Enfin *je puis* parler en liberté;
Je puis dans tout son jour mettre la vérité.—(*Racine.*)
Je ne *puis* bien parler, et ne saurais me taire.—(*Boileau.*)
. . . . Je ne *puis* songer
Que cette horloge existe, et n'ait point d'horloger.—(*Voltaire.*)
Je puis être un serviteur inutile.—(*Massillon.*)

We say: *je ne puis*, and *je ne puis pas*. In the first phrase, the negative is less strong: *Je ne puis* implies difficulties. *Je ne puis pas* expresses impossibility.

PRÉVALOIR, *to prevail;* see *Valoir.*

PROMOUVOIR, *to promote;* see *Mouvoir.*

264. RAVOIR, *to have again, to get again,* is only used in the Present of the Infinitive.

Figuratively, and familiarly, we say *se ravoir,* in the sense of *to recover, to gather new strength:*

Allons, monsieur, tâchez un peu de vous *ravoir*.—(*J. J. Rousseau.*)

EXERCISE LXXXIX.

The spring which *moves* the whole machine is very
 ressort m. *mouvoir* ² ¹ ——f.
ingenious.—He *moved* the heart of that unfeeling man.—
         émouvoir *cœur* m.   ²*insensible* ¹

He has been *promoted* to the dignity of chancellor. —
                                                chancelier.

He *will provide* for all your wants. — I *cannot* answer you.—
            à   *besoin* m.

Can I be useful to you? — Save himself who *can*. — *Can* you
         utile   *Sauve*   *

lend me an umbrella?—I *could* not foresee that event. —
prêter   ind-2   *prévoir*   *événement* m.

I *shall* never *be able* to persuade him. — We *would be able*
                     * *persuader*

to go out. — Try to *get* it *again.*
 * 245   *Tâcher de*

OF THE THIRD CONJUGATION.

265. SAVOIR, TO KNOW.

Part. Pres. sachant. Part. Past, su.

Ind. Pres.	Je sais, nous savons,	tu sais, vous savez,	il sait; ils savent.
Imp.	Je savais, nous savions,	tu savais, vous saviez,	il savait; ils savaient.
Pret.	Je sus, nous sûmes,	tu sus, vous sûtes,	il sut; ils surent.
Fut.	Je saurai, nous saurons,	tu sauras, vous saurez,	il saura; ils sauront.
Cond. Pres.	Je saurais, nous saurions,	tu saurais, vous sauriez,	il saurait; ils sauraient.
Imper.	sachons,	sache, sachez,	qu'il sache; qu'ils sachent.
Subj. Pres.	Que je sache, Que nous sachions,	tu saches, vous sachiez,	il sache; ils sachent.
Imp.	Que je susse, Que nous sussions,	tu susses, vous sussiez,	il sût; ils sussent.

Note.—We find *savoir* written *sçavoir* in some old and esteemed works; but now, the *French Academy*, and all the modern Grammarians, suppress the letter *ç* as useless, because it does not affect the pronunciation of the word, nor does it even serve to point out its Latin derivation, since all the best French etymologists derive *savoir* from *sapere*, and not from *scire*.

266. We sometimes employ the Subjunctive of *savoir* instead of the Indicative, but never without a negative; as, JE NE SACHE *rien de plus digne d'éloge*, I know nothing more praiseworthy.

267. *Je ne saurais* is often used for *je ne puis* (I cannot); yet we do not say, *je ne saurais* for *je ne pourrais*, nor *je saurais* for *je puis*.

268. The student must not confound *savoir* with *connaître*, which also signifies *to know*. We do not say *savoir quelqu'un*, but *connaître quelqu'un*, to know, or be acquainted with some one.

269. SEOIR, *to become, to befit*, is never used in the present of the Infinitive. It has only the participle

present *seyant*, and the third persons of some of the simple tenses: *il sied, ils siéent ; il seyait, ils seyaient ; il siéra, ils siéront ; il siérait, ils siéraient ; qu'il siée, qu'ils siéent.*

270. When *seoir* signifies *to sit*, it has only the two Participles, *séant* and *sis*, which last is used in law as an adjective, and generally translated into English by *situate* or *situated*.

Surseoir, *to suspend, to put off;* see No. 275.

EXERCISE XC.

I *know* that he is not your friend, but I *know* likewise
       de pl.   *aussi*
that he is a man of probity. — The wise man *knows* how to
 *   bien.*   *sage* * * *
regulate his taste, his labours, and his pleasures. — Do you
 régler *goût* pl. *travail*
know French? — They do not *know* their lessons. — Milton
 art.   *leçon*
knew Homer almost by heart. — I *shall know* well how to
 Homère presque *cœur.*   * *
(defend myself). — (In order) *that you may know* it. — The
 me défendre. *Afin*
head-dress which that lady wore *became* her very well. —
 coiffure f. *que* *porter* ind-2 ind-2 *lui*
 Colours that are too gaudy *will* not *become* you.
art. *couleur* f. * * *voyant*

271. *VALOIR*, to be worth.

   Part. Pres. valant.   *Part. Past*, valu.

Ind. Pres.	Je vaux, nous valons,	tu vaux, vous valez,	il vaut ; ils valent.
Imp.	Je valais, nous valions,	tu valais, vous valiez,	il valait ; ils valaient.
Pret.	Je valus, nous valûmes,	tu valus, vous valûtes,	il valut ; ils valurent.
Fut.	Je vaudrai, nous vaudrons,	tu vaudras, vous vaudrez,	il vaudra ; ils vaudront.
Cond. Pres.	Je vaudrais, nous vaudrions,	tu vaudrais, vous vaudriez,	il vaudrait ; ils vaudraient.

Imper.	vaux,	qu'il vaille;
valons,	valez,	qu'ils vaillent.
Subj. ⎱ que je vaille,	tu vailles,	il vaille;
Pres. ⎰ que nous valions,	vous valiez,	ils vaillent.
Imp. que je valusse,	tu valusses,	il valût;
que nous valussions,	vous valussiez,	ils valussent.

In the compound tenses, *valoir* takes the auxiliary *avoir*.

Conjugate in the same manner:—

Équivaloir, *to be equivalent.* | revaloir, *to return like for like.*

272. *Prévaloir,* to prevail, follows the same conjugation, excepting that in the Subjunctive Present it makes, *que je prévale, que tu prévales, qu'il prévale; que nous prévalions, que vous prévaliez, qu'ils prévalent;* and not, *que je prévaille, que tu prévailles,* etc.

EXERCISE XCI.

This cloth *is worth* twenty shillings a yard. — Actions
    drap m.   schelling *l'* aune.   art. *effet* m.
are better than words. — His horse *was* not *worth* ten
valoir   art. *parole* f.
guineas.—That victory *procured* him the staff of a marshal
  guinée   victoire f. *valoir* lui   bâton m. * maréchal
of France.—One ounce of gold *is equivalent* to fifteen ounces
         once f.   or
of silver. — That answer *will be equivalent* to a refusal.—
  argent.   réponse f.   refus m.
    Favour often *prevails* over   merit. — His advice
art.   2   1   sur art. *mérite* m.   avis m.
prevailed. — That consideration *has prevailed* over all
                 considération f.   art
others. — Doubt not that truth will *prevail* at last.
          douter   art.   * *ne* subj-1 *à la longue*

273. VOIR, TO SEE.

Part. Pres. voyant.   Part. Past, vu.

Ind. ⎱ Je vois,	tu vois,	il voit;
Pres. ⎰ nous voyons,	vous voyez,	ils voient.
Imp. Je voyais,	tu voyais,	il voyait;
nous voyions,	vous voyiez,	ils voyaient.

Pret.	Je vis,	tu vis,	il vit;
	nous vîmes,	vous vîtes,	ils virent.
Fut.	Je verrai,	tu verras,	il verra;
	nous verrons,	vous verrez,	ils verront.
Cond.	Je verrais,	tu verrais,	il verrait;
Pres.	nous verrions,	vous verriez,	ils verraient.
Imper.		vois,	qu'il voie;
	voyons,	voyez,	qu'ils voient.
Subj.	que je voie,	tu voies,	il voie;
Pres.	que nous voyions,	vous voyiez,	ils voient.
Imp.	que je visse,	tu visses,	il vît;
	que nous vissions,	vous vissiez,	ils vissent.

274. Conjugate in the same manner, *entrevoir*, to have a glimpse of; *revoir*, to see again; and, *prévoir*, to foresee. Observe, however, that this last verb makes in the Future, *je prévoirai, tu prévoiras*, &c., and in the Conditional, *je prévoirais*, &c.

Note.—Many poets, ancient and modern, for the sake of rhyme, write without s, *je voi, j'aperçoi, je prévoi*, etc.

275. *Surseoir*, to put off (a law term), though a compound of *seoir*, is conjugated like *voir*, except in the Future, *je surseoirai*, and in the Conditional, *je surseoirais*.

EXERCISE XCII.

I *see* it now. — I *saw* it with my own eyes.—That
      maintenant.   ind-4 de   propre
reform (will take place), but we *shall* not *see* it. — You *shall*
réforme f. aura lieu
see what I can do. — Let us *see* your purchases.—*See* the
    ce que   sais faire.   emplette f.
admirable order of the universe: does it not announce a
²—— ¹ordre m.   univers m.   annoncer
supreme architect?—When *shall* we *see* your sisters *again?*
                  Quand
— To finish their affairs, it would be necessary *that they*
  Pour   affaire f.   falloir
should see each other.— Wise men *foresee* events.—
    s'entrevoir subj-2 art. ² ¹   art.
I *shall* not *put off* the pursuit of that affair.
                    poursuite f. pl.

OF THE THIRD CONJUGATION.   145

276. *VOULOIR*, TO WILL; TO BE WILLING; TO WISH.

Part. Pres. voulant.   *Part. Past,* voulu.

IND. PRES.	Je veux, nous voulons,	tu veux, vous voulez,	il veut; ils veulent.
Imp.	Je voulais, nous voulions,	tu voulais, vous vouliez,	il voulait; ils voulaient.
Pret.	Je voulus, nous voulûmes,	tu voulus, vous voulûtes,	il voulut; ils voulurent.
Fut.	Je voudrai, nous voudrons,	tu voudras, vous voudrez,	il voudra; ils voudront.
COND. PRES.	Je voudrais, nous voudrions,	tu voudrais, vous voudriez,	il voudrait; ils voudraient.
IMPER.	Veuillez,	{ The second pers. pl. is the only one used, and signifies, *be so good as, be so kind as to.**	
SUBJ. PRES.	que je veuille, que nous voulions,	tu veuilles, vous vouliez,	il veuille; ils veuillent.
Imp.	que je voulusse, que nous voulussions,	tu voulusses, vous voulussiez,	il voulût; ils voulussent.

☞ Observe that the Subjunctive Present is *que je veuille;* but the plural is *que nous voulions, que vous vouliez;* and not *que nous veuillions, que vous veuilliez,* as some writers have it.

EXERCISE XCIII.

I can and   *will* tell the truth. — He *wishes* to set out
     pron.   dire   vérité f.   *

to-morrow. — If you   are willing, he   will be willing also.—
demain.   le   le   aussi.

We *wish* to be free. — He *wished* to accompany me. — They
      *   libre   * accompagner   On

will give you   whatever you *wish*.—I *should wish* (him to come).
            tout ce que   ind-7   qu'il vînt.

— He *would wish* to speak to you in private. —
        *   *   en particulier.

Have the goodness to read this letter. — Heaven *wills* it so.
Vouloir   * lire   art.   ainsi.

---

* Some admit of a second Imperative, *veux, voulons, voulez,* but they use it only in very rare instances, as in this phrase, VOULONS, *et nous pourrons.*

K

§ IV. IRREGULAR AND DEFECTIVE VERBS OF THE FOURTH CONJUGATION.

277. *ABSOUDRE*, TO ABSOLVE.

Part. Pres. absolvant.   *Part. Past,* absous, *m.* ; absoute, *f.*

IND. Pres.	J'absous, nous absolvons,	tu absous, vous absolvez,	il absout ; ils absolvent.
Imp.	J'absolvais, nous absolvions,	tu absolvais, vous absolviez,	il absolvait ; ils absolvaient.

(No Preterite Definite.)

Fut.	J'absoudrai, nous absoudrons,	tu absoudras, vous absoudrez,	il absoudra ; ils absoudront.
Cond. Pres.	J'absoudrais, nous absoudrions,	tu absoudrais, vous absoudriez,	il absoudrait ; ils absoudraient.
Imper.	absolvons,	absous, absolvez,	qu'il absolve ; qu'ils absolvent.
Subj. Pres.	que j'absolve, que nous absolvions,	tu absolves, vous absolviez,	il absolve ; ils absolvent.

(No Imperfect of the Subjunctive.)

278. Conjugate in the same manner, *dissoudre,* to dissolve.

ABSTRAIRE, *to abstract,* is conjugated like *traire,* but is little used; it is more customary to say *faire abstraction de.*

ACCROIRE is used in the Present of the Infinitive only, with any of the tenses of the verb *faire,* when it signifies, *faire croire ce qui n'est pas,* to make one believe what is not true, to impose upon one.

ACCROÎTRE, *to increase,* is conjugated like *croître.*

ADMETTRE, *to admit,* like *mettre.*

ATTEINDRE, *to reach.* See *Peindre.*

279. ATTRAIRE, *to attract, to allure,* is used only in the Infinitive : *Le sel est bon pour attraire les pigeons,* salt is good for attracting pigeons. *Attirer* often supplies its place, and is more harmonious.

280. *BATTRE*, TO BEAT.

Part. Pres. battant.   *Part. Past,* battu.

IND. Pres.	Je bats,	tu bats,	il bat;
	nous battons,	vous battez,	ils battent.
Imp.	Je battais,	tu battais,	il battait;
	nous battions,	vous battiez,	ils battaient.
Pret.	Je battis,	tu battis,	il battit;
	nous battîmes,	vous battîtes,	ils battirent.
Fut.	Je battrai,	tu battras,	il battra;
	nous battrons,	vous battrez,	ils battront.
COND. Pres.	Je battrais,	tu battrais,	il battrait;
	nous battrions,	vous battriez,	ils battraient.
IMPER.		bats,	qu'il batte;
	battons,	battez,	qu'ils battent.
SUBJ. Pres.	Que je batte,	tu battes,	il batte;
	Que nous battions,	vous battiez,	ils battent.
Imp.	Que je battisse,	tu battisses,	il battît;
	Que nous battissions,	vous battissiez,	ils battissent.

281. Conjugate in the same manner:—

Abattre,	*to pull down.*	rabattre,	*to abate.*
combattre,	*to fight.*	rebattre,	*to beat again.*
débattre,	*to debate.*	se débattre,	*to struggle.*

EXERCISE XCIV.

I *pardon* you in consideration of your repentance. —
   absoudre   faveur   repentir.
She was *acquitted.*—These acids *dissolve* metals.—After the
    ind-3 *absoudre*   acide   art.
death of Alexander, his empire was *dissolved.*—Why do you
                                   —— m.
beat my dog? — Our left wing *beat* the right wing
         chien m.   ²gauche ¹aile f. ind-3   ²droit   ¹
of the enemy. — Believe me, general, we *shall beat* them. —
      pl.   *Croyez-moi*   87
The cannon *beat down* the walls of the fortress. —
   canon m. *abattre* ind-3   muraille f.   forteresse f.
They *fought* bravely on both sides. — They have
On   ind-4 *vaillamment de part et d'autre.*   Ils
discussed that question. — *Beat* these mattresses *again.*
débattre   —— f.   matelas m.

282. BOIRE, to drink.

Part. Pres. buvant.   *Part. Past*, bu.

Ind. Pres.	Je bois,	tu bois,	il boit;
	nous buvons,	vous buvez,	ils boivent.
Imp.	Je buvais,	tu buvais,	il buvait;
	nous buvions,	vous buviez,	ils buvaient.
Pret.	Je bus,	tu bus,	il but;
	nous bûmes,	vous bûtes,	ils burent.
Fut.	Je boirai,	tu boiras,	il boira;
	nous boirons,	vous boirez,	ils boiront.
Cond. Pres.	Je boirais,	tu boirais,	il boirait;
	nous boirions,	vous boiriez,	ils boiraient.
Imper.		bois,	qu'il boive;
	buvons,	buvez,	qu'ils boivent.
Subj. Pres.	₂je boive,	tu boives,	il boive;
	♂nous buvions,	vous buviez,	ils boivent.
Imp.	₂je busse,	tu busses,	il bût;
	♂nous bussions,	vous bussiez,	ils bussent.

283. CONCLURE, to conclude.

Part. Pres. concluant.   *Part. Past*, conclu, *m.*; conclue, *f.*

Ind. Pres.	Je conclus,	tu conclus,	il conclut;
	nous concluons,	vous concluez,	ils concluent.
Imp.	Je concluais,	tu concluais,	il concluait;
	nous concluions,	vous concluiez,	ils concluaient.
Pret.	Je conclus,	tu conclus,	il conclut;
	nous conclûmes,	vous conclûtes,	ils conclurent.
Fut.	Je conclurai,	tu concluras,	il conclura;
	nous conclurons,	vous conclurez,	ils concluront.
Cond. Pres.	Je conclurais,	tu conclurais,	il conclurait;
	nous conclurions,	vous concluriez,	ils concluraient.
Imper.		conclus,	qu'il conclue;
	concluons,	concluez,	qu'ils concluent
Subj. Pres	₂je conclue,	tu conclues,	il conclue;
	♂nous concluions,	vous concluiez,	ils concluent.
Imp.	₂je conclusse,	tu conclusses,	il conclût;
	♂nous conclussions,	vous conclussiez,	ils conclussent.

Conjugate in the same manner, *exclure*, to exclude.

EXERCISE XCV.

I have the honour of *drinking* your health. — His best
                  de   inf-1 à   santé f.
wine is *drunk*.—This paper *blots*.—They *drank* two bottles
vin m.   boire   bouteille
of champaign. —I *shall drink* a glass of white wine.—*Let us*
champagne.   verre m.   ²   ¹
drink to the health of our friends. — Come, *drink*.—I never
          santé f.   Allons
drink wine.— Since he has not arrived, I *conclude* that he will
  154   Puisqu'   est   en
not come.—What do you *conclude* from all this?—They have
                Que   101
concluded the bargain.—He was *excluded* from the assembly.
          marché m.   assemblée f.

284. *CONDUIRE*, TO CONDUCT; TO LEAD.

Part. Pres. conduisant. *Part. Past*, conduit, *m.*; conduite, *f.*

IND. } Pres.}	Je conduis, nous conduisons,	tu conduis, vous conduisez,	il conduit; ils conduisent.
Imp.	Je conduisais, nous conduisions,	tu conduisais, vous conduisiez,	il conduisait; ils conduisaient.
Prct.	Je conduisis, nous conduisîmes,	tu conduisis, vous conduisites,	il conduisit; ils conduisirent.
Fut.	Je conduirai, nous conduirons,	tu conduiras, vous conduirez,	il conduira; ils conduiront.
COND.} Pres.}	Je conduirais, nous conduirions,	tu conduirais, vous conduiriez,	il conduirait; ils conduiraient.
IMPER.	 conduisons,	conduis, conduisez,	qu'il conduise; qu'ils conduisent.
SUBJ.} Pres.}	que je conduise, que nous conduisions,	tu conduises, vous conduisiez,	il conduise; ils conduisent.
Imp.	que je conduisisse, que nous conduisissions,	tu conduisisses, vous conduisissiez,	il conduisit; ils conduisissent.

285. Conjugate in the same manner:—

Construire,	*to construct.*	introduire,	*to introduce.*
cuire,	*to cook, to bake.*	produire,	*to produce.*
déduire,	*to deduct.*	reconduire,	*to reconduct.*
détruire,	*to destroy.*	réduire,	*to reduce.*
instruire,	*to instruct.*	traduire,	*to translate.*

286. *Nuire*, to hurt, is conjugated like *conduire;* but its past participle is *nui*, which has no feminine.

EXERCISE XCVI.

This road *leads* to the town. — Moses *conducted* the
chemin m.   Moïse

people of Israel. — They *built* several ships. — This
peuple m. Israël.   construire   vaisseau m.

baker *bakes* twice a day.—*Deduct* what you have
boulanger deux fois par   ce que

received.— Time *destroys* everything.—The overflowing
         art.   tout.   débordement m.

of the river *destroyed* his crop. —Those who *instruct*
    rivière f.   récolte f.   art.

youth, (must arm themselves) with patience.—I *shall inform*
jeunesse f. doivent s'armer   de   instruire

his family of his conduct. —He *introduced* me into the king's
  famille f.   conduite f.   dans   2

closet. —This country has *produced* many great men.—
1cabinet m.   pays m.   beaucoup de

What book are you *translating?*—This is well *translated.—*
       livre m.   101

Translate this. — That affair has *hurt* his reputation.
              96 affaire f.   à

287. *CONFIRE*, TO PICKLE, TO PRESERVE.

Part. Pres. confisant. *Part. Past,* confit, *m.* ; confite, *f.*

Ind. Pres.	Je confis,	tu confis,	il confit;
	nous confisons,	vous confisez,	ils confisent.
Imp.	Je confisais,	tu confisais,	il confisait;
	nous confisions,	vous confisiez,	ils confisaient.
Pret.	Je confis,	tu confis,	il confit;
	nous confîmes,	vous confîtes,	ils confirent.
Fut.	Je confirai,	tu confiras,	il confira;
	nous confirons,	vous confirez,	ils confiront.
Cond. Pres.	Je confirais,	tu confirais,	il confirait;
	nous confirions,	vous confiriez,	ils confiraient

OF THE FOURTH CONJUGATION. 151

Imper.		confis,	qu'il confise;
	confisons,	confisez,	qu'ils confisent.
Subj. Pres.	je confise,	tu confises,	il confise;
	nous confisions,	vous confisiez,	ils confisent.
Imp.	je confisse,	tu confisses,	il confît;
	nous confissions,	vous confissiez,	ils confissent.

288. *Suffire*, to suffice, to be sufficient, is conjugated like *confire*; but its past participle is *suffi*, which has no feminine.

EXERCISE XCVII.

I *shall preserve* some fruits this year. — *Will* you *preserve*
                                       année f.

these cherries with   sugar or with   brandy? — *Preserve*
    cerise f.   à   art.   art. *eau-de-vie* f.

some apricots   and   peaches. — Have you *pickled* any
    abricot m.   32 *pêche* f.

cucumbers? —   Little   *suffices* to the wise. — A hundred
concombre m.   *Peu de bien*   s.   *

pounds   a   year *suffice* him for his maintenance. —
livres sterling par   an   subsistance f.

If he lose that lawsuit, all his property *will* not *suffice.* —
   perd   procès m.   bien m.   y

That *would* not *suffice* me. — That sum   *is* not *sufficient* to
                       somme f.   pour

pay your debts. — Here are three thousand francs, *will* that
      dette f.   Voici

be *enough?* — That *is enough.* — Do you like   *pickled* walnuts?
 · *suffire*   aimer art.   [2]   [1]noix f.

289. *CONNAÎTRE*, to know.

Part. Pres. connaissant.   *Part. Past*, connu.

Ind. Pres.	Je connais,	tu connais,	il connaît;
	nous connaissons,	vous connaissez,	ils connaissent.
Imp.	Je connaissais,	tu connaissais,	il connaissait;
	nous connaissions,	vous connaissiez,	ils connaissaient.
Pret.	Je connus,	tu connus,	il connut;
	nous connûmes,	vous connûtes,	ils connurent.

Ind. Fut.	Je connaîtrai, nous connaîtrons,	tu connaîtras, vous connaîtrez,	il connaîtra; ils connaîtront.
Cond. Pres.	Je connaîtrais, nous connaîtrions,	tu connaîtrais, vous connaîtriez,	il connaîtrait; ils connaîtraient
Imper.	connaissons,	connais, connaissez,	qu'il connaisse; qu'ils connaissent.
Subj. Pres.	que je connaisse, que nous counaissions,	tu connaisses, vous connaissiez,	il connaisse; ils connaissent.
Imp.	que je connusse, que nous connussions,	tu connusses, vous connussiez,	il connût; ils connussent.

☞ See No. 268, for Remark on *Savoir* and *Connaître*.

290. Conjugate in the same manner :—

Disparaître,	*to disappear.*	reconnaître,	*to know again.*
paraître,	*to appear.*	reparaître,	*to appear again.*

EXERCISE XCVIII.

I *know* him perfectly. — He *knows* his (weak side.)—
    parfaitement.   *faible* m.
We *know* nobody in this neighbourhood. — Do you *know* our
     116   *voisinage* m.
house?— He *knew* me by my voice. — I *would know* him
      à   * art. *voix* f.
among a thousand. — The compass was not *known* to the
entre *   *boussole* f.   *de*
ancients.—At the approach of our troops, the enemy *disappeared.*
      approche f.   pl.
— It seems you are wrong. — You do not appear
  paraître que   *avoir tort.*
convinced.—Do you not *recognise* me?—I *recognise* you.—
convaincu   *reconnaître*
Do they *acknowledge* their errors?—He *knew* his horse *again.*
  reconnaître

Contredire, *to contradict;* see *Dire.*

291. *COUDRE*, to sew.

Part. Pres. cousant.   *Part. Past*, cousu.

IND. } *Pres.* }	Je couds, nous cousons,	tu couds, vous cousez,	il coud : ils cousent.
Imp.	Je cousais, nous cousions,	tu cousais, vous cousiez,	il cousait ; ils cousaient.
Pret.	Je cousis, nous cousîmes,	tu cousis, vous cousîtes,	il cousit ; ils cousirent.
Fut.	Je coudrai, nous coudrons,	tu coudras, vous coudrez,	il coudra ; ils coudront.
COND. } *Pres.* }	Je coudrais, nous coudrions,	tu coudrais, vous coudriez,	il coudrait ; ils coudraient.
IMPER.	 cousons,	couds, cousez,	qu'il couse ; qu'ils cousent.
SUBJ. } *Pres.* }	que je couse, que nous cousions,	tu couses, vous cousiez,	il couse ; ils cousent.
Imp.	que je cousisse, que nous cousissions,	tu cousisses, vous cousissiez,	il cousît ; ils cousissent.

292. *Découdre*, to unsew, and *recoudre*, to sew again, are conjugated in the same manner.

293. *CRAINDRE*, to fear.

Part. Pres. craignant.   *Part. Past*, craint, *m.*; crainte, *f.*

IND. } *Pres.* }	Je crains, nous craignons,	tu crains, vous craignez,	il craint ; ils craignent.
Imp.	Je craignais, nous craignions,	tu craignais, vous craigniez,	il craignait ; ils craignaient.
Pret.	Je craignis, nous craignîmes,	tu craignis, vous craignîtes,	il craignit ; ils craignirent.
Fut.	Je craindrai, nous craindrons,	tu craindras, vous craindrez,	il craindra ; ils craindront.
COND. } *Pres.* }	Je craindrais, nous craindrions,	tu craindrais, vous craindriez,	il craindrait ; ils craindraient.
IMPER.	 craignons,	crains, craignez,	qu'il craigne ; qu'ils craignent
SUBJ. } *Pres.* }	que je craigne, que nous craignions,	tu craignes, vous craigniez,	il craigne ; ils craignent.
Imp.	que je craignisse, que nous craignissions,	tu craignisses, vous craignissiez,	il craignît ; ils craignissent.

294. Conjugate after the same manner, all verbs ending in *aindre* and *oindre;* as, *plaindre*, to pity, and *joindre*, to join.—When *plaindre* is used reflectedly, it signifies to complain: *Je vous plains, mais* JE ne ME PLAINS *pas de vous*, I pity you, but I do not complain of you.

EXERCISE XCIX.

That girl *sews* well.—My sisters *were sewing* all yesterday.—
             ind-3   hier.
Sew a button on this waistcoat. — That is badly *sewed*. —
  bouton m. à   gilet m.   mal
Ilis coat was torn, but his tailor *sewed* it *again* very
 habit m.   déchiré   tailleur
  neatly. — He *is afraid* of being discovered.—He was a man
proprement. craindre d' inf-1 découvert. C'
who *feared* nothing. — I *pity* his family. — He *complains*
  ind-2   famille f.   se plaindre
without cause.—They *were* always *complaining*.—They united
  sujet.   ²toujours ¹ind-2   joindre
their efforts. — *Let us unite* prudence with courage.
  —— m.   art. —— f. à art. —— m.

295. *CROIRE*, to believe.

Part. Pres. croyant.   *Part. Past,* cru, *m.* ; crue, *f.*

Ind. Pres.	Je crois,	tu crois,	il croit;
	nous croyons,	vous croyez,	ils croient.
Imp.	Je croyais,	tu croyais,	il croyait;
	nous croyions,	vous croyiez,	ils croyaient.
Prct.	Je crus,	tu crus,	il crut;
	nous crûmes,	vous crûtes,	ils crurent.
Fut.	Je croirai,	tu croiras,	il croira;
	nous croirons,	vous croirez,	ils croiront.
Cond. Pres.	Je croirais,	tu croirais,	il croirait ;
	nous croirions,	vous croiriez,	ils croiraient.
Imper.		crois,	qu'il croie;
	croyons,	croyez,	qu'ils croient.
Subj. Pres.	Que je croie,	tu croies,	il croie ;
	Que nous croyions,	vous croyiez,	ils croient.
Imp.	Que je crusse,	tu crusses,	il crût ;
	Que nous crussions,	vous crussiez,	ils crussent.

OF THE FOURTH CONJUGATION. 155

296. REMARK.—Some people put the preposition *de* after the verb *croire*, when followed by an infinitive; but this is contrary to the practice of the best writers; we must say: *j'ai cru bien faire*, and not *j'ai cru* DE *bien faire*, I thought I was doing well.

297. CROÎTRE, TO GROW.

Part. Pres. croissant.   Part. Past, crû, m.; crûe, f.

IND. } Pres. }	Je crois, nous croissons,	tu crois, vous croissez,	il croit; ils croissent.
Imp.	Je croissais, nous croissions,	tu croissais, vous croissiez,	il croissait; ils croissaient.
Pret.	Je crûs, nous crûmes,	tu crûs, vous crûtes,	il crût; ils crûrent.
Fut.	Je croîtrai, nous croîtrons,	tu croîtras, vous croîtrez,	il croîtra; ils croîtront.
COND. } Pres. }	Je croîtrais, nous croîtrions,	tu croîtrais, vous croîtriez,	il croîtrait; ils croîtraient.
IMPER.	croissons,	crois, croissez,	qu'il croisse; qu'ils croissent.
SUBJ. } Pres. }	que je croisse, que nous croissions,	tu croisses, vous croissiez,	il croisse; ils croissent.
Imp.	que je crûsse, que nous crûssions,	tu crûsses, vous crûssiez,	il crût; ils crûssent.

298. Conjugate in the same manner, *accroître*, to increase, and *décroître*, to decrease.

_{Accru and décru, past Participles of accroître and décroître, are written without any accent.—(Acad.)}

EXERCISE C.

I *believe* you. — She *believes* only what she sees. — Do
                  ne   que ce qu'
you *think* that I wish   to deceive you?—He *thought*
   croire   vouloir subj-1 * tromper   ind-2
to gain his lawsuit.—They *thought* they heard some cries.—
* gagner   ind-3   * inf-1   cri m.
I *should think* (I would be wanting) in my duty. — *Believe*
               manquer   à   devoir m.
nothing of all that. — He *thought* he was doing well. — The
                        ind-4

vine does not *grow* in cold countries. — These plants
vigne f.   art. ² ¹*pays* m.   *plante* f.
grow on the margin of streams. — His fortune *increases*
           bord m.   art. *ruisseau* m.   —— f. *s'*
every day. — The river has *fallen* two inches. —
tous les jours.   *rivière* f. *décroître de* *pouce* m

After Midsummer, the days begin to *shorten.*
       la Saint-Jean   *décroître.*

299. *DIRE*, TO SAY, TO TELL.

Part. Pres. disant.   *Part. Past,* dit, *m.*; dite, *f.*

IND. Pres.	Je dis, nous disons,	tu dis, vous dites,	il dit; ils disent.
Imp.	Je disais, nous disions,	tu disais, vous disiez,	il disait; ils disaient.
Pret.	Je dis, nous dîmes,	tu dis, vous dîtes,	il dit; ils dirent.
Fut.	Je dirai, nous dirons,	tu diras, vous direz,	il dira; ils diront.
Cond. Pres.	Je dirais, nous dirions,	tu dirais, vous diriez,	il dirait; ils diraient.
Imper.	disons,	dis, dites,	qu'il dise; qu'ils disent.
Subj. Pres.	que je dise, que nous disions,	tu dises, vous disiez,	il dise; ils disent.
Imp.	que je disse, que nous dissions,	tu disses, vous dissiez,	il dît; ils dissent.

300. *Redire*, to say again, is conjugated like *dire;* but

contredire, *to contradict,* ⎫ make in the 2d   ⎧ contredisez.
dédire,   *to disown,*   ⎬ pers. plur. of the ⎨ dédisez.
interdire, *to prohibit,*   ⎪ pres. of the Ind. ⎪ interdisez.
médire,   *to slander,*   ⎪ and of the Imper. ⎪ médisez.
prédire,   *to foretell,*   ⎭   ⎩ prédisez.

301. *Maudire*, to curse, is conjugated like *dire*, except that it takes double *s* in the Part. pres. *maudissant;* in the IND. pres. *nous maudissons, vous maudissez, ils maudissent;* in the Imperf. *je maudissais*, etc.; in the IMPER. *qu'il maudisse, maudissons,* etc., and in the SUBJ. *que je maudisse, que tu maudisses,* etc.

EXERCISE CI.

He *tells* all he knows. — Those who *say:* I shall not
    ce qu'   *savoir*   *Ceux*

work, are the most miserable.—*Tell* us which you would
travailler

prefer. —You always *contradict* me.—That physician *prohibits*
préférer   ³   ²   ¹   *médecin*

wine to all his patients. — He *slanders* everybody.
art.   *malade*   *de tout le monde.*

— The makers of almanacs *foretell* rain and fine
      faiseur   *almanach*   art. *pluie* f.   art.

weather. — Do not *say:* That man is of one people, and
temps m.   *Celui-là*   *peuple* m.

I am of another people: for all peoples have had on
moi   *car*   art.

earth the same father, who was Adam, and have in
art.   ind-2

heaven the same father, who is God.
art. *ciel* m.

DISSOUDRE is conjugated like *absoudre*; see p. 146.

302. ÉCLORE, *to be hatched, as birds,* or *to blow like a flower,* is used only in the present of the Infinitive; in the Part. past, *éclos,* f. *éclose,* and in the third persons of the following tenses:—IND. pres. *il éclôt, ils éclosent;* Fut. *il éclôra, ils éclôront;* COND. *il éclôrait, ils éclôraient;* SUBJ. pres. *qu'il éclose, qu'ils éclosent.* But its compound tenses, which are formed with *être,* are much in use.

The primitive of *éclore* is *clore,* to close, to shut. Another compound is *enclore,* to enclose.

303. *ÉCRIRE,* TO WRITE.

Part. Pres. écrivant.   *Part. Past,* écrit.

IND. } *Pres.* }	J'écris, nous écrivons,	tu écris, vous écrivez,	il écrit; ils écrivent.
Imp.	J'écrivais, nous écrivions,	tu écrivais, vous écriviez,	il écrivait; ils écrivaient.
Pret.	J'écrivis, nous écrivîmes,	tu écrivis, vous écrivîtes,	il écrivit; ils écrivirent.

Fut.	J'écrirai,	tu écriras,	il écrira;
	nous écrirons,	vous écrirez,	ils écriront.
Cond. Pres.	J'écrirais,	tu écrirais,	il écrirait;
	nous écririons,	vous écririez,	ils écriraient.
Imper.		écris,	qu'il écrive;
	écrivons,	écrivez,	qu'ils écrivent.
Subj. Pres.	que j'écrive,	tu écrives,	il écrive;
	que nous écrivions,	vous écriviez,	ils écrivent.
Imp.	que j'écrivisse,	tu écrivisses,	il écrivît;
	que nous écrivissions,	vous écrivissiez,	ils écrivissent.

304. Conjugate in the same manner:—

Circonscrire,	*to circumscribe.*	proscrire,	*to proscribe.*
décrire,	*to describe.*	récrire,	*to write again.*
inscrire,	*to inscribe.*	souscrire,	*to subscribe.*
prescrire,	*to prescribe.*	transcrire,	*to transcribe.*

EXERCISE CII.

Silk-worms *are hatched* in the beginning of
art. *ver à soie* ind-1 à *commencement* m. art.
spring. — These flowers *will* soon *blow*. — That man
printemps m. ²*bientôt* ¹
speaks well, but he *writes* badly. — Saint John *wrote* his
mal. ind-3
gospel at the age of ninety, and joined the quality of an
évangile m. *ans* ind-3 *qualité* f. *
evangelist to that of an apostle and a prophet. — I *shall*
* *apôtre* *de* *
write to you from Naples. — *Write* that on a sheet of paper. —
feuille f.
This poet *describes* a battle well. — His physician has
² ³*bataille* f. ¹ *médecin*
prescribed to him another regimen. — Sylla *proscribed* three or
86 *régime* m. ind-3
four thousand Roman citizens. — He *is* not *writing again*, it is
²*romain* ¹*citoyen* m. c'
a sign that he is coming. — I *shall subscribe* for that atlas. —
* *signe* — m.
I have *transcribed* several passages from Cicero and Tacitus.
Cicéron *de Tacite*.

Ensuivre (s'), *to follow from, to ensue;* see *Suivre.*

Être, *to be,* is conjugated at length, p. 64.

305. *FAIRE*, TO DO, TO MAKE.

Part. Pres. faisant. *Part. Past,* fait.

IND. Pres.	Je fais, nous faisons,	tu fais, vous faites,	il fait; ils font.
Imp.	Je faisais, nous faisions,	tu faisais, vous faisiez,	il faisait; ils faisaient.
Pret.	Je fis, nous fîmes,	tu fis, vous fîtes,	il fit; ils firent.
Fut.	Je ferai, nous ferons,	tu feras, vous ferez,	il fera; ils feront.
COND. Pres.	Je ferais, nous ferions,	tu ferais, vous feriez,	il ferait; ils feraient.
IMPER.	faisons,	fais, faites,	qu'il fasse; qu'ils fassent.
SUBJ. Pres.	que je fasse, que nous fassions,	tu fasses, vous fassiez,	il fasse; ils fassent.
Imp.	que je fisse, que nous fissions,	tu fisses, vous fissiez,	il fît; ils fissent.

Note.—The diphthong *ai* having the sound of *e* mute, in *faisant, nous faisons, je faisais,* as well as in the derivatives *bienfaisant, bienfaisance, contrefaisant,* etc. *Voltaire,* and many writers, after his example, have substituted *e* mute instead of *ai.* But *Dumarsais, Condillac, Girard, Beauzée, D'Olivet,* and *Domergue,* have constantly opposed the adoption of this change, and the *French Academy,* the best judges in this matter, have formally rejected it.

306. Conjugate like *faire:*—

contrefaire, *to counterfeit, to [mimic.* | refaire, *to do again.*
défaire, *to undo, to defeat.* | satisfaire, *to satisfy.*
 | surfaire, *to exact, to overcharge.*

EXERCISE CIII.

I *do* my duty; *do* yours.—Everything she *does,* she
    devoir m.   Tout   ce qu'

does well.—Pliny relates that Cæsar *took* above
le   Pline rapporter   faire ind-3 *plus de*

800,000 prisoners. — The emperor has *made* him a knight
                                                       * chevalier

of the legion of honour.—She *mimics* everybody. — What
                                     tout le monde.   Ce que

the one *does*, the other *undoes*.—Penelope *undid*, at night,
le Pénélope ind-2 * art.
the work she had *done* during the day.—The fleet
ouvrage m. qu' * flotte f.
of the enemy was completely *defeated.*—If it were
pl. ind-3 complétement c' ind-2
to *do again,* I *would* not *do* it.—That scholar *pleases* all
à satisfaire
his masters.—You *ask too much* for your goods.
surfaire * marchandise f.

FEINDRE, *to feign,* is conjugated like *peindre.*

307. FRIRE, *to fry,* besides the Present of the Infinitive, is used only in the singular of the Present of the Indicative, *Je fris, tu fris, il frit;* in the Future, *Je frirai, tu friras, il frira, nous frirons, vous frirez, ils friront;* in the Conditional, *Je frirais, tu frirais, il frirait, nous fririons, vous fririez, ils friraient;* in the second person singular of the Imperative, *fris;* and in the compound tenses, which are formed with the Participle past, *frit, frite.*

To supply the persons and tenses which are wanting, we make use of the verb *faire* prefixed to the Infinitive *frire;* as, *Nous faisons frire, vous faites frire, ils font frire; je faisais frire,* etc.

308. *LIRE*, TO READ.

Part. Pres. lisant.   *Part. Past,* lu.

IND. } PRES. }	Je lis,	tu lis,	il lit;
	nous lisons,	vous lisez,	ils lisent.
Imp.	Je lisais,	tu lisais,	il lisait;
	nous lisions,	vous lisiez,	ils lisaient.
Pret.	Je lus,	tu lus,	il lut;
	nous lûmes,	vous lûtes,	ils lurent.
Fut.	Je lirai,	tu liras,	il lira;
	nous lirons,	vous lirez,	ils liront.
COND. } PRES. }	Je lirais,	tu lirais,	il lirait;
	nous lirions,	vous liriez,	ils liraient.
IMPER.		lis,	qu'il lise;
	lisons,	lisez,	qu'ils lisent.

OF THE FOURTH CONJUGATION. 161

| Subj. Pres. | je lise, nous lisions, | tu lises, vous lisiez, | il lise; ils lisent. |
| Imp. | je lusse, nous lussions, | tu lusses, vous lussiez, | il lût; ils lussent. |

Note.—The regular mode of interrogation is, *lis-je bien?* and not *lisé-je bien?* If *lis-je bien* be thought harsh to the ear, another turn of expression may be adopted. —(ACAD., *Th. Corneille.*) See page 87, Rem. 6th.

309. *Élire*, to elect, and *relire*, to read again, are conjugated like *lire*.

310. LUIRE, TO SHINE.

Part. Pres. luisant. *Part. Past*, lui, *m.* *No feminine.*

| Ind. Pres. | Je luis, nous luisons, | tu luis, vous luisez, | il luit; ils luisent. |
| Imp. | Je luisais, nous luisions, | tu luisais, vous luisiez, | il luisait; ils luisaient. |

(No Preterite Definite.)

| Fut. | Je luirai, nous luirons, | tu luiras, vous luirez, | il luira; ils luiront. |
| Cond. Pres. | Je luirais, nous luirions, | tu luirais, vous luiriez, | il luirait; ils luiraient. |

(No Imperative.)

| Subj. Pres. | Que je luise, que nous luisions, | que tu luises, que vous luisiez, | qu'il luise; qu'ils luisent. |

(No Imperfect of the Subjunctive.)

311. *Reluire*, to shine, to glitter, is conjugated like *luire*, but the Participle present has never been used in a figurative sense.

MAUDIRE, *to curse;* see page 156.

EXERCISE CIV.

Get that fish fried.—The soles are not yet fried.—
Faites ² ³poisson m. ¹inf-1   —f.   encore

I am reading the Roman history.—She reads well.—They read
                         ²   ¹

distinctly. — What author do you read in your class?—
distinctement.   auteur m.   classe f.

We are reading Don Quixote. — He is a man who has read
                   — Quichotte. C''   ²

L

(a great deal).—He can neither *read* nor write.—*Read* that
¹*beaucoup*   *ne sait ni*   *ni*

letter *again*.—They *elected* him for their representative.—We
                ind-3   *représentant.*

shall elect the most worthy.—The sun *shines* for everybody. —
                       digne.   *tout le monde.*

Everything *shines* in that house.—All that *glitters* is not gold.
Tout   *ce qui*

312. *METTRE*, TO PUT.

Part. Pres. mettant.   *Part. Past*, mis.

IND. ⎱ Pres. ⎰	Je mets,	tu mets,	il met;
	nous mettons,	vous mettez,	ils mettent.
Imp.	Je mettais,	tu mettais,	il mettait;
	nous mettions,	vous mettiez,	ils mettaient.
Pret.	Je mis,	tu mis,	il mit;
	nous mîmes,	vous mîtes,	ils mirent.
Fut.	Je mettrai,	tu mettras,	il mettra;
	nous mettrons,	vous mettrez,	ils mettront.
COND. ⎱ Pres. ⎰	Je mettrais,	tu mettrais,	il mettrait;
	nous mettrions,	vous mettriez,	ils mettraient.
IMPER.		mets,	qu'il mette;
	mettons,	mettez,	qu'ils mettent.
SUBJ. ⎱ Pres. ⎰	que je mette,	tu mettes,	il mette;
	que nous mettions,	vous mettiez,	ils mettent.
Imp.	que je misse,	tu misses,	il mît;
	que nous missions,	vous missiez,	ils missent.

313. Conjugate in the same manner:—

Admettre,	*to admit.*	emettre,	*to omit.*
commettre,	*to commit.*	permettre,	*to permit.*
compromettre,	*to compromise.*	promettre,	*to promise.*
se démettre,	{ *to resign; to put out of joint.*	remettre,	*to put again; to put* [*off.*
		soumettre,	*to submit.*
s'entremettre,	*to intermeddle.*	transmettre,	*to transmit.*

EXERCISE CV.

Put on your *hat*. — You have *put* (the cart before the
     *   *chapeau* m.   *la charrue devant les*

horse).—I do not *admit* that principle. — They *committed*
bœufs.   *principe* m   ind-3   *de*

OF THE FOURTH CONJUGATION. 163

great excesses. — I *shall* not *compromise* you. — Diocletian
  excès m.   *Dioclétien*
resigned the empire.—I *shall omit* nothing that depends
 ind-3 *de*   ——m.   *de ce qui dépendre*
  upon me to serve you.—The law of Mahomet does not
ind-7 *de* *pour*   ——
allow wine.—*Allow* me to tell you.—He *promises* enough,
permettre art.   *de*   *assez*
but he seldom keeps his word. — Do not *defer* till to-
  ²*rarement* ¹   *parole* f.   *remettre à*
morrow what you can do to-day. — They *submit* to your
  ce que   *aujourd'hui.* *se*
decision.—His actions *will transmit* his name to posterity.
       ——   art.

314. *MOUDRE*, TO GRIND (corn, coffee, &c.)

Part. Pres. moulant.   *Part. Past,* moulu.

IND. } *Pres.* }	Je mouds, nous moulons,	tu mouds, vous moulez,	il moud; ils moulent.
Imp.	Je moulais, nous moulions,	tu moulais, vous mouliez,	il moulait; ils moulaient.
Pret.	Je moulus, nous moulûmes,	tu moulus, vous moulûtes,	il moulut; ils moulurent.
Fut.	Je moudrai, nous moudrons,	tu moudras, vous moudrez,	il moudra; ils moudront.
COND. } *Pres.* }	Je moudrais, nous moudrions,	tu moudrais, vous moudriez,	il moudrait; ils moudraient.
IMPER.	 moulons,	mouds, moulez,	qu'il moule; qu'ils moulent.
SUBJ. } *Pres.* }	Que je moule, Que nous moulions,	tu moules, vous mouliez,	il moule; ils moulent.
Imp.	Que je moulusse, Que nous moulussions,	tu moulusses, vous moulussiez,	il moulût; ils moulussent.

315. Conjugate in the same manner:—

Émoudre, *to grind* (knives, razors, &c.) | rémoudre, *to grind again*
remoudre, *to grind again* (corn, &c.) | (knives, razors, &c.)

316. *NAÎTRE*, TO BE BORN.

Part. Pres. naissant.   *Part. Past,* né.

IND. } *Pres.* }	Je nais, nous naissons,	tu nais, vous naissez,	il naît; ils naissent.

Ind. } Imp. }	Je naissais, nous naissions,	tu naissais, vous naissiez,	il naissait; ils naissaient.
Pret.	Je naquis, nous naquîmes,	tu naquis, vous naquîtes,	il naquit; ils naquirent.
Fut.	Je naîtrai, nous naîtrons,	tu naîtras, vous naîtrez,	il naîtra; ils naîtront.
Cond. } Pres. }	Je naîtrais, nous naîtrions,	tu naîtrais, vous naîtriez,	il naîtrait; ils naîtraient.
Imper.	naissons,	nais, naissez,	qu'il naisse; qu'ils naissent.
Subj. Pres.	Que je naisse, Que nous naissions,	tu naisses, vous naissiez,	il naisse; ils naissent.
Imp.	Que je naquisse, Que nous naquissions,	tu naquisses, vous naquissiez,	il naquît; ils naquissent.

317. This verb takes the auxiliary *être;* but *renaître,* to be born again, has no participle past, and, therefore, no compound tenses.

Nuire, *to hurt;* see page 150, No. 286.

Instruire, *to instruct,* is conjugated like *Conduire.*

EXERCISE CVI.

This mill does not *grind* fine enough. — *Grind* some
    moulin m.   ²*fin*   ¹

pepper. — Are my scissors   *ground?*—From   labour
poivre m.   *ciseaux* m. pl.   art. *travail* m.

springs health; from health contentment, source of
naître art.   art.   art.   —

every joy. — Abraham *was born* about three hundred and
tout joie f.   ind-3   *environ*   *

fifty years after the deluge. — Moses *was born* a hundred years
    an m.   *Moïse*   *

after the death of Jacob. — Napoleon Bonaparte *was born* at
          —   *Napoléon*   —

Ajaccio, in Corsica, on the 15th of August 1769. — They
         —   *en Corse*   *   *

were born on the same day. — Many   diseases *spring*
    *   *Beaucoup de maladie*

from intemperance. — Everything *revives* in   spring.
                        Tout   *renaître* à art.

OF THE FOURTH CONJUGATION.

318. *PAÎTRE*, TO GRAZE.

Part. Pres. paissant.   *Part. Past*, pu, *m.*   *No feminine.*

IND. } Pres. }	Je pais, nous paissons,	tu pais, vous paissez,	il pait; ils paissent.
Imp.	Je paissais, nous paissions,	tu paissais, vous paissiez,	il paissait; ils paissaient.

(No Preterite Definite.)

Fut.	Je paîtrai, nous paîtrons,	tu paîtras, vous paîtrez,	il paîtra; ils paîtront.
COND. } Pres. }	Je paîtrais, nous paîtrions,	tu paîtrais, vous paîtriez,	il paîtrait; ils paîtraient.
IMPER.	paissons,	pais, paissez,	qu'il paisse; qu'ils paissent.
SUBJ. } Pres. }	que je paisse, que nous paissions,	tu paisses, vous paissiez,	qu'il paisse; qu'ils paissent.

(No Imperfect of the Subjunctive.)

319. *Repaître*, to feed, is conjugated in the same manner, and has, besides, a Preterite Definite, *je repus*, and an Imperfect of the Subjunctive, *que je repusse.*

PARAÎTRE, *to appear*, is conjugated like *Connaître.*

320. *PEINDRE*, TO PAINT.

Part. Pres. peignant.   *Part. Past*, peint, *m.*; peinte, *f.*

IND. } Pres. }	Je peins, nous peignons,	tu peins, vous peignez,	il peint; ils peignent.
Imp.	Je peignais, nous peignions,	tu peignais, vous peigniez,	il peignait; ils peignaient.
Pret.	Je peignis, nous peignîmes,	tu peignis, vous peignîtes,	il peignit; ils peignirent.
Fut.	Je peindrai, nous peindrons,	tu peindras, vous peindrez,	il peindra; ils peindront.
COND. } Pres. }	Je peindrais, nous peindrions,	tu peindrais, vous peindriez,	il peindrait; ils peindraient.
IMPER.	peignons,	peins, peignez,	qu'il peigne; qu'ils peignent.
SUBJ. } Pres. }	que je peigne, que nous peignions,	tu peignes, vous peigniez,	il peigne; ils peignent.
Imp.	que je peignisse, que nous peignissions,	tu peignisses, vous peignissiez,	il peignît; ils peignissent.

321. Conjugate after the same manner all verbs ending in *eindre;* as,

Astreindre, *to bind, to subject.* | éteindre, *to extinguish, to put*
atteindre, *to attain, to reach.* | feindre, *to feign.* [*out.*

EXERCISE CVII.

The sheep   quietly   feed on the grass
   mouton m. ³*tranquillement* ¹*paître* * ²*herbe* h m.
under the care   of the shepherd   and the dogs. — The
sous   garde f.   berger m.   pr.
flocks   *were grazing* in the meadows.—He *feeds himself*
troupeau m.   prairie f.   *se repaître*
with vain hopes.   — She *paints* from nature.— Joy
    d'   ² ¹*espérance* f.   *d'après* —— art. *se*
was painted in his eyes.—He has *attained* his fifteenth year. —
    ind-2   *année* f.
We *shall reach* that village before night. — *Put out* all
                —— m.   art.
the candles. — The fire is *out*.—He *feigns* to be sick.
    chandelle f.   d'   *malade.* .
— He *pretended*   not to see him.
    feindre ind-3 *de ne pas* *

322. *PLAIRE,* TO PLEASE.

Part. Pres. plaisant.   *Part. Past,* plu.

IND. ⎫ Pres. ⎭	Je plais, nous plaisons,	tu plais, vous plaisez,	il plaît; ils plaisent.
Imp.	Je plaisais, nous plaisions,	tu plaisais, vous plaisiez,	il plaisait; ils plaisaient.
Pret.	Je plus, nous plûmes,	tu plus, vous plûtes,	il plut; ils plurent.
Fut.	Je plairai, nous plairons,	tu plairas, vous plairez,	il plaira; ils plairont.
COND. ⎫ Pres. ⎭	Je plairais, nous plairions,	tu plairais, vous plairiez,	il plairait; ils plairaient.
IMPER.	 plaisons,	plais, plaisez,	qu'il plaise; qu'ils plaisent.
SUBJ. ⎫ Pres. ⎭	que je plaise, que nous plaisions,	tu plaises, vous plaisiez,	il plaise; ils plaisent.
Imp.	que je plusse, que nous plussions,	tu plusses, vous plussiez,	il plût; ils plussent.

323. Conjugate in the same manner, *déplaire*, to displease, and *complaire*, to humour.

324. PRENDRE, TO TAKE.

Part. Pres. prenant.   *Part. Past*, pris.

Ind. Pres.	Je prends, nous prenons,	tu prends, vous prenez,	il prend; ils prennent.
Imp.	Je prenais, nous prenions,	tu prenais, vous preniez,	il prenait; ils prenaient.
Pret.	Je pris, nous prîmes,	tu pris, vous prîtes,	il prit; ils prirent.
Fut.	Je prendrai, nous prendrons,	tu prendras, vous prendrez,	il prendra; ils prendront.
Cond. Pres.	Je prendrais, nous prendrions,	tu prendrais, vous prendriez,	il prendrait; ils prendraient.
Imper.	prenons,	prends, prenez,	qu'il prenne; qu'ils prennent.
Subj. Pres.	Que je prenne, Que nous prenions,	tu prennes, vous preniez,	il prenne; ils prennent.
Imp.	Que je prisse, Que nous prissions,	tu prisses, vous prissiez,	il prît; ils prissent.

325. Conjugate in the same manner:—

Apprendre, *to learn.* [prehend.
comprendre, *to understand, to com-*
désapprendre, *to unlearn, to forget.*
entreprendre, *to undertake.*

se méprendre, *to mistake.*
reprendre, *to take back*
to reply; to censure.
surprendre, *to surprise.*

☞ The *n* of the above verbs is always doubled, as in *prendre*, when it comes before the *mute* terminations *e, es, ent.*

EXERCISE CVIII.

That painting pleases me more than the other. — Let us
    tableau m.

not *give offence* by airs of haughtiness. — He *took*
    déplaire 32 —   *hauteur*, h a.   32

guides who conducted him.—I shall *take* a hackney-coach.—
    fiacre m.

Take the first street on the right. — The cat has *caught* a
    rue f. à * *droite*.   *prendre*

mouse. — The place was *taken.—Let us learn* our lesson.—
souris f. — f. ind-2

I do not *understand* these two words. — Philosophy
mot m. art.

comprehends logic, ethics, physics, and
art. *logique* f. art. *morale* f. s. art. *physique* f. s.

metaphysics. — They *undertake* (too many) things at
art. *métaphysique* f. s. trop de à

once. — I *took* up my gun again. — You *surprise* me
art. *fois* f. * *fusil* m.

very much by telling me that. — Virtue *pleases* everybody.
beaucoup en art. à

326. RÉSOUDRE, TO RESOLVE.

Part. Pres. résolvant.   *Part. Past,* résolu, or résous.

IND. Pres.	Je résous, nous résolvons,	tu résous, vous résolvez,	il résout; ils résolvent.
Imp.	Je résolvais, nous résolvions,	tu résolvais, vous résolviez,	il résolvait; ils résolvaient.
Pret.	Je résolus, nous résolûmes,	tu résolus, vous résolûtes,	il résolut; ils résolurent.
Fut.	Je résoudrai, nous résoudrons,	tu résoudras, vous résoudrez,	il résoudra; ils résoudront.
Cond. Pres.	Je résoudrais, nous résoudrions,	tu résoudrais, vous résoudriez,	il résoudrait; ils résoudraient.
Imper.	résolvons,	résous, résolvez,	qu'il résolve; qu'ils résolvent.
Subj. Pres.	que je résolve, que nous résolvions,	tu résolves, vous résolviez,	il résolve; ils résolvent.
Imp.	que je résolusse, que nous résolussions,	tu résolusses, vous résolussiez,	il résolût; ils résolussent.

327. *N.B.*—When *résoudre* signifies to determine, to decide, the Part. past, *résolu*, m. *résolue*, f. is to be employed; but if it mean to change, to reduce, or turn one thing into another, then the Participle *résous* (without feminine), is to be used:

Ce jeune homme *a résolu* de changer de conduite.	*This young man* has resolved *to change his conduct.*
Le soleil *a résous* le brouillard en pluie.	*The sun* has turned *the fog into rain.*

328. *RIRE*, TO LAUGH.

Part. Pres. riant.	*Part. Past*, ri, *m.*	*No feminine*
Ind. Pres. } Je ris,	tu ris,	il rit;
nous rions,	vous riez,	ils rient.
Imp. Je riais,	tu riais,	il riait;
nous riions,	vous riiez,	ils riaient.
Pret. Je ris,	tu ris,	il rit;
nous rîmes,	vous rîtes,	ils rirent.
Fut. Je rirai,	tu riras,	il rira;
nous rirons,	vous rirez,	ils riront.
Cond. Pres. } Je rirais,	tu rirais,	il rirait;
nous ririons,	vous ririez,	ils riraient.
Imper.	ris,	qu'il rie;
rions,	riez,	qu'ils rient
Subj. Pres. } que je rie,	tu ries,	il rie;
que nous riions,	vous riiez,	ils rient.
Imp. que Je risse,	tu risses,	il rît;
que nous rissions,	vous rissiez,	ils rissent.

Rire is also used with a double pronoun, in the sense of to laugh at, to ridicule; as, JE ME RIS *de ses menaces,* I laugh at his threats.

Sourire, to smile, is conjugated in the same manner.

SUFFIRE, *to suffice, to be sufficient;* see No. 288.

EXERCISE CIX.

We *resolved* to set out immediately. — Have they *resolved*
    ind-3 *de*   *sur-le-champ.*   *A-t-on*
on peace or war? — Everybody *is laughing* at his
* art.   art.   *Tout le monde*   *à*
expense. — She *was laughing* most heartily. — They *were*
dépens m. pl.   *de tout son cœur.*
laughing (in their sleeves).—They *laughed* even to tears.—
    sous cape.   * art. *larme*
You make me *laugh.* — Fortune *smiles* on him.—She *smiled*
    art. ——f.   * *lui*   ind-2
at my embarrassment.—He *smiled* to him, in sign of approbation.
de   embarras m.   ind-3   *en*   ——
—He came up to me *smiling.*
    ind-3 *au-devant · de moi en*

329. *SUIVRE*, to follow.

Part. Pres. suivant.   *Part. Past,* suivi.

IND. Pres.	Je suis,	tu suis,	il suit ;
	nous suivons,	vous suivez,	ils suivent.
Imp.	Je suivais,	tu suivais,	il suivait ;
	nous suivions,	vous suiviez,	ils suivaient
Pret.	Je suivis,	tu suivis,	il suivit ;
	nous suivîmes,	vous suivîtes,	ils suivirent
Fut.	Je suivrai,	tu suivras,	il suivra ;
	nous suivrons,	vous suivrez,	ils suivront.
Cond. Pres.	Je suivrais,	tu suivrais,	il suivrait ;
	nous suivrions,	vous suivriez,	ils suivraient.
Imper.		suis,	qu'il suive ;
	suivons,	suivez,	qu'ils suivent.
Subj. Pres.	que je suive,	tu suives,	il suive ;
	que nous suivions,	vous suiviez,	ils suivent.
Imp.	que je suivisse,	tu suivisses,	il suivît ;
	que nous suivissions,	vous suivissiez,	ils suivissent.

Conjugate in the same manner, *poursuivre,* to pursue, to prosecute.

S'ensuivre, to ensue, to result, follows the same conjugation, but is used only in the third persons singular and plural of every tense; as,

Un grand bien *s'ensuivit.*—(ACAD.) | *Much good* resulted from it.

SURVIVRE, *to survive,* is conjugated like *Vivre.*

330. *TAIRE*, to conceal, to keep secret.

Part. Pres. taisant.   *Part. Past,* tû, *m.* ; tue, *f.*

IND. Pres.	Je tais,	tu tais,	il tait ;
	nous taisons,	vous taisez,	ils taisent.
Imp.	Je taisais,	tu taisais,	il taisait ;
	nous taisions,	vous taisiez,	ils taisaient.
Pret.	Je tus,	tu tus,	il tut ;
	nous tûmes,	vous tûtes,	ils turent.
Fut.	Je tairai,	tu tairas,	il taira ;
	nous tairons,	vous tairez,	ils tairont.
Cond. Pres.	Je tairais,	tu tairais,	il tairait ;
	nous tairions,	vous tairiez,	ils tairaient.
Imper.		tais,	qu'il taise ;
	taisons,	taisez,	qu'ils taisent.

OF THE FOURTH CONJUGATION.   171

SUBJ. ⎱ Que je taise,   tu taises,   il taise;
Pres. ⎰ Que nous taisions,   vous taisiez,   ils taisent.
 Imp.   Que je tusse,   tu tusses,   il tût;
        Que nous tussions,   vous tussiez,   ils tussent.

Conjugate in the same manner, *se taire*, to be silent, to hold one's tongue.

EXERCISE CX.

An ass-driver said: I am not what I *follow*, for if I were
    ânier m.   ce que   car   étais
what I *follow*, I would not be what I am. — Trouble
                                                 art. *embarras* m.
attends   riches.   — Several princes of Germany
suivre art. *richesses* f. pl.   *Allemagne*
follow the doctrine of Luther. — I *shall follow* you   very
       — f.   —   de fort
closely.—Always *follow* the advice of   your father.—
  près.   ²   ¹   avis m.   monsieur
Let us pursue our journey. — Well! what (*is the consequence*)?
              chemin m. Eh bien! que   *s'ensuivre*
I *shall* not *conceal* from you my way   of thinking. — After
                    *   façon f.   inf-1
having said that, he *held his tongue*.—*Let us be silent*
                                                         inf-1

331. TRAIRE, TO MILK.

  Part. Pres. trayant.   Part. Past, trait, m.; traite, f.

IND. ⎱ Je trais,   tu trais,   il trait;
Pres.⎰ nous trayons,   vous trayez,   ils traient.
 Imp.   Je trayais,   tu trayais,   il trayait;
        nous trayions,   vous trayiez,   ils trayaient.
             (*No Preterite Définite.*)
 Fut.   Je trairai,   tu trairas,   il traira;
        nous trairons,   vous trairez,   ils trairont.
COND. ⎱ Je trairais,   tu trairais,   il trairait;
Pres. ⎰ nous trairions,   vous trairiez,   ils trairaient.
IMPER.   trais,   qu'il traie;
        trayons,   trayez,   qu'ils traient.
SUBJ. ⎱ Que je traie,   tu traies,   il traie;
Pres. ⎰ Que nous trayions,   vous trayiez,   ils traient.
             (*No Imperfect of the Subjunctive.*)

332. Conjugate in the same manner:—

Abstraire, *to abstract.* | rentraire, *to finedraw, to darn.*
distraire, *to distract, to divert.* | retraire, *to redeem.*
extraire, *to extract.* | soustraire, *to subtract.*

(See Remarks on *Abstraire* and *Attraire*, p. 146.)

333. *VAINCRE*, to vanquish, to conquer.

Part. Pres. vainquant.   *Part. Past,* vaincu.

Ind. Pres.	Je vaincs,	tu vaincs,	il vainc;
	nous vainquons,	vous vainquez,	ils vainquent.
Imp.	Je vainquais,	tu vainquais,	il vainquait;
	nous vainquions,	vous vainquiez,	ils vainquaient.
Prét.	Je vainquis,	tu vainquis,	il vainquit;
	nous vainquîmes,	vous vainquîtes,	ils vainquirent.
Fut.	Je vaincrai,	tu vaincras,	il vaincra;
	nous vaincrons,	vous vaincrez,	ils vaincront.
Cond. Pres.	Je vaincrais,	tu vaincrais,	il vaincrait;
	nous vaincrions,	vous vaincriez,	ils vaincraient.
Imper.	(*The 2d pers. s. is not in use.*)		qu'il vainque;
	vainquons,	vainquez,	qu'ils vainquent.
Subj. Pres.	Que je vainque,	tu vainques,	il vainque;
	Que nous vainquions,	vous vainquiez,	ils vainquent.
Imp.	Que je vainquisse,	tu vainquisses,	il vainquît;
	Que nous vainquissions,	vous vainquissiez,	ils vainquissent.

The Present and Imperfect of the Indicative of this verb are seldom used.

Convaincre, to convince, to convict, is conjugated in the same manner.

EXERCISE CXI.

Is the cow *milked?* — The least thing *diverts* his
    vache f.   *moindre*   *le*   *

attention.—He has *extracted* that passage from a dialogue of
   *   m.   m.

Plato.   —   Arithmetic   teaches   to   add,
Platon.   art.   *arithmétique* f.   *à*   *additionner,*

    subtract,   multiply, and   divide. — Scipio *vanquished*
pr.   pr. *multiplier,*   pr. *diviser. Scipion*   ind-3

Hannibal at the battle of Zama, in Africa. — The Greeks
Annibal   *Afrique.*   *Grec*

vanquished the   Persians   at   Marathon,   Salamis,
   ind-3   *Perse*   *à*   —   pr. *Salamine,*

   Platea, and   Mycale.—How many   people cannot be
pr. *Platée,*   pr.   —   *Combien de gens ne peuvent*

convinced but by   experience!—He was *convicted* of treason.
 m. pl.   *que*   art.

OF THE FOURTH CONJUGATION.

334. *VIVRE*, TO LIVE.

Part. Pres. vivant.   *Part. Past,* vécu.   *No feminine.*

IND. ⎫ Pres. ⎭	Je vis, nous vivons,	tu vis, vous vivez,	il vit ; ils vivent.
Imp.	Je vivais, nous vivions,	tu vivais, vous viviez,	il vivait ; ils vivaient.
Pret.	Je vécus, nous vécûmes,	tu vécus, vous vécûtes,	il vécut ; ils vécurent.
Fut.	Je vivrai, nous vivrons,	tu vivras, vous vivrez,	il vivra ; ils vivront.
COND. ⎫ Pres. ⎭	Je vivrais, nous vivrions,	tu vivrais, vous vivriez,	il vivrait ; ils vivraient.
IMPER.	vivons,	vis, vivez,	qu'il vive ; qu'ils vivent.
SUBJ. ⎫ Pres. ⎭	que je vive, que nous vivions,	tu vives, vous viviez,	il vive ; ils vivent.
Imp.	que je vécusse, que nous vécussions,	tu vécusses, vous vécussiez,	il vécût ; ils vécussent.

So are conjugated, *revivre*, to revive ; and *survivre*, to survive.

Ils ont vécu, in the sense of *ils sont morts* (they are dead), is an expression purely Latin : the Romans avoided, from superstition, the use of words reckoned inauspicious. We say more generally, *ils sont morts ;* however, *ils ont vécu* has become a French phrase, owing to its adoption by a great number of authors ; besides, it produces a finer effect than the expression for which it stands.

335. To live *on* or *upon*, is expressed by *vivre* DE ; as, *Il vit* DE *légumes* (ACAD.), he lives upon vegetables.

C'est une fille accoutumée à *vivre* DE salade, DE lait, DE fromage et DE pommes.—(*Molière.*)

VIVE *le Roi !* is an exclamation to express that we wish the king long life and prosperity. *Vive* is also a term made use of to mark that we highly esteem a person, or set a great value upon something.

Vive la liberté !   *Vivent* nos libérateurs !—(*Acad.*)
Malgré tous les chagrins, *vive* la vie !—(*Gresset.*)
Vivent les gens d'esprit !—(*Palissot.*)
Vivent les gens qui ont de l'industrie !—(*Pluche.*)

Vive or *vivent*, in the above and similar phrases, is the third person of the present of the Subjunctive of the verb *vivre*. (ACAD., *Féraud, Trévoux,* etc.)

EXERCISE CXII.

I *live* with economy. — He *lives* like a great lord. — She
                        en   *   seigneur.
lives upon her income. — We *live* in the country. — Those
      rentes f. pl.   à
animals *live upon* herbs and roots. — Saint Louis (Louis
              herbe f.   pr. racine f.
IX.) *lived* in the thirteenth century. — So good a prince *will*
    ind-2 à   siècle m.   ² ³ ¹
live for ever in history. — It is dear *living* in this
    éternellement dans art.   fait   inf-1 dans
town. — The people shouted, Long *live* the Emperor! —
        peuple m. crier ind-3
Fathers *live again* in their children. — He *will* never
art.   revivre dans
survive the loss of his reputation. — The husband has
   à   perte f.
survived his wife. — He did not long *survive* a person who
  à   ind-3 à   f.
was so dear to him. — Let us *live* as good Christians.
ind-2   86   en

EXERCISE CXIII.

He was in great dejection of mind; but the news
ind-2 un   accablement m.
which he has just received, have *revived* him. — Homer
      vient de   inf-1   fait   inf-1   Homère
lived probably about eight hundred and fifty years before
ind-2   environ   *   avant
the Christian era. — That man *lives on* little. — He *lives* from
     ² ¹   peu.   au
hand to mouth. — She *lives on* bread and water. — They *live* at
jour le jour.   d'
the expense of others. — She *lived* more than a hundred years.
   dépens pl.   115   ind-4   *
— The Latin tongue *will live* for ever. — Long *live* Champagne
              ² ¹   toujours.
and Burgundy for good wines. — They called out to him, Who
                                        crier
goes there? he replied, France. — This work *will live.*
   vivre

CHAPTER VI.

OF THE ADVERB.

336. The *Adverb* is an invariable word, so called, because it is most frequently added to a verb, to express some quality, manner, or circumstance; as, *il écrit* BIEN, he writes well; *elle parle* DISTINCTEMENT, she speaks distinctly.

The adverb serves also to modify an adjective, and even another adverb; as, *il est* TRÈS *éloquent*, he is very eloquent; *elle chante* FORT *bien*, she sings very well.

Some adverbs consist of a single word, as *bien*, well; *toujours*, always; others are compound, and consist of two or more words, and are commonly called, *adverbial expressions;* such are, *pêle-mêle*, promiscuously; *sur-le-champ*, immediately; *tout-à-coup*, suddenly.

337. PLACE OF THE ADVERB.

Adverbs, in French, are generally placed after the verb, in *simple tenses*, and between the auxiliary and the participle, in *compound tenses;* as,

Il parle *souvent* de vous.	He often *speaks of you*.
Il a *souvent* parlé de vous.	He has often *spoken of you*.

But *adverbial expressions* are placed after the participle in compound tenses; as,

Vous avez jugé *à la hâte*.	You have *judged* hastily.

338. CLASSIFICATION OF ADVERBS.

Adverbs may be classified according to their different uses; we shall give a list of those most in use.

339. *Adverbs of Affirmation and Consent.*

Certes,	certainly.	soit,	be it so.
oui,	yes.	volontiers,	willingly.
sans doute,	undoubtedly.	d'accord,	done, agreed.

340. *Adverbs of Denial.*

Non, ne, ne pas, } *no, not.* | nullement, *by no means.*
ne point, | point du tout, *not at all.*

341. *Adverbs of Doubt.*

Peut-être, *perhaps.* | probablement, *probably.*

EXERCISE CXIV.

That is *undoubtedly* a very fine action. — You wish it: *be it*
C'est là   — f.

so.—I *willingly* consent to that bargain. — *No, no,* I shall *not*
                                                     marché m.

consent to it.—Will you give up your rights to him?—*By no*
 109   céder   droit m.

means. — Do you fear his resentment? — *No, not at all.*—
                                  ressentiment m.

You *perhaps* think that he is one of your friends; you are in a
        croire   *   *

 mistake. — He will *probably* succeed in his undertaking.
art. erreur f.   réussir

342. *Adverbs of Interrogation.*

☞ These adverbs are always placed before the verb.

Combien, *how much, how* | d'où,   *whence.*
comment, *how.* [*many.*] | pourquoi, *why.*
où,   *where.* | quand,   *when.*

343. *Adverbs of Quantity.*

Assez,   *enough.* | peu,   *little.*
beaucoup,   *much, very much.* | presque, *almost.*
bien, fort, très,   *very.* | tant,   *so much, so many.*
davantage,   *more.* | trop,   *too, too much, too*
                                                          [*many.*

EXERCISE CXV.

How much have you got in your purse? — *How many*
                        *

 verbs have you learned?—*How* is he?—*Where* do you
de verbe m.   se porter

live? — *Whence* do you come?—*Why* do you make *so much*
demeurer   faire

 noise? — *When* shall I have the pleasure of seeing you
de   inf-1

EXERCISE ON ADVERBS OF COMPARISON. 177

again?—You have played *enough*.—Gentlemen, *where* are you
                jouer   monsieur
running to?—I am *very* glad to meet you.—   Science is
courir *   de   art. ——f.
estimable, but   virtue is much *more* so. —*Almost* all the
——   art.   *l'*   *bien*   *
philosophers think so. — He has *so many* friends! — He
                 ainsi.   d'
drinks *too much*.—She speaks *much* and reflects *little*.

344. *Adverbs of Comparison.*

			[*better.*
Ainsi,	*thus, so.*	de mieux en mieux,	*better and*
aussi,	*as, too, also.*	moins,	*less.*
autant,	*as much, as many.*	pis,	*worse.*
comme,	*as, like.*	plus,	*more*
mieux,	*better.*	si,	*so.*

EXERCISE CXVI.

The president spoke *thus*. — That book has merit; but
     président   du
there are others *as* good. — If he has done that, I can do
   en   *   d'   en
as much. — There were *as many* ladies as   gentlemen.—
                      ind-2   de   que de monsieur
Don't read *like* him. —   Women speak *better* than they
                        art.   qu'
  write.—She sings *better and better*.— Since the invention of
n'   Depuis   ——f.
  powder,   battles are *less* bloody than they   were.—
art. poudre f. art.   sanglant qu'   ne l' ind-2
His affairs are going from bad to *worse*. — You do not offer
                        mal en
enough, give something   *more*. — I was *so* far from them!
                           de   ind-2   loin   86

345. *Adverbs of Order, or Rank.*

Premièrement,	*first.*	après,	*after.*
secondement, &c.	*secondly, &c.*	ensuite,	*afterwards.*
d'abord,	*at first, first.*	auparavant,	*before.*

178 EXERCISE ON ADVERBS OF ORDER, AND PLACE.

346. *Adverbs of Place.*

Ailleurs,	*elsewhere.*	loin,	*far.*
ici,	*here.*	partout,	*everywhere.*
là,	*there.*	y,	*there.*

REMARK.—*Y* adverb comes from the Latin *ibi*, there; it must not be confounded with the relative pronoun *Y*, which has the sense of *to him, to her, to it, to them*, &c.—See No. 109.

EXERCISE CXVII.

Do *first* what we have agreed upon. — Work *first*, you
            ce dont   252   *   d'abord
will amuse yourself *afterwards.* — You will go before, and he
                                            devant   lui
after.—The painter had brought together in the same picture
                      ind-2 *rassembler*   *un*   *tableau* m.
several different objects; *there* a troop of bacchants, *here* a
             2   1   *bacchante*
group of young people; *there* a sacrifice; *here* a disputation of
         gens   —— m.   *dispute* f.
philosophers.—Alexander gave to Porus a kingdom larger
                Alexandre ind-3 ——   *plus grand*
than the one he had *before.* — Don't go *far.* — I have
      celui qu' ind-2
looked for it *everywhere.* — Will you go *there after* dinner?
chercher   *Vouloir*   *y*

347. *Adverbs of Time.*

Present.

| Aujourd'hui, | *to-day.* | maintenant, | *now.* |

Past.

| Autrefois, | *formerly.* | hier, | *yesterday.* [terday. |
| dernièrement, | *lately.* | avant-hier, | *the day before yes-* |

Future.

Demain,	*to-morrow.*	bientôt,	*soon, very soon.*
après-demain,	*the day after*	désormais,	*hereafter.*
	to-morrow.	dorénavant,	*henceforth.*

Indeterminate.

Alors,	*then.*	rarement,	*seldom.*
longtemps,	*long.*	souvent,	*often.*
quelquefois,	*sometimes*	toujours,	*always*

EXERCISE CXVIII.

We expect him *to-day* or *to-morrow*. — *Formerly*, the
    attendre
education of females was neglected, but *now* it is very much
   art. *femme* ind-2 *négligé*   on * ³*beaucoup*
(attended to). — He set out *the day before yesterday*.—Let us
¹*s'en* ²*occupe*   *est parti*
be wiser *hereafter*. — Be more exact *henceforth*.—Where were
     ²   ¹   —   ind-2
you *then ?*—He goes *sometimes* on foot, *sometimes* in a coach.—
             à   en * *voiture*.
That *seldom* occurs. — People *often* deceive themselves by
     arriver   On   *se tromper*   en
judging from appearances. — The wisest kings are *often*
       sur art. *apparence* f.
deceived. — The moon *always* revolves round the earth.
tromper   *tourner autour de*

348. *Adverbs of Manner and Quality.*

Bien,	well.	à la mode,	fashionably.
mal,	badly, ill.	à tort,	wrongfully.
à la hâte,	hastily.	exprès,	on purpose.

To this class must be added the adverbs formed from adjectives, by annexing *ment*. There are, in French, few adjectives, from which adverbs of this nature have not been formed. This termination in *ment* corresponds to the *ly* of the English, and comes from the Italian substantive *mente*, itself derived from the Latin substantive *mens, mentis*, which signifies *mind, intention, manner;* so that *tendrement, fortement*, have the same meaning as "in a tender manner," "in a strong manner."

These adverbs are formed from adjectives in the following manner:—

349. RULE I. When the adjective ends with a vowel, in the masculine, the adverb is formed by simply adding *ment* to it; as,

poli,	polite;	poliment,	politely.
sage,	wise;	sagement,	wisely.
vrai,	true;	vraiment,	truly.

Exception.—*Impuni,* unpunished, makes *impunément,* with impunity.

The six following adverbs take an *é* accented before the termination *ment,* instead of the *e* mute of the adjectives:—

Aveuglément, *blindly.*	énormément, *enormously.*
commodément, *commodiously.*	incommodément, *incommodiously.*
conformément, *conformably.*	opiniâtrément, *obstinately.*

Bellement, softly; *follement,* foolishly; *mollement,* effeminately; and *nouvellement,* newly, are formed from the adjectives, *bel, fol, mol, nouvel,* according to the following rule.

350. RULE II. When the adjective ends with a consonant, in the masculine, the adverb is formed from the feminine, by adding *ment* to it; as,

franc, *m.*	franche, *f.*	*frank;*	franchement,	*frankly.*
heureux, *m.*	heureuse, *f.*	*happy;*	heureusement,	*happily.*
naïf, *m.*	naïve, *f.*	*artless;*	naïvement,	*artlessly.*

Exception.—*Gentil,* makes *gentiment,* prettily.

The six following adverbs take an *é* accented, instead of the *e* mute of the feminine of the adjectives from which they are formed:—

Communément, *commonly.*	obscurément, *obscurely.*
confusément, *confusedly.*	précisément, *precisely.*
expressément, *expressly.*	profondément, *profoundly.*

351. RULE III. Adjectives ending in *ant* or *ent,* in the masculine, form their adverbs by changing *ant* into *amment,* and *ent* into *emment;* as,

constant, *constant;*	constamment,	*constantly.*
éloquent, *eloquent;*	éloquemment,	*eloquently.*

Lent, slow, and *présent,* present, are the only exceptions to this rule; they follow the second rule, making *lentement,* slowly, and *présentement,* presently.

N.B. Most adverbs of manner, and a few of the other classes, have the three degrees of comparison, which are formed as in the adjectives.

352. The following adverbs are irregular in French, as well as in English:—

Positive.	Comparative.	Superlative.
bien, *well*.	mieux, *better*.	le mieux, *the best*.
mal, *badly*.	pis, *worse*.	le pis, *the worst*.
peu, *little*.	moins, *less*.	le moins, *the least*.

(See previous Remarks on these Adverbs, No. 70.)

EXERCISE CXIX.

(*N. B.*—In the two following Exercises, some Adjectives are given, from which the Student will form Adverbs, according to the foregoing rules.)

All goes *well*. — I say it *on purpose*. — He has done that
   aller   dire   faire

very *cleverly*. — He acts *conformably* to your orders. — Speak
fort habile   agir

to me *frankly*. — He is *dangerously* wounded. — Corneille and
                                             dangereux

Racine are the two best French tragic poets; the pieces of
                                   ³ ²*tragique* ¹   pièce f.

the former are *strongly*, but *incorrectly* written; those of the
  premier   ²fort   ³ ⁴incorrect ¹

latter are more *regularly* beautiful, more *purely* expressed,
 dernier   régulier   beau   pur   exprimé

and more *delicately* conceived. — You walk too *slowly*.
         délicat   pensé

EXERCISE CXX.

I want shoes that I can put on *easily*. — He receives
 vouloir 32   subj-1   *   aisé

²*everybody* ¹(very *politely*).—Read *attentively*.—The lion is
tout le monde   attentif

naturally courageous.—The ancients believed that the swan
 naturel   ancien ind-2   cygne m.

sang *melodiously*, when it was about to die.—We see *evidently*
ind-2 mélodieux lorsqu' ind-2 près de   évident

that three times three make nine.—That affair goes *badly*.—
         fois   affaire f.

Sit upon this sofa; you will be *better* than on that
Asseyez-vous   —— m.

chair.—Of all our great writers, he is the one I like *best*.
chaise f.   écrivain d'   celui que   le

CHAPTER VII.

OF THE PREPOSITION.

353. The *Preposition* is an invariable part of speech, so called, because, as its Latin derivation implies, it is generally *placed before* the word whose relation to other words it points out.

It is by means of *prepositions* that we supply the *cases* which are wanting in the French language; for instance, the preposition *de* often corresponds to the genitive or ablative of the Latin. *Le livre* DE *Pierre.*—*Je viens* DE *Rome.*

Prepositions are either *simple* or *compound*. The simple consist of a single word; as, *à*, to; *de*, of; *avec*, with. Compound prepositions consist of two or more words; such are, *quant à*, as to; *vis-à-vis*, opposite; *à l'égard de*, with regard to.

The prepositions are divided into classes, according to the manner in which they express relation or connexion.

354. *To denote Place.*

Auprès,	near.	près,	near.
autour,	round, around.	proche,	near.
chez,	at.	sous,	under.
dans,	in.	sur,	on, upon, over.
devant,	before.	vers,	towards.
derrière,	behind.		(*Vers* is also a prep.
entre,	between.		of time.)
hors,	out.	vis-à-vis,	opposite.
jusque,	till, until.	voici,	behold, *here is* or *are.*
parmi,	among.	voilà,	behold, *there is* or *are.*

EXERCISE CXXI.

Chicanery prowls incessantly *around* justice, envy
art. *chicane* f. *rôder sans cesse* *de Thémis* art.
around prosperity, calumny *around* virtue,
de art. art. *de* art. art.

error *around* the mind of man, and injustice *around*
de esprit m. art. art. —— f.
his heart: what ravages do these monsters not commit
de —— m. * ne font-ils pas,
when once they can gain access! — *In* prosperity it is
 une fois pénétrer! art. il
agreeable to have a friend; *in* misfortune it is a necessity.—
 d' art. malheur m. c' besoin m.
Write injuries *upon* sand, and benefits *upon*
 art. art. art. bienfait m. art.
brass. — The loadstone points *towards* the north. —
airain m. aimant m. se tourner
Paper was invented *towards* the end of the fourteenth
art. ind-4 fin f.
century; and printing *towards* the middle of the
siècle m. art. imprimerie f. milieu m
fifteenth century.—Go *before* me, and not *behind* him.

355. *To denote Order.*

Avant, *before.* | depuis, *since.*
après, *after.* | dès, *from.*

356. *To denote Union.*

Avec, *with.* | outre, *besides.*
durant, *during.* | selon, ⎫
pendant, *whilst, during.* | suivant, ⎬ *according to.*

EXERCISE CXXII.

Augustus began to reign forty-two years *before* Jesus Christ.—
Auguste ind-3 Jésus ——
I fear God, and *after* God, I fear principally those who do not
  ceux
fear him. — Man *from* his birth has the feeling of
 art. sentiment m. art.
pleasure and of pain. —The soldier defends his country
 art. douleur f. * art. patrie f.
with his sword; the man of letters enlightens it *with* his pen.—
  éclairer
It is *during* youth that we must lay the foundations of
 pendant art. il faut poser fondement

an honourable and happy life. — The wise man acts
      2   3   4   1   * *se conduire*
according to the dictates of reason. — Talents
             maxime f.   art.   art.   —— m.
(are productive) *according to* their cultivation.
  produisent   *   art. *culture* f.

357. To denote Separation or Privation.

Sans, *without.* | hors, *except, save.*
excepté, *except.* | hormis, *except, but.*

358. To denote Opposition.

Contre, *against.* | nonobstant, *notwith-*
malgré, *in spite of.* | [*standing.*

EXERCISE CXXIII.

No virtue *without* religion, no happiness *without* virtue.—
Point de   ——

A child *without* innocence is a flower *without* perfume.—Where
        ——   *parfum.*

(will you find) roses *without* thorns ?—We must always be
  trouver inf-1 *des* ——   *Il faut*   2   1

ready to serve our friends, *except against* our conscience. —
               ses   *sa*   ——f.

All is lost *save* honour. — Truth, *notwithstanding*
                art.   art.

prejudice, error and falsehood, (clears its way)
art. *préjugé* m. art.   art. *mensonge* m. *se fait jour*

and penetrates at last. — The hedgehog knows how to
  percer à la fin.   *hérisson* m. *h* a. 265 * *

defend himself *without* fighting.—He has done it *in spite of* me.
 se   *combattre.*

359. To denote the End.

Envers, *towards.* | concernant, *concerning.*
pour, *for.* | touchant, *about, respecting.*

360. To denote Cause and Means.

Par, *by.* | attendu, *on account of.*
moyennant, *by means of.* | vu, *considering.*

EXERCISE CXXIV.

Fulfil your duties *towards* God, *towards* your parents,
Remplir
and *towards* your country. — That letter is not *for* you.
                   *   art. *patrie* f.
— It was at the entrance of Edward III. into Calais,
Ce ind-3   *entrée* f.   *Edouard*   *dans*
in 1347, that (the drum was heard to beat) *for* the first
l'an   *l'on entendit battre le tambour*
time. — He has written to him *respecting* that business. — She
fois f.   *affaire* f.
charms everybody *by* her kindness and her gentleness. —
       tout le monde   *bonté* f.   *douceur* f.
They will succeed *by means of* your counsels. — The fleet
       réussir   *avis* m.
cannot sail *on account of* contrary winds.
      partir   art. ²   ¹

361. The preposition à is used to express several relations, the principal of which are:—

1. *place;* as, *aller à Paris,* to go *to* Paris; *demeurer à Londres,* to live *in* London.
2. *time;* as, *se lever à six heures,* to rise *at* six o'clock.
3. *matter;* as, *bâtir à chaux,* to build *with* lime.
4. *manner;* as, *s'habiller à la française,* to dress *after* the French fashion.
5. *cause;* as, *un moulin à vent,* a windmill; *des armes à feu,* firearms.
6. *use, destination;* as, *un moulin à papier,* a paper-mill; *un sac à ouvrage,* a work-bag.
7. *means;* as, *peindre à l'huile,* to paint *in* oil.
8. *possession;* as, *ce livre est à Alfred,* this book belongs *to* Alfred.

EXERCISE CXXV.

There are two railways from Paris *to* Versailles.—How far
       186   *chemin de fer*   ——   *Combien*
is it from London *to* Edinburgh?—The neglect of all religion
y a-t-il   *Edimbourg?*   *oubli* m.   ——f.
soon leads *to* the neglect of all the duties of man.—
bientôt   284   *devoir* m.   art.

Hypocrisy is a homage that vice pays *to*
art.   *hommage* m.   art. —m. *rendre*   art.
virtue. — Come back *at* six o'clock. — We left   him
            Revenir   *heure*   *quitter* ind-4
at (twelve o'clock).—That is *at* the rate of five per cent.—
    midi.   *C'*   * *raison*   *pour*
The walls of this ancient castle are built *with* lime and
     mur m.   *château* m.   *bâtir*   prep.
cement.—It is a steam-engine of (twenty-horse power).
ciment.   *C'*   *machine à vapeur* f.   *la force de vingt chevaux.*

362. The principal use of DE is to express:—

1. *place;* as, *venir* de *Lyon,* to come *from* Lyons.
2. *time;* as, *il est parti* de *jour,* he went away *in* the day-time.
3. *matter;* as, *une table* de *marbre,* a marble table; *une tabatière* d'*or,* a gold snuffbox.
4. *possession;* as, *le livre* de *Berthe,* Bertha's book.
5. *subject;* as, *parlons* de *cette affaire,* let us speak *of* that affair.
6. *cause, motive;* as, *je suis charmé* de *sa fortune,* I am happy *at* his fortune.

EXERCISE CXXVI.

We come *from* Dublin, where we have spent a week very
          ——   *où*   *passer huit jours*
agreeably.—I intend to go *from* France to Switzerland;
          se proposer d'   *en*   *Suisse*
and *from* Switzerland to Italy.—The seven wonders *of* the
                Italie.   *merveille* f.
world were, the walls and gardens *of* Babylon; the
     ind-2   *muraille* f.   art.   *Babylone*·
pyramids *of* Egypt; the pharos *of* Alexandria; the
pyramide f.   *Egypte;*   *phare* m.
mausoleum which Artemisia erected for Mausolus, her husband;
tombeau m.   *Artémise fit élever*   *Mausole*
the temple *of* Diana at Ephesus; the statue *of* Jupiter
        —— m.   *Ephèse;*   —— f.   ——
Olympius, by Phidias; and the colossus at Rhodes.
Olympien,   ——   *colosse* m. de   ——

363. The preposition EN serves to mark the relations of *place, time, situation, &c.*, and is variously expressed in English.

    1. *place;* as, *voyager* en *Allemagne,* to travel *in* Germany; *aller* en *Italie,* to go *to* Italy.
    2. *time;* as, en *hiver, in* winter; en *temps de paix, in* time of peace.
    3. *situation, manner;* as, *être* en *bonne santé,* to be *in* good health; *agir* en *maître,* to act *as* a master.

364. REMARK.—The noun which follows *en* seldom admits of the article, whereas the noun which comes after *dans* is generally preceded by the article.

EXERCISE CXXVII.

²(The same prejudices) ¹(are found) *in* Europe, *in* Asia, *in*
   préjugé m.   *on trouve*   ———
Africa, and even *in* America. — I have travelled *in* England,
          jusqu'   *Amérique.*
Scotland, and Ireland. — Queen Elizabeth was born
pr. *Ecosse*   pr. *Irlande.* art.   *Elisabeth*   *naître* ind-3
in 1533, and died *in* 1603. — Narcissus was metamorphosed
            ind-3   *Narcisse* ind-3 *métamorphosé*
into a flower. — He has acted, on this occasion, *like* a great
  *   *agir dans*   ———f.   *
man. — Conscience warns us *as* a friend before punishing
         art. ———f. *avertir*   *   *de* inf-1
us *as* a judge. — My grandmother is alive and *in* good health
    *

EXERCISE CXXVIII.

My father is *in* Russia, my brother *in* Prussia, and my sister *in*
           Russie   *Prusse*
Austria. — (It is computed) that there are *in* France four hundred
Autriche.   *On compte* *   *   *
towns, and forty-three thousand villages. — I can go *in* one
                                   pouvoir
day from Edinburgh to London, and *in* two days from London to
                    à
Geneva. — He spends the whole day in going from house *to*
         passer   à inf-1
house, from street *to* street, and from place *to* place.

CHAPTER VIII.

OF THE CONJUNCTION.

365. The *Conjunction* is an invariable part of speech, which serves to connect words or sentences. When I say :—

Travaillons, SI nous voulons acquérir des talents, CAR le temps s'enfuit, ET persuadons-nous bien QU'il ne revient plus.	*Let us work, if we wish to possess acquirements, for time flies, and let us never forget that it returns no more.*

In this phrase the words *si*, if, *car*, for, *et*, and, *que*, that, are conjunctions, as they serve to unite the different parts of the sentence.

366. Some conjunctions are *simple*, that is, they consist of a single word; as, *ou*, or; *mais*, but; others are *compound*, that is, composed of two or more words, such are, *au reste*, besides; *à moins que*, unless.

Some grammarians reckon as many sorts of conjunctions as there are ways in which the sentence is affected by them, but as these properties are common to both languages, we shall content ourselves with giving here a list of the conjunctions most in use in the French language.

367. TABLE OF CONJUNCTIONS.

Afin de,	*to, in order to.*	ni,	*nor, neither.*
afin que,	*that, in order that.*	or,	*now, then.*
ainsi,	*so, thus.*	ou,	*or.*
car,	*for.*	ou bien,	*or else.*
cependant,	*however, yet.*	parce que,	*because.*
c'est-à-dire,	*that is to say.*	pendant que,	*while, whilst.*
comme,	*as.*	pourtant,	*however, yet.*
d'ailleurs,	*besides.*	pourvu que,	*provided that.*
de plus,	*moreover.*	puisque,	*since.*
de sorte que,	*so that.*	quand,	*though, although.*
donc,	*then, therefore.*	que,	*that.*
et,	*and.*	quoique,	*though, although.*
jusqu'à ce que,	*till, until.*	savoir,	*namely, to wit, viz*
lorsque,	*when.*	si,	*if.*
mais,	*but.*	sinon,	*if not, or else.*
néanmoins,	*nevertheless.*	soit,	*whether.*

EXERCISE CXXIX.

I have brought this book *in order* to consult it.—To listen
       livre m.   Ecouter
with joy to a slanderer, *and* to applaud him, is to cherish
   * médisant m. *   lui c' réchauffer
the serpent that stings, *in order that* he may sting more
 ——m.   piquer
effectually.—David was a king *and* a prophet.—All the
sûrement. ——ind-2 *   *
evils are (long ago) out of the box of Pandora, *but*
mal m. depuis longtemps hors   boîte f.
 hope is yet within.—The compass was not
art. encore dedans.   boussole f. n' ind-4 *point*
invented by a mariner, *nor* the telescope by an astronomer, *nor*
trouvée marin m.   télescope m.
the microscope by a (natural philosopher), *nor* printing
 ——m.   physicien m.   art. imprimerie f.
by a man of letters, *nor* gunpowder by a military man.
homme de lettres art. poudre à canon f.   *

EXERCISE CXXX.

Which of the two was most intrepid, Cæsar *or* Alex-
     ind-3 le
ander?—The memory of Henry IV. is *and* always will be
       Henri
dear to the French, *because* he placed his glory *and*
   pl.   mettre ind-2   91
happiness in rendering his people happy.—*Provided* you
  à inf-1   qu' on
know the ruling passion of anyone you are sure to
sache ³dominant ¹——f. quelqu'un, on assuré de
please him.—The Gauls worshipped Apollo, Minerva,
 lui   Gaulois adorer ind-2 Apollon,
Jupiter, *and* Mars; they believed *that* Apollo kept off
 ——   ——   ind-2   chasser ind-2
 diseases; *that* Minerva presided over works; *that*
art. maladie f.   ind-2 à art. travail m.
Jupiter was the sovereign of heaven; *and* Mars the arbiter
  ind-2   art. pl.
of war.—*If* you wish to be happy, love virtue.
 art.   276 *

CHAPTER IX.

OF THE INTERJECTION.

368. The *Interjection* is a word which serves to express some sudden emotion of the mind.

The interjections most commonly used in French, are:—

I. *For Joy.*
Ah! ah!
bon! well!

II. *For Grief and Pain.*
Ah! ah!
aïe! ay! oh dear!
hélas! alas!

III. *For Fear.*
Ah! ah!
hé! oh!

IV. *For Aversion, Contempt, and Disgust.*
Fi! fy!
fi donc! fy! fy!

V. *For Derision.*
Oh! oh!
hé! hah!
zest! pshaw!
bah! nonsense!

VI. *For Surprise.*
Oh! oh!
ha! ha!

VII. *For Admiration.*
Oh! oh!
ah! ha!

VIII. *For Silence.*
Chut! hush!
st! hist!

IX. *For Encouraging.*
Çà! } now! well!
oh çà! } go on!

X. *For Warning.*
Gare! take care!
holà! hold!
hem! hem!
oh! oh!

XI. *For Calling.*
Holà! holla!
hé! eh! ho!

XII. Ô (with a circumflex accent) is an interjection which serves to express various emotions of the mind; it is seldom used but in conjunction with a substantive.

Although several of the preceding interjections are the same for different emotions, yet they vary much in the utterance.

Certain words and phrases that are not interjections in their nature, become such when expressed with emotion, and in an unconnected manner; as, *paix!* peace! *courage!* cheer up! *tout beau!* gently! not so fast! Such are also many words used by the great dramatist *Molière;* as, *morbleu! parbleu! corbleu!*

EXERCISE CXXXI.

Ah! how glad I am to see you! — *Ah!* the cowards,
que ²aise ¹ de lâche
exclaimed Pompey. — *Ay!* you hurt me! — *Alas!* I have
s'écrier Pompée. blesser
lost everything. — *Ha!* you (are there). — *Oh, oh!* I
² ¹tout voilà.
thought the contrary. — *Hush!* some one is coming.—
croire ind-2 quelqu'un
Holla! who is there? — O my son, adore God. — O supreme
là?
pleasure to practise virtue!—Come, my friends, *cheer up!*
de pratiquer art. Allons,

EXERCISE CXXXII.

Ha! how beautiful that is! — *Now!* do tell me what
que ³ ¹cela ² * ce que
you think. — *Hush! peace!* — *Hah!* I think your lordship
penser croire que
(is making game) of me. — *Holla!* where are you? — *Ah* my
se moque
friend! why dost thou wish to undertake that fatiguing
vouloir * ²fatigant
journey? — *Beware* of the bomb! — *Fy!* what infamy!
¹royage m. * bombe f.
plague take the rogue, to wish to beat his wife.—*Fy! fy!*—
soit du coquin de *
Gently, Sir, speak of him with more respect. — *Courage,*
lui 344 de
soldiers, fear nothing!

END OF PART I.

PART II.

OF SYNTAX.

369. The word *Syntax* comes from a Greek word which means *arrangement, construction.* Syntax teaches the regular construction of the different parts of speech, conformably to the rules of grammar, and the genius of a language.

CHAPTER I.

OF THE ARTICLE.

370. GENERAL PRINCIPLE.—The article is to be used, in French, before every *common* noun, taken *in a determinate sense,* unless there be another word performing the same office; but it is not to be used before nouns taken *in an indeterminate sense.*

CASES IN WHICH THE ARTICLE IS TO BE USED.

371. RULE I. The article is used, in French, before all nouns employed in a general sense, or in the full extent of their signification, although not used in English; as,

L'homme est mortel.	*Man is mortal.*
La guerre est un fléau.	*War is a scourge.*

Man is here employed in a general sense for all mankind, and *War* is taken for war in general, and not for any particular war.

EXERCISE CXXXIII.

Ladies have always reverenced *fashion*. — *Liberty* is the
　　　　　révérer　　　　mode f.

natural state　of *man*. — *Heroes* have their moments of fear,
　　　¹*état* m.　　　　　　*héros*　　　　　　　　　　crainte,

and *cowards* their moments of bravery. — *Children* owe
　　　lâche　　　　　　　　bravoure.　　　　　　　　doivent

respect to their masters. — *Fear* and *ignorance* are the sources
　maître

of *superstition*. — *Interest* is the　touchstone　of *friendship*.
　　　—— f.　　 intérêt m.　pierre de touche f.

— *Honour*　is badly guarded, when *religion* is not at the
　honneur h m u.　mal　gardé, lorsque

out-posts. — *Contentment* prolongs *life*. — *Vice* is odious.
avant-postes.　　prolonger　　　　　　　m.　　　odieux.

EXERCISE CXXXIV.

Bread is the staff　of *life*. — *Necessity* is the mother of
　　　　　soutien m.　　f.

invention. — *Custom* is the legislator　of *languages*. —
　　　　　　　usage m.　　législateur m.　　langue f.

Success　repays us for all our troubles. — There is nothing
succès m.　paie　de　　　　peine f.　　　Il

that *man* gives so　liberally　as *counsel*. — *Innoculation*
que　　　　　　aussi libéralement que conseil pl.　　—— f.

passed　from Constantinople to London in 1721, and to
passer ind-3　　　　　　　　à　　　　en

Paris in 1755. — The Persians who worshipped　*fire*, and the
　　　　　　　　Perse　qui　adorer　ind-2

Egyptians who worshipped *crocodiles*, were idolaters.
Egyptien　　　　　　　　—— m. ind-2 *idolâtre*

　372. RULE II. The article is used in both languages before nouns denoting a particular thing or object, one particular individual or class; as,

LA terre tourne autour du soleil, et LA lune tourne autour de la terre. L'homme dont vous parlez, est un de mes amis.	The *earth* turns round *the sun*, and the *moon* turns round *the earth*. The *man of whom* you speak *is* a friend *of mine*.

EXERCISE CXXXV.

The diseases of the mind are more difficult to cure than
      maladie f.   âme f.   difficile   guérir que

those of the body. — *The* empire of Alexander was divided
99   — m.   ind-3 *partagé*

among his generals.—*The* Parthenon was in *the* citadel of
entre   Parthénon m. ind-2   citadelle f.

Athens. —*The* city of Rome was founded 753 years before
Athènes.   ville f.   a été fondé   an m.

Jesus Christ. — Fabius was appointed dictator in *the* war
Jésus-Christ.   ——   ind-3 *nommé dictateur*

against Hannibal. — *The* Roman empire extended from *the*
Annibal.   ²   ¹   s'étendait depuis

Western Ocean to the Euphrates. — (According to)
²occidental ¹Océan m. jusqu' à   Euphrate.   Selon

the poets, *the* car of Venus was drawn by doves.
   poëte m.   char m. Vénus ind-2 attelé de colombe f.

EXERCISE CXXXVI.

The birth of JESUS CHRIST is *the* era of the Christians,
     naissance f.   ère f.

and *the* flight of Mahomet is that of the Mahometans,
     fuite f.   99   mahométan

commonly called *the* hegira. — *The* first year of
²ordinairement ¹appelée hégire h mu.   année f.

the hegira corresponds to *the* year 622 of JESUS CHRIST.—
            répond

In *the* time of Philip the Fair†, there were only *the* dukes,
De   Philippe-le-Bel, il n'y avait que   duc

the counts, and *the* barons whose ladies had the
   comte   ——   dont art. femme eussent

right to (treat themselves) with four gowns a year. —
droit m. de se donner   *   robe f. par an.

The invention of *the* barometer is due to Pascal.
    —— f.   baromètre m.   ——

---

† Ascended the throne in 1285; died in 1314.

SYNTAX OF THE ARTICLE. 195

373. RULE III. The article is used, in French, before the names of arts, sciences, virtues, vices, metals; and also before adjectives, infinitives, adverbs, prepositions, and conjunctions, used substantively; as,

L'ivrognerie est un vice affreux.	Drunkenness is a dreadful vice.
LE vert plaît aux yeux.	Green pleases the eye.
LE savoir a son prix.	Knowledge has its value.

374. *N.B.*—Adjectives, verbs, adverbs, etc. used substantively, are masculine in French.

EXERCISE CXXXVII.

Before studying *navigation* and *fortification* (it is necessary to)
Avant d' étudier —— f. —— pl. *il faut*

know *mathematics.* — *Grammar* teaches to speak correctly,
265 *mathématiques* pl. *apprendre à correctement*

rhetoric to speak elegantly. —*Chronology* and *geography*
rhétorique f. *élégamment. chronologie* f. *géographie* f.

are the eyes of history.—*Faith, hope,* and *charity* are
yeux art. foi f. espérance f. des

cardinal virtues. — *Intemperance* and *idleness* are the two
²théologale ¹ paresse f.

most dangerous enemies of life.—The principal metals are:
plus ennemi m. art. f.

gold, silver, copper, tin, iron, and *lead.* — He
or m. argent m. cuivre m. étain m. fer m. plomb m.

knows *Latin* and *French.* — She (is fond of) *blue.* — *Eating,*
savoir aime bleu. manger

drinking, and *sleeping,* are necessary to man.
boire dormir art.

375. RULE IV. The article is put before the names of countries, provinces, islands, mountains, rivers, and winds; but countries having the same name as their capitals do not take the article; as,

L'Angleterre et LA France sont deux états puissants.	England and France are two powerful states.
Naples est un pays délicieux.	Naples is a delightful country.

EXERCISE CXXXVIII.

Europe contains the following states: on the north,
contenir ²*suivant* ¹*état* m. à nord m.
Norway, Sweden, Denmark, Russia, and the *British*
Norwége f. *Suède* f. *Danemark* m. *Russie* f. ²*Britanniques*
Islands; in the middle, *France, Belgium, Holland,*
¹*îles* à milieu m. ──f. *Belgique* f. *Hollande* f.
Germany or the (German States), *Prussia, Poland,*
Allemagne f. * *Confédération germanique, Prusse* f. *Pologne* f.
Hungary, Austria, and *Switzerland;* on the south,
Hongrie f. *h* asp. *Autriche* f. *Suisse* f. à midi m.
Spain, Portugal, Italy, Greece, and *Turkey* in Europe.
Espagne f. ──m. *Italie* f. *Grèce* f. *Turquie* f. d'
—*Lapland* is the country of the reindeer. — *Burgundy*
Laponie f. patrie f. renne m. *Bourgogne* f.
produces excellent wine.—*Sicily* is the granary of *Italy.*
produire d' *Sicile* f. grenier m.

EXERCISE CXXXIX.

France is separated from *Italy* by *the* Alps, and from
séparé *Alpes* f. pl.
Spain by *the* Pyrenees. — The principal rivers of *Europe*
Pyrénées f. pl. rivière f.
are: *the* Volga, *the* Dnieper or Boristhenes, *the* Don or
── m. *Dniéper* m. *Borysthènes* ── m.
Tanaïs, in Russia; *the* Danube, *the* Rhine, and *the* Elbe,
── en ── m. *Rhin* m. ── m.
in Germany; *the* Vistula, in Poland; *the* Loire, *the* Seine,
Vistule f. ──f. ──f.
the Rhone, and *the* Garonne, in France; *the* Ebro, *the*
Rhône m. ──f. *Èbre* m.
Tagus, and *the* Douro, in Spain; *the* Po, and *the* Tiber,
Tage m. ── m. *Pô* m. *Tibre* m.
in Italy; *the* Thames, *the* Mersey, and *the* Severn, in England;
Tamise f. ──f. *Saverne* f.
and *the* Shannon, in Ireland. — The first pheasants came
── m. *Irlande.* faisan m. sont venus
from the banks of *the* Phasis, a river of *Colchis.*
bord m. *Phase* m. * fleuve m. *Colchide* f.

EXCEPTIONS AND REMARKS.

376. (1.) The article is not used before the names of countries when they are preceded by the preposition *en;* as, *Demeurer* en *Angleterre,* to live *in* England; *Aller* en *Allemagne,* to go *to* Germany.

With the names of towns, the preposition *à,* and not *en,* is used; as, *Demeurer* à *Londres,* to live *in* London; *Etre* à *Paris,* to be *in* Paris.

377. (2.) When the names of countries are governed by some preceding noun, and have the meaning of an adjective, they are used without the article; as, *roi d'Espagne,* king of Spain; *vins de France,* French wines; *laine d'Angleterre,* English wool.

378. (3.) The article is not used when we speak of countries as of places one comes or sets out from; as, *Il vient d'Italie,* he comes from Italy; *j'arrive de France,* I am just arrived from France. In this case, however, we use the article before the names of the five great divisions of the world; as, *je viens de l'Asie, il arrive de l'Amérique.*

379. (4.) Most names of countries out of Europe, keep the article; therefore, instead of the prepositions *en* and *de,* used alone, as in the preceding cases, we employ the prepositions *à* and *de,* with the article; thus we say, *je vais* au *Japon* (and not *en* Japon), I am going to Japan; *j'arrive* du *Canada* (and not *de* Canada), I am just arrived from Canada.

EXERCISE CXL.

In *Norway,* they cover the houses with the bark of the
En on *couvrir* avec *écorce* f.
birch-tree. — We intend going *to Switzerland* and
bouleau m. *se proposer d'* inf-1 *en*
Italy. — Three English miles are a little more than
²*d'Angleterre* ¹*mille* m. *font* plus *d'*
one French league. — My brother will soon return *from*
²*de France* ¹*lieue* f. *revenir*
Russia. — I sailed from *Holland* for the Cape of
partir ind-3 *cap* m.

Good   Hope. — We had set out *from Africa,* when he
Bonne-Espérance.   ind-2 *partir*

arrived there. — He is gone *to China.* — Chocolate   was
ind-3   *y*   *aller*   *Chine* f.   *chocolat* m. ind-3

brought *from Mexico to Europe* by the Spaniards.
apporter   *Mexique* m. *en*   *Espagnol*

380. RULE V. Nouns used in a *partitive* sense, that is, denoting only a *part* of anything, which is marked in English by the words *some* or *any,* sometimes expressed and oftener understood, must be preceded in French by *du, de la, de l', des,* according to the gender and number of the noun.

EXAMPLES.

Donnez-moi *du* pain, *de la* viande, et *des* habits.	Give me some *bread, meat, and clothes.*
A-t-il *de l'*argent ou *des* amis?	Has he any *money* or any *friends?*

381. *Exception.*—When a noun in the *partitive* sense is preceded by an adjective, instead of *du, de la, de l', des,* the preposition *de* only is used; as,

Donnez-moi *de* bon pain, *de* bonne viande, et *de* bons habits.	Give me some *good bread, good meat, and good clothes.*

(For farther explanations, see No. 32, and the Remarks, p. 63.)

In these expressions: *des petits pois, des petites raves, des petits-pâtés, des petits-maîtres, des jeunes gens,* etc., the substantives are so united with the adjectives, as to form but one and the same word, and take the article according to Rule V.

We likewise say: *l'opinion* DES *anciens philosophes; la suite* DES *grandes passions; le propre* DES *belles actions,* etc., because, in expressions of this kind, the nouns are not used in a *partitive* but in a *general* sense.

EXERCISE CXLI.

I have bought *some* books. — Have you *any* change? —
                                                     monnaie f.

Provence and Languedoc produce *oranges, olives, almonds,*
—— f.   —— m. *produire* —— f. —— f. *amande* f.

SYNTAX OF THE ARTICLE. 199

chesnuts,   figs,   peaches, apricots,   and grapes. — He asks
châtaigne, f. figue f. pêche f. abricot m.   raisin m.

for red wine. — To write well, one must have good paper, good
 *   *   1   Pour *   1   il faut   *

ink, and good pens. — A great heart,   said a king of Persia,
encre f.   cœur m. ind-2   Perse

receives little presents with one hand, and makes large ones
                          d'   en faire grand   *

with the other. — (He is always seen) with   wits   or
 de   On le voit toujours   beaux-esprits

   great lords.   — Have you any green peas?
grands-seigneurs.   petits pois

382. RULE VI. The English make use of the indefinite article *a* or *an*, before nouns of measure, weight, and number; but the French use the article *le*, *la*; as,

Un schelling L'aune.	A shilling a yard.
Six sous LA livre.	Six-pence a pound.
Cinq schellings LE cent.	Five shillings a hundred.

383. But, in speaking of time, *a* or *an* is expressed in French by *par*; as, so much *a*-week, *tant* PAR *semaine*.

<small>A-head, is rendered by *par tête*;—so much each, *tant par personne*;—so much a lesson, *tant par leçon*.</small>

EXERCISE CXLII.

   Corn   sells at seven shillings *a* bushel. — The best
art. blé m. se vend *   boisseau m.

   French wines   sell   for five shillings *a* bottle. — That
²de France   ¹   se vendent *   bouteille f.

grocer, sells   sugar at three   pounds   *a* hundred-weight,
épicier m. vend art.   *   livres sterling   quintal m.

     coffee at two shillings *a* pound, and   pepper   at two-pence
art.   *   livre f.   art. poivre m. *

an ounce. — How much *a*   dozen? — (Here are) excellent
   once f.   douzaine f.   Voici

oysters at one shilling *a* hundred. — He gives him a hundred
huître f.   *

    pounds   *a* year; it is more than eight pounds *a* month.
livres sterling   d'   de

384. Rule VII. When the article is used before the first of a series of nouns, it must be repeated before each; as,

Je vis hier *le* roi, *la* reine, et *les* princes. | *I saw the king, queen, and princes, yesterday.*

So you will not say: *les officiers et soldats; le père et mère; les frères et sœurs;* but you will say: *les officiers et les soldats; le père et la mère; les frères et les sœurs.*

Note.—This rule applies to the prepositions *à* and *de*, and to all the words which hold the place of the article. We must therefore say: *J'ai parlé à la reine et à la princesse*, I have spoken to the queen and the princess. *Son père et sa mère,* his father and mother.

EXERCISE CXLIII.

The gentleman and lady are gone. — Gold, silver,
    monsieur   *dame*   *partis.* art.

health, honours, and pleasures, cannot make a man happy,
santé f.   *ne peuvent rendre l'*

without virtue. — Self-love and pride are
  art.   art. *amour-propre* m.   *orgueil* m.

always the offspring of a weak mind. — Innocence of
          partage m.   ²*faible* ¹*esprit* m. art. —— f.

    manners, sincerity, and abhorrence of vice
art. *mœurs* pl.   *horreur* h *mu.* art. — m.

inhabit this happy region. — Poetry painting, and music
habiter   *région* f. art. *poésie* f. *peinture* f. *musique* f.

are (sister arts).—The love for one's father and mother is
   sœurs.   *amour* m.   *son*

the basis of every virtue.—The city of Andrew and Peter
   base f. *tout* art. pl.   *ville* f.

385. Rule VIII. When two adjectives are united by the conjunction *et* (and), and one of them is intended to qualify a substantive expressed and the other a substantive understood, the article must be repeated, in French, before each adjective; as,

L'histoire ancienne et LA moderne. | *Ancient and modern history.*
Le premier et LE second étage. | *The first and the second floor.*
Les philosophes anciens et LES modernes. | *Ancient and modern philosophers.*

There are *two histories, two floors, philosophers* both ancient and modern; the one expressed, the other understood; therefore the article must be repeated.

☞ Observe that the substantive is not put in the plural: *l'histoire ancienne* et *la moderne, le premier* et *le second étage,* because these phrases are elliptical, and stand for *l'histoire ancienne* et *l'histoire moderne, le premier étage* et *le second étage.*

386. But, when the adjectives united by *et* (and), qualify only one substantive, and no other is understood, the article is not repeated; so we say with the modern grammarians: *Le sage et pieux Fénélon,* the wise and pious Fénélon; and with Boileau:

Le doux et tendre *ouvrage*—(The sweet and tender work)—

because it is the same person that is wise and pious, and the same work which is sweet and tender.

Note.—This rule, on the repetition or non-repetition of the Article, applies also to *mon, ton, son, leur, ce, cet, un, une,* etc.

EXERCISE CXLIV.

The first *and* the second volume.—The first *and* the fourth
　　　　　　　　　　　　　　　　　　　　　　　— m.

class.—The fifteenth *and* the sixteenth century　were marked
classe f.　　　　　　　　　　　　　　　　　*siècle* m.　ind-4 *marqué*

by great discoveries. — The faults　of Peter the Great
　381　　*découverte* f.　　　*défaut* m.　*Pierre*

tarnished　his great *and* admirable qualities. — Can anyone
ternir ind-4　　　　　　　*qualité* f.　　　　　*Peut-on*

contemplate the heavens,　without being convinced that
contempler　　*ciel* m. sing.　　　inf-1　*convaincre*

the universe is governed　by a supreme *and* divine Intelligence?
　　　　　　　gouverner　　　　　　　　　—　　—f.

— Homer has described men such as they were with *their*
　Homère　　*peindre*　　　*tel qu'*　　ind-2

good *and* bad qualities.—*My* brother and sister are going to Pau.
　　　　qualité f.

CASES IN WHICH THE ARTICLE IS NOT USED.

387. RULE I. The article is omitted before substantives, when, in using them, nothing is said as to the extent of their signification.

EXAMPLES.

Un tyran n'a ni *parents* ni *amis*.	*A tyrant has neither* relations *nor* friends.
Les chemins sont bordés de *lauriers*, de *grenadiers*, de *jasmins*, et d'autres *arbres* toujours verts et toujours fleuris.—(*Fénélon.*)	*The highways are bordered with* laurels, pomegranates, jessamines, *and other* trees *which are always green, and always in bloom.*

It follows from this rule that the article is not used before substantives:—

388. (1.) When they are in the form of a title or an address; as,

OBSERVATIONS sur l'état de l'Europe.	*Observations on the situation of Europe.*
Il demeure RUE Piccadilly, QUARTIER Saint-James.	*He lives in Piccadilly, St James's.*

389. (2.) When they are governed by the preposition *en;* as,

Etre en *ville*.	*To be in town.*
Vivre en *prince*.	*To live like a prince.*

390. (3.) When they are used as an apostrophe or interjection; as,

Courage, soldats, tenez ferme! | Courage, soldiers, *stand firm!*

We say, however, to a person whom we do not know, and with whom we are on no ceremony: *Ecoutez, l'homme!* Hark ye, my man!—*La fille, arrêtez!* Stop, girl! etc.—(*Dict. de l'Elocution Française.*)

391. No article is used, but simply the preposition *de*, after the words *sorte, genre, espèce, mélange,* and such like; as, *une sorte* DE *fruit,* a kind of fruit.

EXERCISE CXLV.

(We see there) neither *marble,* nor *columns,* nor *pictures,* nor
   On n'y voit   marbre   colonne   tableau
statues.—The fleets   of Solomon, under the conduct   of the
                 flotte f.   Salomon   conduite f.
Phœnicians, made frequent voyages to the land   of Ophir and
   Phénicien   ind-2   m.   terre f.   ——
     Tharsis, in Ethiopia, whence they returned   at the end
de ——   en   d'où   revenir ind-2   bout m.

of three years, laden with *gold, silver, ivory, precious*
                               chargé de   ivoire m.   ²

stones, and other *kinds* of merchandise. — I will pay you *in*
   ¹   espèce f.   marchandises.   en

gold. — He lived   and died *like a* philosopher. — Come,
              vivre ind-3   ind-3   *Allons*,

children, work. — That *kind*   of work does not please
                            genre m.   *ouvrage*   *plaire*

everybody. — *History* of the Roman emperors.
à tout le monde.   ²   ¹

392. RULE II. No article is used before proper names of deities, persons, animals, towns, and particular places.

EXAMPLES.

Dieu est tout-puissant.	God *is all-powerful.*
Jupiter et *Vénus* étaient des divinités païennes.	Jupiter *and* Venus *were heathen divinities.*
Edimbourg est une belle ville.	Edinburgh *is a fine city.*

Some proper names of towns and particular places always keep the article as an inseparable part of the name; as, *La Rochelle, La Flèche, la Haye, le Caire, la Mecque*, &c.

393. Proper names, however, take the article, when used in a particular sense, or to denote an individual distinction; as,

Le Dieu des Chrétiens.	The *God of the Christians.*
Le Jupiter d'Homère.	*Homer's Jupiter.*
La Vénus de Médicis.	The *Venus de' Medici.*

394. *Observation.*—In imitation of the Italians, the French use the article before the names of several celebrated Italian poets and painters, the word *poëte* or *peintre*, being then understood; as, *le Dante, le Tasse, l'Arioste, le Titien, le Guide*. However, we say *Pétrarque, Bocace, Michel-Ange, Raphaël*, etc.; it is usage that decides here, as in many other cases.

EXERCISE CXLVI.

God said. let there be light, and there was light. — *The*
     ind-3   *que la lumière soit*,   *   ²ind-3 ¹

God of *Abraham, Isaac*, and *Jacob*, was the only true God.
                                    ind-2   *seul vrai*

—*Plato, Aristotle, Homer, Demosthenes, Cicero, Virgil*, and
   Platon, Aristote,   *Démosthène, Cicéron, Virgile*,

Livy, are classical authors.—*Achilles* is the hero
Tite-Live, des ²classique ¹ *Achille héros* h *asp.*
of the Iliad; *Æneas* is the hero of the Eneid. — *Helen* was
Iliade f. *Enée Enéide* f. *Hélène* ind-4
the ruin of *Troy.* — *Bucephalus* (would carry none but) *Alex-*
Troie. Bucéphale ne voulait porter qu'
ander. — *Carthage* was the rival of *Rome.* — *Dante, Tasso,*
ind-2 *rivale* f.
and *Ariosto,* hold the first rank among the Italian poets.
tenir rang m. *parmi* ² ¹

395. RULE III. The article is not used, in French, before the ordinal numbers *first, second, third, fourth,* etc., when they come after the name of a sovereign, or after the words *book, chapter,* or such like; as,

Édouard premier.	*Edward* the *first.*
Richard trois.	*Richard* the *third.*
Livre premier.	*Book* the *first.*
Chapitre second.	*Chapter* the *second.*

396. Observe that, in French, we make use of the *cardinal* numbers instead of the *ordinal,* in speaking of sovereigns, with the exception of the *first* of the series. With the *second,* it is optional to use *deux* or *second,* for we say indifferently *Henri deux* or *Henri second.*—(*Acad.*)

397. The cardinal or ordinal numbers are indifferently used, the *first* excepted, after the words *livre, chapitre, page,* or such like. We say, *livre premier, section première,* and not *livre un, section une.* But we say either *livre huit* or *huitième; chapitre dix* or *dixième; page trois* or *troisième; tome second* or *tome deux,* etc.—(*Acad.*)

(For further Remarks, see pages 34, 35.)

EXERCISE CXLVII.

Pope Leo *the tenth* and Luther were cotemporaries. —
art. *pape Léon* —— *contemporain*
William *the third* married the princess Mary, daughter
Guillaume épouser ind-3 *Marie*
of James *the second,* and granddaughter of Charles *the first.*
Jacques petite-fille

—Louis *the eleventh* had a Scotch guard. — Louis *the fifteenth*
ind-2 ²*écossais* ¹*garde* f.

was the great grandson of Louis *the fourteenth.*—Book *the*
ind-2 *arrière-petit-fils*

sixth, chapter *the* fifth.—Volume *the* third, section *the* seventh,
—— f.

article *the* first. — Rule *the* fourth, page *the* ninth.
règle f.

398. RULE IV. No article is used before nouns preceded by any of the possessive, demonstrative, or indefinite adjectives *mon, ton, son, notre, votre, leur, ce, nul, aucun, chaque, tout* (used for *chaque*), *certain, plusieurs, tel,* nor before those which are preceded by a cardinal number; as,

Mon frère et *ma* sœur apprennent la géographie.	My brother and sister are learning geography.
Cette montre est bonne ; donnez-la à *votre* sœur.	This watch is good ; give it to your sister.
Tout homme peut mentir, mais *tout* homme ne ment pas.	Every man can lie, but every man does not lie.
J'ai *trois* chevaux.	I have three horses.

(See Observations, pp. 42, 43, and Rule, p. 44.)

EXERCISE CXLVIII.

It is *my* turn to speak. — Give me the number of *his*
C' à *tour* m. à *numéro* m.

house. — The Seine has *its* source in Burgundy, and *its*
f. —— f. en

mouth at Havre-de-Grâce. — All the husbands were at
embouchure f. *au* *mari* ind-2

the ball with *their* wives. — *These* ladies (are waiting for)
bal m. *femme* *dame* *attendent*

their carriages. — Those *two* boys have lost *their* hats. —
voiture f.

The Saracens occupied Spain during *several* centuries. —
Sarrasins ont occupé *pendant* *siècle* m.

The city of Troy sustained a siege of *ten* years. —
ville f *Troie soutint* *an* m.

The pound sterling (is worth) about *twenty-five* francs.
vaut *environ*

399. Rule V. The indefinite article, *a* or *an*, used in English, before nouns expressing *title, profession, trade, country*, or any attribute of the noun preceding, is omitted in French; as,

Le duc d'York, prince du sang.	The Duke of York, a prince of the blood.
Je suis médecin.	I am a physician.
Il est libraire.	He is a bookseller.
Etes-vous Français?	Are you a Frenchman?
Je viens de Caen, ville de Normandie.	I come from Caen, a town of Normandy.

400. But when an adjective is joined to the noun, or when it is specified by some circumstance, then *a* or *an* must be expressed in French; as,

Je suis un prince infortuné.	I am an unfortunate prince.
M. Walewski est un Polonais d'une illustre maison.	M. Walewski is a Pole of an illustrious family.

A or *an* is also expressed in French after *c'est*; as,

C'est un évêque.	He is a bishop.

401. Rule VI. The English indefinite article *a* or *an* is omitted in French, after *quel, quelle,* what, used as an exclamation; as,

Quel malheur!	What a misfortune!
Quelle beauté!	What a beauty!
Quelle belle maison!	What a beautiful house!
Quelle folie d'agir ainsi!	What a folly to act thus!

EXERCISE CXLIX.

Napoleon was (at once) an emperor, a warrior, and a
        ind-2 *à la fois*   *guerrier,*
statesman. — Socrates was a philosopher; Apelles, a
homme d'état.   *Socrate* ind-2   *Apelle*
painter; Phidias, a sculptor; Cicero, an orator; Livy, an
peintre   *Tite-Live*
historian; and Virgil, a poet. — His father was a barrister.—
historien   *poète.*   ind-2   *avocat.*
I am an Englishman, and a merchant. — The best coffee
                          négociant.   *café* m.
comes from Mocha, a town of Arabia Felix. — I am an
       Moka,   *heureuse.*

unhappy Spaniard, who seek an asylum, where I may
malheureux Espagnol, cherche *asile* m. où puisse
end my days in peace.—He is *an* officer.—He is *a* captain.—
finir *en* *C'* *officier.* *Il*
What *a* noise you make!—What *a* beautiful morning!
bruit m. *matinée* f.

402. RULE VII. No article is used, but only the preposition *de,* after the following adverbs:—

assez,	*enough.*	moins,	*less, fewer.*
autant,	*as much, as many.*	pas or point,	*no.*
beaucoup,	*much, very much,*	peu,	*little, few.*
	many.	plus,	*more.*
combien,	} *how much, how*	rien,	*nothing.*
que,	} *many.*	tant,	*so much, so many*
jamais,	*never.*	trop,	*too much, too many.*

EXAMPLES.

Beaucoup DE nations. | *Many nations.*
Plus D'effets et moins DE paroles. | *More deeds and fewer words.*
Trop DE peine. | *Too much trouble.*

Bien, in the sense of *beaucoup,* is the only adverb of quantity which, besides the preposition *de,* requires the article; as,

Elle a bien DE L'esprit. | *She has a great deal of wit.*
Il a bien DES amis. | *He has many friends.*

But, should the substantive that comes after the adverb be particularized by what follows, it requires the article; as,

J'ai encore beaucoup DE L'argent | *I have still a good deal of the*
que j'ai apporté de France. | *money which I brought from France.*

EXERCISE CL.

I have *enough* money.—The elephant has *much* intelligence.—
éléphant —— f.

For one Plato in opulence, *how many* Homers and Æsops
dans —— f. *Homères* h m. *Esopes*

in indigence!—The honest man is esteemed, even by those
dans —— f. *honnête* *estimé* *de*

who have *no* probity. — There is *no* church (that can be)
    pas   Il *n'y a point église* *qu'on puisse*
compared to Saint Peter's of Rome. — He has *few* friends.—
 inf-1

Mothers have often *too much* indulgence for their children.—
371   —— f.

 Study presents *so many* advantages that one cannot
371 *étude* f. *offrir*   *avantage* m.   *on ne saurait*
(give himself up to it) with *too much* ardour.
 s'y livrer

 403. RULE VIII. No article is used before nouns joined to verbs with which they express but one idea, and form idiomatical expressions; as,

Ajouter foi, *to give credit.*
Avoir besoin, *to want, to be in need of.*
— carte blanche, *to have full power.*
— chaud, *to be warm.*
— froid, *to be cold.*
— compassion, *to commiserate.*
— dessein, *to intend.*
— envie, *to wish.*
— faim, *to be hungry.*
— soif, *to be thirsty.*
— honte, *to be ashamed.*
— patience, *to have patience.*
— peur, *to be afraid.*
— pitié, *to pity.*
— raison, *to be in the right.*
— tort, *to be in the wrong.*
— soin, *to take care.*
Donner carte blanche, *to give full power.*
Faire attention, *to attend, to mind.*
— peur, *to frighten.*
Faire plaisir, *to do a favour.*
— semblant, *to pretend, to feign.*
— tort, *to wrong.*
— voile, *to set sail.*
Mettre fin, *to put an end.*
Parler allemand, *to speak German.*
— anglais, *to speak English.*
— français, *to speak French.*
Porter bonheur, *to bring good luck.*
— malheur, *to bring bad luck.*
— envie, *to bear envy.*
Prendre courage, *to take courage, to cheer up.*
— garde, *to take care.*
— jour, *to appoint a day.*
— patience, *to take patience, to bear or wait patiently.*
— plaisir, *to delight.*
— racine, *to take root.*
Rendre visite, *to pay a visit.*
Tenir tête, *to cope with one, to oppose.*

 404. REMARK.—The article is sometimes omitted before substantives, in order to render the language more striking and expressive. When we say, *Pauvreté n'est pas vice; Contentement passe richesse*, we express ourselves with more life than if we were to say, *La pauvreté n'est*

pas un vice; Le contentement passe la richesse. See also this phrase of FLÉCHIER: *Citoyens, étrangers, ennemis, peuples, rois, empereurs, le plaignent et le révèrent.* It has much more liveliness, energy, and grace, than it would have by re-establishing the articles: *Les citoyens, les étrangers,* etc., *le plaignent et le révèrent.*

EXERCISE CLI.

I *want* a hat. — We *intend* to travel. — We must always
    d'   de   Il faut
pity the unfortunate. — I (do not know) who *is in the wrong.*
de   malheureux pl.   ne sais   qui
— The king has *given full power* to that general. — That man
                                            général.
pretends to sleep. — The night *put an end* to the battle. —
    de   ind-3   combat m.
Take care of yourself. — He will come in a moment, *have*
Prendre   à vous.   ind-7 dans   prendre
patience. — Towers, *spires,* trees, *flocks,* huts, houses,
       Tour f. clocher m.   troupeau m. cabane f.
palaces, everything was swallowed up by the waves of the sea.
        tout   ind-3 englouti   flot m.   mer f.

EXERCISE CLII.

You *are wrong,* it is he who *is right.* — The fox sometimes
     c'   lui
feigns to be dead. — *Speak French* to us. — She *speaks Italian,*
 d'
Spanish, German, and *English.* — Let us say no ill of Boileau,
espagnol,   de mal
said Voltaire, that *brings bad luck.* — My vine *wants* cutting. —
                 cela   d' être taillée.
Are you *cold?* I am neither *cold* nor *warm.* — *Are* you *hungry,*
                      ni
my boy? No, but I *am* very *thirsty.* — *Mind* what he says to
              mais   à
you. — We must not *wrong* our neighbour. — The service that
     Il   à son prochain.   m.
I have rendered him seems to have *brought* me *good luck.*
                    sembler *
— Vice cannot *take root* in a heart like his.
art. — m. *ne saurait*   comme 94

CHAPTER II.

OF THE SUBSTANTIVE OR NOUN.

§ I. FUNCTIONS OF THE SUBSTANTIVE.

405. The Substantive is either the subject of the verb, or is governed by the verb, in which case it is called the regimen.

In this phrase: *la mère aime ses enfants*, the mother loves her children; *la mère* is the subject, or nominative case; and *enfants* is the regimen, object, or accusative case. *Ses enfants* is also called the *regimen direct*, because there is no preposition intervening between it and the verb *aime*.

In *les enfants obéissent à la mère*, the children obey the mother; *les enfants* is the subject, and *à la mère* is the regimen; and this regimen is called *indirect* because it has a preposition (*à*) before it.

§ II. OF THE GENDER OF SUBSTANTIVES.

406. We have already said (p. 11) that there are in French only two genders, the *masculine* and the *feminine*.

The masculine gender expresses the male kind, and the feminine gender denotes the female kind.

The French language has no neuter; consequently, inanimate objects are either masculine or feminine.

407. Generally speaking, French substantives have but one gender; a few of them, however, are masculine in one signification, and feminine in another. The following are those most in use:—

AIGLE (eagle) is feminine in the sense of a standard, an ensign in war: *l'aigle* ROMAINE, *l'aigle* IMPÉRIALE. In every other sense it is masculine: *Aigle* NOIR; *aigle* ROYAL; *l'aire* D'UN *aigle*. *C'est* UN *aigle*, in speaking of a man of genius, of superior talent.

OF THE GENDER OF SUBSTANTIVES. 211

COUPLE is feminine when it means a brace, two of a sort; as, UNE *couple de perdrix;* UNE *couple d'œufs.* It is masculine when speaking of a man and wife; as, *Ce fut* UN HEUREUX *couple.*

CRÊPE, *masc.* crape; *fem.* pancake.

ENFANT is masculine, when speaking of a boy: *c'est* UN *bon enfant;* and feminine, when it is said of a girl: *voilà* UNE *belle enfant.*

GENS (people) requires all words preceding it and relating to it to be in the feminine, and all words following it to be in the masculine: *les* VIEILLES *gens sont* SOUPÇONNEUX; TOUTES *les* MÉCHANTES *gens.* However, instead of *toutes, tous* is employed, 1*st,* When that adjective is the only one that precedes the substantive *gens:* TOUS *les gens qui raisonnent;* TOUS *les gens pieux.* 2*dly,* When *gens* is preceded by an adjective which has only one and the same termination for both genders, such as *aimable, brave, honnête,* etc. TOUS *les honnêtes gens;* TOUS *les habiles gens.*—(*Acad.*)

LIVRE, *masc.* a book; *fem.* a pound.

MANCHE, *masc.* the handle of a tool; *fem.* a sleeve, the English Channel.

MÉMOIRE, *masc.* a memoir, a bill; *fem.* the memory.

MOUSSE, *masc.* a young apprentice sailor; *fem.* moss, froth.

PAGE, *masc.* a page, an attendant; *fem.* the page of a book.

PERSONNE (nobody, a person), see No. 116, p. 52.

PIQUE, *masc.* spade at cards; *fem.* a pike, or long lance.

QUELQUE CHOSE is masculine, when it signifies *something: Quelque chose m'a été* DIT; *quelque chose de* MERVEILLEUX. It is feminine, when it means *whatever thing: Quelque chose qu'il ait* DITE, etc.—(*Acad.*)

☞ Observe that when *Quelque chose* (something) is immediately followed by an adjective, it takes the preposition *de* before that adjective; as, *Quelque chose* DE *curieux,* something curious.—(*Acad.*)

212 EXERCISES ON THE GENDER OF SUBSTANTIVES.

Souris, *masc.* a smile; *fem.* a mouse.
Tour, *masc.* a tour, turn, trick; *fem.* a tower.
Trompette, *masc.* a trumpeter; *fem.* a trumpet.
Voile, *masc.* a veil; *fem.* a sail.

(For the gender of some particular words, see pp. 22, 23, and 24.)

EXERCISE CLIII.

Several Roman *eagles* were taken by the Germans, after the
       ind-3   *Germains*
defeat   of Varus, under the reign   of Augustus.—A *couple*
défaite f. ———   *règne* m. *Auguste.*
of sheep   which they   roasted   themselves, composed the
 mouton m. qu' *faisaient rôtir*   ind-2
feasts   of the heroes of Homer. — We have shot a *brace* of
festin m. *héros* d'   *tué*
pheasants.—Dear *child*, said a mother to her daughter, without
      ind-2
thee there   is no happiness for me.—What wicked *people!*—
toi *il n'* *point*   *Quel méchant*
They are the best *people* in the world. —   Young *people* are
Ce   *de*   art.
often lazy.—   Military men wear the *crape* (round their) arm.
    art. * *porter*   *au*

EXERCISE CLIV.

We have eaten excellent *pancakes*.—This *book* is stereotyped
             stéréotypé.
—At Paris and in the greatest part of   France, the *pound*
        partie f. art.
  was   sixteen ounces.—The *Memoirs* of Sully are (very much)
ind-2 *de*   *fort*
esteemed. — That passage is at the bottom of   page 164.—
           bas m. art.
Nobody is more unhappy than a miser. — Have you seen the
     qu' *avare* m.
person that I   sent   to you?—I will give you *something*
    que ²*ai* ³*envoyée* * ¹
good. — The *tower* of Cordouan serves as a lighthouse at
         de * *phare*
the   mouth   of the Gironde.
 embouchure f. f

§ III. OF NUMBER IN SUBSTANTIVES.

408. Although there be plurality in the idea, certain French substantives do not take the mark of the plural; these are:—

409. (1.) Proper names; as, *l'Espagne s'honore d'avoir vu naître les deux* SÉNÈQUE. *Les deux* CORNEILLE *sont nés à Rouen.* Except when they are used as *common nouns*, that is to say, to designate individuals similar to those whose name is employed; as, *la France a eu ses* CÉSARS *et ses* POMPÉES; that is, generals such as Cæsar and Pompey. *Les Corneilles et les Miltons sont rares;* that is, poets such as CORNEILLE and MILTON.

REMARK. — It sometimes happens that poets and orators place the article *les* before proper names which designate but one individual. This is an irregularity, or at least a license, which can only be tolerated when productive of a fine effect, as in the following phrase of *Voltaire:*

Il manque à CAMPISTRON *ces expressions heureuses qui font l'âme de la poésie et le mérite des* HOMÈRE, *des* VIRGILE, *des* TASSE, *des* MILTON, *des* POPE, *des* CORNEILLE, *des* RACINE, *des* BOILEAU.

You discover that there is unity in the idea when the sense permits to suppress the article *les;* here we might say: *le mérite d'Homère, de Virgile,* etc.

☞ Although a proper name cannot, in French, take the mark of the plural, with the exception of the case in which it is used as a common noun, yet we write with the sign of the plural *les Stuarts, les Bourbons,* and some others, for the same reason that we say *les Allemands, les Italiens,* because these words are no longer the proper name of an individual, but the proper name of a class of individuals.

410. (2.) Words taken from the Latin, or from any foreign language, and which have not yet been naturalized by frequent use; as,

des *adagio*.	des *quiproquo*.
des *alibi*.	des *solo*.
des *auto-da-fé*.†	des *Te Deum*.
des *post-scriptum*.	des *vade-mecum*.

☞ The French Academy write des *bravos*, des *duos*, des *opéras*, des *pensums*, because these words are frequently used.

411. (3.) Words naturally invariable, and which are only accidentally employed as substantives; such as, les *pourquoi*, les *car*, les *oui*, les *non*, les *on dit*, etc.

Les *si*, les *car*, les *pourquoi*, sont la porte
Par où la noise entra dans l'univers.—(*La Fontaine*.)

EXERCISE CLV.

Spain is proud of having produced Lucan, Martial, the
       s'honore   inf-1   *Lucain*,
two *Senecas*, etc. — The first of the four *Williams* came
   Sénèque   *Guillaume est venu*
from Normandy. — *Ciceros* and *Virgils* will always be
                art.   art.
scarce. — The *mistakes* of apothecaries are very
rare   *quiproquo* m. *apothicaire* sing. *très*
dangerous. — After the victory, they sung *Te Deums* in all the
                             on ind-3
churches. — It was Cardinal Mazarin who introduced in
 église f. *C'est* art.   ind-3
France the taste for *operas*.—That violinist performed
        goût m. *de* art.   *violiniste* m. *a exécuté*
several *solos* at the last concert. — He puts *postscripts* to all
                         —— m.   32
his letters. — Where shall we now find *Bonapartes* and
                                     trouver
Wellingtons? — He was the friend of the *Bourbons*.

---

† *Auto-da-fé*; three Spanish words which signify Act of Faith.

§ IV. OF THE FORMATION OF THE PLURAL OF COMPOUND SUBSTANTIVES.

412. Compound substantives which have not yet passed to the state of words, that is to say, whose distinct parts are connected by a hyphen, are written in the singular or in the plural, according as the nature and particular sense of the words of which they are composed require the one or the other number.† Such is the general principle, whose application will be facilitated by the following rules.

413. RULE I. When a word is composed of a substantive and an adjective, both take the mark of the plural; as,

un petit-maître,	a dandy,	pl. des petits-maîtres.
une chauve-souris,	a bat,	— des chauves-souris.
une basse-cour,	a poultry-yard,	— des basses-cours.

To this rule there are a few exceptions; as, UNE grand'mère, plural DES grand'mères.

☞ GRAND, without apostrophe, always agrees in gender and number with its substantive, but GRAND' is always invariable.

414. RULE II. When a compound word is formed of two substantives placed immediately one after the other, both take the mark of the plural; as,

un chef-lieu,	a county town,	pl. des chefs-lieux.
un chou-fleur,	a cauliflower,	— des choux-fleurs.
une dame-jeanne,	a large bottle,	— des dames-jeannes.

The exceptions to this rule are but few, among which is UN *Hôtel-Dieu* (un hôtel de Dieu), a name given to the principal hospital, or infirmary, of several towns in France; plural DES *Hôtels-Dieu*.

415. RULE III. When a compound word is formed of two substantives joined by a preposition, the first only takes the mark of the plural; as,

un arc-en-ciel,	a rainbow,	pl. des arcs-en-ciel.
un chef-d'œuvre,	a master-piece,	— des chefs-d'œuvre.

---

† In compound nouns, the only words susceptible, by their nature, of taking the mark of the plural, are the *substantive* and the *adjective*.

Exceptions.—Un *tête-à-tête*, a conversation or interview between two persons; plural des *tête-à-tête*. Un *coq-à-l'âne*, an unconnected, nonsensical speech, passing from one thing to another quite opposite, as from a *cock to an ass*; plural des *coq-à-l'âne*.

EXERCISE CLVI.

Those two men are *brothers-in-law*. — I know his two
        beau-frère

grand-fathers. — There are in France eighty-six *capitals* of
 grand-père Y avoir   *chef-lieu* m.
departments.— *Rainbows* are formed by the reflection of the
 sing.   art.   *réflexion* f.
(rays of the sun) in the clouds. — In warm countries
rayons solaires dans *nuage* m. Dans art. ² ¹*pays* m.
  ²*silk-worms* ¹(are reared) upon (mulberry trees). —
art. *ver-à-soie* m. *on élève* *sur des* *mûrier* m.
The *great nightshade* (originally came) from Mexico. —
 belle de nuit pl. *sont originaires* art. *Mexique* m.
He is always making *cock and bull stories.*
  *   *fait* 32 *coq-à-l'âne*

416. Rule IV. When a compound word is formed of a substantive joined either to a verb, a preposition, or an adverb, the substantive only takes the sign of the plural, if there be plurality in the idea. So we write with an *s* in the plural:

un avant-coureur, *a forerunner,* pl. *des* avant-coureurs.
un contre-coup, *a counter-blow,* — *des* contre-coups.
une contre-danse,† *a country-dance,* — *des* contre-danses.

But we write without an *s* in the plural, because the expressions are elliptical, and there is unity in the idea:

Des réveille-matin (clocks which } *alarm-clocks.*
 awake in *the morning*),
Des contre-poison (remedies against } *counter-poisons.*
 poison),

---

† On croit que ce mot est une altération de l'anglais, *country-dance* 'danse de la contrée, de la campagne).

Finally, we write with an *s*, in the singular as well as in the plural, because there is always plurality in the idea:

un essuie-mains (that which wipes *the hands*) } a towel, pl. *des* essuie-mains.
un porte-mouchettes (that which carries *the snuffers*) } A *snuffers stand*, — *des* porte-mouchettes.

417. RULE V. When a compound substantive contains only such parts of speech as the *verb, preposition,* or *adverb*, none of its components takes the mark of the plural; as,

un passe-passe, *a sleight of hand,* pl. *des* passe-passe.
un passe-partout, *a master-key, a pass-key,* — *des* passe-partout.

EXERCISE CLVII.

The Cossacks are generally the scouts of the Russian
  Cosaque ordinairement avant-coureur ²russe
armies.—Rear-admirals are below vice-admirals.
  ¹ contre-amiral au-dessous de art. vice-amiral
—Snow-drops bear flowers in the midst of the
  perce-neige f. porter de art. à milieu m.
rigours of winter.—In time of war, the savages of
rigueur f. art. En sauvage m. art.
America are armed with *tomahawks*.—Gold is the surest of all
   de casse-tête
   pass-keys. — These (are mere) hearsays.
art. Ce ne sont que de art. ouï-dire

§ V. THE KING'S PALACE; THE QUEEN'S CROWN, ETC.

418. This form of the possessive or genitive case, is rendered in French in an inverted manner, the last word coming first, as if it were *the palace* OF THE *king, le palais* DU *roi; the crown* OF THE *queen, la couronne* DE LA *reine*

EXERCISE CLVIII.

(Here are) Joséphine's gloves and Alfred's hat. — Where is
  Voici
John's book?—My uncle's house. — The mayor's authority. —
          maison f.   maire autorité f.

The king of England's palaces. — The queen's presence of
     palais m.
mind. — Helen's beauty (was the cause of) Troy's
esprit *Hélène* h *mu.*   *causa*   *Troie*
destruction.—Have you read Milton's Paradise Lost?— Will
          Paradis m. *Vouloir*
you lend me La Fontaine's Fables?— Are you going to Mrs
  prêter   — f.
Bell's party?— Paul's sister's son entered into the castle.
 soirée f.   *dans* *forteresse* f.

§ VI. EAR-RINGS; DINING-ROOM, ETC.

419. These are a kind of compound words, the order of which is likewise inverted in French. *Boucles d'oreilles. Salle à manger.*

Here also, two different prepositions are used, *à* and *de*, the choice of which depends upon the nature of the expression.

420. *De* is used when *of, of the, made of, composed of, coming from*, can be understood.

EXAMPLES.

Boat-builder, i. e. builder *of* boats,	Constructeur de bateaux.
The house-door, i. e. the door *of the* house.	La porte de la maison.
Silk-stockings, i. e. stockings *made of* silk.	Bas de soie.
Madeira wine, i. e. wine *coming from* Madeira.	Vin de Madère.

EXERCISE CLIX.

The *golden age* is one of the (most agreeable) fictions
   âge m.   ²*les plus agréables* ¹—— f.
of mythology.—He has bought a *country-house.*—He is a
 art.   *campagne*
wine-merchant.—The *garden-seat* is broken.—My uncle has
 marchand   *banc* m.
given me a *gold watch*, and a *silver chain.* — Do you like
           chaîne f.

OF COMPOUND SUBSTANTIVES.

Newfoundland cod? — I like *Burgundy wine.*—The English
Terre-Neuve morue f.   *Bourgogne*

import a great quantity of *Malta oranges* and *Turkey figs.*
importer   *Malte*   *figue* f.

421. *A* is used in compound words, when *for, for the purpose of, by means of, with,* may be understood.

EXAMPLES.

Paper-mill, i. e. mill *for the purpose of* making paper.   Moulin à papier.

Steam-boat, i. e. boat moved *by means of* steam.   Bateau à vapeur.

Three thread-stockings, i. e. stockings *with* three threads.   Bas à trois fils.

Note. — Some compound words take the article besides the preposition *à*; as, *un pot* AU *lait,* a milk-jug. In the following Exercise, when the article is required it has been pointed out.

EXERCISE CLX.

The inventor of *gunpowder* was a German monk, named
                canon poudre f. ind-2   ² ¹*moine*

Schwartz.—I have always *fire-arms* in my   *bed-room.* — Give
                                  coucher chambre f.

me a *wine glass,* and a *soup spoon.* — The *hay-market*
     verre m.   *cuiller* f.   *au foin marché* m.

is on your left, and the   *horse-fair*   is before you.—There
 à   *gauche*   *aux* pl. *foire* f.   *devant*

are (a great many) *windmills* in France. — Have you ever
    beaucoup de   *jamais*

seen a *steam-mill?* No; but I have seen several *water-mills.*—
                mais   *plusieurs eau*

Honour to the inventor of the *steam-engine!* — I like *rice-soup.*
Honneur   *machine* f.   *au riz*

— Take the *coffee cups* into the *dining-room.* — Where is
  Porter   *café tasse*   *manger salle* f.   *Où*

my sister's *work-bag?* — My brother has given me a penknife
      ouvrage sac m.   *canif* m.

with an *ivory handle.* — The waiter has broken the *milk-jug*
    * *ivoire manche* m.

CHAPTER III.

OF THE ADJECTIVE.

§ I. CONCORD OF THE ADJECTIVE WITH THE NOUN.

422. General Rule.—The Adjective, in French, must be of the same gender and number as the noun or pronoun to which it relates, for which purpose it often changes its termination. In English, on the contrary, the adjective is never varied on account of gender or number.

EXAMPLES.

Le BON père.	The GOOD *father*.
La BONNE mère.	The GOOD *mother*.
De BEAUX jardins.	FINE *gardens*.
De BELLES fleurs.	FINE *flowers*.

Bon is masculine singular, because *père* is masculine, and in the singular; *bonne* is feminine singular, because *mère* is feminine, and in the singular.

Beaux is masculine plural, because *jardins* is masculine and plural; *belles* is feminine plural, because *fleurs* is feminine and plural.

(For the formation of the feminine, and plural of the adjectives, see p. 20—25.)

EXERCISE CLXI.

The *formidable* empire which Alexander conquered,
       2   1   *avait conquis*

(did not last)   longer   than his life, which was very *short*.
ne dura pas plus longtemps   f.   ind-3   *court*

—The victory which Cæsar obtained   on the plains
          f.   *remporter* ind-3   *dans*   *plaine* f.

of Pharsalia was *baneful* to his country, *pernicious* to the
   Pharsale ind-3 *funeste*   *pays* m. *pernicieux*

Romans, and *disastrous* to mankind.— (It is believed)
Romain *désastreux pour* art. *genre humain* m. *On croit*
that the *first* bayonets were made at Bayonne. — That
baïonnette f. ind-3 *fabriquer*
custom is very *ancient* among us.—It is a *mere* evasion, for
coutume f. *parmi* C'' *franc défaite* f. *car*
the thing is *public*. — Give these *fine* roses to those *good* girls.

423. 1st REMARK.—When the adjectives *demi*, half, *nu*, bare, are placed *before* a substantive, and when the adjective *feu*, late, comes *before* the article or a pronominal adjective, they always remain invariable; as, *une* DEMI-*livre*, half-a-pound; *il va* NU-*pieds*, he goes bare-foot; FEU *la reine*, the late queen. But the agreement takes place, if *demi* and *nu* be placed *after* the substantive, and *feu* after the article or pronominal adjective; as, *une livre et demie*, one pound and a half; *il a les pieds nus*, his feet are bare; *la feue reine*, the late queen; *ma feue nièce*, my late niece.

Observation.—The adjective *demi*, placed after the substantive, never takes the mark of the plural; because it does not agree with the substantive which precedes it, but with a substantive following, which is understood, and which is always of the singular number. This phrase: *Il a étudié quatre ans et demi*, he has studied four years and a half, is equivalent to this: *Il a étudié quatre ans et un demi an*, he has studied four years and one half year.

424. 2d REMARK.—Adjectives used adverbially are invariable, that is to say, remain always in the masculine singular; as, *Ces dames parlent* BAS, those ladies speak low; *ces fleurs sentent* BON, these flowers smell well.

EXERCISE CLXII.

An Irishman said to a Scotchman: Lend me three guineas.-
Irlandais ind-2 *Ecossais Prêter* *guinée* f.
That is impossible, for I (only possess) *half* a guinea.—Well,
Cela *car* *ne possède qu'* *
lend it me, and you will owe me two guineas and a
toujours *devoir*
half. — They go *bare*-foot and *bare*-headed. — I have heard
tête f. *ouï dire*

your *late* sister say that her daughter and I were born the
à ²   ¹   *moi naquîmes*
same year. — The *late* princess was universally regretted. —
   année f.   ind-3
She sings (*out of tune*).—They spoke *loud*.—Mary, speak *low*.
          faux   fem. ind-3 *haut*

425. Besides the general rule upon the agreement of the Adjective with the substantive which it qualifies, there are particular rules which it is indispensable to know, because they serve to explain the general rule.

426. (I.) An adjective referring to two or more substantives singular, of the same gender, must be put in the plural, and agree with them in gender; as,

Le riche et le pauvre sont *égaux* devant Dieu.	*The rich and the poor are* equal *before God.*
La rose et la tulipe sont *belles*.	*The rose and the tulip are* beautiful.

427. If the substantives are of *different* genders, the adjective is to be put in the masculine plural; as,

Ma sœur et mon frère sont *attentifs*.	*My sister and brother are* attentive.
Il a montré une prudence et un courage *étonnants*.	*He has shown* astonishing *prudence and courage.*

428. Remark.—When the substantives are of *different* genders, and the adjective qualifying them has not the same termination for the masculine and feminine, the ear requires that the masculine substantive should be placed last in French, that is to say, immediately before the adjective; so it is better to say: *la bouche et les yeux* ouverts, than, *les yeux et la bouche* ouverts.

EXERCISE CLXIII.

Pilpay and Confucius are very *celebrated* among the nations
————— —————   *célèbre*   *parmi*   *peuple* m.
of   Asia.—Uprightness and piety are (very much) *esteemed*,
art.   †*droiture*   †*piété* f.   *très*
even by the wicked. — Ignorance and   self-love   are
même de   *méchant* pl. †——— f.   †*amour-propre* m.

---

† See No. 371, page 192.

equally *presumptuous*.—The inhabitants of   (Davis' Strait)
    présomptueux   *habitant*   art. *détroit de Davis* m.

cat their flesh   and their fish   raw. — The room and
    viande f.   *poisson* m. *cru*   *chambre* f.

the closet   are *open*, but the window and the drawer are
 cabinet m.   *ouvert*   *fenêtre* f.   *tiroir* m.

shut. — His sister and brother are very polite.
fermé   *poli*

429. (II.) The Adjective placed after two or more substantives which are synonymous or nearly so, agrees with the last substantive only; as,

Toute sa vie n'a été qu'un travail, qu'une occupation CONTINUELLE. (*Massillon*.)	*His whole life has been nothing but continual labour and occupation.*

In this case, there is really but one word to qualify, because there is only one and the same idea expressed, and it is with the last substantive that the agreement takes place, as striking the mind most.

430. (III.) When substantives are united by the conjunction *ou* (or), the adjective agrees with the last; as,

Un courage ou une prudence ÉTONNANTE.	*An astonishing courage or prudence.*

That conjunction *ou* gives the exclusion to one of the substantives, and it is upon the last, as fixing the attention most, that the qualification falls.

431. REMARK.—When an adjective relates to two or more substantives, and is one of those that must absolutely be placed before the substantive, it is repeated, in French, before each substantive, and agrees with it; as,

De GRANDS événements, et de GRANDES révolutions suivirent la mort de César.	GREAT *events and revolutions followed the death of Cæsar.*

EXERCISE CLXIV.

Our Queen honours literature with that attachment and
                     les lettres de   m. *attachement,* * de

patrouage *capable* of ⁴making ¹it flourish. — Birds
cette protection f.   inf-1 †*les fleurir.*   oiseau m.
   build their nests with ³*admirable* ¹art and ²address.
construire   nid m. avec un   art, * une adresse f.
—The demi-gods of the ancients were only men who
                        ancien m. ind-2 ne que des
(had distinguished themselves) by ⁴*extraordinary* ¹valour ²or
   s'étaient distingués   une
³virtue. — Louis XIV. had in France an ³*absolute*
une   ind-2   un absolu
¹power and ²authority.
pouvoir, * une

§ II. PLACE OF ADJECTIVES.

432. Some Adjectives are placed before the noun, and some after it; others are either put before or after, according as taste or ear may require. However, it may be laid down as a rule that the French more generally place the Adjective after the noun.

ADJECTIVES WHICH ARE PLACED BEFORE THE NOUN.

433. (1.) *Adjectives* of one syllable, as *beau, bon, grand, gros,* etc., generally precede their substantive. We say, un BEAU *jardin,* un BON *ouvrage,* un GRAND *chapeau,* un SAINT *personnage,* etc.

434. (2.) Plural *Adjectives* generally unite harmoniously with substantives beginning with a vowel; as, BRILLANTS *atours.* It is the same with the *Adjectives* which, although singular, terminate with an *x* which is pronounced like a *z;* as, HEUREUX *artifice,* etc.

(See Remark 5th, p. 227.)

EXERCISE CLXV.

Have you seen the *beautiful* lake   of Geneva? — The Loire
                        lac m.   Genève
is a *fine* river. — You arrive at a *good* moment.—The Turks
      rivière f.   le   —— m.   Turc
make a *great* use   of opium.—The *big*   fishes   eat the
            usage m.   ——   gros poisson m.

---

† It is only when *les* is an *article,* that the contraction of *de les* into *des* takes place. The same rule applies to *de le,* and to *à le, à les.*

little ones. — What a *holy* man   father Bernard is! —
                  * *saint*   *que* art.   *

He is an *old* soldier. — My *dear* friend, you are mistaken. —
C'   *vieux*   *cher*   *se méprendre*

He is in   *continual* alarms. — That child has   *fine* eyes.
Il   *dans de*   *alarme* f.   132

ADJECTIVES WHICH ARE PLACED AFTER THE NOUN.

435. The *Adjectives* which are placed after the substantive are : —

1st, *Adjectives* which express names of nations; as, *Le gouvernement* ANGLAIS, the English government; *La révolution* FRANÇAISE, the French revolution.

REMARK. — When the name of a nation is an *adjective*, it does not require a capital letter in French, but it takes one if it be a *substantive*. So we write: *La nation française, anglaise, espagnole, italienne, allemande*. And, with a capital, *un Anglais* (an Englishman), *un Espagnol* (a Spaniard), etc. — (ACAD.)

EXERCISE CLXVI.

English bravery; *Spanish* gravity; *Italian* policy; *Roman*
          bravoure f.   f.   *politique* f.
beauty; *German* music;   *Dutch*   manners;   *Prussian*
f.   *hollandais* *mœurs* f. pl. *prussien*
troops; *Swedish* soldiers; *Chinese* ceremonies. — The *French*
troupe f. *suédois* *soldat*   *chinois*   f.
monarchy   began under Pharamond, in the year 420. — That
monarchie f. ind-3   *en l' an*
young *German* requests you to inscribe your name in his
              prier   *d' inscrire*   *sur*
album. — Paul spoke to them in the *Hebrew* tongue. — I have
——— m.   86   *en * hébraïque*
seen Moscow with its *Chinese* pagodas, its *Italian* terraces, and
     Moscou   *pagode* f.   *terrasse* f.
its *Dutch* farms. — Nothing   stops the *Russian* coachman, his
    ferme f.   n'   *russe*   *cocher*
driving   is a steeple chase; ditch, hillock, overturned tree,
course f.   *course au clocher fossé   tertre* ²*renversé* ¹
he leaps over everything. — Long live the *Irish* nation!
  franchir   *tout*.   335   *irlandais* ——— f.

P

436. *2dly, Adjectives* denoting colour are placed after the noun; as, *un habit* NOIR, a black coat; *une robe* BLANCHE, a white dress; *un ruban* BLEU, a blue ribbon.

In poetry, and in a figurative sense, *Noir* may be placed before the substantive; as, *un* NOIR *attentat*, a black crime.

Some compound words, as, *rouge-gorge*, a Robin-redbreast; *du blanc-manger*, blancmange, can scarcely be considered as exceptions to this rule.

EXERCISE CLXVII

She has   *blue* eyes. — The Spanish soldiers wear a *red*
      art.   *porter*
cockade. — (Here is) a beautiful statue of *white* marble. —
cocarde f.   *Voici*   ―― f.   *blanc marbre* m.
The marigold is a *yellow* flower. — Saddle my *black* horse. — I
   souci m.   *jaune*   *Seller*
shall put on my *brown* coat, and my American boots. —
     mettre *   *brun*   *américain botte* f.
Almost all the trees of   Florida,   particularly the
             arbre m.   art. *Floride* f. *en particulier*
cedar   and the *green* oak,   are covered with a *white* moss.
cèdre m.   *vert chêne* m.   d'   *mousse* f.

437. *3dly, Adjectives* formed from the present participle of verbs, are *generally* placed after the substantive; as,

Un ouvrage *divertissant*.	An entertaining work.
La mode *régnante*.	The reigning fashion.

438. But, *Adjectives* formed from the past participle are *always* placed after the substantive; as,

Un homme *instruit*.	A well-informed man.
Une figure *arrondie*.	A round figure.

EXERCISE CLXVIII.

(That is) an *amusing* book. — The *smiling* images of
  Voilà   *riant*   ―― f.
Theocritus, Virgil, and Gessner, excite in the soul a gentle
  Théocrite   †   † ――   *porter*   *doux*
   feeling. — There are   *striking* examples of English
sensibilité f.   *des frappant*

---

† See *Note* to Rule VII. p. 200.

generosity. — *Grateful* people are like those
78 f. art. *reconnaissant personne* f. *ressemblent à*
fruitful lands which give more than they receive. — He has
²*fertile* ¹f. *rendre* *ne*
made *astonishing* progress. — An *affected* simplicity is a
des étonnant progrès m. pl. *affecté* f. 78
refined imposture. — She is a *well-informed* woman.
²*délicat* ¹—— f. C'

439. 4*thly*, Adjectives are placed after the substantive, when expressing some physical or natural quality, such as *chaud*, hot; *froid*, cold; *humide*, damp; and when expressing form, as *une table carrée*, a square table.

440. 5*thly*, Adjectives of several syllables seldom go well before substantives of one syllable; so, instead of saying *les champêtres airs*, rural airs; *les imaginaires lois*, imaginary laws, say *les airs champêtres, les lois imaginaires*.

441. 6*thly*, When two or more adjectives qualify the same noun, they are almost always placed after that noun. So, instead of adopting the English construction, *ces deux rivales et guerrières nations*, those two rival and warlike nations, say: *ces deux nations guerrières et rivales*.

EXERCISE CLXIX.

Will you give me some *warm* water? — Bring me some *cold*
chaud
milk. — Put it on the *round* table. — Never sleep in a *damp*
lait m. *rond* *coucher*
room.— ²Arts ¹(are divided) into *liberal* Arts and *mechanical*
art. *on divise en* m. *mécanique*
Arts. — The king of Spain is styled the *Catholic* king. — She
appeler catholique *Elle*
has an *harmonious* voice.—She is a *good* and *charitable* woman.
voix f. C'
—He is an *amiable* and *virtuous* man. Do you not know him?—
C' *vertueux* 289
Denmark is, in general, an *agreeable* and *fertile* country.
375 *pays* m

442. Finally, the placing of a great many Adjectives, before or after the substantive, holds so much to the genius of the French language, that from their being placed before or after, often depends the meaning of the substantive; and usage dictates so imperiously the law, that by infringing it we would not be understood.

LIST OF ADJECTIVES

which impart a different meaning to the noun, according as they are placed before, or after it.

Un bon homme, most frequently means *a simple man.*	Un homme bon, *a good man.*
Un brave homme, *an honest man.*	Un homme brave, *a brave man.*
Une commune voix, *a unanimous voice.*	Une voix commune, *a common voice.*
Une fausse clef, *a false key.*	Une clef fausse, *a wrong key.*
Une fausse porte, *a private door.*	Une porte fausse, *a false door.*
Un furieux menteur, *a terrible liar.*	Un fou furieux, *a furious madman.*
Un grand homme, *a great man.*	Un homme grand, *a tall man.*
Le grand air, *noble manners.*	L'air grand, *a noble look.*
Une grosse femme, *a big stout woman.*	Une femme grosse, same as une femme enceinte.
Le haut ton, *an arrogant manner.*	Le ton haut, *a loud tone of voice.*
Un honnête homme, *an honest man.*	Un homme honnête, *a polite man.*
Des honnêtes gens, *respectable people.*	Des gens honnêtes, *polite people.*
Mauvais air, *a vulgar appearance.*	L'air mauvais, *an ill-natured look.*
Une méchante épigramme, *a bad epigram.*	Une épigramme méchante, *a wicked epigram.*
Du mort bois, *wood of little value.*	Du bois mort, *dead trees.*
Morte eau, *ebb tides.*	Eau morte, *still water.*
Le nouveau vin, *the wine newly come.*	Le vin nouveau, *the wine newly made.*

PLACE OF ADJECTIVES. 229

De nouveaux livres, *other books.* } Des livres nouveaux, *new books.*

Un nouvel habit, *another coat.* { Un habit nouveau, *a new-fashioned coat.* / Un habit neuf, *a new coat.*

Un pauvre homme, *a man without genius.* } Un homme pauvre, *a poor man.*

Un plaisant homme, *a whimsical ridiculous man.* Un homme plaisant, *a pleasant facetious man.*

Un plaisant personnage, *a contemptible person.* Un personnage plaisant, *an amusing person.*

Un plaisant conte, *an unlikely story.* Un conte plaisant, *an amusing story.*

Un petit homme, *a little man.* Un homme petit, *a mean man.*

Les propres termes, *the exact words.* Les termes propres, *correct expressions.*

Une sage-femme, *a midwife.* { Une femme sage, *a prudent woman.*

Un seul homme, *a single man.* Un homme seul, *a man alone.*

Unique tableau, *a single picture.* { Tableau unique, *a picture, the only one of its kind, incomparable.*

Un vilain homme, *a disagreeable man.* } Un homme vilain, *a mean man.*

EXERCISE CLXX.

He opened the presses with *false* keys. — As an actor
   ind-3   armoire f.   de

was walking on tiptoe to represent the *great*
  marcher ind-2 le bout des pieds pour

Agamemnon, they cried out to him that he was making him a
          on ind-3 * 86

tall man, and not a *great* man. — Bonaparte had *a loud*
         non pas   ind-2

tone of voice.—He has (got on) a *new-fashioned* coat.—A lady,
                              mis

seeing Chapelain and Patru, said that the first was an author
                           ind-3   ind-2   auteur

without genius, and the second a *poor* author.
  pauvre

§ III. GOVERNMENT OF ADJECTIVES.

One of the difficulties of the French language is to know what preposition must be used after an adjective, as the French prepositions are not always in this instance correlative to the English prepositions.

443. *Adjectives which govern the preposition A.*

Adonné à,	addicted to.	pareil à,	like.
ardent à,	ardent in.	prêt à,	ready to.
bon à,	good for.	prompt à,	prompt in, quick at.
cher à,	dear to.	propre à,	fit for.
conforme à,	conformable to.	semblable à,	similar to.
égal à,	equal to.	sensible à,	sensible of.
enclin à,	inclined to.	sourd à,	deaf to.
lent à,	slow to, and in.	sujet à,	subject to.
nuisible à,	hurtful to.	utile à,	useful to.

And in general all adjectives denoting *inclination, habit, aptness, fitness.* And, when followed by a verb, it is most commonly put in the present of the infinitive.

EXERCISE CLXXI.

Your intentions are *conformable to* my wishes. — He is *slow*
                désir m.

to punish, and *prompt in* rewarding. — Are you *ready to* go out?
      récompenser.   sortir

— He is *fit for* anything. — He is *deaf to* remonstrances.—
     tout.   art. remontrance f.

Sicily is *subject to* great earthquakes. — That man is *useful*
Sicile f.   ‡ m. tremblement de terre.

and *dear to* his famíly. — That is *easy to* say. — It is ridiculous
     famille f. Cela facile   Il ridicule

to put oneself in a passion against objects which are *insensible*
de se† en* colère § objet m.

of our anger. — Your dress is *like* mine.
  colère.   robe f.

---

† Place of *Se*, No. 88.   ‡ Rule V. No. 381.   § No. 380.

444. Adjectives which govern the preposition DE.

Agréable de,	agreeable to.	exempt de,	exempt from.
aise de,	glad to.	fatigué de,	fatigued with.
avide de,	greedy of.	heureux de,	happy to.
capable de,	able to.	inconsolable de,	inconsolable at.
chargé de,	loaded with.		
charmé de,	charmed with.	inquiet de,	uneasy about.
chéri de,	beloved by.	libre de,	free from.
content de,	pleased with.	mécontent de,	dissatisfied with.
coupable de,	guilty of.	plein de,	full of.
curieux de,	curious to.	reconnaissant de,	grateful for.
digne de,	worthy of.		
enchanté de,	delighted with.	satisfait de,	satisfied with.
ennuyé de,	weary of.	sûr de,	sure of.

As likewise adjectives expressing *plenty* and *scarcity*, and in general all those which are followed in English by the prepositions *of, from, with*, or *by*.

EXERCISE CLXXII.

I am very *glad to* see you in good health. — Voltaire was
      bien   santé f.   ind-3

always *greedy of* praise. — The vine is *loaded with* grapes.—
        louange pl.   vigne f.   raisin

I am *pleased with* your answer. —   Virtuous men are always
                réponse f. art. ²*vertueux* ¹

worthy of esteem. — I am *tired with* running after him. — A
     estime.   fatigué   inf-1

heart *free from* cares   enjoys the greatest felicity possible.—
          soin m. jouir de   f.

He is very *grateful for* the services   you have rendered him.
      fort   que   ²*rendus* ¹

— Here is a purse *full of* louis† and napoleons.‡ — I am
       bourse f.   m.   napoléon m.

satisfied with my lot. — Are you *pleased with* your horse?
      sort m.

445. Some Adjectives are often followed in French by the preposition *envers*, and in English by the preposition

---

† A gold coin of France, worth about twenty shillings; so called, since Louis XIII., from the name of the kings who coined it.

‡ A gold piece of twenty or forty francs, with the effigy of Napoleon. It is more commonly said of pieces of twenty francs.

to; such are, *affable, bon, complaisant, cruel, généreux, indulgent*, or any other expressing kindness or unkindness of feeling towards individuals; as,

Il faut être *poli* ENVERS tout le monde.	*We must be* civil TO everybody.

446. Adjectives expressing gladness or regret at a thing, such as *aise, charmé, enchanté, fâché, contrarié*, etc., require the infinitive with DE, or the subjunctive mood; as,

Je suis bien *aise* D'être de retour à temps.	*I am very glad that I have returned in time.*
Je suis bien *aise* que vous soyez de retour.	*I am very glad that you have returned.*

In the first example, there is only one subject, *Je*, and the second verb is in the infinitive.

In the second example, there are two subjects, *Je* and *vous*; the verb, therefore, is put in the subjunctive mood.

447. IL EST, impersonal, joined to an adjective, requires *de* before an infinitive. C'EST requires *à*; as,

Il est horrible DE penser, DE voir.	*It is horrid to think, to see.*
C'est horrible A penser, A voir.	*It is horrid to think of, to be seen.*

EXERCISE CLXXIII.

We must be charitable *to* the poor. — I do not like people
  Il faut   pauvre pl.   aimer ceux
who are cruel *to* animals.—Scipio Africanus was respectful
                               Scipion *l'Africain* ind-2 *respectueux*
to his mother, liberal *to* his sisters, good *to* his servants, just
                                                domestique juste
and affable *to* everybody. — He will be delighted *to* see you. —
                                enchanté
I am very sorry you cannot come. — It is agreeable *to*
    bien fâché   pouvoir subj-1   Il
live with one's friends.—It is noble *to* die for one's country.—
vivre   ses   Il   beau   sa   patrie.
This is painful *to* see and *to* hear. — Be kind *to* every-
  C'   pénible   entendre.   obligeant
body.—It is easy *to* prove it to you.—That is easy *to* be proved.
                 C'   prouver

§ IV. ADJECTIVES OF NUMBER.
(The numbers are given at full length, page 31.)

448. (1.) Of all the *cardinal* numbers, *un* is the only one that takes an *e* for the feminine: UN *homme*, UNE *femme*.

449. (2.) *Unième*, first, is never used but after *vingt, trente, quarante, cinquante, soixante, quatre-vingt, cent*, and *mille. C'est la vingt et* UNIÈME *fois*, it is the twenty-first time.

450. (3.) We say *second*, or *deuxième*, but we cannot say *vingt-second, trente-second;* we must say *vingt-deuxième, trente-deuxième, quarante-deuxième*, etc.

There is this difference between *le second*, and *le deuxième*, that this last makes you think on the *third*, it awakens the idea of a series, whereas *le second* awakens the idea of order without that of series. We say, therefore, of a work which has only two volumes: *Voici le* SECOND *tome*, and not *le deuxième;* and, of a work which has more than two volumes: *Voici le* DEUXIÈME *tome*, or also *voici le* SECOND *tome.—(Chapsal, Boniface*, etc.)

451. (4.) We say, *le onze, le onzième, du onze, du onzième, au onze, au onzième, vers les onze heures, vers les une heure*, or *sur les une heure*, pronouncing the words *onze, onzième*, and *une*, as if they were written with an *h* aspirate.

NOTE.—*Dumarsais* thinks, that if we write and pronounce *le onze*, it is in order not to confound *l'onze* with *l'once*.

Vers les une heure is an elliptical phrase, for, *vers les moments qui précèdent ou qui suivent une heure*. The article is allowed to remain in the plural, although the substantive is not expressed.

452. (5.) When a cardinal number is preceded by the pronoun *en*, the *adjective* or *participle* which follows that number must be preceded by the preposition *de;* as,

Sur mille habitants, il n'y EN a pas un DE riche.	*Of one thousand inhabitants, there is not a rich one.*

453. (6.) *Cent* and *mille* are sometimes used for an indefinite, but very large number; as,

Il nous fit *cent* caresses.	*He showed us a hundred marks of kindness.*

Heureux, heureux *mille* fois,
L'enfant que le Seigneur rend docile à ses lois!—(*Racine.*)

☞ For several important Remarks on Nouns and Adjectives of Number, see pp. 33, 34, 35.

EXERCISE CLXXIV.

One of the nine Muses is called Terpsichore. — It was in
————   f. *s'appeler*   ————   *Ce* ind-3
the *thirty-first* year after the peace, that war (broke out again).
                année f.   *paix* f.   *se rallumer* ind-3
— William, surnamed the Conqueror, king of England and
  Guillaume, surnommé   *Conquérant,*
duke of Normandy, was one of the greatest generals of the
                                ind-3
eleventh century. — Of ten thousand combatants, there were
  siècle m.   *Sur*   *combattant*   il y EN eut
one thousand *killed*, and five hundred *wounded*. — The admiral
             *   *blessé*
showed me a *thousand* civilities. — About *eleven* o'clock.
faire   *   *caresse*

§ V. ADJECTIVES OF DIMENSION.

454. Adjectives of dimension, such as *haut*, high; *long*, long; *large*, wide or broad; *épais*, thick; *profond*, deep; which come after the word of measure in English, come before it in French, and are followed by the preposition *de;* as,

Un mur *haut* DE sept pieds.	A wall seven feet high.
Une chambre *longue* DE vingt pieds.	A room twenty feet long.

Another construction, frequently used, is to let the words remain in French as in English, and to put *de* both before the number and before the word of measure or dimension. In this case, the substantive of dimension is often used instead of the adjective; as,

Un mur DE sept pieds DE haut, or DE hauteur.	A wall seven feet high.
Une chambre DE vingt pieds DE long, or DE longueur.	A room twenty feet long.

455. The English manner of expressing *dimension* is to use the verb *to be;* but the French, in general, make use of the verb *avoir*. In this case, *de* is left out before the number, and the phrase is rendered thus :—

Ce mur A sept pieds de haut, or de hauteur.	That wall is *seven feet high*.

EXERCISE CLXXV.

The walls of Babylon　*were* two hundred feet *high* and fifty
　　　　Babylone avaient　　†

broad.—The great wall,　　on the north of China, *is* about
largeur.　　　　*muraille* f. *à*　　　　　　*Chine* f. *a environ*

twelve hundred miles *long.* —The highest of the pyramids　of
　　　　　　　　　†　　　　　　　　　　　　　　　*pyramide* f.

Egypt *is,* at least, five hundred feet *high.* —The Monument of
　a au moins　　　　†　　　　　　　　　　—— m.

London is a round pillar　two hundred feet *high.*—The Tiber
　　　‡*rond pilier* m.　　　　†

is three hundred feet *wide* at Rome.—The famous mine　of
a　　　　†　　　*largeur*　　　　　　　　　　　—— f.

Potosi, in Peru,　*is* more than fifteen hundred feet　deep.
　　dans Pérou m. *a*　　*de*　　　　†　　　　*profondeur.*

§ VI. ADJECTIVES IN THE COMPARATIVE DEGREE.

456. (1.) BY, after a comparative, is expressed by DE; as,

Il est plus grand DE deux pouces. | *He is taller* BY *two inches.*

457. (2.) In English, when the adverbs *more* and *less* are repeated to express a comparison, they are preceded by the article; as, THE MORE *difficult a thing is,* THE MORE *glorious it is to do it well.* But, in French, the article is omitted; as, PLUS *une chose est difficile,* PLUS *il est glorieux de la bien faire.*

§ VII. ADJECTIVES IN THE SUPERLATIVE DEGREE.

458. (1.) An adjective in the superlative degree governs the preposition DE; as,

Le plus grand empire DU monde. | *The greatest empire* in *the world.*

---

† See Remarks on *Cent,* p. 34.　　‡ See No. 439, p. 227.

459. (2.) When the substantive precedes the superlative, both take the article; but the substantive takes no article, if the superlative goes first; as,

Les *gens* les plus habiles.
Les plus habiles *gens*. } *The most able men.*

460. (3.) The article placed before *plus* and *moins* is always invariable, when there is no comparison; as, *La lune ne nous éclaire pas autant que le soleil, même quand elle est* LE PLUS *brillante,* The moon does not light us so much as the sun, even when it shines brightest. But the article takes gender and number, when there is a comparison; as, *La lune est* LA PLUS *brillante de toutes les planètes,* The moon is the most brilliant of all the planets.

EXERCISE CLXXVI.

She is taller than her sister *by* the whole head.—*The more*
                          ² ¹*tout tête* f.

one reads La Fontaine, *the more* one admires him.—Seneca
on   Sénèque

was *the richest* man *in* the empire.—*The highest* mountains
ind-2   ²   ¹   montagne f.

are the reservoirs (from which) issue *the largest* rivers.—
       réservoir m.   d'où   sortir   grand fleuve m.

Those whom I have always seen *most struck* with the writings
Ceux   que   vus   frapper de   écrit m.

of Homer, Virgil, Horace, and Cicero, are minds of the first
       †   †   *   †   des esprit m.

order.—Although the Chinese boast of being *the most ancient*
      Quoique   Chinois se vanter inf-1   ²

nation, they are far from being *the most enlightened.*
¹——f.   loin   inf-1   éclairé

EXERCISE CLXXVII.

That man is *the best* creature *in* the world.—That is the
                            f.   Voilà

cleverest boy *in* the school.—His father is the most learned
habile   savant

man *in* the kingdom.—His mother is the most sensible wo-
                                          spirituel

man *in* the whole town.—Her grandfather is the richest

merchant *in* London.—*The* more you study, *the* more you
négociant

learn.—Astronomy is one of the sciences which does *most*
                                          f.

honour to the human mind.

---

† See *Note* to Rule vii. p. 200.

CHAPTER IV.

OF PRONOUNS.

§ I. OF PERSONAL PRONOUNS.

Place of Personal Pronouns.

461. THE Personal Pronouns, whether *subjects* or *objects*, are placed before the verb in simple tenses, and before the auxiliary in compound tenses; except, 1*st*, When the pronouns take a preposition before them in French; 2*dly*, In interrogative sentences; 3*dly*, When the verb is in the imperative *affirmative* (the third persons excepted). Such is the general principle of the position of personal pronouns, which will be fully developed in this chapter.

<small>(See what has already been stated on this subject, p. 38.)</small>

OF PERSONAL PRONOUNS AS SUBJECTS.

462. (I.) The *personal* pronouns, *I, thou, he* or *it, she* or *it, we, you, they,* are expressed in French by *je, tu, il, elle, nous, vous, ils* m., *elles* f., when they are the subjects or nominatives of the verb; as,

Je parle, I *speak; il* chante, he *sings.*	*Elle* danse, she *dances;* nous jouons, we *play.*

463. (II.) *I, thou, he, they* m. are rendered by *moi, toi, lui, eux:*—

1*st*, When used in answer to a question; as,

Qui a fait cela?—*Moi.*	*Who has done that?*—I.

2*d*, When joined to a noun or pronoun by a conjunction, or when a verb has two or more pronouns as subjects; as,

Mon frère *et* moi.	*My brother* and *I.*
Lui *et* moi.	*He* and *I.*
Vous, lui, et moi, nous irons.	*You, he, and I will go.*

3*d*, When they come after a comparative; as,

Il est plus riche que *lui*, qu'*eux* et *moi*. | *He is richer than* he, they, *and* I.

4*th*, When followed by the relatives *qui*, *que*, the adjective *seul*, or a present participle; as,

Moi QUI suis son fils.	I who *am his son*.
Eux QUE j'aimais tant.	They whom *I loved so much*.
Lui SEUL respecte la vertu.	He alone *respects virtue*.
Eux, VOYANT qu'ils avaient tort.	They, seeing *that they were in the wrong*.

5*th*, When they mark opposition or distinction, or point out the part taken in an action by different persons; as,

EUX l'ont relevé, et LUI l'a pansé.	They *raised him up, and* he *dressed his wounds*.

6*th*, When coming after these expressions, *It is, it was, it will be, it would be*, or similar ones, whether in the affirmative, negative, or interrogative; as,

It is I,	C'est *moi*.	*It is* thou,	C'est *toi*.
It is he,	C'est *lui*.	*It is* they,	Ce sont eux, *n.* elles, f.

EXERCISE CLXXVIII.

I come from Dover. — *You* like the town, and *I* the
                                   Douvres.
country. — Who read last? — *He*. — *I* am not so tall
campagne f.   ind-4 *le dernier*   fem.   *si grand*
as your sister, but *she* is older than *I*. — They alone have
que   *âgé*   *seul*
fought the enemy; *they alone* deserve to be rewarded. —
combattre   *mériter* d'   *récompensé*
He, perceiving their intentions, gave up his project. —
     s'apercevoir de   †   *abandonner*   *projet* m.
Your uncles and your brother take charge of the enterprise;
                              se charger
they find the money, and *he* will manage the work. —
     fournir   *fonds* pl.   *conduire* ind-7   *travail* m.
Was it *he* that was singing? — No, it was *I*.
ind-2 *ce*   *qui*   ind-2   *c'* ind-2

---

† Most words ending in *ion* are alike in both languages. See p. 30.

464. (III.) Personal pronouns used as *subjects*, are placed after the verb, although no interrogation is meant:—

1*st*, When the verb is in the present or imperfect of the Subjunctive without any conjunction being expressed. In such a case, the final *e* of the first person is marked with an acute accent, for the sake of euphony; as,

Puissé-*je* de mes yeux, &c. (CORNEILLE.)	*May I with my eyes*, &c.
Dussé-*je* mourir! (RACINE.)	*Were I to die!*

2*d*, When the verb is preceded by any of these words, *aussi, peut-être, encore, en vain, du moins, au moins, à peine;* as,

Peut-être avez-*vous* raison.	*Perhaps you are right.*
En vain prétendons-*nous*.	*It is in vain that we pretend.*

We might also say: *Peut-être* vous *avez raison;*—*en vain* nous *prétendons,* but then the expression possesses neither the same grace, nor the same energy.

3*d*, In narrations, as in English:—

Où allez-vous? lui dis-*je*.	*Where are you going? said I to him.*
Je le veux bien, lui répondit-*il*.	*I am very willing, replied he to him.*

☞ Observe that in the foregoing examples a *hyphen* is put after the verb when followed by the pronoun its subject.

EXERCISE CLXXIX.

(Oh that I may) see him! — (Though you were) more
   Puissé-je   Fussiez-vous
numerous, you will meet with resistance. — This
nombreux   éprouver ind-7 32
lace is beautiful, (*but then*) it is dear. — The rose is
dentelle f.   aussi   coûter† ‡   ——f.
the queen of flowers; *therefore* it is the emblem of
       art.   aussi   emblème m.   art.
beauty. — *Perhaps* I shall go. — You were *hardly* gone when
        Peut-être   ind-2 *à peine partir que*
your brother arrived. — What would you have? *said he* to me.
          ind-3   ind-1   *
Life, *replied* I. — *Scarcely* had I arrived.
art.   répondre   fus

---

† See the 3d Remark, p. 87.   ‡ See the 2d Remark, p. 221.

465. IV. Personal pronouns, when subjects or nominatives, must be repeated:—

1st, When we pass from negation to affirmation; as, JE *ne plie pas et* JE *romps* (I do not bend and I break.) But we can say: JE *plie et* JE *ne romps pas,* or *je plie et ne romps pas,* the first verb being in the affirmative.

2d, When the verbs are connected by any conjunction except *et* (and), *ou* (or), *ni* (nor), *mais* (but).

Except in those two cases, the personal pronouns *subjects,* are either repeated or not, according as the harmony, energy, and especially the perspicuity of the phrase may require.

EXERCISE CLXXX.

You gain *nothing,* and *you* spend (a great deal). — *1*
      gagner   dépenser   beaucoup.

(am *not* ignorant) that one cannot be happy without virtue,
  n'ignore pas   on ne saurait   art.

and *I* (am firmly resolved) always to practise it.—*We* detest
     me propose bien   de   *   ²   ¹

the wicked, *because we* fear them.—*He* is learned *although*
  méchant parce que   *craindre*   *quoique*

he is very young.—I wish to see you happy, *because I* am
  subj-1 *bien*   *désirer* *

attached to you.—*You* will be truly esteemed, *if you* are wise
  attaché *   *vraiment*

and modest.—*You* are *not* happy, and *you* have saved Rome.
    modeste

OF PERSONAL PRONOUNS AS OBJECTS.

466. A Personal pronoun, when the regimen† or object of the verb, is either *direct* or *indirect.* A pronoun is the direct object of the verb, when it is governed by the verb without any preposition, either expressed or understood; as, *Je la vois,* I see her. But, when a pronoun is the indirect object, it is always preceded by *à* (to), or

---

† REGIMEN. The word or member of a sentence governed by a verb; as, *Evil communication corrupts good manners,* where *good manners* may be said to be the regimen, or part of the sentence governed by the verb *corrupts.*—*Walker.*

de (of), either expressed or understood; as, *Je lui parle*, I speak to him; *J'en parle*, I speak of him.

467. (I.) When personal pronouns are in the accusative, or in other words, the *direct objects* of the verb, they are expressed in French thus:—

me,	by me		*us,*	by nous
thee,	„ te		*you,*	„ vous
him, it,	„ le		*them,*	„ les, *m.* and *f.*
her, it,	„ la			

and are placed before the verb in simple tenses, and before the auxiliary in compound tenses, whether the sentence be affirmative, negative, or interrogative; as,

Il *me* flatte.	*He flatters* me.
Vous ne *la* surprendrez pas.	*You will not surprise* her.
Ils *nous* ont trompés.	*They have deceived* us.
Ne *les* connaissez-vous pas?	*Do you not know* them?

REMARK.—When *me, te, se, le, la,* come before a vowel, or *h* mute, the elision of the *e* takes place, as explained in the chapter of the apostrophe, page 9.

N.B.—The pronouns *le, la, les,* are also called *relative* pronouns, because they relate to a substantive already expressed.

EXERCISE CLXXXI.

You suspect *me* (without reason).—He has rewarded *me*
    soupçonner   mal à propos.   récompenser
generously. — God is a father to those who love *him*, and a
généreusement.   le   de ceux   le
protector to those who fear *him*. — (As soon as) my sister
  78   de   craindre   Dès que
(shall have) arrived, I will go and see *her*. —   Vice often
  sera   ind-7   *   art.
deceives *us* under the mask of virtue. — We shall go and
    masque m. art.   *
see *you* after dinner. — Do you not see *them?* — Whoever
    après dîner.   112
flatters his masters betrays *them*. — I know *it*.
    maître trahir   265

468. (II.) When personal pronouns are the *indirect objects* of the verb, and governed by the preposition *à* (to),

understood, they are expressed by *me, te, lui,* m. and f.; *nous, vous, leur,* m. and f., and placed before the verb, in the same manner as when they are the direct objects; as,

Elle *me* parle.	*She speaks* to me.
Il *lui* donne.	*He gives* him (*i. e.* to him).
Je *leur* écrirai.	*I will write* to them.

469. (III.) When the preposition *à* is to be expressed before the pronouns, they are then rendered by *moi, toi, lui, elle, nous, vous, eux, elles,* and placed after the verb. This happens only in the following cases:—

1st, With the verbs *aller,* to go; *courir* and *accourir,* to run to; *marcher,* to walk; *penser* and *songer,* to think; *venir,* to come; *viser,* to aim at; *être* (in the sense of to belong); *avoir,* to have, used with the words *affaire, égard, rapport, recours ;* as,

Votre frère vint à nous.	*Your brother came* to us.
Ce livre est à moi.	*This book belongs* to me.
J'aurai recours à eux.	*I will have recourse* to them.

2d, When a verb has two or more indirect regimens, and likewise with all reflected verbs; as,

Je parle à *lui* et à *elle*.	*I speak* to him *and* to her.
Il s'adressa à *moi*.	*He applied* to me.

EXERCISE CLXXXII.

Do you not speak *to her,* when you meet her?—Few
         quand rencontrer Peu
people are wise enough to prefer the blame that is useful
de gens   pour
to them, to the praise which betrays them.—They came *to us*
      louange f. trahir
when we (were not thinking) *of* them. — That horse was
   ne pensions pas à   ind-2
formerly *mine,* but I sold it to your cousin.—If you don't
autrefois à moi   ind-4 *l'*
behave better, you will have to do *with me.*—He speaks
se conduire   affaire à
to you and *to him.*—We trust *to them.*—She applied *to him.*
      se fier

470. (IV.) When a personal pronoun, used as a direct

or indirect object, accompanies a verb in the imperative mood, in the first person plural, or in the second person singular or plural, it is put in French, as in English, immediately after the verb, and *moi, toi,* are used instead of *me, te.* But, if a negation attends the imperative, the pronoun follows the general rule, and is placed before the verb, and again *me, te,* are used.

EXAMPLES.

Affirmatively.		*Negatively.*	[them.
Aimons-*les,*	*Let us love* them.	Ne *les* aimons pas,	*Let us not love*
Sauvez-*moi,*	*Save* me.	Ne *me* sauvez pas,	*Don't save* me.
Dites-*lui,*	*Tell* him.	Ne *lui* dites pas,	*Don't tell* him.

471. REMARKS.—(1.) When two imperatives are joined by the conjunction *et* or *ou,* and without a negative, it is considered more elegant to place the second pronoun before the verb; as,

Polissez-*le* sans cesse, et *le* repolissez.—(*Boileau.*) | *Polish and repolish it continually.*

472. (2.) When an imperative has two pronouns for regimens, one direct and the other indirect, the direct regimen is expressed first; as,

Donnez-le-moi. | *Give it me.*
Prêtez-le-lui. | *Lend it to him.*

Negatively, we would say, *Ne me le donnez pas; Ne le lui prêtez pas.*

473. (3.) When *moi, toi,* are placed after the imperative, and followed by the pronoun *en,* they are changed into *m', t';* as,

Donnez-*m'en, Give me* some. | Retourne-*t'en, Go back.*

Note.—Observe again how a hyphen is introduced in the foregoing examples. The rule is thus laid down by *Beauzée* and *Féraud.* When the first and second persons of the imperative have for *complement* (or *regimen*) one of these words: *moi, toi, nous, vous, le, la, lui, les, leur, en, y,* they are joined together by a *hyphen,* and a second *hyphen* is introduced when there are two of those words as complement of the imperative. Examples:—*Donnez-moi, dépêchons-nous, accordez-la-leur, rendons-la-lui.*

But we write: *faites-moi lui parler,* and not *faites-moi-lui parler,* because *lui* is the regimen of *parler,* and not of *faites; venez me parler,* because *me* is not governed by *venez,* but by the infinitive *parler.*

EXERCISE CLXXXIII.

Whatever thing (you have promised), give *it*. —
127   *que vous ayez promise,*

Listen to *me;* do not condemn *me* without a hearing. —
Ecouter *   *condamner*   *m'entendre.*

Tell *me* the truth. — Don't speak *to me.* — Repeat *to them*
vérité f.   *Répéter*

continually, that, without honesty, one can never succeed in
sans cesse   *on*   *réussir*

the world. — Don't repeat *to them* the same things. — Take
    Prendre

them, or leave *them,* it is (all one) to me. — My innocence
laisser   *cela égal*   —— f.

is the only good that remains to me: leave *it to me.*
seul bien m. *qui*

474. (V.) Personal pronouns, whether direct or indirect objects, are repeated, in French, before every verb; as,

Il *vous* estime et *vous* honore. | *He esteems and honours* you.

Son visage odieux *m'*afflige et *me* poursuit. (RACINE.)

EXERCISE CLXXXIV.

He beseeches and entreats *me* not to do it. — I say and
prier conjurer *de*

declare to *you.* — The idea that they believe him guilty,
*   *pensée* f.   *on croire coupable*

pursues, torments, and overwhelms *him.*—He wearies and
poursuivre, tourmenter, accabler   *ennuyer*

torments *us* incessantly. — A ²well brought up ¹son never
obséder sans cesse.   *bien élevé*

rebels against his father; he loves, honours, and respects *him.*
se révolter   *respecter*

475. (VI.) The pronouns *it, they, them,* which the English use with reference to animals and inanimate things, are expressed in French by *il, elle, ils, elles,* when they are the subject or nominative of the verb, and by *le, la, les,* when they form the accusative or direct object of the verb.

Be careful to make these pronouns agree in gender and number with the nouns to which they refer. It is almost

SYNTAX OF PERSONAL PRONOUNS. 245

unnecessary to repeat that the French language has no neuter gender, consequently inanimate objects are either masculine or feminine; so, in speaking of the *rose*, which is feminine, we say ELLE *est belle*, it is beautiful; and of a book, *livre*, which is masculine, *vous a-t-*IL *amusé ?* has it amused you?

476. REMARK.—When these pronouns come after a preposition, they are usually left out in French; then the preposition becomes an adverb, and conveys the idea sufficiently; as,

| Approchez-vous du feu.—Je suis tout *auprès*. | Come near the fire.—I am quite near it. |

EXERCISE CLXXXV.

Look at that magnificent building; *il* unites grace
Regarder * *magnifique bâtiment* m. *réunir* art. *grâce* f.
with beauty, and elegance with simplicity. — Where
à art. art. *à* art.
is my pen? *It* is upon the table. — Give *it* me. — Never
plume f. *sur*
judge from appearances, for *they* are often deceitful. —
juger sur art. *apparence* f. *car* *trompeur*
(There is) a good book, read *it*. — My house is new; I will
Voilà *maison* f. *neuf*
not sell *it*; but I will let *it*.—His cot was solitary;
ind-7 *louer* ind-7 *cabane* f. ind-2 *isolé*
near *it* flowed a spring of pure water.
couler ind-2 *source* f. ²*vif* ¹

477. (VII.) When *to it, to them*, relate to inanimate things, they are expressed by *y ;* as,

| Ce tableau est très-bon; mettez-Y un cadre. | That picture is very good; put a frame to it. |

But, when the pronouns *it, them*, are in the dative case, that is, used for *to it, to them*, and have reference to animals, plants, and ideal substances, in which we suppose an active principle, such as some virtues and vices, or are preceded by the verb *to owe*, or *to be indebted*, they are translated by *lui* for the singular, and *leur* for the plural; as,

Ce chien a faim, donnez-LUI du pain.	That dog is hungry, give IT some bread.
Ces orangers vont périr, si vous ne LEUR donnez point d'eau.	These orange-trees will die, if you do not give THEM water.

(For the proper place of *y*, see *N.B.* p. 50.)

EXERCISE CLXXXVI.

I study   botany, and   apply myself seriously *to*
   art. *botanique* f.   pron. *s'appliquer sérieusement*
it.—History and geography are his delight, he (gives himself up)
  373   *délices* pl.   *se livre*
to them entirely.—I leave you the care of that goldfinch;
     entièrement. laisser   *soin* m.   *chardonneret* m.
do not forget to give *it* water.—When virtue appears in all
   oublier de   *paraître dans*
its beauty, we cannot refuse *it* our homage and respect.—
        ne pouvons refuser   —— m.
This book cost me (a great deal), but I (*am indebted*) *to it* for
    coûte   *cher*   *dois*   *
my knowledge.—Bring my horses, and give *them* some hay.
 instruction f. *Amener*   *foin* m.

478. (VIII.) The pronoun *le*, which makes *la* for the feminine, and *les* for the plural of both genders, may supply the place of a substantive, or an adjective, or even of a part of a sentence.

When this pronoun supplies the place of a substantive or an adjective used substantively, it takes the gender and number of that substantive or adjective used substantively. In such a case, the English equivalent is almost always understood.

EXAMPLES.

Êtes-vous madame de Genlis?— Je ne *la* suis pas.	Are you madame de Genlis?—I am not.
Êtes-vous la mère de cet enfant?— Oui, je *la* suis.	Are you the mother of that child? —Yes, I am.
Êtes-vous la malade?—Je *la* suis.	Are you the patient?—I am.
Mesdames, êtes-vous les parentes de monsieur?—Oui, nous *les* sommes.	Ladies, are you the relations of this gentleman?—Yes, we are.

EXERCISE CLXXXVII.

Are you Dr Kitto's sister? Yes, I am.—Are you Marshal
     sœur   maréchal m.
Ney's daughter? No, I am not.—Are you Lady Melville?
     Non   Lady †
Yes, I am.—Are you the mistress of this house? I am.—Are
        maîtresse
you the king's ministers? We are.—Madam, are you the bride?
   ministre   mariée
Yes, I am.—Are those your gloves? Yes, they are. Give
     -ce là gant m.   ce
them to me.—Are you my sister's dressmaker? I am.
           couturière f.

479. (IX.) The pronoun *le* remains invariable, when it has reference to a verb, an adjective, or a substantive used adjectively. The English equivalent, which is generally *so* or *it*, is almost always understood.

EXAMPLES.

Madame, êtes-vous malade?—Oui, monsieur, je *le* suis.	*Madam, are you ill?—Yes, Sir, I am.*
Êtes-vous mère?—Je *le* suis.	*Are you a mother?—I am.*
Mesdemoiselles, êtes-vous prêtes? —Oui, nous *le* sommes.	*Young ladies, are you ready?— Yes, we are.*

EXERCISE CLXXXVIII.

Madam, are you pleased with that speech? Yes, I am.—
      444   discours m.
Madam, are you married? Yes, I am.—Are you mistress of
    mariée   maîtresse
your actions? I am not.—Ladies, are you glad to have seen
             bien aise
the little Princess? Yes, we are.—Have we ever been so
   princesse   jamais
quiet as we are?—Do you know if they are rich? No,
tranquille que   265   riche
they are not.—The poor will not always be *so.*
     pauvre pl.

---

† Mot emprunté de l'anglais. On prononce *Lédi.*—(*Acad.*)

SYNTAX OF PERSONAL PRONOUNS.

OF THE PRONOUNS *se*, *soi*.

(For the various meanings, see No. 88.)

480. The pronoun *se* (*s'* before a vowel) is of both numbers and genders; it is always placed before the verb of which it is the regimen; as *il* SE *connaît,* he knows himself; *elle s'imagine,* she fancies.

Les yeux de l'amitié *se* trompent rarement.—VOLTAIRE.

481. The pronoun *soi* is of both genders, and is generally preceded by a preposition, or by the conjunction *que.*—When applied to persons, it is employed only in a vague and indeterminate sense; as, *Il faut prendre garde à* SOI, it is necessary to take care of oneself.

EXERCISE CLXXXIX.

They lost *themselves* in the wood. — This flower is fading.
    s'égarer ind-3   *fleur* f. *se flétrir*
These trees are dying.—A good deed carries its reward
        se mourir   *bienfait* m. *porter*   *récompense* f.
with *itself.*—Frankness is good of *itself*, but it has its excesses.
avec   *franchise* f.   *de*   *excès* m.
When a man   loves nobody but *himself*, he is not fit for
Quand * *on n'*   *   *que*   *on*   *propre*
society. — To be too much dissatisfied with *ourselves* is a
           *   444   *soi*
weakness; but to be too much pleased with *ourselves* is a
faiblesse f.   *   444
folly. — It always depends on *ourselves* to act honourably.
sottise f.   *de*   *d'*

RESPECTIVE PLACES OF THE PERSONAL PRONOUNS.

482. When a verb (the imperative *affirmative* excepted) governs two or more pronouns without a preposition, they are always placed before it, and before its auxiliary in compound tenses, in the following order:—

me, te, se, nous, vous,	before all others.
le, la, les,	before *lui, leur, y, en.*
lui, leur,	before *y, en.*
y,	before *en.*
en,	is always the last.

SYNTAX OF PERSONAL PRONOUNS.

483. When the sentence is not interrogative, the pronoun which is the subject of the verb is always placed at the head; as,

Vous ne *me le* conseillez pas.	*You do not advise* me so.
Je ne *le lui* dirais pas.	*I would not tell* it him.
Nous *les en* avertirons.	*We shall warn* them of it.
Nous *lui en* parlerons.	*We will speak* to him about it.
Ils ne *s'y* soumettront pas.	*They will not submit* to it.

484. In an imperative sentence, when affirmative, *le, la, les,* are always placed first; as, *donnez-le-moi,* give it me. *Moi* is placed after *y;* as, *menez-y-moi,* take me thither: but *nous* must precede *y;* as, *menez-nous-y,* take us thither.

EXERCISE CXC.

Do not say to a friend, who asks something of you: Go,
_{see p. 211}   *

and come again to-morrow, and I will give *it you;* when you
    revenir   *demain*   *   *lorsque*

can   give *it him* immediately.—It is certain that   old
pouvoir   *lui sur-le-champ.*   *art.*

Géronte has refused his daughter to Valère; but because he
                                            parce qu'

does not give *her to him,* (it does not follow) that he will give
                    il ne s'ensuit pas

her to you.—I will give *you some.*—I have a letter for you.
                  en   *lettre* f. *pour*

Your brother has sent *it me* to bring *it you.* Give *it me.*
                 envoyée   *pour*

§ II. OF POSSESSIVE PRONOUNS.

Under this head we shall place the POSSESSIVE ADJECTIVES, as we have already done, page 42.

485. *Possessive adjectives* agree in gender and number with the noun to which they are joined.

486. They are repeated before every noun of the same sentence; as, MON *père,* MA *mère,*† *et* MES *frères sont venus,* my father, mother, and brothers have come.

---

† *Mes père et mère, ses père et mère,* instead of *mon père et ma mère, son père et sa mère,* are phrases extremely incorrect, and though used by many people, are most certainly contrary to the principles of the French language, and are condemned by *Vaugelas, Wailly,* by the modern Grammarians, and finally by the French Academy.

487. *Possessive adjectives* are repeated also before the adjectives that do not qualify the same noun; as, MON *grand et* MON *petit appartement*, which is equivalent to *mon grand* APPARTEMENT *et mon petit appartement*. But I would say: MON *grand et bel appartement*, without repeating *mon*, were I speaking of an apartment both large and beautiful.

<small>(See what is said upon the repetition of the Article, p. 200 and 201.)</small>

EXERCISE CXCI.

Cyrus knew all the soldiers of *his* army, and could
—— ind-2   *soldat*   93 *armée* f.   *pouvoir* ind-2
designate them by *their* names.—²Four ³things ¹(are required)
désigner   *nom* m.   *on demande*
of a woman: that virtue (should dwell) in *her* heart; that
à   *femme*   que 371   *habite*   dans
modesty (should shine) on *her* forehead; that   gentleness
 371   *brille*   *front* m.   371 *douceur* f.
(should flow) from *her* lips, and that   work   (should occupy)
découle   *lèvre* f.   371 *travail* m.   *occupe*
her hands.—*Her* father and mother are dead.—*My* uncle and
                                                       235
aunt are in Paris.—He (showed him) both *his* fine and   ugly
tante   *lui a montré*   *   beau*   *vilain*
dresses. — He showed him *his* beautiful and rich dresses.
habits m.

488. The French make use of the article, and not of the possessive adjective, when the sense clearly points out who is the possessor; as,

J'ai mal à LA tête.	*I have a pain in* MY *head.*
Pierre a reçu un coup de feu AU bras droit.	*Peter has received a shot in* HIS *right arm.*

As there can be no doubt as to whose head is aching, and whose arm has received the shot, the French deem the article sufficient.

But, to avoid ambiguity, I must say,

Je vois que MON bras enfle.	*I see my arm is swelling.*
Pierre a perdu SON argent.	*Peter has lost his money.*

Because, were I to say, *Je vois que* LE *bras enfle;*

Pierre a perdu L'*argent*, one would not know whether it is my arm or that of another that I see swelling; or, whether it is his own money or John's that Peter has lost.

The possessive adjective is also used in speaking of an habitual complaint known to the person spoken to; as,

MA migraine m'a repris.	*My headache has returned.*
SA goutte le tourmente.	*His gout torments him.*

Reflected verbs generally remove all ambiguity; as,

Je me suis blessé à LA main.	*I have hurt my hand.*
Je me lave LES mains.	*I wash my hands.*

The use of the possessive adjective would here be an error; custom, however, authorizes a few familiar expressions in which the possessive seems to be redundant; as, *Je me suis tenu toute la journée* SUR MES JAMBES;—*il se tient ferme* SUR SES PIEDS.

489. The French use the article, not the possessive adjective, before a noun forming the regimen, when a personal pronoun, which is the indirect regimen, sufficiently supplies the place of the possessive; as,

Vous LUI avez cassé LE bras.	*You have broken his arm.*
Vous ME blessez LA main.	*You hurt my hand.*

EXERCISE CXCII.

Of all ²living ¹creatures, man is the only one who (has not)
    art. *vivant* f.   *seul* *   *n'ait pas*

his face turned towards the earth; he walks with *his* eyes
     — f. *tourné vers*   *marcher* *   m.

directed towards heaven, as if to indicate the superiority
dirigé   art. *ciel* m. *comme pour indiquer*

of his origin.—*My* gout does not allow me a moment's repose.
son   *laisser*   *repos.*

—You will cut *your* finger. — A cannon-ball
     se couper   *doigt* m.   *boulet de canon* m. *lui*

carried off *his* arm.—Our carriage passed over *his*
emporter ind-3   *voiture* f. *lui* ind-3   *sur*

body, and bruised *his* right shoulder.
corps m.   *lui meurtrir* ind-3   ²*droit* ¹*épaule* f.

SYNTAX OF POSSESSIVE ADJECTIVES.

490. When *its* or *their* relate to inanimate objects, they are expressed by *son, sa, ses, leur,* or *leurs :*—

1st, When the possessor, substantive or pronoun, is expressed, as the subject, in the same member of a sentence; as,

| Londres a *ses* beautés. | London has its *beauties.* |

2d, When preceded by any preposition whatever; as,

| J'admire la largeur DE *ses* rues. | I admire the *width* OF its *streets.* |

3d, When joined to a noun qualified by an adjective, unless the noun form the regimen; as,

| *Ses* bâtiments *réguliers* plaisent au premier coup d'œil. | Its regular *buildings please at first sight.* |

4th, When joined to the subject of the verb, the latter is, or may be, followed in French by the preposition *de;* as,

| *Son* commerce produit D'immenses ressources. | Its *trade produces immense resources.* |

On all other occasions, *its* and *their* are expressed by *en,* before the verb, and by the article before the noun. So, still speaking of London, I would say:

| *La* situation *en* est très-commode pour le commerce. | Its *situation is very convenient for trade.* |

EXERCISE CXCIII.

A new custom was a phenomenon in Egypt: (for which
  coutume f. ind-2   *prodige* m. *en*   *aussi*
reason) (there never was) a people that preserved   so long
  n'y eut-il jamais de   *conserver* subj-3
its laws, and even *its* ceremonies. — The   pyramids   of Egypt
             pyramide f.
astonish,   both   by the enormity of *their* bulk, and by the
   également et   *masse*
justness   of *their* proportions.—The Thames is a magnificent
justesse f.   ——   *superbe*
river: *its* channel is so wide and so deep   below   London-
   lit m.   *large*   *au-dessous de*
bridge, that several thousand   vessels lie at their ease in it.
      millier de   *être*   *l'*   109

SYNTAX OF POSSESSIVE ADJECTIVES. 253

491. REMARKS.—1. *A friend of mine; a book of yours*, are turned in this manner in French, *un de mes amis; un de vos livres.* As if it were, one of my friends, one of your books; and so on with all other phrases of the same kind.

2. *Mine, thine, his, hers, ours, yours, theirs*, used with the verb *to be*, in the sense of *to belong*, are expressed, in French, by *à moi, à toi, à lui, à elle, à nous, à vous, à eux,* m., *à elles,* f.; as, this book is MINE, *ce livre est À MOI*; that watch is HERS, *cette montre est À ELLE.*

3. The forms *my brother's, your sister's,* etc. are also rendered by *à mon frère, à votre sœur.*

4. In speaking to a person of his relations or friends, we generally put *monsieur, madame, mademoiselle, messieurs, mesdames, mesdemoiselles,* before the possessive adjectives; as,

J'ai rencontré *monsieur* votre père.	*I met your father.*
Comment se porte *madame* votre mère?	*How does your mother do?*

But this is a mere form of politeness, and has nothing to do with the rules of grammar.

EXERCISE CXCIV.

His mother is an old acquaintance *of ours.* — *ancienne connaissance* f.

That gentleman is a relation *of mine.* — I am going to *monsieur parent*

dine with an aunt *of his.*—A sister *of hers* is dead. — Is this *tante* 161

house *yours* or *his?* It is not *mine.* It is *my uncle's* or *oncle*

my mother's. — Is *your sister* in town? — No, she is in 161 *en* à

the country, with a cousin *of mine.* — These keys are *his* or f. *clef* f.

hers.—They are not *mine,* they are *my father's* or *my mother's.*

§ III. OF DEMONSTRATIVE PRONOUNS.

492. *Ce* before *être*, requires this verb to be in the singular, except when it is followed by the third person plural. So we say, C'EST *moi*, C'EST *lui*, C'EST *nous*, C'EST *vous*. But we must say, *Ce* SONT, C'ÉTAIENT, *ce* FURENT, *ce* SERONT *eux, elles, les parents, qui*, etc.

Such is the rule of the best grammarians. With the third person plural, however, some respectable authors use the verb *être*, sometimes in the plural, and sometimes in the singular.

493. *Ce* is often used instead of *il, elle, ils, elles*, in reference to a person or thing mentioned before. *Ce* is preferred when the verb *être* is followed by a substantive, accompanied by the article, or the adjective *un;* as,

Lisez Homère et Virgile; CE SONT LES plus grands POÈTES de l'antiquité.	*Read Homer and Virgil; they are the best poets of antiquity.*
C'est UN César. C'est UN Cicéron.	*He is a Cæsar. He is a Cicero.*

But, when the verb *être* is followed by an adjective without a noun, or by a noun taken adjectively, *il, elle, ils, elles*, must be used; as,

Lisez Démosthène et Cicéron; ILS SONT très *éloquents*.	*Read Demosthenes and Cicero; they are very eloquent.*
J'ai vu le Louvre; IL EST *magnifique*, et digne d'une grande nation.	*I have seen the Louvre; it is beautiful, and worthy of a great nation.*

EXERCISE CXCV.

It is we who have restored tranquillity.—*It is* you, brave
                           rétablir
soldiers, who fought gloriously.—*It was* the Egyptians
  soldat   combattre ind-4   ind-3   Egyptiens
who first observed the course of the stars, regulated
    les premiers   ind-3   cours m.   astre m.   régler
the year, and invented arithmetic.—Read attentively Plato
  année f.   Lire
and Cicero; *they are the* two *philosophers* of antiquity, who
                             philosophe
have given us ²(the most sound and luminous) ¹ideas upon
        art.   sain   lumineux idée f.
morality.—I have seen the city of Edinburgh; *it is beautiful.*
  morale f.   ville f.

SYNTAX OF DEMONSTRATIVE PRONOUNS.

494. *Ce qui*, as the subject, and *ce que*, as the object, are much used in the sense of *what, that which, that thing which.*

When *ce qui* or *ce que* begin a sentence of two parts, *ce* must be repeated in the second part of the sentence, if it begins with the verb *être;* as,

Ce *qui* m'attache à la vie, C'EST vous.	What *keeps me attached to life, is you.*
Ce *que* je désire le plus, C'EST d'aller vous voir.	What *I wish most, is to come and see you.*

The repetition of *ce* is not indispensable when the verb *être* is followed by a substantive singular. Thus, we may say,

Ce qui mérite le plus notre admiration, C'EST or EST la vertu.	*That which deserves our admiration most, is virtue.*

Even in this case, however, it is better, in general, to repeat *ce*, which gives more energy to the expression.

But when the verb *être* is followed by an adjective or a past participle without a noun, the demonstrative *ce* is not repeated; as,

CE que vous dites EST vrai.	*What you say is true.*

EXERCISE CXCVI.

What I fear, *is* to displease you.— *What* pleases in the
Ce que craindre de déplaire   Ce qui   dans
ancients, *is* that they have painted nature with a noble sim-
ancien   peindre
plicity.—*What* we ²justly ¹admire in Racine, *are* those
Ce qu' on avec justice   dans
characters always   natural   and always well sustained.—
caractère m.   dans la nature   * soutenu
That which sustains man in the midst of the greatest reverses,
Ce qui   soutenir   à   milieu m.
is hope. — *What* I say *is* true.—*What* is true *is* beautiful.
espérance f.   beau.

495. *Celui, celle, ceux, celles,* are frequently used with the relatives *qui, que, dont, auquel, à laquelle,* in the sense of *he who, she who, they who, whoever, whichever,* etc.; as,

Heureux *celui qui* craint le Seigneur!	*Happy is* he who *fears the Lord!*
Celle *qui* aime la vertu est heureuse.	She who *loves virtue is happy.*

EXERCISE CXCVII.

Happy is *he who* lives contented with his lot!—*He who* has
   *   vivre content 444 sort* m.

never been acquainted with adversity, says Seneca, has seen
  * éprouvé * art.   *n'a vu*

the world but on one side.—*She who* did it was punished.
    que d' côté m. ind.-4 ind.-4

—*He who* thinks (of nobody but himself), excuses others
  ne   qu'à lui-même   dispenser les autres

from thinking of him. — *He who* renders a service should
 inf-1 à   *rendre   doit*

forget it, *he who* receives it, remember it.
oublier   *s'en souvenir.*

496. In the very familiar style, *cela* is sometimes contracted into *ça;* as, *Donnez-moi ça.*—(*Acad.*)

§ IV. OF RELATIVE PRONOUNS.

497. The relative pronouns *who, which,* and *that,* are expressed by *qui,* when they are the subject or *nominative* of a verb; as,

L'homme *qui* parle.	*The man* who *speaks.*
La dame *qui* chante.	*The lady* who *sings.*
La chaise *qui* vient.	*The chaise* which *comes.*

498. *Whom, which,* and *that,* are expressed by *que* when they are in the *accusative,* or in other words, the regimen or direct object of a verb; as,

L'homme *que* je vois.	*The man* whom *I see.*
Les chevaux *que* je vois.	*The horses* which *I see.*
La maison *que* j'ai.	*The house* that *or* which *I have.*

499. *Whom* is expressed by *qui,* when it has no antecedent, and means *what person;* as,

Qui appelez-vous?	*Whom do you call?*
Je sais *qui* vous voulez dire.	*I know* whom *you mean.*

☞ Remember that the *e* of *que* is cut off before a vowel; *qui* is never changed.

Observation.—Should *qui* or *que* be divided from its antecedent by a noun, and any uncertainty arise as to which of the two nouns it may relate to, use *lequel, laquelle*, instead of *qui;* as,

C'est un effet de la Providence, LEQUEL attire l'admiration.	*It is an effect of Providence which draws forth admiration.*

Here *lequel* is preferable to *qui*, as a doubt might arise whether it was *effect* or *Providence* to which it related.

EXERCISE CXCVIII.

Pythagoras was the first among the Greeks *who* took the
Pythagore   *est*   *d'entre*   *ait pris*
name of philosopher. — ²Synonymous ¹terms are words *which*
                art. *synonyme*   *terme*   *des mot*
signify the same thing. — (You must have) a man *who* loves
signifier   *Il vous faut*   *n'*
(nothing but) truth and you, and *who* (will speak) the truth
   que   *vous dise*
(in spite of) you.—Here is a lady *whom* you know. — Where
  malgré   *Voici*   *connaître*
is the horse *that* he has bought? — *Whom* shall we invite?
                        acheter

500. The relative pronoun *qui* is always of the gender, number, and person of its *antecedent;* that is, of the noun or pronoun to which it relates.

Moi *qui* suis estimé.	*I* who *am esteemed.*
Elle *qui* est estimée.	*She* who *is esteemed.*
Nous *qui* sommes estimés.	*We* who *are esteemed.*
Vous *qui* riez.	*You* who *laugh.*

On the same principle we say : *Vous parlez comme un homme* QUI ENTEND *la matière* (you speak like a man who understands the subject), and not, QUI ENTENDEZ *la matière*—because the relative *qui* does not represent the pronoun *vous*, but represents the substantive *homme* which immediately precedes *qui*.

REMARK.—An adjective, or a cardinal number, cannot serve as an antecedent to a relative pronoun; so, instead of saying : *Nous étions* DEUX *qui étaient du même avis* (we were two who were of the same opinion), we must say : *Nous étions deux qui* ÉTIONS *du même avis,* thus making *nous,* the subject of the preceding verb, the antecedent of the relative pronoun.

501. The relative pronoun ought always to be placed near its antecedent; any other place occasions ambiguity. So *Boileau* is not to be imitated when he says:

> La *déesse*, en entrant, *qui* voit la nappe mise.

He ought to have said: *la* DÉESSE QUI, *en entrant, voit la nappe mise,* in order to bring the relative *qui* near its antecedent *déesse*.

EXERCISE CXCIX.

You *who* are esteemed.—We *who* study. —I *who* believe the
                          étudier   croire
soul immortal.—The greatest men *who* were the ornament
                                    ind-4   ornement m.
and glory of Greece, Homer, Pythagoras, Plato, even Lycurgus
                                                 même Lycurgue
and Solon, went to learn wisdom in Egypt.—The [2]mo-
              —— ind-3 * apprendre sagesse f. en
dern [1]writers *who* attack the ancients, are children *who* beat
     écrivain   attaquer ancien   des   battre
their nurse. — I see only us *two who* are reasonable.—It is
  nourrice.   ne   que   subj-1 *raisonnable* C'
I *alone who* am guilty. — We were *ten who* were of the
   seul   coupable.   ind-2   ind-2
same opinion. — You *who* have spoken so well.
  avis m.   3   1   2

502. The relative pronouns, *whom, that, which,* and also the conjunction *that,* are frequently understood in English, but *que* is always expressed in French; as,

L'homme *que* nous avons vu.	*The man* (whom *or* that) *we saw.*
Le vin *que* nous avons bu.	*The wine* (that *or* which) *we drank.*
Je crois *que* vous parlez français.	*I think* (that) *you speak French.*

Note.—The student will already have observed, that the English make much greater use of the ellipsis (or omission of some words) than the French, and that, in general, the words which are understood in English, are expressed in French. For previous instances of the ellipsis occurring in English, and not in French, see Nos. 31, 32, 65, 66, 67, 91, 97, 180.

EXERCISE CC.

The lady you have married is my cousin.—The tea we
femme épousée thé m.

drink is very good.—I will never forget the favour you have
prendre oublier grâce f.

done me.—Have you received the letter I wrote to you?—
faite ai écrite

I think he will come.—Titus spent eighty millions in the
croire dépensa dans

²public ¹games he ²once ¹gave to the Roman people. —
jeu m. *une fois peuple* m.

I thank you for the trouble you have taken.
de peine f. *prise.*

503. Whose, of whom, of which, are generally expressed in French by *dont*, both in speaking of persons and things; as,

Le ciel, *dont* le secours est nécessaire.	Heaven, whose *assistance is necessary.*
L'homme *dont* il se plaint.	The man of whom *he complains.*
La maison *dont* vous parlez.	The house of which *you speak.*

But, when the relative requires to be separated from its antecedent, instead of *dont*, we use *duquel* and *de laquelle* in speaking of *things* or *animals*; as,

La Tamise, dans le lit *de laquelle*, etc.	*The Thames, in the bed* of which, &c.

In speaking of *persons*, it is generally a matter of indifference whether we use *de qui*, or *duquel, de laquelle*; as,

Le prince à la protection DE QUI ou DUQUEL je dois ma fortune.	The prince to whose *patronage I owe my fortune.*

From whom is rendered by *de qui*, and not by *dont*.

504. *N.B.* Dont can only be used when the antecedent is expressed; for, in the beginning of an interrogative phrase, *of whom* would be rendered by *de qui*, and *of which* by *duquel, de laquelle*; as,

De qui parlez-vous?	Of whom *do you speak?*
Duquel vous plaignez-vous?	Of which *do you complain?*

505. Whose, used without reference to a noun expressed before, implies the word *person* understood.

If it can be changed into *of whom*, it is expressed by *de qui;* as,

De qui êtes-vous fils?	Whose *son are you?* i. e. of whom are you the son?

If WHOSE can be changed into *to whom*, it is expressed by *à qui;* as,

A qui est ce chapeau?	Whose *hat is this?* i. e. to whom does this hat belong?

EXERCISE CCI.

There is the gentleman *whose* horse has won the race. —
Voilà   monsieur   gagner prix de la course.
He is a man *of whom* I have a good opinion. — The lady *of whom*
C'   *   dame
you are speaking is gone. — Here is the book *of which* you
            ind-1   partir   Voici
made me a present. — The daughter of Minos gave a thread to
ind-4   * présent.   ind-3   fil m. ,
Theseus, (by means) *of which* he got out   of the labyrinth. —
Thésée   au moyen   sortir ind-3   labyrinthe m.
The people *from whom* you expect so many services deceive
            gens   attendre tant de   tromper
you. — *Whose* daughter is she? — *Whose* house is that?

506. When the pronouns WHOM or WHICH come after any preposition (except *of*), *whom* is expressed by *qui,* and *which* by *lequel, laquelle, lesquels, lesquelles;* as,

Le monsieur à QUI j'écris est très riche.	*The gentleman to whom I write is very rich.*
Il y a un Dieu, *par* QUI tout est gouverné.	*There is a God,* by whom *all things are governed.*
Le cheval *sur* LEQUEL il est.	*The horse* on which *he is.*
La disposition *dans* LAQUELLE il est.	*The disposition* in which *he is.*
Le bonheur *après* LEQUEL j'aspire.	*The happiness* after which *I aspire.*

It follows from the foregoing rule, that *qui*, preceded by a preposition, is never said of things, but only of persons. So, we can say: *La personne à qui j'ai donné ma confiance;* but we cannot say: *Les sciences à qui je m'applique.* We must say: *Les sciences auxquelles je m'applique.*

EXERCISE CCII.

The man, *for whom* you speak, is gone to Paris.—He is a
                                               aller   C°
friend *in whom* I put my confidence. — There are two things
      en   *mettre*   *confiance* f.   *y avoir*
to which we must (accustom ourselves) under pain of finding
             falloir   *s'accoutumer*   *peine*   inf-1
life insupportable: the injuries of time and the injustices of
                           injure f.
men. — Regulus, in his expedition against Carthage, had to
       Régulus   ind-3
combat a prodigious serpent, *against which* it was necessary
combattre   m.   *falloir* ind-3
to employ ²the ¹whole Roman army.

§ V. OF INDEFINITE PRONOUNS.—See p. 51.

507. The pronoun ON is generally followed by a masculine singular; as,

On n'est pas toujours HEUREUX. | People *are not always fortunate.*

Yet, when it is quite evident that a female is spoken of, *on* should be followed by a *feminine* singular; as,

On n'est pas toujours JEUNE et JOLIE.—(*Acad.*) | A woman *cannot be always young and pretty.*

On may likewise be followed by an adjective or substantive *plural*, when the sense clearly indicates that this pronoun relates to several persons: the verb, however, remains singular; as,

On se battit en *désespérés*. | They *fought like desperate men.*
Ici ON est *égaux*. (*Inscription sur la porte d'un cimetière.*)

508. *On* must be repeated before every verb of which it is the subject or nominative; as,

On le loue, on le menace, on le caresse; mais, quoi que l'on fasse, on ne peut en venir à bout. | They *praise, threaten, and caress him; but whatever they do, they cannot master him.*

N. B.—When *they* is used with reference to a plural noun *expressed* before, it is rendered in French by *ils* or *elles*, and not by *on*.

☞ Observe also, that although ON frequently represents WE, THEY, PEOPLE, which are all of the plural number, yet ON is always followed by a verb in the *third* person *singular*.

509. The English have an indefinite manner of expressing themselves, by means of the *indefinite* pronoun IT, which the French express by ON, at the same time changing the verb from the passive into the active sense; as,

ON dit. ON pense. ON rapporte. | It *is said*. It *is thought*. It *is reported*.

510. *On* is much used in French as the subject of an active verb, when the passive voice is used in English. So, instead of saying as the English: *I am deceived;—I have been told;* the French say: *On me trompe;—On m'a dit;* as if it were, *They deceive me;—They have told me.*

511. CHACUN, *each, every one.* This pronoun is always singular, but when preceded by a plural, it is sometimes followed by *son, sa, ses,* and sometimes by *leur, leurs.*

Chacun takes *son, sa, ses,* when it is placed after the direct regimen, or when the verb has no regimen of that nature; as,

Ils ont apporté leurs offrandes, chacun selon *ses* moyens.	They have brought their *offerings,* every one according to his *means.*
Les deux rois se sont retirés, chacun dans *sa* tente.	The two kings have retired, each to his *tent.*
Ils ont opiné, *chacun* à *son* tour.	They voted, each *in* his *turn.*

Chacun takes *leur, leurs,* when it is placed before the direct regimen; as,

Ils ont apporté, *chacun, leur* offrande.	Each *of them has brought* his *offering.*
Ils ont donné, *chacun, leur* avis.	Each *of them gave* his *opinion.*

EXERCISE CCIII.

When a *woman* is *handsome,* she (is not ignorant of it).—
Quand * on on ne l'ignore pas.
We are not slaves, to endure such ill treatment.—In
On des pour endurer de si mauvais pl.
that house, *they* laugh, play, dance, and sing.—*It is believed*
rire danser *
that peace (will be made) this year. — *We* have been much
se fera année f. bien
deceived.—*He is said* to have succeeded.- Return those medals,
trompés. réussi. Remettre médaille f.
each to *its* place. —²*Each* ¹(of them has fulfilled) *his* duty.
Ils ont rempli

CHAPTER V.

OF THE VERB.

§ 1. Agreement *of the* **VERB** *with its* **subject** *or* **nominative.**

512. General Rule.—A verb must agree with its subject in number and person; as,

Nous *lisons;* vous *lisez.*	*We* read; *you* read.
La haine *veille,* et l'amitié *s'endort.*	*Hatred* is awake, *and friendship* is [asleep.

513. *Observation.* — When a verb has more than one subject, it is put in the plural; as,

Mon frère et lui *parlent* français. | *My brother and he* speak *French.*

And, should the subjects be of different persons, the verb must agree with the first person in preference to the other two, and with the second rather than with the third. In this case, the pronoun *nous* (not expressed in English) is *generally*† placed before the verb, if one of the subjects is in the *first* person; and, the pronoun *vous*† if the *second* person is used with the *third,* without a *first* person; as,

Vous et moi, nous *avons* fait notre devoir. (*Acad.*)	*You and I,* have *done our duty.*
J'ai appris que vous et votre frère vous *partiez* bientôt. (*Ibid.*)	*I have heard that you and your brother were soon to set out.*

† Observe, I say *generally,* and not *always,* as most grammarians do; for *nous* or *vous* may sometimes be understood, as in this sentence of *Fénélon: Narbal et moi* admirions *la bonté des dieux.* Narbal and I were admiring the goodness of the gods.

EXERCISE CCIV.

²Riches ¹often *attract* friends, and poverty *keeps* them
richesses pl.   *attirer* art.   *éloigner*
away.—Religion *watches* over ²secret ¹crimes; the laws *watch*
   *   ——f. *veiller*   ——m.

over ²public ¹crimes. —Virgil, Horace, and Tibullus *were* friends.
——   *Tibulle* ind-2

—He and she *will go* to the country with my father —
campagne f.

You, your cousin, and I, *have* each a ²different ¹opinion.—
——   114   ——f.

You and he *shall accompany* me to the botanical garden.
accompagner

EXCEPTION.

514. When two subjects singular are joined by the conjunction *ou* (or, either), the verb is put in the singular; as,

    Jean OU Jacques le FERA. | *John* or *James* will do *it.*

When, however, the words joined by *ou* are of different persons, usage requires the verb to be in the plural, and that it should agree with the person that has priority, that is, with the first person rather than with the other two, and with the second rather than with the third; as,

    Vous ou moi PARLERONS.   *You or I shall speak.*
    Vous ou votre frère VIENDREZ.   *You or your brother will come.*

REMARKS.

515. (1.) As the words *l'un et l'autre* (both) express plurality, the verb should be put in the plural; as,

    L'un et l'autre SONT venus. | *Both are come.*
    L'un et l'autre *ont* promis.—(*Racine.*)
    L'un et l'autre *ont* le cerveau troublé.—(*Boileau.*)

516. (2.) *Ni l'un ni l'autre* (neither, neither the one nor the other), and all subjects joined together by *ni* repeated, require also the verb in the plural; as,

J'ai lu vos deux discours : ni l'un   *I have read your two speeches: nei-*
ni l'autre ne SONT bons.   *ther the one nor the other is good.*

Ni l'or ni la grandeur ne nous *rendent* heureux.—(*La Fontaine.*)

Exception.—When one of the words united by *ni* can alone perform the action expressed by the verb, the verb is then put in the singular; as,

NI l'un NI l'autre n'OBTIENDRA   *Neither the one nor the other will*
le prix.   *obtain the prize.*
NI M. le Duc, NI M. le Comte   *Neither the Duke nor the Count*
ne SERA nommé ambassadeur   *will be appointed ambassador to*
à Saint-Pétersbourg.   *St.-Petersburg.*

☞ Observe that *Ni*, and *Ni l'un ni l'autre* take NE before a verb.

AGREEMENT OF THE VERB WITH ITS SUBJECT. 265

EXERCISE CCV.

It was either Pitt *or* Fox who *said* that.—*Either* mildness,
C" ind-1   *   ind-4   douceur f.

or force *will do* it.—I have seen A. and B., *either* the one *or* the
— f.   273

other *will write* to you.—It was either he *or* I that *did* that.—
ind-7   ind-1   *   ind-4

I send you my two servants, *both are* honest. —*Neither has*
domestique   honnête

done his duty. —*Neither* of them *shall marry* my daughter.
devoir m.   * *   épouser

517. We have already seen (page 17) that there are
two sorts of collective nouns: the *collective general,* and
the *collective partitive.*—The *collective general* are those
which express the totality of the persons or things of
which we speak; as, *l'armée,* the army; *la foule,* the
crowd; or a determinate number of those same persons
or things; as, *la moitié,* the half.—The *collective partitive*
are those which express only a partial number; as, *une
quantité,* a quantity, *une foule,* a crowd.

La troupe de voleurs s'est introduite, the gang of thieves
got in:—*Une troupe de voleurs se sont introduits,* a
gang of thieves got in. In the first sentence *troupe* is
a collective *general;* in the second it is a collective
partitive.

518. RULE I. When a *collective general* is followed by
the preposition *de* (of) and a noun, the adjective, pronoun,
participle, and verb, *agree with the collective general;* as,

L'armée des infidèles FUT entière- | The army *of the infidels* was en-
ment détruite. | *tirely destroyed.*
Il a fourni LE NOMBRE d'exem- | *He has furnished* the number *of*
plaires CONVENU.—(*Acad.*) | *copies* agreed upon.

519. RULE II. When a *collective partitive* is followed
by the preposition *de* (of) and a noun, the adjective, pronoun, participle, and verb, *agree with the last noun,* because

it expresses the principal idea, and more particularly fixes the attention; as,

LA PLUPART du monde le CROIT.	*Most people believe it.*
LA PLUPART des hommes le PENSENT.	*Most men think so.*
UN grand NOMBRE d'ennemis PARURENT.	*A great many enemies appeared.*
Il trouva UNE PARTIE des abricots mangés, UNE PARTIE des liqueurs BUES.	*He found a part of the apricots eaten, a part of the liquors drunk.*

520. *Observations.*—(1.) Adverbs of quantity, as *peu*, few; *beaucoup*, many; *assez*, enough; *plus*, more; *trop*, too many, etc. are considered as collectives partitive. Consequently we write:—

Peu de gens *négligent* leurs intérêts.	*Few people neglect their interests.*
Beaucoup de monde *était* à la promenade.	*Many people were walking.*

521. (2.) *Peu, beaucoup,* and *la plupart,* used by themselves, require the verb in the plural; as,

Le sénat fut partagé, LA PLUPART VOULAIENT que...	*The senate was divided, the majority wished...*

The noun which here regulates the agreement of the verb is understood: *La plupart des* SÉNATEURS *voulaient que,* etc.; the majority of the SENATORS wished...

EXERCISE CCVI.

It was with James the First, that *began that series* of
   C' ind-1   à   395   *que* ind-1   *chaîne* f.
misfortunes which *gave* to the house of Stuart the title of
 malheur   ind-4   *titre* m.
unfortunate. — *A troop* of nymphs, crowned with flowers,
 infortuné   *troupe* f.   *nymphe* f.   *de*
swam behind her car. — *Few* men *reason,* and all wish to
ind-2 *derrière*   *char* m.   *raisonner*   *vouloir* *
decide. — *Most were* of that opinion. — An infinite *number* of
               ind-3   *avis* m.
birds *made* those groves resound with their sweet songs.
        2   3   1   *de*   *chant* m. 8

Additional Remarks upon the General Rule.

522. (1.) When the words forming the subject are synonymous, the verb agrees, in French, with the last noun; as,

Son courage, son intrépidité *étonne* les plus braves.—(*Domergue.*)

☞ Synonymous nouns must never be joined, in French, by the conjunction *et*.

523. (2.) The verb agrees also with the last noun only, although the nouns be not synonymous, if we dwell more upon the last than upon the others, either because it explains the preceding nouns—is more energetic, or is of such moment that the others are forgotten; as,

Le fer, le bandeau, la flamme EST toute prête.—(*Racine.*)
Le Pérou, le Potose, Alzire EST sa conquête.—(*Voltaire.*)

524. (3.) The verb is put in the singular, although preceded by plurals, when there is an expression which sums up all the nouns into one, such as *tout, rien, personne, nul, chacun;* or when the conjunction *mais* is placed before the last noun, and this noun is in the singular; as,

Paroles et regards, *tout* EST charme dans vous.—(*La Fontaine.*)	*Words and looks*, everything is *a charm in you*.
Crainte, périls, *rien* ne m'A retenu.—(*Racine.*)	*Neither fear nor dangers*, nothing could *restrain me*.
Non-seulement toutes ses richesses, *mais* toute sa vertu *s'évanouit*.	*Not only all his riches*, but *all his virtue* vanished.

525. (4.) When two subjects are joined by the following and similar conjunctions, *comme, de même que, ainsi que, aussi bien que*, the verb agrees with the first subject, the second being the subject of a verb understood; as,

Cette bataille, *comme* tant d'autres, ne *décida* de rien.—(*Voltaire.*)	*That battle*, like *so many others*, decided *nothing*.
Aristophane, *aussi bien que* Ménandre, *charmait* les Grecs.	*Aristophanes*, as well as *Menander*, delighted *the Greeks*.

It is as if it were:

Cette bataille ne décida de rien, comme tant d'autres batailles ne décidèrent de rien.

Aristophane charmait les Grecs, aussi bien que Ménandre charmait les Grecs.

EXERCISE CCVII.

Vanity, says Pascal, is so rooted in the ²human ¹heart, that
              ancré   *de l'homme*
a scullion, a porter even boasts, and *wishes* to have
  marmiton   *crocheteur*   *   *se vanter*   *vouloir*   *
his admirers. — Games, conversation, shows, *nothing*
  admirateur   404   *jeu*   *spectacle*
diverts her. — The strength of the mind, *like* that of the
ne distraire   *force* f.   *âme* f.
body, *is* the fruit of   temperance. — Alcibiades, *as well as*
       art.   *Alcibiade*
Plato, *was* among the disciples of Socrates.
     au nombre de

§ II. PLACE OF THE SUBJECT OF THE VERB.

526. RULE.—The subject or nominative is generally placed *before* the verb, in French, as in English; as,

Le maître enseigne, et *l'écolier* apprend.	The master *teaches, and* the scholar *learns.*
Nous irons vous voir.	We *shall come and see you.*

527. There are a few cases in which the subject is placed *after* the verb; they are the following:—

1*st,* When, in any interrogative sentence, the subject is a *pronoun;* as,

Quand-viendra-t-*elle?*	*When will* she *come?*

But if, in asking a question, the subject of the verb is a *noun*, the noun is placed *before* the verb; and to show that a question is asked, one of the pronouns, *il, elle, ils, elles,* is placed immediately *after* the verb; as,

Votre *frère* parle-t-il *français?*	*Does your* brother *speak French?*
Vos *sœurs* sont-*elles* arrivées?	*Have your* sisters *arrived?*

Remark.—When an interrogative sentence begins with *que, à quoi, où,* we generally place the noun subject *after* the verb, without adding a pronoun to it; as,

Que fait votre frère?	What *is* your brother *doing?*
À quoi s'occupe votre sœur?	What *is* your sister *busy with?*
Où demeure votre oncle?	Where *does your uncle live?*

(See the *Preliminary Remarks* on Interrogation, p. 87.)

PLACE OF THE SUBJECT OF THE VERB. 269

2*d*, When, as in English, we quote the words of another person ; as,

Que ferai-je ? *dit Télémaque.* | *What shall I do ?* said Telemachus.

3*d*, When the subjunctive mood is used without any conjunction being expressed ; as,

Fasse LE CIEL que vous soyez heureux ! | *Heaven grant you may be happy !*
Dussé-JE y périr, j'irai. | *Should I perish there, I will go.*

This turn of expression has more vivacity than if we had said : *Je souhaite* QUE *le ciel fasse que vous soyez heureux.* QUOIQUE *je dusse y périr, j'irai.*

4*th*, When the sentence begins with a unipersonal (or impersonal) verb, or with one of these words, AINSI, *thus, so ;* TEL, *such ;* as,

Il est arrivé d'heureux change- | *Happy changes have taken place.*
ments.
Ainsi finit cette tragédie. | *Thus ended that tragedy.*
Tel fut le résultat de sa folie. | *Such was the result of his folly.*

(See Rule III, p. 239.)

5*th*, When the subject is followed by several words which are dependent upon it ; as in this phrase of *Fénélon:*—

Là *coulent* mille RUISSEAUX qui dis- | *There flow a thousand rivulets that*
tribuent partout une eau claire. | *carry everywhere a clear water.*

This transposition of the subject is sometimes indispensable, and sometimes only the effect of taste.

EXERCISE CCVIII.

The violet is the emblem of modesty.—Are *they* gone?
 violette f. emblème m.   partir
Does your *cousin* often come to see you?—Is your governess
           venir
English or French?—*What* will posterity think?—You are
          ind-7   avoir
wrong, *said* her *father* to her. — *May* you succeed in your
tort   Pouvoir réussir
projects!—²(Great misfortunes) ¹(have happened).—*So* goes the
      malheur m.
world. — *Such* was his advice.—On one side was seen a river
monde m.   avis m. D'   on ind-2
(from which) *sprung islands* lined with lime-trees in bloom.
 où se former   bordé de tilleul fleuri

§ III. GOVERNMENT OF VERBS.

528. The *object, regimen,* or *complement* of a verb, is a word which completes the idea begun by the verb.

529. There are two sorts of regimens, the one called *direct,* the other *indirect.*

530. The *direct regimen* denotes the immediate object of the action of the verb, without the help of any preposition, and answers to the question *qui ?* (whom?) for persons, and *quoi ?* (what?) for things; as, *J'aime mon père,* I love my father. *J'aime,* QUI? *mon pere.—Il aime l'étude,* he likes study. *Il aime,* QUOI? *l'étude. Mon père* and *l'étude* then are the direct regimens of the verb *aimer,* since they complete, without the help of any preposition, the idea begun by the verb.

531. The *indirect regimen* completes, in an *indirect* manner, the idea begun by the verb; that is, it completes it only by means of a preposition expressed or understood; it answers to the question *à qui ? de qui ? pour qui ? par qui,* etc., for persons; and *à quoi ? pour quoi ? de quoi ?* etc., for things; as, *Il parle à son frère,* he speaks to his brother. *Il parle, à* QUI? *à son frère. A son frère* is then the indirect regimen of *parler,* and completes the action expressed by that verb, by means of the preposition *à.*

532. The *direct regimen* corresponds to the *accusative;* the *indirect regimen* to the *genitive, dative,* or *ablative* of the Latin.

533. RULE I. When a verb has two regimens, the one direct and the other indirect, the shorter must be placed first; as,

Les hypocrites parent *le vice des* dehors de la vertu.	*Hypocrites* deck vice *with the exterior of virtue.*
Les hypocrites parent *des dehors de la vertu* les vices les plus honteux et les plus décriés.	*Hypocrites* deck with the exterior of virtue *the most shameful and odious vices.*

GOVERNMENT OF VERBS. 271

534. Rule II. If the regimens are of equal length, the direct regimen must be placed first; as,

L'ambition sacrifie *le présent* à l'avenir, mais la volupté sacrifie *l'avenir* au présent.	Ambition sacrifices the present *to the future, but pleasure sacrifices* the future *to the present*.

EXERCISE CCIX.

He has sent a circular to all his correspondents. — He
      circulaire f.   *correspondant* m.

devotes his talents to the defence of ²public ¹liberty. — Give
consacrer   pl.

to study all the time that you can. — I delivered the letter
étude f.   *remettre* ind-4

to the tutor of the prince. — Show your governess the
  précepteur   à

letter that you have written. — I have given a ring to my sister. —
                f.

Alexander, in dying, said that he left his empire to the most
        ind-3 ind-2

worthy. — Have you lent my brother any money?

535. Rule III. *Passive* verbs require *de* or *par* before the noun or pronoun which they govern.

536. *De* is used, when the verb expresses an action *wholly of the mind;* as,

L'honnête homme est estimé, même DE ceux qui n'ont pas de probité.	An honest man *is esteemed, even* by *those who have no probity*.

537. *Par* is required, when the *bodily faculties* participate in the action; as,

Carthage fut détruite PAR les Romains.	*Carthage was destroyed* by *the Romans*.

REMARK. — *Par* is also used to avoid the repetition of *de* in the same sentence; as, *Son ouvrage a été censuré* D'*une manière sévère* PAR *les critiques*.

☞ Remember that it is a GENERAL RULE to make every past participle used with the verb *être*, agree in *gender* and *number* with the subject of that verb.

EXERCISE CCX.

Your brother is honoured and respected *by* all who know
                           honorer   *ceux*
him.—He is loved *by* all his masters.— Misers are tormented
                                               371 *avare*
with the fear of losing what they have.— Bombs
      crainte f. *perdre* inf-1 *ce qu'*   371 *bombe* f.
were invented *by* Gallen, a bishop of Munster, about the
ind-3   399   *vers*
middle of the 16th century. — The city of Troy was
                                    ville f.   ind-3
taken, plundered, and destroyed *by* the Greeks, 1184 years
       saccager   *détruire*
B. C. This event has been celebrated *by* the
avant J.-C.   *événement* m.
two greatest poets of Greece and Italy.
                        art.   31

538. The preposition TO, before a second verb in the infinitive, is expressed in French by À, DE, or POUR, but not indiscriminately. Sometimes also there is no preposition at all in French.

EXAMPLES.

J'aime *à* lire.	*I* like to read.
Je crains *de* tomber.	*I* fear to *fall*.
Je le fais *pour* vous obliger.	*I* do it to *oblige you*.
Ou laissez-moi périr, ou laissez-moi régner.—(*Corneille*.)	*Either* allow me to *perish*, or allow me to reign.

It is important to observe, that when in French a preposition is required before an infinitive, it is the foregoing verb, noun, or adjective that determines which is to be used, according as that verb, noun, or adjective governs one or another preposition. This government must therefore be ascertained. This is one of the principal difficulties of the French language, and, in order to remove it, we give two Lists of Verbs with the prepositions that they respectively govern, and a third List of those Verbs that require no preposition.

539. *N.B.* After prepositions,* the French use the present infinitive, and not the present participle; as,

Amusez-vous à lire.	*Amuse yourself* with *reading.*
Il m'empêche de le faire.	*He hinders me* from *doing it.*

The only exception is EN; as,

Nous causerons en marchant.	*We shall talk as we walk.*
Il donna cet ordre en partant.	*He gave that order* in *going away.*

540. LIST I. *Verbs which require the preposition* A *before the infinitive which follows them.*

s'Abaisser à,	*to stoop* to.	Demander à, de,‡	*to ask* to.
aboutir à,	*to end* in, *tend* to.	destiner à,	*to destine* to.
s'accorder à,	*to agree* in.	se déterminer à,	*to resolve* upon.
accoutumer à,	*to accustom* to.	disposer à,	*to dispose* to.
aider à,	*to help* to, *assist* in.	donner à,	*to give* to.
aimer à,	*to like* to. [with.	s'Efforcer à, de,‡	(*physical*) *to endeavour* to.
s'amuser à,	*to amuse oneself*		
animer à,	*to excite* to.	employer à, *to employ* to, *use* to.	
s'appliquer à,	*to apply* to.	s'empresser à, de,‡ *to be eager* to.	
apprendre à,	*to learn* to.	encourager à,	*to encourage* to.
s'apprêter à,	*to get ready* to.	engager à,	*to induce* to.
aspirer à,	*to aspire* to.	enhardir à,	*to embolden* to
s'attendre à,	*to expect* to.	enseigner à,	*to teach* to.
autoriser à,	*to authorise* to.	s'étudier à,	*to study* to.
avoir à,	*to have* to.	exceller à,	*to excel* in.
Balancer à,	*to hesitate* to.	exciter à,	*to excite* to.
Chercher à,	*to seek* to.	exercer à,	*to exercise* in.
commencer à,†	*to begin* to.	exhorter à,	*to exhort* to.
condamner à,	*to condemn* to.	exposer à,	*to expose* to.
condescendre à,	*to condescend* to.	se Fatiguer à,	*to get tired* with.
consentir à,	*to consent* to.	forcer à, de, ‖	*to force* to, *compel*
consister à,	*to consist* in.	Gagner à,	*to gain* by. [to.
continuer à, de, ‡	*to continue* to.	Habituer à,	*to accustom* to.
contraindre à, de, ‖	*to compel* to.	haïr à,	*to hate* to.
contribuer à,	*to contribute* to.	se hasarder à,	*to venture* to.

---

* To ascertain which preposition to use, consult the Lists.

† Some writers occasionally use *de*, and establish a shade of difference between *commencer à* and *commencer de;* but, according to the latest decisions of the *French Academy*, *à* may be properly used in all cases.

‡ As it sounds best, i. e. *de* to avoid several *a*, and *a* to avoid several *de*.

‖ *A* or *de*, as it sounds best in the *active* sense, but always *de* in the *passive*.

VERBS WHICH GOVERN à.

hésiter à,	to hesitate to.	persister à,	to persist in.
Inviter à,	to invite to.	se plaire à,	to delight in.
se Mettre à,	to set about to, be-	préparer à,	to prepare to.
montrer à,	to show to. [gin to.	provoquer à,	to incite to. [to.
Obliger à, de,†	to oblige to.	Recommencer à,	to begin again
s'obstiner à,	to persist in.	renoncer à,	to renounce to.
s'offrir à,	to offer to.	se résoudre à,	to resolve to.
oublier à,	to forget how.	réussir à,	to succeed to, in.
Parvenir à,	to succeed in.	Servir à,	to serve to.
passer à,	to spend in.	songer à,	to think of.
penser à,	to think of.	Tâcher à,	to aim at.
perdre à,	to lose in.	tendre à,	to tend to.
persévérer à,	to persevere in.	Viser à,	to aim at.

EXERCISE CCXI.

I *shall* not *stoop to* justify myself.—He *likes to* be flattered.
    ne point   se justifier.

—He *amuses himself with* making ²chemical ¹experiments.
                      32 de chimie expérience

—I *expect to* meet with many difficulties.—I *have to* thank
                * bien des

you.—I *begin to* understand.—Liberality *consists* less *in* giving
              comprendre.

much, than *in* giving seasonably.—He *is asking to* come in.—
beaucoup   à propos.   entrer.

They *encouraged* me *to* continue.—The example of his ancestors
        ind-3   ancêtre

excites him *to* distinguish himself. — I *offer to* serve you.
              se distinguer.

541. List II. *Verbs which require the preposition* DE *before the infinitive which follows them.*

s'Abstenir de,	to abstain from.	appréhender de,	to fear to.
accuser de,	to accuse of.	avertir de,	to warn to.
achever de,	to finish to.	s'aviser de,	to bethink of.
affecter de,	to affect to.	Blâmer de,	to blame for.
s'affliger de,	to be grieved at.	brûler de,	to be anxious to.
ambitionner de,	to be ambitious to.	Cesser de,	to cease to.

---

† *A* or *de*, as it sounds best; but with the meaning of *doing a service*, or in a *passive* sense, always *de*.

charger *de*,	to *charge* to.	Jurer *de*,	to *swear* to.
commander *de*,	to *command* to.	Manquer *de*,	to *fail* to.
conjurer *de*,	to *conjure* to.	menacer *de*,	to *threaten* to.
conseiller *de*,	to *advise* to.	mériter *de*,	to *deserve* to.
se contenter *de*,	to be *content*	Négliger *de*,	to *neglect* to.
convenir *de*,	to *agree* to. [with.	Offrir *de*,	to *offer* to.
craindre *de*,	to *fear* to.	omettre *de*,	to *omit* to.
Dédaigner *de*,	to *disdain* to.	ordonner *de*,	to *order* to.
défendre *de*,	to *forbid* to.	oublier *de*,	to *forget* to.
défier *de*,	to *defy* to.	Pardonner *de*,	to *forgive* for.
se dépêcher *de*,	to *make haste* to.	permettre *de*,	to *permit* to.
désespérer *de*,	to *despair* to, of.	persuader *de*,	to *persuade* to.
différer *de*,	to *defer* to, to de-	se piquer *de*,	to *pretend* to.
dire *de*,	to *tell* to. [lay to.	plaindre *de*,	to *pity* to, for.
discontinuer *de*,	to *discontinue*	prescrire *de*,	to *prescribe* to.
disconvenir *de*,	to *disown* to. [to.	presser *de*,	to *press* to, *urge* to.
dispenser *de*,	to *dispense* with.	prier *de*,	to *request* to.
dissuader *de*,	to *dissuade* from.	promettre *de*,	to *promise* to.
Écrire *de*,	to *write* to. [vour to.	proposer *de*,	to *propose* to.
s'efforcer *de*,	(moral) to *endea-*	Recommander *de*,	to *recommend*
empêcher *de*,	to *prevent* to.	refuser *de*,	to *refuse* to. [to.
enrager *de*,	to be *enraged* to.	regretter *de*,	to *regret* to.
entreprendre *de*,	to *undertake*	se réjouir *de*,	to *rejoice* to.
essayer *de*,	to *try* to. [to.	remercier *de*,	to *thank* for.
s'étonner *de*,	to be *astonished*	se repentir *de*,	to *repent* of, to.
éviter *de*,	to *avoid* to. [at.	reprocher *de*,	to *reproach* for.
excuser *de*,	to *excuse* for.	résoudre *de*,	to *resolve* to.
exempter *de*,	to *exempt* from.	rire *de*,	to *laugh* at.
Feindre *de*,	to *feign* to.	risquer *de*,	to *run the risk* to.
féliciter *de*,	to *congratulate*	rougir *de*,	to *blush* to.
finir *de*,	to *finish* to. [upon.	Sommer *de*,	to *summon* to.
se flatter *de*,	to *flatter oneself* to.	soupçonner *de*,	to *suspect* to.
frémir *de*,	to *shudder* to.	se souvenir *de*,	to *remember* to.
se Garder *de*,	to *take care not* to.	suggérer *de*,	to *suggest* to.
gémir *de*,	to *lament* to.	supplier *de*,	to *entreat* to.
se glorifier *de*,	to *glory* in.	Tâcher *de*,	to *endeavour* to.
gronder *de*,	to *scold* for.	tenter *de*,	to *attempt* to.
se Hâter *de*,	to *hasten* to.	se Vanter *de*,	to *boast* of.

542. REMARK.—Verbs generally require, before a noun, the same preposition that they require before an infinitive; as,

Il faut *accoutumer* les enfants à *obéir*—à *l'obéissance*.	*We must* accustom *children* TO obey —TO *obedience*.
Je l'*accuse* DE *négliger* ses études. Je l'*accuse* DE *négligence*.	*I* accuse *him* OF neglecting *his studies*. *I* accuse *him* OF *negligence*.

EXERCISE CCXII.

Abstain from injuring your enemies.—The courtiers of Darius
         nuire à   *sing.*   *courtisan*

accused Daniel *of* having violated the laws of the Persians.—
ind-2   *violer*   *Perse*

Your brother *will* never *cease to* think of you.—Zerbinette has
                   ind-7

charged me *to* come and tell you that..—God *commands* us *to*
              *   *que..*

love him.—I *would advise* you *to* speak to him.—Reason
              conseiller

forbids us *to* commit an injustice.—Who *told* you *to* do it?
             —f.   ind-4

— He has *undertaken to* translate Homer and Virgil.
                          traduire

EXERCISE CCXIII.

I *shall* not *fail to* do what you wish.—I *ordered* him *to*
                  ce que   *vouloir*   ind-4

go and see him.—You *forgot to* come this morning.—They
  *   ind-4   *matin* m.   *On*

have *persuaded* him *to* marry.—I *promise to* observe what
                 lui   *se marier.*

the law orders me.—We should *blush to* commit faults,
     ordonner   *Il faut*   *commettre* 32

but not *to* acknowledge them.—I will *endeavour to* satisfy you.
  non   *avouer*   *tâcher*

—*Make haste to* breakfast.—I *congratulate* myself *on* having
                                           me

made so good a choice.—The king *orders* me *to* set out with
        choix m.   *partir*

the fleet.—*Recommend* to your children *to* shun vice, *to* love
                                     fuir m.

virtue.—General Desaix *contributed to* the gaining of the
                       ind-3   *gain* m.

battle of Marengo.—I *thank* you *for* your kindness.
bataille f.   *bonté* f.

543. LIST III. *Verbs which require no preposition in French before the infinitive which follows them, whether a preposition be used in English or not.*

Aimer mieux,*	*to like better.*	J'*aime mieux* voir mon fils. (*J. B. Rousseau.*)
Aller,	*to go.*	Le Rhin *ira* grossir la Loire. (*Boil.*)
Compter,	*to intend.*	Il *compte* partir demain. (*Acad.*)
Croire,	*to think.*	Elle *croyait* servir l'état. (*Bossuet.*)
Daigner,	*to deign.*	*Daignez* leur parler. (*Boileau.*)
Devoir,	*to owe.*	Le jour qui *doit* nous rendre heureux. (*L. Racine.*)
Entendre,	*to hear.*	J'en ai *entendu* parler. (*Acad.*)
Envoyer,	*to send.*	*Envoyez* demander. (*Ib.*)
Espérer,†	*to hope.*	Il *espère* revivre en sa postérité. (*Racine.*)
Faire,	*to make, to cause.*	Je le *fis* nommer chef. (*Le même.*)
Falloir,	*to be necessary.*	Il *faut* voir. (*Acad.*)
s'Imaginer,	*to fancy.*	Il *s'imagine* être un grand docteur. (*Ib.*)
Laisser,	*to leave, to let.*	Il *laisse* opprimer l'innocence. (*Rac.*)
Oser,	*to dare.*	Qui suis-je pour *oser* murmurer? (*L. Racine.*)
Paraître,	*to appear.*	Il *paraît* être satisfait. (*Acad.*)
Pouvoir,	*to be able.*	Rien ne *peut* prospérer sur des terres ingrates. (*L. Racine.*)
Prétendre,	*to pretend.*	Il *prétend* donner la loi. (*Acad.*)
Savoir,	*to know.*	Je *sais* lire et écrire. (*Molière.*)
Sembler,	*to seem.*	L'ennui *semble* dire aux humains... (*Voltaire.*)
Souhaiter,‡	*to wish.*	Je *souhaiterais* pouvoir vous obliger. (*Acad.*)
Valoir mieux,*	*to be better.*	Il *vaut mieux* attendre un peu. (*Ibid.*)
Venir,§	*to come.*	Je *viens* adorer l'Éternel. (*Racine.*)
Voir,	*to see.*	Il n'aime pas à *voir* souffrir. (*Acad.*)
Vouloir,	*to be willing.*	*Voulez-vous* du public *mériter* les amours? Sans cesse en écrivant variez vos discours. (*Boil.*)

---

* *Aimer mieux; valoir mieux*, followed by two verbs in the infinitive, require DE before the *second* infinitive; *J'aimerais mieux mourir, que* DE *faire une si mauvaise action.—Il y a beaucoup d'occasions où il vaut mieux se taire que* DE *parler.*

† *Espérer*, being in the present infinitive, and followed by another verb also in the present infinitive, requires DE: *Peut-on espérer de vous revoir?*

‡ It is also used with DE: *Je souhaite* DE *vous voir.—(Racine.)*

§ *Venir*, in the sense of *to be just, to have just*, requires *de* before the next infinitive; when used for *to happen*, it requires *à*; as,

    Il vient *de* sortir. | *He has just gone out.*
    S'il venait *à* mourir. | *If he should happen to die.*

EXERCISE CCXIV.

I *like better*   *to* pardon than *to* punish you.—She *is going to*
             vous

sing.—When do you *intend to* go?—A man of honour *ought to*
   Quand   *partir*   ind-1

keep his word.—I *hope to* see you often.—I will *show* you
   parole f.   *faire voir*

all the curiosities of the town.—He *appeared to* hesitate, but
   curiosité f.   ind-2

we encouraged him.—My sister *wishes* very much *to* go to
   ind-3

France.—*It is better to* work than *to* beg.—Cæsar ordered
                               mendier.   ind-3

Labienus to *come* and join him.—She *will* not stay.
à   *   *rester.*

General Rule for the use of POUR.

544. To, before an INFINITIVE, is expressed by POUR, when *in order to*, is either expressed or understood in English; as,

Je suis venu *pour* le complimenter. | *I came* in order to *congratulate him.*
Je vais à la campagne *pour* chasser. | *I am going into the country to shoot.*

The English present participle, preceded by the preposition FOR, explaining the motive of an action, is also expressed in French by the INFINITIVE with POUR; as,

Il a été chassé POUR avoir menti. | *He was expelled* FOR *telling lies.*

EXERCISE CCXV.

They ²all ¹agree   to deceive me.—He will do anything *to*
     s'accorder   *tout*

oblige you.—I was going to write to you *to* ask a favour of
                                            grâce f. *

you.—I want money *to* buy a horse.—I have not ²money
   ai besoin d'

¹enough *to* buy one.—I shall do it *in order* not *to* displease you.
     en   *déplaire*

—I have done all (I could) *to* gain his friendship.—He was
           mon possible   ind-3

banished for life *for having* robbed on the highway.
  bannir à perpétuité   *voler*   *grand chemin.*

§ IV. MOODS AND TENSES.

INDICATIVE MOOD.

545. The INDICATIVE *mood* simply declares a thing; as, *Elle* CHANTE *bien*, she sings well; or it asks a question; as, CHANTE-*t-elle bien ?* does she sing well ? This mood has eight tenses—the *present*, the *imperfect*, the *preterite definite*, the *preterite indefinite*, the *preterite anterior*, the *pluperfect*, the *future absolute* (or *simple*), and the *future anterior*.

546. The PRESENT *tense* expresses something doing or existing at the present time; as, *J'écris*, I am writing; *Nous sommes*, we are. It is also used to express a *habit* or *custom;* as, *Il fume*, he smokes.

547. In historical narration, the *present* tense is used for the *past*, in order to awaken the attention, and make the thing, as it were, present; as,

César *quitte* la Gaule, *passe le* Rubicon, et *entre* en Italie avec cinq mille hommes.	Cæsar leaves *Gaul*, crosses *the Rubicon, and* enters *Italy with five thousand men.*

548. The *present* is also sometimes used to express a *future* near at hand; as,

Je SUIS de retour dans un moment.	*I shall be back in a moment.*
Où ALLEZ-VOUS ce soir ?	*Where are you going this evening?*

549. *N.B.* In English there are *three* different ways of expressing the PRESENT: *I speak, I do speak, I am speaking;* but in French there is only one way, *Je parle.* There is likewise but one expression in French for any other tense, when the verb *to be* is used with the present participle; thus, *I shall be writing*, must be rendered by *j'écrirai*, and *I should be doing* by *je ferais.* The verb which is in the present participle is thus put in the tense expressed by the auxiliary *to be*.

EXERCISE CCXVI.

My sister *is* in her room, where she *is reading* the celebrated
où
discourse   of Bossuet on   Universal History. — Everybody
discours m.   art.   ²   ¹

thinks that either ³your ⁴brother ²or ¹you have written that song.
penser   *

— It ²seldom ¹rains in Egypt. — Seamen *smoke* a great deal. —
          en   marin   beaucoup.

The battle *begins*, and immediately a cloud of arrows *darkens*
              aussitôt   nuée f.   trait m. obscurcir
the air, and *covers* the combatants. — I *shall be* with you
                                                                       à
in a minute. — I *set out* to-morrow for the country.
          la   partir

550. The IMPERFECT (*je parlais*, I was speaking, I spoke, I did speak, I used to speak) expresses a thing having been done at the moment that another took place; as,

| Je PENSAIS à vous, quand vous êtes entré. | *I was thinking of you, when you came in.* |

551. The *Imperfect* is also used when we wish to denote that the action of which we speak was *habitual*, or has been *reiterated;* as,

| Quand j'étais à Paris, je me PRO-MENAIS ordinairement dans les Champs Élysées. | *When I was in Paris, I generally walked in the Champs Élysées.* |
| J'y RENCONTRAIS souvent des Anglais. | *I often met Englishmen there.* |

552. Finally, the *Imperfect* is used in describing the *qualities* of persons or things, the *state, place*, and *disposition* in which they were in a *time past*, but without fixing the time of its duration; as,

| Alfred *était* un grand roi. | *Alfred was a great king.* |
| Carthage *était* sur le bord de la mer. | *Carthage was on the sea-coast.* |

553. *Note.*—Suppose you have to translate into French, *I spoke, I wrote*, and you are in doubt whether to use the Imperfect or Preterite, see whether you can turn the expression into, *I used to speak, I used to write*, or into, *I was speaking, I was writing*—if you can, the *Imperfect* is your tense. This rule is infallible.

EXERCISE CCXVII.

Montezuma *reigned* over the Mexicans, when Fernando
                  régner   lorsque Fernand-
Cortez attacked Mexico.—Socrates, wishing to harden himself,
            ind-3   s'endurcir

went barefoot in the depth of winter. — In ²ancient ¹times,
423   plus fort   ancien
those who *were* taken in war *lost* their liberty and *became* slaves.
                           à   devenir
— Among the Romans, the plebeians *attached* themselves, under
        Chez   plébéien   s'
the name of clients, to some patrician whom they *called* their
                         ———   quelque patricien
patron. — The temple of Delphi *had* for an inscription this
                       Delphes   *
maxim: KNOW THYSELF. — The pyramids of Egypt *were*
        Connais-toi toi-même.
intended as   burying-places   for the kings.
destiner à art. sépulture f. s. de

554. The PRETERITE DEFINITE *(je parlai, je reçus)* serves to express something done at a time completely past, and of which no part remains unexpired; hence it cannot be used when speaking of anything done during the present day, week, month, year, or century; as,

J'*écrivis* hier à Bordeaux.	*I wrote yesterday to Bordeaux.*
Nous nous *rencontrâmes* l'année dernière à Genève.	*We met last year at Geneva.*

555. As the events related in history are considered as facts, completed in a time entirely elapsed, the *preterite definite* is principally used in that style; as,

Les Juifs *quittèrent* l'Égypte sous la conduite de Moïse.	*The Jews left Egypt under the conduct of Moses.*

EXERCISE CCXVIII.

Amenophis *conceived* the design   of making   his son a
                      dessein m.   inf-1   de
conqueror. He *set about* it after the manner   of the Egyptians,
conquérant.   s'y prendre à   manière f.
that is, with great ideas.   All the children who were born
c'est-à-dire   pensée f.   316
on the same day as Sesostris, *were* brought to   court, by order
 *   que   amener   art. cour f.
of the king: he *had* them educated   as his own children, and
                faire   élever inf-1

with the same care as Sesostris. When he *was* grown up,
  soin pl. que   grand

he ²*made* ¹him serve his apprenticeship in a war against the
 lui faire apprentissage m. par

Arabs. This young prince *learned* there to bear hunger
Arabe   y supporter faim f.

and thirst, and *subdued* that nation, till then invincible.
 soif f. soumettre   jusqu'

He ²*afterwards* ¹*attacked* Libya, and *conquered* it.
  ensuite   Libye f.

EXERCISE CCXIX.

After these successes, Sesostris *formed* the project of
     succès m.

subduing the ²whole ¹world. In consequence of this,
subjuguer inf-1 entier   En   • •

he *entered* Ethiopia, which he *rendered* tributary. He
   dans Ethiopie   se rendre

continued his victories in Asia. Jerusalem *was* the first to feel
        Jérusalem f.   à

the force of his arms. the rash Rehoboam *could* not
    arme f. téméraire Roboam

²*resist* ¹him, and Sesostris *carried away* the riches of Solomon.
 lui   enlever   richesse pl. Salomon.

He *penetrated* into the Indies farther than Alexander did
      Indes   ne

afterwards. The Scythians ²*obeyed* ¹him as far as the
ensuite.   Scythe   lui jusqu'à

Tanais: Armenia and Cappadocia *were* subject to him. In
      Cappadoce f. sujettes   En

a word, he *extended* his empire from the Ganges to
 mot m. étendre   —— m. depuis Gange m. jusqu'à

the Danube.—(BOSSUET.)

556. The PRETERITE INDEFINITE *(j'ai parlé)* is the past tense most used in French; it expresses something done in the course of the day, week, month, year, or century in which we are; as,

J'AI REÇU cette semaine la visite de monsieur votre père.	*I have this week received a visit from your father.*
Je lui AI ÉCRIT ce matin.	*I wrote to him this morning.*

557. The *Preterite indefinite* is also used in speaking of a past action, without *specifying* the TIME in which it happened; as,

J'AI VENDU mon cheval.	*I have sold my horse.*
Il A VOYAGÉ en Allemagne.	*He has travelled in Germany.*
J'en AI PARLÉ à votre maître.	*I mentioned it to your master.*

This tense is sometimes used instead of the *future;* as,

AVEZ-VOUS bientôt FAIT?	*Will you have done soon?*
Attendez, J'AI FINI dans un moment.	*Wait, I shall have done in a moment.*

558. The PRETERITE ANTERIOR *(j'eus parlé)* denotes a thing past and done before another also past, and is, for this reason, called *anterior*. It is generally preceded by a conjunction, or an adverb of time, such as *quand, lorsque, dès que, aussitôt que;* as,

Quand J'EUS RECONNU mon erreur, j'en fus honteux.	*When I had seen my error, I was ashamed of it.*

Note.—There is another *preterite*, called the *preterite anterior indefinite*: *J'ai eu parlé, tu as eu parlé,* etc., but it is little used.

559. PLUPERFECT *(j'avais parlé)* represents a thing as *past* before another event happened; as,

J'*avais dîné* quand il entra.	*I had dined when he came in.*

This tense, like the Imperfect, serves to describe, and to express repetition, habit or custom; as,

Dès que *j'avais dîné* j'allais à la pêche.	*As soon as I had dined, I went fishing.*

EXERCISE CCXX.

I *was* (at your house) this morning; I *saw* your brother, and
    chez vous
spoke to him.—We *have written* to him to-day.—The [2]present
je
[1]century *began* on the first day of the year 1801, and will end
   *   année f.
aujourd'hui.   actuel

on the last day of the year 1900.—He *resided* six months
*   demeurer
at Rome.—When I *had done* that, I set out.—I *had finished*
                                            partir
my work when he arrived.—During his stay in the country,
                            Pendant   séjour m. à
as soon as he *had breakfasted,* he went hunting.

560. The Future absolute *(je parlerai,* I shall *or* will speak) represents the action as yet to come; as, *Je vous* écrirai, I shall write to you.

561. The Future anterior *(j'aurai parlé)* intimates that a thing will be done before another takes place; as,

J'aurai fini mon thème avant votre retour.	*I* shall have finished *my exercise before your return.*

562. *N.B.* The English often use the *present* tense after *when, as soon as, after,* or similar words, when they want to express a thing to come: the future, however, must always be used in French; as,

Passez chez moi, *quand* vous serez prêt.	*Call on me* when *you* are *ready.*

Conditional Mood.

563. The Conditional *mood* has two tenses, the *present* and the *past.*

564. The *Conditional present (je parlerais,* I should *or* would speak) expresses that a thing would be done on a certain condition; as,

J'irais avec vous si j'avais le temps.	*I* would go *with you if I had time.*

565. The *Conditional past (j'aurais parlé,* or *j'eusse parlé†)* expresses that a thing *might, could, would,* or *should,* have happened, at a time now passed, if another thing had taken place; as,

Le ministre lui aurait donné cette place, s'il l'avait demandée.	*The minister* would have given *him that place, if he had asked for it.*

566. Remark. — When si (if) signifies *supposé que* (suppose that), the French use the present indicative instead of the future, and the imperfect instead of the conditional; as,

J'irai demain à la campagne, s'il fait beau.	*I shall go to the country to-morrow, if it be fine weather.*
Si j'allais en France, je vous en préviendrais.	*If I should go to France, I will let you know.*

---

† Some writers often use this form, but the student will do well to follow the first.

Imperative Mood.

567. The IMPERATIVE *mood* commands, exhorts, entreats, or permits. It has only one tense.

EXERCISE CCXXI.

I *shall wait for* you till six o'clock.—*When* I *have done*,
    attendre   jusqu'à   heure

I *shall go out.*—I *will call* on you, *as soon as* I *have dined.*
              passer chez   aussitôt que

—I *would sing*, if I could.—I *should have found* him (at home),
                                                            chez lui

if I had arrived a little sooner. — *If* he *should come*, what
être   plus tôt.

should I *say* to him?—*Do* good, if you wish to be
                   art. *bien* m.   vouloir

happy; *do* good, if you wish that your memory should be
                                                     subj-1

honoured; *do* good, if you wish that   heaven should open to
                                  art.   subj-1

you its [2]eternal [1]gates.
               porte f.

Subjunctive Mood.

568. The INDICATIVE is the *mood* of affirmation, and the SUBJUNCTIVE that of doubt and indecision.

The Subjunctive is used:—

569. (I.) After any verb expressing *doubt, fear, surprise, admiration, will, wish, desire, consent*, or *command;* because then this verb denotes nothing affirmative, nothing positive with regard to the following verb; as,

| Il veut, il exige, il désire que vous FASSIEZ votre devoir. | *He wishes, he requires, he desires* you to do your duty. |

There is an uncertainty whether you will comply with his wish, his request, or his desire.

570. (II.) After an *interrogation*, and after a verb

accompanied by a *negation*, because then there is doubt, uncertainty, etc. ; as,

Croyez-vous QU'IL VIENNE?	*Do you think he will come?*
Je ne crois pas QU'IL VIENNE.	*I do not think he will come.*

571. REMARK. ¶.—Sometimes an interrogation is used only to affirm or deny with more energy. In this case, the second verb is put in the *Indicative*, because there is no doubt expressed; as,

CROYEZ-vous que les Limousins SONT des sots?	*Do you think that the Limousins are blockheads?*

That is :—

Are you simple enough to believe that the Limousins are blockheads?

572. (III.) After unipersonal verbs, or those used unipersonally; as,

Il convient qu'il VIENNE.	*It is proper that he should come.* [there.
Il importe que vous y SOYEZ.	*It is of importance that you should be*

573. REMARK.—*Il semble*, accompanied by an indirect regimen of persons, *il y a, il paraît, il résulte*, and some other unipersonal verbs which express something positive, follow this rule when used *negatively* or *interrogatively*, else they require the *Indicative ;* as,

Il me semble		*It seems to me*	
Il vous semble	qu'il A raison.	*It seems to you*	*that he is right.*
Il paraît		*It appears*	
Il est sûr		*It is certain*	

EXERCISE CCXXII.

I *tremble* lest he *should come*.—I *wish* you *may succeed*.—
    qu' ne   souhaiter

I *consent* that you *do* it.—Do you think *it will rain* to-day?—
                                            croire

I do not think *it will rain* much.—Although the wicked some-
                                         Quoique

times prosper, do not think that they *are* happy. — ¶Do you
    penser

believe that the guilty man *sleeps* tranquilly, and that he
                coupable   *   tranquille

can stifle the remorse with which he is racked?—*It is enough*
étouffer   *remords* pl.   dont   déchirer   suffire
that you   *order*   me. — *I think* I *see* him. — *It often*
        commander   Il me semble
happens that we *are* deceived.
arriver   on

574. (IV.) The *Subjunctive* is used after the relative pronouns *qui, que, dont, où,* etc., when they are preceded by *peu,* or by an adjective in the *superlative relative* degree. Among such adjectives are included *le seul, l'unique, le premier, le dernier;* as,

Il y a PEU d'hommes *qui* SACHENT supporter l'adversité.	*There are few men who can support adversity.*
Le MEILLEUR cortége *qu'*un roi PUISSE avoir, c'est le cœur de ses sujets.	*The best retinue that a king can have is the love of his subjects.*
Le chien est LE SEUL animal *dont* la fidélité SOIT à l'épreuve.	*The dog is the only animal whose fidelity is proof.*
C'est LA SEULE place *où* vous PUISSIEZ aspirer.	*It is the only place to which you can aspire.*

575. (V.) The *Subjunctive* is used after the relative pronouns *qui, que, dont, où,* etc., when we wish to express something doubtful and uncertain; as,

Je cherche quelqu'un *qui* me RENDE ce service.	*I seek some one who may render me that service.*
Je sollicite une place *que* je PUISSE remplir.	*I solicit a place which I may be able to fill.*
J'irai dans une retraite *où* je SOIS tranquille.	*I shall retire to a place where I may be quiet.*

It is possible that the person I am seeking may not render me that service; that I may not be able to fill the place I solicit; and, that I may not be tranquil in the retreat where I shall go; it is the subjunctive that expresses this doubt and uncertainty.

Observe that we could also say: *qui me* RENDRA *ce service; que je* PEUX *remplir; où je* SERAI *tranquille;* but the sense would no longer be the same: the action marked by the verbs *rendre, pouvoir,* and *être,* would then be represented as certain and positive.

288 OF THE SUBJUNCTIVE.

576. (VI.) The *Subjunctive* is required after *quel que, quelque*. . . *que, qui, que, quoi, que ;* as,

Quels que SOIENT VOS talents.	*Whatever your talents may be.*
Quelque riche *que* vous SOYEZ.	*However rich you may be.*
Qui que vous SOYEZ, parlez.	*Whoever you be, speak.*

*Quoi qu'*on DISE, un âson ne deviendra qu'un âne.—(*Grozelier.*)

(See what has already been said on *Quelque*, p. 57-58.)

Finally, The *Subjunctive* is required after certain conjunctions, see Chapter VIII.

EXERCISE CCXXIII.

He is the *only* man *who lives* in that manner.—The example
 C°   de la sorte.
of a good life is *the best* lesson *that* one *can* give to
                vie f.   on   art.
mankind. — The siege of *Azoth* lasted 29 years: it is the
genre humain m.   ———   c'
longest siege   mentioned   in ancient history. — Show me
             DONT être question
a road   *that   will lead* to London. — *However* clever
chemin m. qui   conduire   habile
²(those two writers) ¹*be,* neither the one nor the other will
          écrivain   †
obtain the vacant seat   in the French Academy.—*Whatever*
              place f. à   Quoi que
you *study,* you must (apply   yourself   to it) with ardour.
              il   vous y livrer

CONCORD BETWEEN THE TENSES OF THE SUBJUNCTIVE AND
THOSE OF THE INDICATIVE AND CONDITIONAL.

577. The Subjunctive mood being always subordinate to a verb that precedes it, its tenses are *regulated* by this *foregoing verb ;* as,

Je ne CROIS pas que vous VENIEZ.	*I do not think you will come.*
Je ne CROYAIS pas que vous VINSSIEZ.	*I did not think you would come.*

---

† See *Remarks* on *Neither*, No. 516.

578. Rule I. After the present and future of the Indicative, we use the *present* of the Subjunctive to express a thing present or future ; but we use the *preterite* of the Subjunctive to express a thing past :—

  Je doute   } que vous *étudiiez* maintenant.
  Je douterai

  Je doute   } que vous *ayez étudié* hier.
  Je douterai

579. Remark.—After the present and future of the Indicative, we use the *Imperfect* of the Subjunctive instead of the present, and the *Pluperfect* instead of the preterite, when some conditional expression is introduced in the sentence :—

  Je doute   } que vous *étudiassiez* maintenant, demain, si
  Je douterai   l'on ne vous y contraignait.

  Je doute   } que vous *eussiez étudié* hier, si l'on ne vous
  Je douterai   y eût contraint.

EXERCISE CCXXIV.

Do you doubt that I *am* your friend?—*Does he think* I
               douter
shall have time?—I *don't think* you *have learned* mathe-
 art.   art.
matics.—He *will wait* till you *are* ready.—She *will wish*
         que   vouloir que
your sister *to be* one of the party.—I *shall* always *doubt* that
    *   partie f.
you *have used* all your endeavours.—*Do you think I might*
  faire   effort m.   pouvoir
speak to him, were I to go now?—*I doubt* whether my
     si y ind-2   que
brother *would have succeeded,* (had it not been for) your
    réussir   sans
assistance.

580. Rule II. After the Imperfect, the Pluperfect, any of the Preterites or Conditionals, we use the *Imperfect* of the Subjunctive, if we mean to express a thing present or future; but to express a thing that is past, we use the *Pluperfect* :—

Je doutais Je doutai J'ai douté J'avais douté Je douterais J'aurais douté	que vous *étudiassiez* aujourd'hui, demain.
Je doutais Je doutai J'ai douté J'avais douté Je douterais J'aurais douté	que vous *eussiez étudié* la semaine passée.

581. REMARK.—With a *Preterite indefinite* the following verb is put in the *Present* of the Subjunctive, if we intend to express a thing which is, or may be done at all times; as,

Dieu A ENTOURÉ les yeux de tuniques fort minces, transparentes au dehors, afin que l'on PUISSE voir à travers.	*God has surrounded the eyes with very thin tunics, transparent on the outside, that we may see through them.*

And in the *Preterite* of the Subjunctive, if we intend to express something past; as,

Il A FALLU qu'il se SOIT DONNÉ bien de la peine.	*He must have given himself a great deal of trouble.*

EXERCISE CCXXV.

He *was waiting* till I *should be* ready.—*Would* you *wait* till
    attendre   que   que
we *should be* ready?—Sparta *was* sober before Socrates *had*
                      Sparte   avant que
praised sobriety; before he *had praised* virtue, Greece abounded
                    avant qu'   abonder
in virtuous men.—William III. *left*, at his death, the reputa-
                                         laisser
tion of a great politician, although he *had* not *been* popular,
            politique   populaire
and of a general (to be feared), although he *had lost* many
                à craindre,
battles.—You must *have had* (a great deal) of patience
        Il   a fallu   beaucoup

OF THE PRESENT PARTICIPLE.

582. The *Present Participle* always terminates in *ant*, and is invariable :—

Un homme *lisant;* des hommes *lisant.*	*A man reading; men reading.*
Une femme *lisant;* des femmes *lisant.*	*A woman reading; women reading.*

We say, however :—

Des hommes *obligeants;* une femme *charmante.*	Obliging *men;* a charming *woman.*

But the words *obligeants, charmante,* are not here present participles ; they are *verbal* adjectives.

583. We call *verbal* adjectives, those adjectives which are derived from verbs; as, *charmant, menaçant,* &c. These adjectives always agree in gender and number with the nouns which they qualify.

The verbal adjective simply expresses a *quality;* the present participle expresses an *action.*

N.B. In English, the verbal adjective is placed *before* the noun, and the present participle *after* it. In French, both are generally placed *after.* See No. 437.

584. REMARK.—The present participle is often used in English as a noun, which is never the case in French :—

Le jeu et la chasse sont la ruine de bien des gens.	GAMING and HUNTING *are the ruin of many people.*

EXERCISE CCXXVI.

⁴David ¹is ³often ²represented *playing* on the harp. — She
              on   ind-1   de
is a woman of a good disposition, *obliging* her friends, whenever
                    caractère m.   quand
an occasion (presents itself).—Those men *foreseeing* the danger,
l'   s'en présente.   prévoir
put themselves on their guard.—Those *foreseeing* men have
                          pl.
perceived the danger. — The *ruling* passion of Cæsar was
apercevoir   dominant

ambition. — Your sister is *charming;* how *obliging* she is! —
               que

Her *singing*   was much admired.
 chant m. ind-3 *fort*

OF THE PAST PARTICIPLE.

585. (I.) The *Past Participle* employed without an auxiliary, agrees, like an adjective, in gender and number, with the noun or pronoun to which it relates; as,

Les méchants ont bien de la peine à demeurer UNIS.—(*Fénélon.*)	*The wicked have much difficulty in remaining* united.

   Que de ramparts *détruits!* que de villes *forcées!*—(*Boileau.*)

586. (II.) The *Past Participle,* accompanied by the auxiliary verb *être,* agrees with its subject or nominative in gender and number; as,

Mon frère est *venu.*	*My brother is* come.
Ma sœur est *venue.*	*My sister is* come.
Mes frères sont *venus.*	*My brothers are* come.
Mes sœurs sont *venues.*	*My sisters are* come.
L'armée a été† *vaincue.*	*The army has been* conquered.
Les ennemis ont été *vaincus.*	*The enemies have been* conquered.

Sometimes the subject is placed after the participle, but this construction does not alter the agreement of the participle: *Quand il vit l'urne où étaient* RENFERMÉES *les* CENDRES *d'Hippias, il versa un torrent de larmes. (Fénélon.)*

587. (III.) When the *Past Participle* follows the verb *avoir,* it never agrees with its *subject;* as,

Mon père a *écrit.*	*My father has* written.
Ma mère a *écrit.*	*My mother has* written.
Mes frères ont *écrit.*	*My brothers have* written.
Mes sœurs ont *écrit.*	*My sisters have* written.

EXERCISE CCXXVII.

A quarrelsome dog has always a *torn* ear.—The ceiling
 * *hargneux*   *l' déchirer*   *plafond* m.
of the Egyptian temples was *painted*   blue. — That letter is
               en

---

† The participle *été* never varies. We say *il* or *elle a été,* he or she has been; *ils* or *elles ont été,* they have been.

OF THE PAST PARTICIPLE.

well *written*. — The city of London, having been *burnt* in
                     ville f.
1666, was *rebuilt* in three years, more beautiful and more
       rebâtir   *année* f.
regular than before.—The ancient Greeks were *persuaded* that
    auparavant.   *persuader*
the soul is immortal.—It is to Jenner that ²(the discovery of
                                               découverte f.
vaccination) ¹(is *due*). — Artemisia survived ²(Mausolus, her
vaccine f.   *Artémise n'* ind-4   *à Mausole*
husband), ¹(only two years). — The Amazons have *acquired*
        que   *an* m.   *Amazone*
celebrity.—They have *executed* the orders of Your Excellency.
32

☞ To make a right application of the following rules, the student must distinguish well a *direct regimen* from an *indirect regimen*, for this is the pivot on which turn the principal difficulties of the *past participle*. For the meaning of *regimen*, see Nos. 405, 466, 500.

588. (IV.) The *Past Participle* accompanied by the auxiliary *avoir*, always agrees with its *direct regimen*, when that regimen is placed *before* the participle; as,

La lettre *que* vous avez *écrite.*	*The letter* which *you have* written.
Voici les lettres *que* j'ai *reçues.*	*Here are the letters* which *I have* received.
Où est votre livre?—je *l'ai perdu.*	*Where is your book?—I have* lost it.
Où est votre plume?-je *l'ai perdue.*	*Where is your pen?—I have* lost it.
Où sont vos livres?-je *les* ai *perdus.*	*Where are your books?—I have* lost
Ils m'ont *félicité.*	*They have* congratulated me.[them.
Il nous a *félicités.*	*He has* congratulated us. [taken?
Quelle affaire avez-vous *entreprise?*	What business *have you* under-
Que de désagrêments ils m'ont *causés!*	What vexations *they have* caused *me!*
Combien de livres avez-vous *lus?*	How many books *have you* read?

These Examples show that the direct regimen which precedes the participle is expressed either by one of these pronouns *que, le, la, les, me, nous, te, vous, se,* or by a noun preceded by *quel, que de,* or *combien de.*

In the first example *écrite* agrees with *que*, of which the antecedent is *lettre*, feminine and singular. In the fifth example, *perdus* agrees with *les*, which stands for its antecedent *livres*, masculine and plural.

A lady would say,

   Ils m'ont *félicitée*. | They have congratulated *me*.

Félicitée agrees with *me*, of which the antecedent *dame* is understood.

The same analysis applies to the other and similar cases.

☞ Observe that the rule says *direct regimen*, for although we say, *Il nous a* vus, he has seen us; we could not say, *Il nous a* dits *cela*, he has told us that: we must say, *Il nous a* dit *cela*; because *nous* is here used for *à nous*, and is an *indirect* regimen.

EXERCISE CCXXVIII.

Here is the answer which I have received.—The sciences
    réponse f.   —— f.
which you have *studied*, will prove infinitely useful to you.—
      être

  General Villars often said, that the two ²(most lively)
art.   *vif*
¹pleasures he had *felt* in his life, had been the first
     subj-2 *ressentir* ind-2
prize which he had *obtained* at college, and the first victory
prix m.   ind-2
which he had *gained* over the enemy.—Where is my
  ind-2 *remporter*
watch?—I have not *seen* it.—They have *deceived* us.—What
montre f.   *tromper*
answer have they *given* you?—How many enemies has he not
    on *faire*
conquered!—The house which her father has *bought*.
vaincre   *que*

589. (V.) After the auxiliary *avoir*, the *Past Participle* remains invariable when the *direct regimen* is placed AFTER the participle, or when there is no direct regimen; as,

 Nous avons *reçu* votre *lettre*. | We have received *your* letter.
 Ils ont *perdu* leurs *livres*. | They have lost *their* books.
 J'ai *récompensé* mes *fils*. | I have rewarded *my* sons.

No agreement here takes place, because the direct regimens *votre lettre, leurs livres, mes fils*, are placed *after* the participles *reçu, perdu, récompensé*.

In the same manner, we write without varying the participle:

Elle a *dansé*.	*She has* danced.
Nous avons *chanté*.	*We have* sung.
Ils ont *répondu* à notre attente.	*They have* answered *our expectation*.

Because the verbs *danser, chanter, répondre,* have not here any direct regimen.

590. REMARK.—It follows from the preceding rule, that the participle of neuter verbs, which are conjugated with *avoir*, never varies, since that class of verbs has no direct regimen. Thus, in *Les cinq heures que j'ai* DORMI (the five hours that I have slept), *les dix ans qu'il a* VÉCU (the ten years that he has lived), the participle of the neuter verbs *dormir* and *vivre* does not vary, and the relative *que* which precedes, although presenting itself under the form of a direct regimen, is in reality but an indirect regimen, equivalent to *pendant lequel: les cinq heures* PENDANT LESQUELLES *j'ai dormi, les dix ans* PENDANT LESQUELS *il a vécu.*

Note.—Sometimes *neuter* verbs are employed *actively,* then their participles agree, if preceded by a direct regimen; as, *La langue que Cicéron a* PARLÉE, the language which Cicero has spoken.

EXERCISE CCXXIX.

I have *received* no answer.—He has *named* several persons.
   plusieurs

—Cromwell *governed* England under the title of Protector.—
   ind-4

Men have never *reaped* the fruit of happiness from the tree of
   cueillir   *sur*

injustice. — The Romans *triumphed* successively over the
   ind-4   *successivement*   *de*

³(most warlike) ¹nations.—They *danced* a great deal at the
   belliqueux   f.   ind-4

last ball. — We have *laughed* heartily. —We must deduct
   bal m.   *de bon cœur. Il*   *retrancher*

from life the hours we have *slept*.
   on

591. (VI.) The verb *être* being used instead of *avoir* in pronominal or reflected verbs, the participle of these verbs follows exactly the same rules as the participle conjugated with *avoir;* that is, the participle of a reflected verb agrees with the direct regimen when preceded by it, but remains invariable, when the direct regimen is placed after it, or when there is none.

So we write with agreement:—

| Nous *nous* sommes *blessés.* | *We have* hurt ourselves. |
| Lucrèce *s'est tuée.* | *Lucretia* killed herself. |

Because the participles *blessés, tuée*, are preceded by their direct regimens *nous, se.*

But we write without agreement:—

| Lucrèce s'est *donné* la mort. | *Lucretia* destroyed *herself.* |

Because the participle *donné* is followed by its direct regimen *la mort.* In this example, *se* is an indirect regimen or dative.

We write also without varying the participle:—

| Il se sont *écrit.* | *They have written to each other.* |
| Nous nous sommes *succédé.* | *We have succeeded one another.* |

Here, the participles *écrit* and *succédé* have no direct regimen. It is as if it were: *Ils ont écrit à* EUX: *Nous avons succédé à* NOUS.

592. REMARK.—It follows from the foregoing rule, that verbs essentially pronominal, that is, verbs which cannot be conjugated without two pronouns of the same person, as *je me repens, je m'abstiens*, require their participles always to agree, because these verbs have for direct regimen their second pronoun; as,

| Nous *nous* sommes *abstenus* de toute reflexion. | *We have abstained from all reflections.* |
| Mes amis, vous *vous* êtes *repentis.* | *My friends, you have repented.* |

EXERCISE CCXXX.

Madame de Sévigné *has rendered herself* celebrated by the
                                se rendre
graces of her style.—She *perceived*   *herself* in that glass.
        —— m.   *s'apercevoir* ind-4   *glace* f.

— That lady has *given herself* fine dresses. — Some
robe f.   Quelques-uns
of our modern authors have *imagined* that they surpassed the
s'imaginer   ind-2
ancients. — They have *spoken to one another.* — They have
se parler
succeeded one another.—Those boys have *repented.* —The
se repentir
troops have *seized* the town.
s'emparer de

593. (VII.) The participle of a unipersonal (or impersonal) verb is always invariable:—

Les chaleurs qu'il a FAIT cet été.	*The heat which we have had this summer.*
La disette qu'il y a EU l'hiver dernier.	*The scarcity which there was last winter.*

Here the verbs *faire* and *avoir* have not their active signification, but simply express existence, and the *que* which precedes is not the regimen of any verb, for we do not say *faire des chaleurs*, as we say *faire des habits*. That *que* must be considered a *gallicism*.

594. (VIII.) The *Past Participle*, followed by an infinitive, agrees with the antecedent noun, when that noun is the regimen or object of the participle, but it remains invariable when the noun is the object of the infinitive; as,

La lettre *que* je lui ai DONNÉE à copier.	*The letter* which *I have* given *him to copy.*
La lettre *que* je lui ai DIT de copier.	*The letter* which *I have* told *him to copy.*

Note.—The regimen or object is known to belong to the participle when the antecedent can be placed after the participle, as in the first example, which may be turned, *Je lui ai donné la lettre à copier.*

As we cannot say, *Je lui ai dit la lettre de copier*, but we may say, *Je lui ai dit de copier la lettre*, it follows that the regimen belongs to the infinitive.

For the same reason, the participles DÛ, *owed, ought;* PU, *been able,* and VOULU, *been willing,* remain invariable when an infinitive is understood after them; as,

Je lui ai rendu tous les services que j'ai PU (lui rendre *understood.*)	*I have rendered him all the services that I have been able.*

298 OF THE PAST PARTICIPLE.

595. REMARK.—When the French participle happens to be placed between two *que*, the first *que* is not the regimen of the participle, but of the verb which follows it, consequently the participle is invariable ; as,

| Les raisons *que* vous avez CRU *que* j'approuvais. | The reasons which you thought I approved. |
| Les mathématiques *que* vous avez VOULU *que* j'étudiasse. | The mathematics which you would have me to study. |

EXERCISE CCXXXI.

The heavy rains which we *had* in the spring, have
    grand pluie f.   * *il faire* ind-4

been the cause of many diseases.—That young lady sings well;
    maladie f.

I have *heard* her sing. — That song is charming; I *heard* it
                                                                                  ind-4

sung. — I have used all the endeavours I *could*. — He has
inf-1   *faire*   *effort* m. † ind-4

obtained all the favours he *wished*. —These are the answers
           grâce f. †   *vouloir* ind-4   *Voilà*

which I had *foreseen* they would give you.—The difficulties
que   †   *faire*   *embarras* m.

which I knew you were in have accelerated my departure.
     ind-4 †   *avoir* *   *départ* m.

EXERCISE CCXXXII.

The rain which has *fallen* has prevented me from going out
    f.   *fait*   *empêché*   *sortir*

to-day. — Have you finished the letter which I *gave* you to
                                                                 ind-4

write?—Have you finished the letter which you had *begun* to
                                                                       ind-2

write? — Have you read the books which I *advised* you
                                                                conseiller ind-4

to read?—Is that the actress whom we *heard* sing?—Sing the
        de   -*ce là*   *actrice*   ind-4

song which we *heard* her sing. — Imitate the virtues which
               ind-4 *lui*

you have *heard* praised.

---

† See *Rule* and *Note*, foot of page 266.

CHAPTER VI.

OF THE ADVERB.

596. (I.) Adverbs, in French, are generally placed after the verb in the *simple tenses*, and between the auxiliary and the participle in the *compound tenses*, but never between the subject and the verb, as is frequently the case in English; as,

Je pense SOUVENT à vous.	*I* often *think of you.*
J'ai TOUJOURS pensé à vous.	*I have* always *thought of you.*

Compound adverbs are usually placed *after* the participle; as, *Vous êtes venu* à PROPOS, you have come seasonably. In some instances, however, the ear alone is consulted; for we say, *Je l'avais* TOUT À FAIT *oublié*, I had quite forgotten it.

597. (II.) The adverbs AUJOURD'HUI, *to-day;* DEMAIN, *to-morrow;* HIER, *yesterday*, may be placed either before or after the verb, but never between the auxiliary and the participle; as, *Il fait* AUJOURD'HUI *beau temps, il pleuvra* DEMAIN; or, AUJOURD'HUI *il fait beau temps,* DEMAIN *il pleuvra,* To-day, it is fine; it will rain to-morrow.

598. (III.) The adverbs BIEN, *well;* MIEUX, *better*; MAL, *ill*; PIS, *worse*, may be placed either before or after an *infinitive;* as, BIEN *faire son devoir*, or *Faire* BIEN *son devoir*, to do one's duty well. But they are always placed after the verb in the simple tenses; as, *Vous fîtes* BIEN, *il fit* MAL, you did well, he did ill. And, with the compound tenses, they are placed between the auxiliary and the participle; as *Vous avez* MAL *fait,* you have done wrong.

599. (IV.) The adverbs, *comment, où, combien, quand, pourquoi,* are always placed before the verb; as,

Comment se porte monsieur votre frère?	How *is* your brother?
Où allez-vous ?	Whither *are you going?*

Remarks on some Adverbs.

600. (1.) BEAUCOUP is not, as the English *much*, susceptible of being modified by any preceding adverb; thus, *très beaucoup, trop beaucoup, si beaucoup*, would be barbarisms.

601. (2.) BIEN before another adverb means *very, much, quite*, etc.; as, *Bien tard*, very late; *bien moins*, much less; *bien assez*, quite enough. After the adverb, it signifies *well;* as, *Assez bien*, pretty well; *moins bien*, not so well.

602. (3.) PLUS and DAVANTAGE, both mean *more*, but they are not used indiscriminately. *Davantage* can never modify an adjective, and cannot, like *plus*, be followed by the preposition *de* nor the conjunction *que*. We say:—

Il a PLUS de brilliant que de solide.	He has more *brilliancy than solidity.*
Il se fie PLUS à ses lumières qu'à celles des autres.	He relies more *on his own knowledge than on that of others.*

We could not say, *Il a* DAVANTAGE *de brillant, il se fie* DAVANTAGE *à ses lumières*, etc.

Davantage is always used absolutely, either at the end of a sentence, or at the end of a member of a sentence; as,

Le cadet est riche, mais l'aîné l'est *davantage*.	*The youngest is rich, but the eldest is still more so.*

603. (4.) PLUS TÔT means *sooner*, and has for its opposite PLUS TARD, *later*. PLUTÔT signifies *rather*.

EXERCISE CCXXXIII.

I *very seldom* go out. — Homer *sometimes* slumbers in the
      sortir   *sommeiller à*
midst   of his gods and heroes. — She has sung *very well.*—
milieu m.   *très*
Where hatred prevails, truth (is sacrificed). — That grieves
     dominer   *fait naufrage.*   *chagriner*
me *very much.* — This letter is *pretty well* written. — I would
            f.
like you *much more*, if you were reasonable. — He has arrived
    bien   ind-2   *est*
sooner than   usual. — I will die *rather* than   suffer it.
     de coutume.   *de*

Remarks on the Negatives.

604. (1.) The negative expressions *ne-pas*, *ne-point*, etc. form only one negation.

605. (2.) *Point* denies more strongly than *pas*.

606. (3.) *Pas* is used in preference to *point;* 1st, Before *plus, beaucoup, moins, si, autant,* and other comparative words; as, *Milton n'est* PAS MOINS *sublime qu'Homère,* Milton is not less sublime than Homer; 2dly, Before nouns of number; as, *Il n'y a* PAS SIX *ans,* it is not six years ago.

607. (4.) *Pas* and *point* may be suppressed after the verbs *cesser,* to cease; *oser,* to dare; and *pouvoir,* to be able; as,

Elle ne CESSE de gronder.	*She does not cease scolding.*
On n'OSE l'aborder.	*They dare not accost him.*
Je ne PUIS me taire.	*I cannot be silent.*

608. (5.) After *savoir,* to know, when this verb is used to express a state of uncertainty, it is better to omit *pas* and *point;* as,

Je ne SAIS où le prendre.	*I do not* know *where to find him.*
Il ne SAIT ce qu'il dit.	*He does not know what he says.*

But, *pas* and *point* must be used when *savoir* is employed to declare anything positively; as,

Je ne SAIS pas le français.	*I do not know French.*

(See former Remarks on *Pouvoir* and *Savoir,* used with a negative, p. 140 and 141).

609. (6.) *Pas* and *point* are suppressed after the conjunction *que,* preceded by the comparative adverbs *plus, moins, mieux,* or some other equivalent; as,

Il écrit mieux qu'il ne parle.	*He writes better than he speaks.*
Il est moins riche, plus riche qu'on ne croit.	*He is less rich, richer than is believed.*
C'est autre chose que je ne croyais.	*It is different from what I thought.*

610. (7.) *Pas* and *point* are omitted with a verb in the preterite, preceded by the conjunction *depuis que,* or by the verb *il y a,* denoting a certain duration of time; as,

Comment vous êtes-vous porté depuis que je ne vous ai vu ?	*How have you been since I saw you?*
Il y a six mois que je ne lui ai parlé.	*I have not spoken to him these six months.*

But they are not omitted when the verb is in the present tense :—

Comment vit-il depuis que nous ne le voyons point ?	*How does he live now that we do not see him?*
Il y a six mois que nous ne nous parlons point.	*It is six months since we do not speak to one another.*

EXERCISE CCXXXIV.

There is *no* happiness without virtue. — The rich are *not*
154 *bonheur* m.   *riche*   153
always happier than the poor. — There will *not* be *much*
                                                              pl.
fruit this year. — You will *not* find two of your opinion.—
année f.   *en*   *avis* m.
You do *not cease* scolding me — I *dare not* speak to him. —
              inf-1
I *cannot* understand what he means. — I do *not know*
                comprendre ce qu' vouloir dire.
what to do. — She sings much *better than* she did.—
                                              que   *ne* ind-2
He is richer *than* he was. — That child has grown
                   ne   ind-2   *grandir*
(very much) *since* I saw it.
   bien   *ne* ind-4

EXERCISE CCXXXV.

Since the world has been a world, said Boileau, one
Depuis que   *est*   *   *   *on*
has *not* seen a great poet, son of a great poet. — She does
              de   *un*
not like (people to flatter her.) — Do you *not* believe what he
         qu'on la flatte.   *ce qu'*
says ? — That is *not* worth *more* than a guinea. — Do *not* go
                       271   *d'*
so fast. — There are I *know not* how many people at the
si   186   402
door. — When Darius proposed to Alexander to divide Asia
                       ind-3   *partager* 375
equally with him, he answered : The earth *cannot* admit of
également   ind-3   *souffrir*
two suns, nor Asia of two kings.

CHAPTER VII.

OF THE PREPOSITION.

611. Rule I. In French, the preposition is always placed immediately *before* its object, whereas in English it is sometimes placed *after* it; as,

A qui parlez-vous ?	To *whom do you speak?* or, *Whom do you speak* to?
De quoi vous plaignez-vous ?	Of *what do you complain?* or, *What do you complain* of?

EXERCISE CCXXXVI.

To whom does that house belong? — What house are you
                     appartenir
speaking *of?* — *Of* that white house. — It belongs to the
                                       ind-1
gentleman *with* whom we are going to dine. — He has two
  monsieur   ind-1
footmen *behind* his carriage. — Tiberius was emperor *after*
 laquais   *voiture* f.   *Tibère* ind-3
Augustus. — The liberty of the Roman republic expired *under*
Auguste.   435   ind-3
Tiberius. — A serpent biting its tail was, *among*
                 qui se mord art. *queue* f. ind-2 *chez*
the Egyptians, the emblem of eternity.
                             art.

612. Rule II. The prepositions *à*, *de*, and *en*, must be repeated in French before every noun, pronoun, or verb which they govern, whether they are repeated or not in English; as,

Il dut la vie à la clémence et à la magnanimité du vainqueur.	*He owed his life to the clemency and generosity of the conqueror.*
Il tâche de mériter et d'obtenir votre confiance.	*He is endeavouring to merit and obtain your confidence.*
J'ai été en France et en Suisse.	*I have been in France and Switzerland.*

613. The other prepositions, especially those of one syllable, are repeated before words which have meanings totally different, but seldom before words that are nearly synonymous; as,

Dans la ville et dans la campagne.	In *the town and* in *the country.*
Par la force et par l'adresse.	By *force and* by *address.*
Dans la mollesse et l'oisiveté.	In *effeminacy and idleness*
Par la force et la violence.	By *force and violence.*

EXERCISE CCXXXVII.

Here is the road from London *to* York and Edinburgh.— *route* f.
You will receive a letter either *from* my father or my brother.— ind-7 *
The celebrity of literary men keeps pace with that *of* f. * *littéraire* * *marcher de pair* art.
great kings and heroes: Homer and Alexander, Virgil and *héros*
Cæsar, equally occupy the voice of fame. — We are *César* *voix* pl. *renommée* f.
going *to* France and Germany.— He is a turner *in* wood and *en* *Allemagne.* 399 *tourneur*
ivory. — I shall come back either *by* the railway or the * *chemin de fer*
canal. — He is *under* the safeguard and protection of the laws. *garde* f

Remarks on the use of some Prepositions.

614. (1.) En is used to express a vague and indeterminate sense; as,

J'ai vécu en pays étranger. | *I have lived* in *a foreign country.*

Dans is employed in a limited and determinate sense; as,

Ce livre est dans ma bibliothèque.	*That book is* in *my library.*
Elle était dans sa chambre.	*She was* in *her room.*
J'ai lu cela dans Buffon.	*I have read that* in *Buffon.*

N.B. When, in English, a noun is preceded by the definite article, or a possessive or demonstrative pronoun,

IN, INTO, are generally expressed in French by *Dans;* as,

Il demeure DANS la maison près du parc.	*He lives* in *the house near the park.*
Il y a du charme DANS sa société.	*There is a charm* in *her society.*
DANS cette guerre malheureuse.	In *that unfortunate war.*

But when the noun is used in an indefinite sense, and without article or pronoun, IN, INTO, are usually expressed by *En ;* as,

| EN paix et EN guerre. | In *peace and* in *war.* |
| Ils sont toujours EN querelle. | *They are always* in *broils.* |

Owing to its indeterminate nature, EN ought not to be followed by the article, except in a few phrases which have been sanctioned by usage; as, *En la présence de Dieu ; Président en la chambre des comptes,* etc.

(See Remark 1st, page 197.)

615. (2.) AUTOUR and ALENTOUR, *around,* must not be confounded. *Autour* is a preposition which requires a regimen ; as,

| *Autour* d'un trône. | Around *a throne.* |

Alentour is an adverb which admits of no regimen; as,

| Il était sur son trône, et les grands étaient *alentour.* | *He was upon his throne, and the grandees were* around. |

616. (3.) AU TRAVERS is always followed by the preposition *de*, and A TRAVERS is not. We say:—

| *Au travers* DE la foule.
 A travers la foule. | Through *the crowd.* |

617. (4.) AVANT, *before,* denotes priority of time; as,

| Il est arrivé *avant* vous. | *He arrived* before *you.* |

It serves also to mark priority of order and place ; as,

Mettez ce chapitre *avant* l'autre. | *Put this chapter* before *the other.*

DEVANT, *before,* is never used, nowadays, with reference to time. It is a preposition of place, and has the meaning of *in presence of, opposite to, in front of ;* as,

| Il a prêché *devant* le roi. | *He has preached* before *the king.* |
| *Devant* la porte ; *devant* l'église. | Before *the door ;* before *the church.* |

Devant serves also to mark order; as,

| C'est mon ancien, il marche *devant* moi. | *He is my senior, he goes* before *me.* |

When *Before* has no noun or pronoun after it, it is generally expressed by the adverb *auparavant;* as,

| Je l'en avais averti longtemps *auparavant.* | *I had warned him of it long before.* |
| Un mois, un an *auparavant.* | *A month, a year* before. |

618. (5.) *Près de* and *prêt à*, are not the same expressions. *Près* is a *preposition* which governs *de ;* as,

| Il est bien PRÈS DE midi. | *It is very* near *twelve o'clock.* |

But *Prêt* is an adjective which governs *à;* as,

| Il est *prêt à* partir. | *He is* ready *to set out.* |

EXERCISE CCXXXVIII.

I was *in* France, *in* the province of Burgundy.—The glory
   ind-2   Bourgogne.
of a sovereign consists less *in* the extent of his states,
   souverain m.   *grandeur* f.   *état* m.
than *in* the happiness of his people. — They ranged themselves
                       peuple pl.   *se ranger* ind-3
around him.—Here is a sad accident for my creditors, said
              Voilà fâcheux m.   *créancier* m. ind-2
a Gascon officer, who had just received a ball *through* his body.
435   *venait de* inf-1 *balle* f.   art.
—I saw that *before* you.—She was walking *before* the house.—
ind-4   *se promener*
He was *near* dying. — I am *ready* to maintain my opinion,
   ind-2   inf-1   *maintenir*
pen in hand, until the last drop of my ink.
art. *à* art.   *jusqu'à*   *goutte* f.

619. (6.) The following prepositions require DE before the noun or pronoun which they govern:—

Auprès, }		au-dessous,	under, below.
près, } near.		autour,	around.
proche, }		le long,	along.
au-dessus,	above.	vis-à-vis,	opposite.

EXAMPLES.

| *Près* DE la poste. | Near *the post-office.* |
| *Autour* DU bras. | Round *the arm.* |

Note.—In the familiar style, and in conversation, the preposition DE is sometimes omitted after *près, proche,* and *vis-à-vis;* as, Je loge PRÈS *l'arsenal,* vis-à-vis *la nouvelle rue.*

620. (7.) The prepositions JUSQUE, *till, until, even, as far as,* and QUANT, *as to, as for,* require the preposition A after them; as,

Depuis Pâques *jusqu'* à la Pentecôte.	From Easter till Whitsunday.
Quant à moi. Quant à elle.	As for *me*. As for *her*.

EXERCISE CCXXXIX.

I live *near* the gate Saint-Martin.—*Above* the door were
  demeurer   porte f.   ind-2
written these words.—In the ²ecclesiastical ¹hierarchy,
  586   mot m.   ecclésiastique hiérarchie f. h asp.
the bishop is *below* the archbishop. — The queen had her
                               archevêque.
daughters *around* her. — We came *along* the river side.—
                        ind-4   rivière f.
He lodges *opposite* my windows.—All   fathers, *even* the most
                                    art.
grave, play with their children. — Let us go together *as far*
                                    jouer
as Oxford. — *As for* him, he (shall act) as he   pleases.
                         en usera   lui ind-7

EXERCISE CCXL.

²Æsculapius ¹(is represented) with a snake   in his hand
 Esculape on représente   couleuvre f. à
or *around* his arm, and a cock *near* him.—The   Falls   of
                        coq   cataracte f. s.
Niagara are *near* the boundaries of the United States
         se trouve   limite f.   Etats-Unis
and   Canada. — The Americans place Washington and
 31   ——— m.
Bolivar *above* Alexander and Cæsar. — The planets are
                              de   planète f.
opaque bodies which turn *around* the sun, from which they
                      tourner   où
derive light and heat. — There are forests of canes
 tirer lumière f.   chaleur f   forêt f.   canne f.
along the Ganges. — I will wait for you *till* two o'clock.
        Gange m.   151

CHAPTER VIII.

OF THE CONJUNCTION.

621. IN French, some conjunctions require the verb which follows them to be in the indicative, some in the subjunctive, and others in the infinitive mood.

622. *The following Conjunctions, and* Conjunctive Locutions, *require the indicative mood:*—

Ainsi que,	*as, as well as.*	depuis que,	*since.*
après que,	*after.* [*as.*	lorsque,	*when.*
attendu que,	*considering that,*	parce que,†	*because.*
aussitôt que,	} *as soon as.*	pendant que,	} *while, whilst.*
dès que,		tandis que,	
autant que,	*as much as* [*what.*	peut-être que,	*perhaps.*
à ce que,	*as, as far as, from*	puisque,	*since.*
à mesure que,	*as, in proportion*	tant que,	*as long as.*
au lieu que,	*whereas.* [*as.*	vu que,	*seeing that.*

They require the indicative, because the principal sentence, which they unite with that which is incidental, expresses affirmation in a direct and positive manner.

† *Observation.—Par ce que* (in three words) is not a conjunction, though sometimes mistaken for one. It signifies, *by that which, by what.*

EXERCISE CCXLI.

As soon as the Khan of Tartary has dined, a herald cries
      kan m.   *héraut*

that all the other princes of the earth may go and dine,
          terre f. ind-1 *

if (they please). — A child ought not to ²obtain ¹anything,
 bon leur semble.   *ne doit* *   *rien*

because he asks for it, but *because* he has need (of it).—
      *   *besoin en*

We must not judge of a man *by what* he (is ignorant of),
 Il falloir   *ignore*

SYNTAX OF THE CONJUNCTION. 309

but *by what* he knows. — *Whilst* we are in prosperity,
  savoir   *on*   art.
we must prepare for adversity. — *As long as* I have
il *se*   *à* art.   ind-7
money, you shall not want any.
     manquer en

623. *The following Conjunctions, and* Conjunctive Locutions, *require the subjunctive mood.*

Afin que,	} *that, in order that.*	pour peu que,	} *however*
pour que,		si peu que,	*little.*
avant que,	*before.*	pourvu que,	*provided that.*
à moins que,†	*unless.*	quoique,	}
au cas que,	*in case that.*	bien que,	} *though, although.*
de crainte que,†	} *for fear, lest.*	encore que,	}
de peur que,†		sans que,	*without.*
jusqu'à ce que,	*till, until.*	soit que,	*whether.*
non que,	} *not that.*	supposé que,	*supposing that.*
non pas que,			

They require the subjunctive, as they always imply doubt, desire, uncertainty.

624. *Remark on the conjunction* QUE. Learners are often mistaken, by supposing that QUE always requires the verb which follows it to be in the *subjunctive mood;* but QUE does not govern any particular mood. It is the positive or doubtful sense of the first verb that requires the second to be in the indicative or subjunctive.‡ There are, however, several cases in which QUE requires the subjunctive after it. These are when QUE is used instead, or in the sense of some conjunctions which themselves always govern the subjunctive, such as *afin que, avant que, à moins que, jusqu'à ce que, quoique, sans que, soit que, supposé que;* as,

Approchez, QUE je vous voie (*afin que.*)	*Come near, that I may see you.*
Attendez QUE la pluie soit passée (*jusqu'à ce que.*)	*Wait until the rain be over.*

---

† *A moins que, de crainte que, de peur que,* require *ne* before the verb which follows them, although not having a negative sense.
‡ See the syntax of this mood, p. 285-288.

EXERCISE CCXLII.

The Apostles received the gift of tongues, *that* they might
       ind-3 *don* m.   *pouvoir*
preach the Gospel to all the nations of the earth. — If my
           Evangile m.
brother come *before* I am up, show him into the dining-
      ind-1   *levé faire entrer*
room, and give him a newspaper to amuse himself with *till*

I come down.— *Unless* you be useful, you will not be sought after.
 descendre   *recherché*
—Speak low, *for fear* anybody should hear you. — *Though*
          on   *entendre*
you are learned, be modest. — Get in *without* his seeing you.
  instruit   *Entrer*

625. *The following Conjunctions govern the infinitive :—*

Afin de,	*to, in order to.*	au lieu de,	*instead of.*
avant de,†	} *before.*	loin de,	*far from.*
avant que de,		de crainte de,	} *for, or from*
à moins de,	} *unless.*	de peur de,	*fear of.*
à moins que de,		plutôt que de,	*rather than.*

† *Avant de*, and *avant que de*, are both correct expressions; but present usage is decidedly in favour of *avant de*.

Note.—*A cause que, devant que, durant que, malgré que*, are found among the Tables of Conjunctions, and in the Exercises of many Grammars; but these are antiquated expressions. *A cause que* is replaced by *parce que; devant que*, by *avant que; durant que*, by *pendant que;* and *malgré que*, by *quoique.*

EXERCISE CCXLIII.

He works *in order to* acquire riches and consideration.—*Before*
        acquérir   f.
granting him my confidence, I shall examine if he is worthy of
       confiance f.
it.—*Instead* of studying, he does nothing but amuse himself.
         ne   * que *se divertir.*
—*Far from* thanking me, he has scolded me. — Charles VII.,
           gronder
king of France, abstained from eating, in fear of
     ind-3   par art. *crainte* f.
being poisoned, and allowed himself to die, *from fear of*
     se laisser ind-3   *peur*
dying. — *Rather* die *than* do a dishonourable action.
     inf-1   *lâcheté* f.

626. The INTERJECTIONS have been treated of in page 190: their construction is the same in French as in English; they require, therefore, no further explanation. The soul is the only syntax for interjections, and they can never embarrass the student, since they do not require any rules.

627. OF ABBREVIATIONS.

There are certain French words which it is customary to abridge and represent by capital letters, as follows:—

J.C.	for	Jésus-Christ.
N.S.	...	Notre-Seigneur.
N.S. J.C.	...	Notre-Seigneur Jésus-Christ.
S.S.	...	Sa Sainteté.
S.M.	...	Sa Majesté.
LL. MM.	...	Leurs Majestés.
S.M.I.	...	Sa Majesté Impériale.
S.M. T.C.	...	Sa Majesté Très-Chrétienne.
S.M.C.	...	Sa Majesté Catholique.
S.M.T.F.	...	Sa Majesté Très-Fidèle.
S.M.B.	...	Sa Majesté Britannique.
S.M.S.	...	Sa Majesté Suédoise.
S.A.	...	Son Altesse.
S.A.R.	...	Son Altesse Royale.
S.A.I.	...	Son Altesse Impériale.
S.Ex.	...	Son Excellence.
S.Em.	...	Son Eminence.
Mgr	...	Monseigneur.
M. or M^r *	...	Monsieur.
MM. or M^{rs} *	...	Messieurs.
Mme	...	Madame.
Mlle	...	Mademoiselle.
M^d	...	Marchand.
M^{de}	...	Marchande.
Nég^t	...	Négociant.
Cie	...	Compagnie.

(*Encycl. méthod.—Gram. des Gram.—Acad.*)

* The first is more used in print, and the latter in writing. *Messrs* is also a good abbreviation of *Messieurs*.

PROMISCUOUS EXERCISES

ON THE NINE PARTS OF SPEECH, AND ON THE PRINCIPAL NICETIES, DIFFICULTIES, AND IDIOMS OF THE FRENCH LANGUAGE.

CCXLIV.—I look upon the silence of the abbé Sieyes, said
regarder
Mirabeau, as a public calamity. — Saying of Peter the Great:
Mot
It requires three Jews to deceive a Russian.—A Swiss proverb:
187   544
Keep at least three paces from him who hates bread, and the
247 *toi*   *à*
voice of a child.—Every Roman knight had a horse maintained
120   *entretenir*
at the expense of the republic, and wore a gold ring as a mark
pl.   419
of his dignity. — I bequeath to surgeon Larrey, 100,000 fr.;
Je lègue
he is the most virtuous man I have known. (*Napoléon's Will.*)
493   ²   ³   ¹   subj-1

CCXLV.—It is related of Alexander that he said of
111   ind-2
Diogenes, that if he had not been Alexander, he (would have)
eût   *eût*
wished to be Diogenes. — It was at the battle of Cressy (1346)
98
that for the first time the English made use of artillery. — Go,
fois f.
my friends, said Napoléon to his grenadiers, fear nothing, the
ind-2   293
ball which will kill me is not yet cast. — The Spaniards
ind-7   *fondre*
compare Charles V. to Solomon for wisdom, to Cæsar for
76
courage, to Augustus for good fortune. — Such was Sheridan!
bonheur m.
he could soften an attorney! There has been nothing like it
since the days of Orpheus.—(*Byron.*)

CCXLVI.—"Soldiers," said Bonaparte, in one of his pro-
               ind-2
clamations, "you have, in a fortnight, gained six victories,
                                        remporter
taken twenty-one standards, fifty pieces of cannon, several
                  drapeau m.
strong places, made fifteen thousand prisoners, killed or
                            75
wounded more than ten thousand men. You have won battles
                                                    de
without artillery, crossed rivers without bridges, performed
                  passer   faire
forced marches without shoes, bivouacked without brandy and
                                bivaquer
often without bread. Thanks be rendered to you, soldiers!
                     Grâce f.
The country has a right to expect great things from you.
    Patrie f.
You have yet combats to wage, towns to take, rivers to cross.
                        livrer
  Friends, be the liberators of the people, do not be
                                    peuple pl.
their oppressors."
en   fléau m.

CCXLVII.—The castle clock struck twelve. At that mo-
                              sonner   En
ment the   buzzings   of the crowd ceased, and a little man,
           bourdonnement m.
dressed in a green uniform,   white trousers, and wearing
  253   d'   d'   chaussé de
  riding-boots, appeared all on a sudden, keeping on his head
à l'écuyère   en 146
a three-cornered hat as fascinating as he was himself. The
  à trois cornes   prestigieux   l'
broad red riband of the Legion of Honour floated on his
                                                  ind-2
breast. A small sword was at his side. He was perceived
poitrine f.   apercevoir
by all eyes, and at once. Immediately, cries of: Long live
                                                       335
the Emperor! were uttered by the enraptured multitude.
                     pousser   enthousiasmer   f.

CCXLVIII.—Botanists assure us that corn is nowhere to
           *   *blé* m.
be found in its primitive state. This plant seems to have
                 543
been confided, by Providence, to the care of man, with the
                  pl.
use of fire, to insure him the sceptre of the earth. With corn
   544
and fire, we can acquire all the other goods. Man, with corn
    on   *bien* m.
alone, can feed all the domestic animals that sustain his life,
     nourrir   248
and share his labours; the pig, the hen, the duck, the pigeon,
   partager
the ass, the sheep, the goat, the horse, the cow, the cat, and
     brebis f. *chèvre* f.
the dog, which give him, in return, eggs, milk, bacon, wool,
       rendre
services, and gratitude.

CCXLIX.—My dear Friend,

Pray, apply yourself diligently to your exercises; for though
   s'appliquer
the doing them well is not supremely meritorious, the doing
               méritoire
them ill is illiberal, vulgar, and ridiculous.
   ignoble
I send you enclosed a letter of recommendation for Marquis
     ci-inclus
Matignon, which will at once thoroughly introduce you
        tout d'un coup
into the best French company. Your character, and conse-
               réputation
quently your fortune, absolutely depends upon the company
               de
you keep, and the turn you take at Paris. I do not,
      tournure f.
in the least, mean a grave turn; on the contrary, a gay, a
 nullement
sprightly, but at the same time an elegant and liberal one.

Keep carefully out of all quarrels. Many young Frenchmen are hasty and giddy. But these young men, when mellowed by age and experience, very often turn out able men. The number of great generals and statesmen, as well as authors, that France has produced, is an undeniable proof of it.—(*Lord Chesterfield to his Son.*)

CCL.—Scotland is a picturesque country.—The country has its amusements and beauties, but I prefer town. — It is very fine weather. — That requires much time. — I saw him to-day for the first time. — I know him, but I do not know where he lives. — If your sisters are at home, bring them with you; we shall be delighted to see them. — Bring me a few French books well bound in calf.—There is some cold veal.—Here is a calf's head.—Cut some bread.—Give me the loaf.—The poorest of the Russians have a tea-pot, a copper tea-kettle, and take tea, morning and evening.—It requires an iron hand in a silk glove.—Andrew was Simon Peter's brother.

CCLI. — Knock at the door.—There is no knocker.—She is always cross.—What a pretty gold cross she wears!—She reads better now, and better books.—If I had better paper and a better pen, I would write better.—She has married my brother.—It was our bishop that married them.—Look at this boy.—He looks well to-day.—I have called at your house.—Tell him to call again. — Call the waiter.—I am a bachelor.—They say the plague is at Smyrna.—Don't plague me.—When Cromwell gave half-a-crown a-day to every dragoon, he readily got recruits for the Parliamentarian armies.

CCLII.—The sons of the emperors of Russia take the title of Grand-duke.—Take my horse to the stable.—Take the saddle to the saddler.—If you are going to Canterbury, take me with you.—Take this bonnet to your sister.—I take a cup of coffee every morning.—It has rained all the morning.—I will go and see you on Friday evening.—I shall spend the evening with you.—He has spent all his money.—I come from Paris, and I will return to-morrow.—I am going to Paris, and I will return next week.—Return me my money.—Have I not returned it to you?—Gardener, have you swept all the walks?—Good bye, ladies; I wish you a pleasant walk.

INDEX.

	Page
A ; with and without accent,	8
Proper names ending in *a*,	37
English indef. art.	14, 199, 206
Preposition,	{ 8, 14, 15, 185, 219, 303.
Verbs which require *à*,	273
Abbreviations in the Exercises,	6
———— of Titles,	311
Abstain (*to*), s'abstenir,	133
Accents ; number and use,	8
Adjective ; Feminine of,	20 to 25
Plural of,	25, 26
Possessive,	42
Demonstrative,	44
Numeral,	31, 233
Cardinal,	31, 233
Ordinal,	31, 34, 233
General Rule on,	66
Concord of the,	220 to 224
Used adverbially,	221
Place of the,	224 to 230
Government of the,	230 to 233
Of Number, its synt,	233
Of Dimension,	234
In the Comparative Degree,	235
In the Superlative Degree,	235
Adverb ; its place,	175, 299
How formed from an adj.	179
Of Quantity,	176, 266
Aïeul ; its plural,	19
All,	17, 26, 56
Aller ; *s'en aller*,	117, 118
Alphabet (*French*),	7
Although, quoique,	309
Always, toujours,	178
Antecedent ; its meaning,	47
Any ; how expressed in French,	16
Apostrophe,	9
Appartenir, see *Tenir*,	133
Around,	305
Article,	13, 14, 15, 16
Contraction of,	14
Partitive,	16, 62, 198
When used,	192 to 202
When not used,	197, 202 to 210
When invariable,	236
Aucun, aucune, none,	55
Autrui, others,	52
Avant, devant,	305

	Page
Avant de, avant que de,	310
Avoir, to have ; its conjugation,	60
*B*arefoot,	221
Beaucoup ; Remark on,	300
Before ; how expressed,	305, 310
Bénir, to bless, Remark on,	122
Best,	30
Better,	30
———— *and better*,	177
Bien, Remarks on,	207, 300
Born (*to be*), naître,	163
Both,	53, 264
*C*a, for *cela*,	256
Can (to be able to), pouvoir,	139
Cases ; if any in French,	11
Ce, demonst. pron.,	45, 254, 255
Cedilla,	10
Cent ; when it takes an *s*,	34
Chacun, every one,	52, 262
Chaque, every, each,	55
Ciel ; its plural,	19
Collective nouns,	17, 33, 34, 265
Comparative degree,	27, 28, 235
Comparison, degrees of,	26
Compound nouns,	215 to 220
Compound tenses ; how formed,	59
Concord between the tenses,	288
Conditional mood,	284
Conjugations ; how distinguished,	59
First in *er*,	69
Second in *ir*,	73
Third in *oir*,	77
Fourth in *re*,	80
Negatively,	83, 84
Interrogatively,	87, 88
Interrogatively & negatively,	90
Conjugation—	
Of *Passive* verbs,	92
Of *Pronom.* or *Reflect.* verbs,	96
Of the same, negatively, 99 ; interrogatively, 101 ; interrogatively and negatively,	102
Of *Impersonal* or *Univers.*	103

INDEX.

Conjugation—
Of verbs in *ger, éer, cer, uer, eler, eter, yer, ier*, 108 to 117
Conjunctions; the principal, 188
  Some govern the indic., 308
  Some the subj. or inf. 309, 310
Connaître, to know, . . 151
  Its difference from *savoir*, 141
Craindre, and verbs in *aindre* and *oindre*, ... 153
Cru; with and without accent, 9

D; takes the sound of *t*, . 90
Dans, en; how used, . . 304
Date, how to, ... 34
De, . 14, 15, 182, 186, 218, 303
  Verbs which require *de*, . 274
Deceive (to), tromper, like *parler*, 69
Degrees of comparison, . . 26
Demi; Remark on, . . 221
Demonstrative adjectives, . 44
———— *pronouns*, 45, 46, 254,
Dès; with and without accent, 8
Devant, avant, . . . 305
Diæresis, ... 10
Die (to), ... 128, 173
Distributive nouns, . . 33, 34
Do, did, ... 69, 83
—— *(to)*, faire, . . . 159
Du; with and without accent, 9

E; gender of nouns ending in, 12
Each, ... 52, 55, 262
Eat (to), manger, . . . 108
Either, ... 264
Elision of vowels, . . . 9
Elle; its derivation, . . 13
Ellipsis; Note on, . . 258
En; pronoun, . . 49, 50
  Preposition, 187, 273, 303, 304
  Governs the Particip. pres. 273
En, dans, ... 304
Entre; when written *entr'*, . 10
Étre, to be; its conjugation, 64
Eye, eyes, ... 19

Faire *(to do, to make)*, . 159
Falloir (to be necessary), . 105
Fleurir, to flourish, Remark on, 125
Foresee (to), see *Voir*, . . 143

Gender, ... 11, 210
Gent, gens, ... 17, 211
Give (to), donner, . . . 71
Go (to), aller, ... 117
— *out (to)*, sortir, . . . 132

Half *(demi)*; its Synt. . . 221
He who, she who, . . . 255
Her, ... 40, 42, 241
Him, ... 40, 241
Hyphen, ... 10, 243

I; when cut off, . . . 9
If, si; Remarks on, . . 9, 284
Imperfect; when used, . . 280
Impersonal verbs, . . . 103
In, into; how expressed, . 304
Indefinite pronouns, . 51, 261
———— pronom. adjectives, . 55
Interjection, . . . 190, 191
Irregular verbs, 1st conj. *er*, 117
  ... ... 2d conj. *ir*, 120
  ... ... 3d conj. *oir*, 136
  ... ... 4th conj. *re*, 146
It, ... 40, 235, 262
Its, their, . . . 42, 43, 252

Know *(to)*, . . . 141, 151

La; la, . . 8, 9, 10, 13, 14
Le, article, . . 9, 10, 13, 14
—, pronoun, . . . 9, 40, 241
—, *la, les*, pronouns, . . 40
Least, ... 30
Less, ... 30
Little, ... 30
Live (to), vivre, . . . 173
Long, adj. 25
———— adv. 178
Lose (to), perdre, . . . 81
L'un l'autre, l'un & l'autre, 53, 54, 264

Make *(to)*, faire, . . . 159
Même, same, self, like, . . 55
Mille; milles; mil, . . 34
Moise; its pronunciation, . 10
Monsieur, . . . 253, 260, 311

318 INDEX.

	Page
Moods and *Tenses,*	279
More,	300
—— (*no*),	83
Much, very much, too much,	176
Mur; with and without accent,	8

*N*ames (proper) see *Proper.*

Near,	306
Negatives,	83, 301
Neither,	264
—— *the one nor the other,*	264
Neuter Verbs,	94
—————— Remark on,	295
Never,	83
No, not,	83, 301
No more,	83
Nobody,	52, 53
Nothing,	83
Nor,	264
Noun, see *Substantive.*	
Nul, nulle, none,	55
Numbers,	11
Cardinal,	31, 34, 204
Ordinal,	31, 34, 204
Rules on,	34, 35, 204, 233

*O*btain (to), obtenir, like *tenir,*	133
Œil; its plural,	19
Of it, on,	49, 50
On; one, they, etc.,	51, 261, 262
Ou; with and without accent,	8
Où; relative pronoun,	49
Owe (to), devoir,	78

*P*arce que, par ce que,	308
Participle Present,	291
——————— Past,	92, 292
Partir, to set out,	129
Partitive article,	16, 198
Parts of speech,	13
Pas, point,	83, 301
Passive verbs,	92, 271
Personal Pronouns,	38, 237
Personne,	52, 53
Plural of Nouns,	17, 213
—— of compound Nouns,	215
—— of Adjectives,	25, 26
Plus, davantage,	300
Plus tôt, plutôt,	300
Plusieurs, several, many,	56

	Page
Possessive adjectives,	42
—————— *pronouns,*	43, 249
—————— *case,*	217
Pour, before a verb,	278
Pouvoir, to be able,	139
Prepositions,	11, 182, 218, 303
Govern the Infinitive,	273
Some govern, *de* or *à,*	273, 306, 307
Present Indic. used for a *past,*	279
... ... for a *future,*	279
Près de, prêt à,	306
Preterite definite,	281
—————— *indefinite,*	282
Primitive Tenses,	67, 68
Pronominal verbs,	95
Pronouns: how divided,	38
Personal,	38
Place of *Pers. pron.*	38, 237, 248
Syntax of *Pers. pron.*	237, 249
Possessive,	42, 43, 249
Demonstrative,	44, 45, 254
Relative,	47, 256
Indefinite,	51, 261
Proper names; definition of	17
Of states, provinces, towns,	12, 197
Of Sovereigns,	35
Ending in *a,*	37
Which take the article,	195, 197, 203, 213
When they take the sign of the plural,	213
Proportional nouns,	34

*Q*ue; when it loses the *e,*	47
Rem. on the conj. *que,*	309
Quel, quelle; when used,	57
Quelconque, whatever,	56
Quelque; quel que,	57, 58
Quelqu'un; somebody,	52
Quiconque; whoever,	51, 52

*R*adical letters,	67
Railroad or *railway,*	304
Rain (to), pleuvoir,	104
Read (to), lire,	160
Reflected Verbs,	95, 99, 101, 102
Regimen,	210, 240, 270, 293
Regular Verbs,	67, 69
Relative pronouns,	47, 256
Repentir (se), see *Sentir,*	180

INDEX. 319

	Page
Résolu ; Résous,	168
Request (to), prier,	116
S*avoir,* to know,	141
Without *pas* and *point,*	301
Say (to), dire,	156
Se,	41, 248
See (to), voir,	143
Sell (to), vendre,	80
Send (to), envoyer,	115
—— back, renvoyer,	115
Serve (to), to help to, servir,	131
Set out, (to), partir,	129
Several, plusieurs,	56
She who, he who,	255
Si, if,	9, 284
Sing (to), chanter,	71
Soi,	41, 248
Some ; how expressed,	16, 198
Something,	211
Sometimes,	178
Sovereigns,	35, 204
Speak (to), parler,	69
Steam-engine ; how translated,	186
Subjunctive mood ; when used,	285
Substantive ; plural of,	17 to 20
Gender of,	11, 210
Number in,	213, 214
Plural of compound,	215
Superlative degree,	28
Sur ; with and without accent,	8
Syntax,	192
T*ake* (to), prendre,	167
Tel, telle, such,	54
Tell (to), dire,	156
Tenses ; formation of,	59, 67, 68
Syntax of,	279 to 291
Their, its,	42, 252
Thousand, mille,	34
To ; how translated,	14, 272
When expressed by *pour,*	278
Tout,	17, 26, 56
Tréma, or *diérèse,*	10
Très ; its derivation,	29

	Page
Tu ; with and without accent,	9
U*nipersonal verbs,*	103
V*enir,* to come,	134
Verb ; how many kinds of *verbs,*	59
Conjugated negatively,	83, 84
Interrogatively,	87, 88
Interrogatively and negativ.	90
Active verbs,	69
Passive,	92, 271
Neuter,	94
Pronominal, reflective, reciprocal,	95
Impersonal or Unipersonal,	103
Verbs ending in *ger, éer, cer, uer, eler, eter, yer, ier,*	108 to 117
Observations on,	67
Agreement of the,	263
Place of the subject of the,	268
Government of the,	270
Verbs which require *à,*	273
Verbs which require *de,*	274
Verbs which require no preposition,	277
Very,	29, 300
Vingt ; when it takes an *s,*	34
Vivre ; remarks on,	173
Vowels,	7, 9
W*;* when used,	7
Wait, wait for, attendre,	81
Who, which,	256
Whom, which,	256, 260
—— (of),	259
Whose, of whom, of which,	259
Words alike in French and English,	36
Worse,	30
Worst,	30
Write (to), écrire,	157
Y,	7, 50, 178

FINIS.

PRINTED BY WILLIAM BLACKWOOD AND SONS, EDINBURGH.

www.ingramcontent.com/pod-product-compliance
Lightning Source LLC
Chambersburg PA
CBHW022022240426
43667CB00042B/1049